HANDBOOK OF VOCATIONAL PSYCHOLOGY

Volume 1

FOUNDATIONS

HANDBOOK OF VOCATIONAL PSYCHOLOGY

Volume 1

FOUNDATIONS

Edited by
W. Bruce Walsh and Samuel H. Osipow
The Ohio State University

LEA LAWRENCE ERLBAUM ASSOCIATES, PUBLISHERS
1983   Hillsdale, New Jersey   London

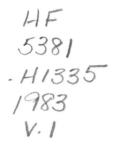

HF
5381
.H1335
1983
V. 1

Lawrence Erlbaum Associates, Inc., Publishers
365 Broadway
Hillsdale, New Jersey 07642

Library of Congress Cataloging in Publication Data
Main entry under title:

Handbook of vocational psychology.

  Includes indexes.
  Contents: v. 1. Foundations.
  1. Vocational guidance—Addresses, essays, lectures.
2. Occupations—Psychological aspects—Addresses,
essays, lectures. 3. Personality and occupation—
Addresses, essays, lectures. I. Walsh, W. Bruce,
1936-   . II. Osipow, Samuel H. [DNLM: 1. Occupations
—Handbooks. 2. Vocational guidance—Handbooks.
3. Psychology—Handbooks. BF 76 H236]
HF5381.H1335 1983   158.6   83-8856
ISBN 0-89859-285-2 (v. 1)

Printed in the United States of America
10 9 8 7 6 5 4 3 2 1

Contents

PART III: RESEARCH ISSUES IN VOCATIONAL PSYCHOLOGY

Preface

The idea to produce a *Handbook of Vocational Psychology* is one that we have thought about for a long time. After almost a decade of planning, commissioning chapters, and editing, we are optimistic about the value of our efforts.

The *Handbook* represents "state of the art" thinking about the field of vocational psychology on the part of important workers in the area. As a result, the effort should advance vocational psychology. The audience we have in mind for these volumes includes both the working professional and advanced students.

We hope to chart new directions toward which vocational psychologists can direct their efforts. In addition, we hope to reinforce already existing positive trends in the field. Vocational psychology is a field which has now clearly emerged that cuts across a number of sub-fields including counseling psychology, industrial/organizational psychology, and rehabilitation psychology. Furthermore, vocational psychology draws on knowledge bases dealing with the psychology of women, the psychology of minority groups, research methodologies, and basic psychological theory.

Each chapter is designed to be more than a literature review. The chapter authors were encouraged not only to review the salient research and theoretical literature in their chapter topic area, but also to analyze and synthesize the current work. Since each author is an expert in the sub-specialty in which they are writing, we think that each chapter offers exciting insights into each sub-specialty topic.

We wish to express appreciation to the contributors for their hard work and their deligence in approaching the task, and to the publisher for his cooperation with the effort.

The editors would also like to express their appreciation to the following individuals who served as reviewers for the chapters in this volume: Frank Fletcher, Bruce Fretz, Gary Gottfredson, Linda Gottfredson, and Patricia Fannin Raskin. Carol Helm's efforts in the collation of the index is also gratefully acknowledged.

W. Bruce Walsh
Samuel H. Osipow

HANDBOOK OF VOCATIONAL PSYCHOLOGY

Volume 1

FOUNDATIONS

I
BACKGROUND ISSUES

The first part of Volume I of this handbook consists of two chapters, one describing the history of vocational psychology as seen through the eyes of Donald E. Super and the other describing current theoretical issues in vocational psychology as prepared by Lenore Harmon and Helen Farmer.

Super's personal perspective on the history and development of vocational psychology suggests that vocational psychology today combines the differential approach of occupational psychology in the strict sense of that term with the developmental approach of career psychology. Super suggests that vocational psychology has gone through two major stages of evolution, having started out as the differential psychology of occupations with a focus on the men and women doing the work and having evolved into the developmental psychology of boys and girls and of men and women considering and pursuing the occupations of which occupational psychology has given us a deeper understanding. In historical perspective, Super suggests that the first half of the twentieth century saw vocational psychology dominated by theories and instruments of differential psychology used to match people and occupations. Several trends contributed to change that emphasis during the years after World War II. These included: (1) the fact that test construction had, technically, nearly reached its peak before computers made possible an even higher level of development; (2) the advancement of the mental hygiene movement and the growth of clinical psychology as an attractive specialty; and (3) the better training in other applied and human aspects of psychology by those going into its application. Vocational psychologists were no longer experimentalists with little knowledge of personality theory, development, and social psychology. Both personnel psychologists and vocational counselors, many of the latter now counseling psychologists, brought more to vocational psychology than a knowledge of psychometrics, individual differences, and research methods. It is in this context that Super, from the perspective of a very active participant, reviews the history of differential psychology applied to occupations, the history of developmental psychology applied to careers, and the history of vocational psychology and practice. Finally, Super suggests that the past still lives in the present. Matching people and jobs is as important as ever, and methods and instruments are far better than they were decades ago. Career development has proven to be more than a fad and has found a permanent place in education and in industry. The past and the present are now producing the inevitable future in vocational psychology. Super suggests that vocational psychology may need to become career psychology in order to provide us with a theory of self-actualization in a combination of roles that evolve as the individual and society change.

In their chapter on theoretical issues, Lenore Harmon and Helen Farmer address several issues in vocational psychology that are important both to researchers and practitioners. Most of these issues reflect the unfinished task of establishing increasingly comprehensive, parsimonious, and valid theory for the field. Harmon and Farmer suggest that to strengthen vocational psychological theory it is important to increase the range of phenomena addressed and at the same time increase parsimony. One means suggested to do this is to incorporate within vocational psychology elements of other theoretical systems that relate to the field. Examples are the achievement motivation literature and the cognitive, personal, and moral development literature. Furthermore, to strengthen vocational psychological theory it seems important that explanations provided by the theory lead to a better understanding of minority groups, females as well as males, and a full range of social classes.

The chapter itself is divided into four major sections: issues related to nonpsychological theories, issues related to other psychological theories, issues related to theories of vocational behavior, and issues of emphasis. Issues related to nonpsychological theories emphasize sociology and labor economics and theories of vocational behavior. Issues related to other psychological theories view vocational behavior in terms of ego development, cognitive development, moral development, work values, achievement motivation, and childhood determinants of achievement motivation. Issues related to theories of vocational development concern themselves with career development, career choice, and adult vocational behavior. The last section points to theoretical gaps in the field's understanding of the process of career development. For example, the lack of longitudinal data providing evidence on the effectiveness of vocational counseling efforts in high school and college for long term adult vocational satisfaction and productivity suggests caution in counseling efforts. In addition, Harmon and Farmer note that the field is particularly unprepared theoretically to counsel adults who are in the process of making career changes as well as being unprepared to counsel minorities, the poor, and the unskilled because of the relative lack of research dealing with these populations.

In summary, time and time again Harmon and Farmer illustrate that research is the cornerstone of both theory and practice. They argue that a broad perspective that takes into account the interface between vocational psychology and other social sciences, between vocational psychology and other fields within psychology, and between theories in vocational psychology will serve to benefit the field of vocational psychology.

1 The History and Development of Vocational Psychology: A Personal Perspective

Donald E. Super
Teachers College, Columbia University

Introduction

"There were giants in the earth in those days," (as *Genesis* says) or so it sometimes seems to those of us who were young psychologists when vocational psychology was first making its mark, and earlier when men like Walter V. Bingham, Harry Dexter Kitson, Donald G. Paterson, Frank Parsons, Rudolph Pintner, Lewis Terman, Edward Thorndike, Morris Viteles, and Robert Yerkes, together with women like Marion Bills, Beatrice Dvorak, and Millicent Pond were actively laying the foundations for a science and a technology of vocational psychology. Giants seem rare nowadays. Were they really giants, or did they just seem great because they were so few and the competition so limited?

Perhaps most were not really great. In fact, one of the second crop of vocational psychologists once said of one of the field's eminent elder statesmen that he was "American psychology's leading mediocrity," a statement that had in it enough truth, and enough falsehood, to cause me not to record here the identities of the speaker and of his subject.

Their real greatness matters not; what does matter is that, great, mediocre, or small, the giants stood out at a time when psychology was strongly laboratory-oriented and highly theoretical. They stood out because they were interested in the applications of psychology, and because for some of them the principal subject of study and object of application was *homo laborans,* people at work.

The giants were earthy. Many were from the Midwest or worked in the Midwest, and prided themselves on being "Dustbowl empiricists." Most of

5

them were the product of the pragmatism that tended to characterize American philosophy, well-exposed to "brass-instrument psychology" and quantitative methods, but interested in counting qualities that count and in the metrics of that which matters. Paterson never completed his doctorate, impatient with departmental requirements at Ohio State; Kitson treasured a bit of apparatus he had made as a graduate student conducting an obscure experiment, but like Pintner he discouraged his doctoral candidates from taking work in physiological and experimental psychology.

What mattered to the founders of vocational psychology was what people do, why they do it, how well they do it, and what satisfactions they get from doing it. In a work-oriented society dominated by the Protestant Work Ethic, work was man's, and woman's, most important activity on 5 or 6 days of the week. Hence the focus on work of many applied psychologists in the United States, some concerned with personal selection, job satisfaction, and productivity, some with occupational choice, satisfaction, and success.

What is Vocational Psychology?

The distinction just made suggests that vocational psychology and personnel psychology have two different focuses and that both differ from other aspects of industrial psychology in their focus on the working individual rather than on the work itself or the organization in which individuals work. The four specialties of *vocational psychology, personnel psychology, engineering* or *human factors psychology,* and *organizational psychology* are closely related and interdependent, but they do have different focuses.

Vocational psychology focuses on people thinking about careers, preparing for occupations, entering the world of work, pursuing and changing occupations, and leaving the world of work to devote what knowledge and energies they have to leisure activities that may resemble in content the work that they did for pay or which may involve quite different types of knowledge and skill. It might be called career psychology, and indeed that term is now occasionally used. It might have been called occupational psychology, a term used in Great Britain to denote the whole field of industrial psychology; if used it would preferably denote occupations rather than the people who pursue them. It would focus on the duties and tasks performed, on the abilities required, and interests and values for which they provide outlets. In the usage now prevailing, vocational and occupational psychology tend to be viewed as one field. It might help to adopt the term *career psychology* in order to make clear the focus on the developing person in search of and pursuing a vocation rather than on the static or (technologically) changing occupation.

Some definitions. It should have become evident that some basic terms need defining before we proceed further. These are: task, position, job, occupation, and career.

A *task* is a specific "job" (colloquial), operation, or project undertaken at work or at play (Super, 1976, p. 20); it is an assignment, a piece of work (Oxford, 1976).

A *position* is a group of tasks to be performed by one person (Shartle, 1946, 1959); a position exists independently of its occupant, it may be filled or vacant; positions are task- and product,-, not person-oriented (Super, 1976).

A *job* is a group of similar paid positions requiring similar attributes, in a single organization (Shartle, 1946, 1959). Jobs are task-, outcome-, and organization-oriented.

An *occupation* is a group of similar jobs found in various organizations; they too are therefore task-, outcome-, and organization-oriented, but they are also, importantly, society-oriented (Super, 1976).

A *career* is a sequence of positions occupied by a person throughout his or her preoccupational, occupational, and postoccupational life. It includes work-related roles such as those of student, employee, and pensioner or annuitant. When qualified by the term "occupational," it should be limited to these. When not so qualified, some would have it denote also complementary or alternate roles such as homemaker, citizen, and leisurite (Super, Crites, Hummel, Moser, Overstreet, & Warnath, 1957; Super, 1976, 1980).

A *vocation* can now be precisely defined as an occupation to which a person has a commitment; it is distinguished from occupation by the psychological meaning it has to the individual rather than its economic meaning to society. Vocations are person-centered (Super, 1976).

It is significant that English and English (1958), in their classic dictionary of psychology, define the terms occupation and vocation, but do not define the words career and job. They cite the religious meaning of vocation, a task in life to which one is called, and also define it as the way in which a person earns a living. This last fails to differentiate vocation from occupation, which is defined as an activity in which a person regularly engages for pay and also much more broadly as whatever one is doing. During the quarter-century since this standard dictionary of psychology was compiled, the scientific vocabulary of industrial psychology has been refined. But the refinements of some specialties have not yet had sufficient impact on psychology as a whole: the APA's *Thesaurus of Psychological Index Terms* (APA, 1977) still equates career, occupation, and vocation, thus handicapping literature searches and scientific communication.

Today *vocational psychology* combines the differential approach of occupational psychology, in the strict sense of that term, with the developmental approach of career psychology. It has itself gone through two major stages of evolution, having started out as the differential psychology of occupations with a focus on the men and women doing the work, and having evolved into the developmental psychology of boys and girls, and of men and women, considering and pursuing the occupations of which occupational psychology has given us a deeper understanding. In the next section we review the history of *differential psychology applied to occupations,* and in the section following we take up the later history that focuses on the *developmental psychology of careers.*

Differential Psychology Applied to Occupations

One who knew the pioneers and worked with some of them is strongly tempted to write about men and women, about the individuals who did the pioneering. Telling stories of the giants one knew while they still trod the earth can become a pleasant vice. Indulging occasionally in the history of people, the focus here is generally on the history of trends and events and on the institutions reflecting and creating them. People will appear in connection with the history they made or helped to make. Even then, this is a personalized history, history as one vocational psychologist saw it at the time and sees it in perspective, not history as gleaned, historiographically, from the archives.

A science and technology of occupations.   Although the beginnings of industrial psychology are generally traced to Hugo Munsterberg a decade or two earlier, it is also generally noted that it was the work of the psychologists serving the United States Army during World War I that actually launched what today is called vocational psychology.

Army classification needs led psychologists to build on the work of pioneers such as Alfred Binet, Arthur Otis, and Lewis Terman who studied individual differences in intelligence and developed tests for their measurement (Memoirs, 1921; Pintner, 1923, 1931). Robert Yerkes and others constructed the Army Alpha Test for use with groups, and Douglas Fryer (1922) and others quickly put the data on civilian occupational groups as seen in the Army into tables widely used as national norms in vocational guidance and personnel selection. It was not just in intelligence testing that the Army pioneered, but also in testing special aptitudes, particularly mechanical ability. The O'Rourke Mechanical Aptitude Test was one direct outcome of this work (Super, 1949, 1962). As Pintner points out, applied psychologists were stimulated by the Army data to collect survey data for many different types of employees in a great variety of companies, usually for personnel selection purposes.

The great impetus given to aptitude testing by World War I arose from the need to classify large numbers of new entrants into the Army and to assign them to appropriate types of military jobs. Civilian occupation and education often gave good leads, but many draftees were inexperienced, and some Army assignments did not resemble civilian occupations, making Army norms and general ability measures most imporant. The utility of the tests in the Army did a great deal to educate managerial personnel as to the possibilities of aptitude tests in personnel work.

Some 20 years later, World War II gave an even greater impetus to the development of aptitude testing. The Army General Classification Test replaced the old Army Alpha; other more specialized tests were developed by the Army (Harrell, 1946), the Air Force (Flanagan, 1948), the Navy (Stuit, 1947), and even the cloak-and-dagger services (Murray, 1948). Norms and cutting scores were developed for military occupational specialities and assignments were made accordingly; as the above sources report, the effectiveness of personnel selection and classification methods was thus greatly increased.

Again a great war had demonstrated the importance of testable individual differences in occupational success. Emergency conditions affecting the entire nation led, in both emergencies, to the assignment of large numbers of talented psychologists to test development and personnel research. In the Aviation Psychology Program alone, during the first 2 years of World War II, three Psychological Research Units each had staffs of about 25 officers and 125 enlisted men, all with at least a bachelor's degree, most with an MA or more, and many with doctorates in psychology or education assigned to test development and to classification testing for aircrew assignments. These units were supported and supplemented by two headquarters units. The leaders of this work were established psychologists, with John C. Flanagan (1947) at the head and Robert L. Thorndike and Frederick Davis and others at HQ with him, and with Laurence Shaffer, Arthur Melton, and J. P. Guilford (two of them later presidents of the American Psychological Association) in charge of the three field units; others in their units, and in other units established later in the war, already had established reputations and later became equally distinguished. The numbers in Dewey Stuit's Navy program and Thomas Harrell's Army program were smaller, but their contributions too wcre notable.

Again, the exposure of many general officers and others in the armed forces to the use of tests during a major war gave their civilian use a great impetus. This time psychology was much better prepared for expansion into the world of work than it had been after World War I, when excessive enthusiasm for its possibilities outran the numbers of qualified and cautious psychologists interested in business and industrial personnel research and application.

Civilian needs and potential thus twice became the focus of vocational psychologists after great wars. Between the two wars another national crisis had done a great deal to further research and development in vocational psychology. This was the Great Depression of the 1930s. This time it was not the need for the quick and efficient assignment of personnel to training and to active duty that was the stimulus; it was the need to understand the possibilities of reassigning men and women to types of employment in which there appeared to be growing opportunities as the fields in which they had been working shrank. The way had been paved for this by several spinoffs of World War I.

The Carnegie Institute of Technology, now part of Carnegie–Mellon, had founded a Division of Applied Psychology under Walter V. Bingham in 1915 (Brewer, 1942), gathering there a number of psychologists who, together with Edward L. Thorndike and Walter Dill Scott, headed up the Army work of World War I reported in *Memoirs* (1921). After the war, some returned to Carnegie Tech to the new but short-lived Personnel Research Foundation or went on to found in 1921, under J. McKeen Cattell, the Psychological Corporation. This corporation, its stock then held exclusively by psychologists and managed by a distinguished board of directors, went on, with Paul S. Achilles and then George Bennett as later presidents, to lead the way in the development of instruments and methods and in their use in personnel selection, training, and vocational counseling. Parallel with the work of this corporation was that of the Scott Company, in which Walter Dill Scott and associates conducted a number of landmark studies of managers, salesmen, clerical workers, and other occupations. When the Carnegie group broke up early in the 1920s, Bruce Moore went to Penn State and Edward K. Strong went first to George Peabody College and then to Stanford, taking with him ideas on the measurement of interests that soon led to his Vocational Interest Blank (Strong, 1927, 1943) and put the measurement of interests for vocational counseling and personnel selection on technical and usage levels approaching those of the measurement of intelligence and aptitudes (Darley, & Hagenah, 1955).

Also early in the 1920s the Minnesota Mechanical Abilities Project (Paterson, Elliott, Anderson, Toops, & Heidbreder, 1930) was launched, conceived of as the study of aptitude testing that might help with the assimilation into the U.S. labor force of the large number of European immigrants whose prior experience in backward rural areas gave little in the way of clues to possible industrial employment and who needed help through vocational counseling and placement. This small project bore fruit in several manual dexterity and mechanical aptitude tests but, more important, it paved the way for part of a major project, the Minnesota Employment Stabilization Research Institute (MESRI; Paterson, & Darley, 1936), which had as its objective, when founded in 1931, the development of psychological tests and methods for the assessment of the abilities and interests of the unemployed, to study the reeducation potential and problems of the unemployed, and to demonstrate methods of retraining and reeducation. The result, as reported in Paterson and Darley (1936) and elsewhere (Super & Crites, 1949, 1962), was the creation of what became known as occupational ability patterns or profiles, providing evidence of the feasibility of measuring many dimensions of individual differences and using these in vocational guidance and placement. Just as important as its substantive contributions, Minnesota, under Donald Paterson's leadership, attracted a large number of outstanding doctoral candidates, some of whom, including John G. Darley and Edmund G. Williamson, made their careers there, whereas others like Arthur Brayfield and Milton Hahn went elsewhere and continued to develop vocational psychology in their teaching and writing.

There were other spinoffs of the early Army work. At Teachers College, Columbia University, Edward L. Thorndike carried on research and development with intelligence and special aptitude tests and created a center that attracted able graduate students and other faculty members such as Harry Kitson. At The Ohio State University, Herbert Toops did pioneer work in measurement in an atmosphere made congenial to vocational psychology by colleagues like Harold Burtt whose text on employment psychology became a classic and Ralph Stogdill and much later Carroll Shartle, who both worked on leadership and, in Shartle's case, for the U.S. Employment Service on occupational analysis and classification (Stead & Shartle, 1940; Shartle, 1946, rev. 1952, rev. 1959). Purdue University, too, belongs in this list of early pioneering universities in vocational psychology, for there Joseph Tiffin, later joined by Ernest J. McCormick, founded another nucleus of occupational psychology researchers and practitioners.

Some business and industrial organizations, employing some of the new breed of personnel psychologists, launched programs of job analysis, test development, norming, and validation that added to the armamentarium of vocational psychologists. The Aetna Life Insurance Company, Life Agency Managment Association, Prudential Insurance Company, Proctor and Gamble, and Scovill Manufacturing Company are only some of the more visible contributors to the early literature on intelligence, special aptitude, interest, and biographical data in relation to type of work and to success in occupations. Among the leaders in applications in companies such as these were Marion Bills, Millicent Pond, Robert Selover, and Richard Uhrbrock.

Certain other psychologists who made important contributions to vocational psychology should be identified here. Clark Hull, later famous at Yale as a learning theorist, was the first to write while still at Wisconsin on the mechanical combination of test scores for vocational guidance and personnel selection, envisaging (Hull, 1928) a machine similar in its essential functions to the computers that today handle regression equations and produce test profiles and behavioral predictions. Morris Viteles at Pennsylvania pioneered the job psychographic method, produced a comprehensive and widely used text on industrial psychology (1932) and led in applications of current principles and methodology to both counseling and selection. Guilford (1936, 1954), even before making his military contribution in World War II, did fundamental research on the structure of mental abilities and of personality at the University of Southern California. This is only a partial list, one that not only leaves out people who made important contributions, but also leaves out details that would, if space permitted, add greatly to the picture of how vocational psychology developed.

It was the Minnesota work of the Great Depression years that undoubtedly made the major contribution of the development of vocational psychology. It had shown, in its construction and applications of aptitude tests, that tests could be developed and used in vocational counseling and in personnel selection for a great variety of occupations. In fact, one single battery could do this if given to appropriate subjects for norming and validation purposes.

The *General Aptitude Test Battery* (GATB; Dvorak, 1947), the *Dictionary of Occupational Titles* (DOT; U.S. Department of Labor, 1940), and the *Occupational Outlook Handbook* (U.S. Department of Labor, 1949) of the U.S. Employment Service, all since revised several times, were the direct outcome of Minnesota's demonstrations. The test research and development work was headed by Beatrice Dvorak, one of Minnesota's staff members. The job description work was directed by Carroll Shartle, a product of Northern Iowa, Columbia, and Ohio State Universities, but clearly influenced by, and funded as a result of, the MESRI work. Carl Heinz headed the outlook, or economic, work. These United States Employment Service and Bureau of Labor Statistics products led one observer to title an article in a professional journal "Vocational Guidance Is Now Possible," hailing the availability of tools that enable counselors to match people and occupations.

The new tools were quickly put to widespread use. Made available as the Great Depression was coming to an end, put to use as the defense industries were tooling up for and moving into wartime production and the armed services were preparing for the large-scale classification and assignment of men and women, they became the principal tools of vocational counselors and of placement workers. They served as models, too, for the development of instruments specifically designed and validated for military personnel in projects briefly described earlier in this chapter.

Again the wartime projects had important postwar byproducts, for again many of the psychologists who had done the work were interested in finding opportunities to carry on similar work in civilian settings, and many nonpsychologists in responsible positions had learned what psychology could do. A few anecdotal illustrations may not be out of place in this personal perspective on history.

Early in World War II, the director of an Air Force Navigation School came storming into the office of Laurence Shaffer, director of one of the three research and classification units, accusing the unit of having sent his school the dregs of the Corps of Aviation Cadets. The psychologist asked to see a roster that, when checked against the roster of recommended assignments, showed the navigator that most of the failing cadets had been recommended for return to regular army assignments because they were unqualified for aircrew: An important ally was won for the unit and its work.

Neal Miller and I, visiting a headquarters in search of some research data and talking with two recently assigned statistical control officers, were told excitedly that these management statisticians had discovered that "stanines" were very good predictors of success in flying training. Miller replied, "Yes, we know, we invented them for that and we make them." The desired research data were quickly forthcoming.

Finally, I was called into command headquarters on another occasion and accused by an air inspector of violating regulations in the performance of my unit's work. Having had some inkling of what was pending, I stated the case for the unit's practices, citing evidence for them, and was upheld. Leaving HQ with my immediate superior, a surgeon, the latter turned to me and said, "Super, you psychologists have a great advantage over the rest of us—you know how to read!" The reply was "Yes, sir, *and* to count."

When the war ended, educational, human factors, personnel, and vocational psychology bloomed, old organizations expanded, and new units and organizations sprouted both in existing organizations and independently.

The prewar Cooperative Test Service developed into the Educational Testing Service, headed by Henry Chauncey and focusing on testing and guidance for college admissions and adjustment. The American College Testing program was founded with similar objectives, and it was there that John Holland, a Minnesota Ph.D. with postwar experience in a veterans hospital, launched the research pursued later at Johns Hopkins on occupational choice as a process of matching oneself with a situation (Holland, 1973). His work is discussed later.

It was not just in serving education, however, that vocational psychology expanded.

The American Institutes for Research (AIR) were founded immediately after World War II by John C. Flanagan, their history reflecting well the developments of this period. One institute at first, based at the University of Pittsburgh in order to have an academic base for accreditation in the eyes of the public, it soon blossomed out into several institutes. Housing under one roof business, industrial, government, military, and educational projects on contract with appropriate organizations, the spinoff institutes specialized, in Pittsburgh under Brent Baxter (long at Prudential) in business and industrial research and development, in Washington in military and other government human factors work, and in Palto Alto in educational research, development, and applications. The first contract obtained by Flanagan was in 1946, when one of the major commercial airlines found that it had overexpanded and needed to release about 100 pilots before their probationary periods expired. AIR was still just a dream for Flanagan, a dream on which he was working, but he immediately recruited a core of full-time staff and a large number of the leading aviation psychologists who had served with him during the war. Robert Thorndike adapted some of the paper-and-pencil aptitude tests; I adapted two of the personality tests; Flanagan and others devised cutting scores; and with the combined efforts of a dozen or so of us who were used to working together on aircrew selection AIR became a young giant in a very few years. Project Talent (Flanagan et al., 1971) was its most important single contribution to vocational psychology with its development of the Career Data Book (Flanagan et al., 1973) and other materials throwing light on the aptitude, interest, and personality patterns of boys and girls tested in high school and followed up into college and into the working world.

It was not just organizations such as these. Science Research Associates was founded by Lyle Spencer and William Burns in Chicago to develop and distribute aptitude and interest tests and educational and occupational information (the last based on U.S. Employment Service data but packaged to make it appeal to the ultimate consumer in high school), and a greatly expanded Psychological Corporation supplemented government efforts to put tools into the hands of vocational psychologists and counselors. Individuals made independent contributions, often as university professors in the research-teach-demonstrate-and-apply tradition and sometimes as directors of small, personalized institutes.

Robert Ladd Thorndike was one of these, son of a distinguished educational psychologist who had done one of the first longitudinal studies of the validity of aptitude tests (E. L. Thorndike, 1931) and himself father of a third-generation psychometric Thorndike. At Teachers College, Columbia University, after World War II experience in aviation psychology, one of his contributions was, with Elizabeth Hagen (Thorndike & Hagen, 1959), a study of the postwar occupations (not careers in the sense of sequences, movement, and stability) of some 10,000 men who took the aviation cadet tests. Like Project Talent it was a developmental study for most of the men had been young, recently out of high school or college, with little significant civilian experience or training before they took the tests. The data were truly predictive, yielding distinctive profiles for many occupations although not predictive of success as assessed by the study: They did prove a tendency to enter fields appropriate to special aptitudes and provided profiles different from those of the U.S. Employment Service's General Aptitude Test Battery in that the latter are postdictive and hence possibly contaminated by training and experience. Many of Thorndike's other contributions were in personnel selection or in educational measurement.

Edwin Ghiselli was another research and development, as well as teaching, psychologist who did much to put good tools in the hands of vocational psychologists, (i.e., person-and-job matching tools in the early differential tradition of vocational psychology). A professor at the University of California at Berkeley after serving as an aviation psychologist, one of his contributions was the scientific synthesis of research findings on occupational abilities leading to helpful conclusions as to which special aptitudes have repeatedly been shown to be related to choice of or success in each of a number of occupations pursued in a variety of settings (Ghiselli, 1966). Ghiselli, like R. L. Thorndike, was primarily a psychometrician; he was unlike him in focusing primarily on industry and occupations and on aptitudes and their role in occupational success.

At Berkeley with Ghiselli, but working on different traditions, were Harrison Gough and Donald MacKinnon, the former a Minnesota clinician by training influenced no doubt by Paul Meehl, and the latter a Harvard theorist who was influenced by collaboration with Murray in selection for the cloak-and-dagger work of World War II. Both set to work to apply personality theory and assessment methods to occupations. Gough did this by producing a deceptively simple but effective adjective rating scale (Gough, 1952) and a "sane man's MMPI" by modifying the terminology of that clinical–diagnostic instrument to make it meaningful to men and women at work and collecting occupational norms for both. MacKinnon developed the first civilian assessment center, modeled after his and Murray's OSS center (1948), and demonstrated the possibilities of using clinical methods with psychometric and sociometric devices to judge human managerial and scientific potential.

Of essentially the same order, but quite different in method and in appeal, was the work of Anne Roe. A clinical psychologist who came to see that occupational roles provide one of the best ways of studying personality, her first vocational research was on the role of alcohol in the creativity of artists (1946); this led her to carry out a series of studies, using interviews, tests, and case or life histories and drawing on neo-Freudian and Maslovian theory, of distinguished natural scientists (1951a, 1951b, 1953). These led her to carry out a systematic review of the research literature on the psychology of occupations and to write a landmark book on the abilities, interests, and personalities of men and women in the various occupational fields (1956). Next came a widely read article on the early determinants of vocational choice (1957), drawing heavily on Maslow and on general child development theory and then research on the origins of interest (Roe & Siegelman, 1964). Her theory was to the effect that the psychological climate of the home, as determined by parental coldness and warmth, involvement and detachment, leads to person- and non-person orientations in children and that these in turn lead to the choice of different types of occupations. This in some ways represents a transition from differential vocational psychology to developmental vocational psychology. Its defect was that, overly influenced by Freud's emphasis on infancy and early childhood, she treated development almost as though it stopped at or soon after entry into school. This is no doubt the principal and sufficient reason for the failure of the large number of studies that her work inspired to support the theory and for the failure of her own well-designed final monographic study to support what was, indeed, a most appealing theory.

Holland, too (cited previously), may be viewed as a transition figure whose neat and simple theory inspired a large number of studies among doctoral candidates in search of topics of current interest that can be handled in a relatively brief span of time. Matching studies in the differential tradition thus have much more appeal than developmental studies that require waiting several years for subjects and data to mature. Building on the work of Strong (1943, 1955), Kuder (1939), Darley and Hagenah (1955), and others, Holland used occupational titles to measure interest in the major fields of work, finding that he could group Strong's and Kuder's larger numbers into six major categories that he called personality types on the basis of the nature of the work involved and, in due course, of the adjectives used by judges to describe the people in those occupations. These occupational fields or types of people, he found, were related to each other in varying degrees leading to a hexagonal arrangement or model of personality types. As his theory evolved it developed into a trait rather than a type theory, a situation as well as a person theory. Much of the research done with it is supportive (Super, 1981), but most of the designs used have been defective in that they use student choice or preference in, for example, the final year of study as the criterion that the predictor predicts, the predictor itself being an expression of occupational preference. A few studies have recently used the criterion of actual occupation entered after school or college with mixed results: More good studies are needed using behavioral (rather than verbal) criteria that are definitive choices.

Holland's theory, like Roe's, might be viewed as transitional from differential to developmental. It does imply development in a person as he or she seeks increasingly better situations in which to express personality and find outlets for interests and abilities. However, development is only implicit, it is not described: Holland's focus is on the mechanics of matching. As a result he has made available to practicing counselors and to counselees instruments that are useful in helping people do a better matching job than they might on their own. It tells vocational psychologists nothing about how people come to be, for example, enterprising and thus to seek entrepreneurial occupations.

Differential psychology applied abroad. Applied fields find it very easy to develop parochially, each country so concerned with what is happening at home and so convinced of the greater relevance of homegrown theories, developments, and products that they tend to disregard what is happening in other countries. This is not to deny the fact of international communication, for there is and long has been much interchange. Until a decade or two ago it was, in psychology, an activity of a small minority. The U.S. psychologists who studied in Germany with Wundt founded their own laboratories in the United States, and it was soon Clark University under G. Stanley Hall, Columbia under Edward L. Thorndike, Chicago under Judd, Pennsylvania under Witmer, and other such universities and personalities that produced America's theoretical and applied psychologists. International congresses attracted only a small number of Americans, of whom too large a percentage were and still are one-time participants and perhaps primarily tourists. The libraries of U.S. universities contained few foreign psychological journals, and many important European and Asian publications are still difficult to find in the United States. A personal example may be so relevant as to be warranted: Although when I returned to the United States from England with a bachelor's degree in 1932 I had learned four other modern languages and found that I could manage to read three more, I used them only three times before 1954; twice during World War II in interviewing Free-French and Polish airmen and once when a commission of French psychologists studying industrial productivity met with applied psychologists at Columbia University (only Robert L. Thorndike and I could converse at all in French). It was only after that experience that I subscribed to a number of French and British journals and bought occasional European books. Active since then in the International Association for Applied Psychology and the International Association for Education and Vocational Guidance, I now get Dutch, Italian, Portuguese, Spanish, German, Polish, Slovakian, and Serbo–Croatian publications (the last two, alas, only to decipher enough to know what to struggle through with a dictionary) and have a better European (although very incomplete) vocational psychology library than most universities.

Despite the problems of obtaining funding for participation in European, Asian, and South American meetings, despite the problems of precise communication in foreign languages, more and more Americans are now aware of what is happening overseas in our fields. It would therefore be pertinent to tell something of the story of vocational psychology in other countries. Space does not permit a real history, and for it the reader must be referred to Brewer (1942), Drapela (1979), Keller and Viteles (1937), and Reuchlin

(1964) for histories of vocational guidance with, in Brewer and in Keller and Viteles, attention to aspects of psychology important to it. The histories of psychology have been so heavily experimental in orientation that vocational psychology has been neglected.

A few institutions that pioneered or are doing important work in the field need to be mentioned. In Britain, the now-defunct National Institute for Industrial Psychology (NIIP) did ground-breaking work in research, development and applications during the 1920s and 1930s, led by F. M. Earle, C. S. Myers, and Cyril Burt (1931). They were followed by Alec Rodger (1952) who developed the "Seven-Point Plan" for assessment and vocational counseling that became basic to the work of Britain's careers officers (vocational counselors). The early pioneering and eminence of the NIIP did not continue, its research and development work ceased, and its contract work with industry was in due course not enough to keep it functioning in any way. Its place has been taken by a variety of researching university teachers in counseling or in occupational psychology such as Barrie Hopson of Leeds, Richard Nelson-Jones of Atson, Peter Herriott of Birkbeck College (University of London), Peter Warr of Sheffield, by training programs in the teaching-oriented polytechnics, and by institutes such as the National Institute for Careers Education and Counseling (NICEC) in Cambridge that are more concerned with career development than with matching approaches (Watts, Super, & Kidd, 1981).

In France, J. M. Lahy was one of the prewar founders of industrial psychology, ably followed by men like R. Bonnardel and women like Suzanne Pacaud in applications to personnel selection in organizations such as the French Railroads and Peugeot. It was Henri Piéron who became the grand old man of vocational psychology, founder of the National Institute for the Study of Work and Vocational Guidance (INOP) in 1928, author of a French classic on differential psychology (Piéron, 1949) and senior author of volumes in the same series that deal with psychometric methods and with using aptitude tests in vocational counseling and selection. Piéron set a testing and matching pattern like Britain's, but implemented by better tests and more highly trained counselors, for the work of vocational counselors, and maintained that pattern until the 1960s, when work in the United States on career development began to have impact on counselors and teachers of counseling willing to risk being branded as heretics. The result of the heresy was, in due course, a revolution that may have saved INOP from stagnation and led to the development of modified centers in a number of other cities, institutes more open to developmentalist ideas and practices than that in Paris where Piéron's distinguished pupil and successor, Maurice Reuchlin, is still dedicated to psychometrics. Private enterprise also plays a role, as in Pichot's Center for Applied Psychology and Guyot's Psychotechnical Institutes, both long-established test developers and publishers.

The Netherlands, like other Western countries, became active in vocational psychology early in its history, a tradition continued today in the Ministry of Social Affairs, the National Foundation for Vocational Guidance in Rotterdam, and the Universities of Amsterdam, Nijmegen, Tilburg, and Utrecht. S. Wiegersma of Amsterdam, Nathan Deen of Utrecht, Jan Grosfeld of Tilburg, and Leo van Geffen of Nijmegen stand out as major contributors. Van Geffen (1977) published a text on occupational choice, using Vroom's (1964) expectancy-value theory as the matching model.

Belgium's Psycho–Socio–Medical Centers are the contemporary followers of pioneer work begun before World War I but completely updated in the quality of staff, the sophistication of their methods, and their approach to assessment and counseling (Super, 1982). Charles Tomas of the School of Ergology in Brussels today leads in training and in research.

Germany, despite a good start under Hugo Munsterberg (1913) in industrial psychology and despite great contributions in experimental psychology before World War II, fell behind in applications and moved even further backwards under Hitler with what sought to be an "Aryan psychology." Since the last great war Germany has made great strides under the Ministry of Labor's Employment Service and with the cooperation of universities and other institutions of higher education. The Arbeitsamt is staffed by well-trained personnel who have developed test batteries, occupational descriptions, and other needed tools. Joachim Schaeffer of the Arbeitsamt in Nuremberg and Ludger Busshof of the Fachhochschule der Bundesanstalt fuer Arbeit in Mannheim are current leaders in the development of services and training of personnel.

In Switzerland, the Universities of Lausanne, Geneva, Neuchatel, and Zurich have provided leadership in developing tests and counseling materials, and Lausanne is a center for training counseling and industrial psychologists. Edouard Claparède (1922) of Geneva is generally viewed as the founder of vocational psychology in his country and as one of the conceptual and methodological leaders in France; he is credited also with having founded the International Association for Applied Psychology later in the 1920s, stressing "psychotechnology" or psychometrics and job analysis at the time of founding and thus contributing to the development of basic vocational psychology with a differential slant. Today, it is people like J. B. Dupont, J. P. Descombes, and F. Gendre of Lausanne and J. Cardinet of Neuchatel who are major contributors in French-speaking Switzerland, whereas in the German-speaking part of the country the older leaders like Franziska Baumgarten and Meili do not seem to have been replaced by young giants: Ernst Stauffer of Biel does stand out as researcher and practitioner.

In Italy the early beginnings of vocational psychology date, as in other

Western countries, from about the time of World War I. Sancto de Santis published on the subject as early as 1911, and in a 1919 work discussed aptitude testing and vocational adjustment. A. Gemelli was another early Italian giant, working, among other things, on the selection of military pilots. A committee, later Center ("Ente") for the Scientific Organization of Work, directed before World War II by M. Ponzo of the University of Rome also played a major role in launching vocational psychology in Italy as a broad-gauge field. Today both the Ministry of Education and the Ministry of Labor actively support applications in the field, but some of the early leadership role of Italian psychologists appears to be lost.

Spain too got off to an early start, first in Barcelona along pre-psychometric lines, but under the leadership of Mira y Lopez the Psychotechnical Laboratory was founded in Barcelona's Institute for Vocational Guidance shortly after 1918. In due course the National Institute for Psychotechnology was founded in the University of Madrid, which became a center for research and applications in personnel selection and vocational guidance. The names of Juan Mallart, José Germain, M. Yela, and Pilar Garcia Villegas stand out in the field, and in universities such as Barcelona, Valencia, and Salamanca faculty members, a number of them trained by Germain in Madrid, continue to carry on the tradition.

In the countries of Eastern Europe it is Poland, Czechoslovakia, and Yugoslavia that seem most interested and active in vocational psychology: Drapela (1979) describes the current picture. It is one in which the Soviet Russian policy of indoctrination and direction, rather than matching or developing, ceased to dominate sometime after the death of Stalin, although it is still dominant in Russia and in certain other Marxist countries such as Benin in West Africa (Super, in press). Choynowski began, in 1958, to develop Polish aptitude, interest, and personality inventories in his Psychometric Laboratory in the Polish Academy of Sciences; consulting and lecturing there and in three leading universities in as many cities in 1960 and 1966 I found widespread interest and considerable competence in an effort to catch up with what the West had done in applied differential psychology. Choynowski has since emigrated and his laboratory was dissolved, but the work is carried on by B. Hornowski and his vocational counselor wife at the University of Poznan. Counselors in schools and in the employment service have some of the training needed to use the tools of differential psychology.

In Czechoslovakia, Prague, Bratislava, and Brno have universities with active units concerned with vocational psychology. Jozef Koščo (1980), head of the Institute for Vocational Psychology at the Comenius University of Bratislava, directs an active program of research and publication in individual differences as related to occupations and, keeping up more than most Eastern Europe with the developmental approach that has spread from North America to Western Europe, as related to careers.

Yugoslavia, too, has kept in close touch with Western trends since World War II. The Ministries of Labor in the several countries have active programs of vocational guidance, from test development and job analysis to counseling and placement, staffed by trained personnel, led in Serbia by Branka Brančič and in Croatia by Dragan Tarbuk. Bujas of the University of Zagreb has dominated the field since World War II in a department of psychology leaning heavily toward quantitative methods and interested in personnel selection, vocational choice, and organizational psychology as pursued by Bramimir Sverko and others.

In the Far East, Japan has long had work under way in vocational psychology, paralleling the early U.S. studies of intelligence and occupation and, since World War II, translating many of America's texts and pursuing in a number of universities such as Tokyo, Kobe, Kyoto, Rikkyo and Osaka, studies of personnel selection and vocational counseling. The American GATB soon was adapted for use in Japan, and in more recent years there has been considerable interest in career development under the association's leadership spearheaded by Kihachi Fujimoto. An autonomous Institute of Vocational Research now provides a more stable base for the development of Japanese theories and tools appropriate to national traditions of organizational, as contrasted with personal, occupational careers.

Other Asian countries, particularly the Philippines, South Korea, Malaysia, and India have also made beginnings since World War II in developing personnel selection and vocational counseling tools and programs. Progress has been slow, due to economic problems, illiteracy, and cultural differences. Occupational choice is typically viewed as determined by the family rather than as a self-actualization process, which hampers even the development of matching methods. Institutions and names that stand out, other than the relevant ministries, include the Central Bureau for Educational and Vocational Guidance in India that dates from 1954 and is now a part of the National Council for Educational Research and Training; there Perin Mehenti Mehta, trained in career development theory and research in the United States, heads the program.

Israel, with many European- and U.S.-trained psychologists, has since achieving nationhood been very active in the field. The Universities of Tel Aviv and the Hebrew University were perhaps the first to offer work in vocational psychology; the Haddassah Vocational Guidance Service of Jerusalem has long had a well-established research and development program in job analysis, occupational information, test development, personnel selection, and vocational counseling, headed, for more than 20 years, by Zev Sardi.

In South America, the development of vocational psychology, whether for personnel selection or for vocational guidance, has generally been sporadic due to abrupt changes in governmental policies and practices. Brazil, despite this fact and despite its vast size and large illiterate population, has made real progress through the research and development staff of the Getulio Vargas Institute in Rio de Janeiro, one department of which has this as its concern. Its staff include members trained in both North America and Europe (France, Italy, or Spain), persons concerned with developing the tools of vocational psychology. In addition, several of the universities, both public (state) and private (Catholic), have counselor training departments and staff members, some of whom carry on research.

Finally, Australia and Canada, both very close to the United States in their development, warrant mentioning. The Australian Council for Educational Research, like the Educational Testing Service in the United States, develops tests for use in educational and vocational guidance. At the various state ministries of education and labor and in the universities staff and individual professors carry out research projects on individual differences and occupational choice and success.

In Canada, N. W. Morton (1935) of McGill University carried out a study of occupational ability profiles that resembled the landmark Minnesota study published 2 years earlier (Trabue, 1933), but with little impact on Canadian psychology or vocational guidance. It was only after the importance of the DOT and GATB in its southern neighbor became clear after World War II that Canada, through its Employment and Immigration Commission in a program headed by D. Stuart Conger, began an aggressive research, development, and applications program. Before that, the YMCA Vocational Guidance Service of Toronto under Gerald Cosgrove led the way in vocational counseling. At about the same time the Ontario Institute of Education began to publish educational tests and guidance materials, and the combined efforts of these and other organizations, including universities such as McGill, Toronto, Calgary, and Laval, quickly enabled Canada to catch up with and, judging by the nature and scope of current efforts, perhaps move ahead of the neighbor that it had for so long followed in so many ways.

Developmental Psychology Applied to Careers

It has been pointed out that from the first decade until the middle of this century vocational psychology was dominated by theories and instruments for the matching of people and occupations, by trait-and-factor theory and its instruments. But several trends contributed to change during the years after World War II. These included: (1) the fact that test construction had, technically, just about reached its apogee even before computers made possible a higher level of development through the more rapid handling of vast amounts of data; (2) the advancement of the mental hygiene movement and the growth of clinical psychology as an attractive specialty; and (3) the better training in other applied and human aspects of psychology of those going into its applications. Vocational psychologists were no longer experimentalists with little knowledge of personality theory, development, and social psychology. Both personnel psychologists and vocational counselors, many of the latter now counseling psychologists, brought more to vocational psychology than a knowledge of psychometrics, individual differences, and research methods.

A science of careers. The beginnings of career psychology (as it is not usually called) were in Europe, in the work of Charlotte Buehler and Paul Lazarsfeld, then of Vienna and later (but before World War II) of the University of Southern California and of Columbia University. They both conducted longitudinal studies of the work and related lives of men and women (Buehler, 1933, 1959; Lazarsfeld, 1931). At about the same time two Americans, a sociologist and a psychologist, published a study of the occupational histories of a representative sample of American men (Davidson & Anderson, 1937) and a few years later two other sociologists, D. C. Miller and W. H. Form (1951) published a study of the careers of another sample of adult males.

It was these works that led me to want to understand better than we did at the time just how careers unfold and why they unfold as they do. Building at that time on the Austrian developmental work, especially Buehler's, and on the Minnesota differential work, I wrote a text on the subject of vocational adjustment (Super, 1942). After World War II and excursions into test development and their vocational applications (Super, 1949), I turned again to the idea of a psychology of careers. The result was the planning of the Career Pattern Study, launched in 1951, the year in which Ginzberg's team at Columbia's School of Business published their occupational choice study (Ginzberg, Ginsburg, Axelrod, & Herma, 1951).

Ginzberg had asked me to prepare a working paper for his team on the theoretical base of American vocational psychology, I found little explicit theory, only implicit: the theory of individual differences and of their import for occupational choice and personnel selection. This strengthened my interest in providing a better theoretical base that called, as I saw it, for incorporating differential vocational psychology in developmental for a psychology of careers. Ginzberg's work did a great deal to prepare vocational psychologists for this broader approach, both in his challenge to us as nontheorists and in the insights that he and his colleagues drew, not so much from their data, as from Freudian and Piagetian theory.

In the basic theory and plan for the Career Pattern Study (CPS), colleagues and graduate students at Teachers College sought to bring together the insights of the several relevant fields of psychology, economics, and sociology. The first CPS monograph (Super, Crites, Hummel, Moser, Overstreet, & Warnath, 1957), a monograph on scientific careers (Super &

Bachrach, 1957), and a more general text (Super, 1957) were the result of this joint effort. Among other things, the term "career" was defined as in this chapter, and the term "vocational (later also called career) maturity" was established as part of the theoretical and working vocabulary of vocational psychology and guidance (Jordaan & Heyde, 1979; Super & Overstreet, 1960) and as an assessment trait (Crites, 1978; Super, Thompson, Lindeman, Jordaan, & Myers, 1981).

The trend thus started at Columbia spread as John Crites (1965, 1969) moved to Iowa, then to Maryland, and now at Kent State carried on a series of studies of career maturity and adjustment; Tiedeman, first at Harvard, then at AIR, at Northern Illinois, and now at the University of Southern California carried out the Harvard Studies of Career Development, and various texts on career development theories and developmental counseling began to appear and to find currency (Osipow, 1973; Tolbert, 1974).

Unaware of the ferment in vocational psychology, but contributing indirectly to it, was work under way in personality theory and social psychology at a number of universities. At Ohio State, Sidney Pressey maintained a long-standing interest in life-span developmental psychology, a voice crying in the wilderness save for that of his former student Raymond Kuhlen of Syracuse University (Pressey, Janney, & Kuhlen, 1939). Since the mid-1970s, in the National Center for Research in Vocational and Technical Education, this tradition is being carried on in studies of occupations and careers with Robert Campbell playing a leading role. In the Department of Psychology, Samuel Osipow (1973) is an active researcher, synthesizer, and editor. In economics, Herbert Parnes has been carrying out, with Department of Labor funds and data, massive studies of occupational mobility and hence of careers in adults. Ohio State thus maintains, somewhat disjointedly as is typical of universities, a leadership role in developmental approaches to careers and occupations.

Harvard, too, continued to contribute in its way, with David McClelland's (1953) work in achievement motivation, Murray's Harvard Study of Adult Development (Murray, 1938; White, 1954), Vaillant's (1977) similar work, and others. Unrelated to the work of Roe and Tiedeman while they were there, most personality theorists have been singularly unaware of the important possibilities for research in careers and occupations, not even mentioning these and related words or concepts in their studies of lives. Psychologists such as Edwin Schein (1978) at MIT, Douglas T. Hall (1976) at Boston University, and Daniel Levinson (1978) at Yale have mined the field with a yield of new insights into the roles that organizations play in career development and, in Levinson's case, into work as a function of personality changes associated with age.

At Stanford University Lewis Terman and Melita Oden (1925, 1947) conducted what proved to be the first long-term study of careers, focusing on

gifted children and their pursuit of educational, familial, social, and occupational careers. John Krumboltz (1979) and associates followed, many
years later, with a social learning theory of career development, not unlike
other current career development theories except in its emphasis on learning
and in its vocabulary.

More important for career psychology is the work of Marjorie Fiske
Lowenthal and a large group of associates at the University of California in
San Francisco (Lowenthal, Thurner, & Chiriboga, 1975). She and her colleagues took samples of four age cohorts in one middle-class community,
studying role and values differences with age and thereby shedding new
light on career development as the interaction of changing personalities and
changing role expectations.

At the American Institute for Research in nearby Palo Alto the
longitudinal style of Project Talent and the dynamic approach of the Career
Pattern Study led J. J. Card et al. (1975), an interdisciplinary team of the
type that has come to be both important, fashionable, and recruitable in the
behavior sciences, to develop a career development model and apply it, with
notable success, to the careers of college students, army cadets, and army
officers. Their use of path analysis brought into the domain of career
psychology a powerful technique for applying the logic of causation to the
use of regression methods.

With funding from the National Institute of Education, Hilton (1973) at
the Educational Testing Service, and then Davis and Levinsohn at the
Research Triangle Institute (1979) carried out the National Longitudinal
Study of High School Students, like Project Talent a massive follow-up of
students studied in high school and traced later in college or the world of
work.

There have been other follow-up studies of youth and adults (Bachman et
al., 1967; Foster & Wilson, 1942; Husen, 1969; Sewell & Hauser, 1975;
Trent & Medsker, 1967) which seem to have had little impact. Project
Talent, for example (Flanagan et al., 1962, 1971), seems to have impressed
people more by its size and scope than by its findings. Certain others have
indeed avoided near-oblivion (Astin & Panos, 1969; Bray, Campbell, &
Grant, 1974; Davis, 1964; Eckert & Marshall, 1938; Ginzberg et al., 1966).
One is inclined to speculate concerning the differences in impact. Perhaps it
is because some of them are census-type pedestrian studies that grasp the
imagination only if a creative thinker uses the data to illuminate hypotheses
or to derive new ones; perhaps in other instances they were published
through channels that did not reach the appropriate public; perhaps they
appeared when their potential readers were otherwise distracted.

A striking observation, however, is that few writers have drawn on many
of these in their work, and that no one has written a synthesis of the
psychology of careers, or of the sociology of careers, that takes them into

account. Few of them existed when I produced my text of that name (Super, 1957); now, perhaps, there are too many! Certainly, when with colleagues in Cambridge (Watts, Super, & Kidd, 1981) I sought to bring together the much scantier British work on career development in Britain with the supported intent of writing my own synthesis in the collaboration of my eventual coeeditors, we found that the task of synthesis would have to take much longer than the 3 years available for it: Instead, we edited a symposium produced by important contributors in education, psychology, and sociology. In my introductory chapter on U.S. approaches, I found myself compelled to limit myself to detailed discussion of two theoretical approaches and their research, omitting all of the studies mentioned in this section except the Career Pattern Study (my own!).

Some musings are prompted by the above, for although there is no doubt that career psychologists, like Osipow (1973) in his comprehensive book on theories, need to synthesize the related work that bears on their field, few developmentalists, personalty theorists, or social psychological theorists have examined the work on career development to see its import for their fields. This, despite Anne Roe's (1956) having pointed out and exploited the study of people at work in order to refine and apply personality development theory, despite Robert White's (1954) masterly use of career data in the development and refinement of his approach to personality theory, and despite Glenn Elder's (1968) use of Career Pattern Study-derived theory, along with Piagetian theory and other approaches, in a helpful chapter on adolescent socialization.

White's (1963) symposium *Festschrift* honoring Henry Murray, in which he was joined by other distinguished former students of that distinguished theorist and clinician, makes no reference to job, career, occupation, or work: The terms are not indexed, nor can they be found anywhere in the text. Baltes and Schaie (1973), Baltes and Brim (1979), and Nesselrode and Baltes (1979), in their landmark volumes on life-span developmental theory and research, seem unaware of what has been going on in the study of careers—this despite, for example, Brim's interest in adolescent and adult socialization (Brim & Wheeler, 1966).

Is the theorizing and researching in the psychology of career development so bad that it is unworthy of notice by psychologists in the other specialities? If so, they owe it to psychology, and to the people and organizations to which career development theory and methods are applied, to pay some attention to it, whether as critics of what has been done or by doing better work in the field.

Developmental psychology applied abroad.   The trends that started in the United States in the 1950s, and began to have real impact there in the 1970s with the career education movement in education and the career development movement in business and industry, began to have impact in Europe and Asia only in the late 1960s and 1970s.

In Great Britain, Barrie Hopson and John Hayes (1968) brought out a book of readings on the theory and practice of vocational guidance, of which the first two chapters were reprints of mine and my students and most of the others were American: The tide had begun to run toward Europe. My text (Super, 1957) was widely read there; Blocher, Hoyt, Samler, and Tiedeman, along with Carl Rogers and the counseling theorists, became familiar names among the school counselors trained at Keele by Gilbert Wrenn, Donald Blocher, and Lyle Schmidt among others; by Lawrence Stewart and Bruce Shertzer at Reading; by C. H. Patterson at Aston; and by Britons like Peter Daws at Leeds and then at Keele; by Hopson at Leeds; Patrick Hughes at Reading; and Hans Hoxter at Northeast London Polytechnic.

There was dissatisfaction however, in many quarters, with the simple importation of American theories and American practices. Watts and Bridgewater of the Careers Research and Advisory Center in Cambridge (a materials and methods publisher and methods trainer) sought and obtained foundation funding to bring an American theorist and researcher to Cambridge to launch and lead a program of research and research training in career development. Innovating in Great Britain, the term career was used in its developmental rather than static occupational sense, and the objective was the development of indigenous theory and indigenous research as a basis for developing or assuring the importation of methods and materials appropriate for the British culture. One result was the symposium volume with chapters recruited for the NICEC seminar on career development in Great Britain, tried out there, and refined by discussion and editing (Watts, Super, & Kidd, 1981). It is of course too early to judge its impact.

In France, too, the influence of American trends was felt. The language barrier prevented the importing of American theorists, researchers, and practitioners. Quasi-bilingualism did make it possible for me to function for a year (1958–1959) as a visiting professor in the Institutes of Psychology and of Vocational Guidance (one in the University of Paris, the other in the Conservatoire des Arts et Métiers), introducing instruction in counseling theories and methods that had hitherto been learned only in internships without formal instruction, and lecturing again when visiting there and at other universities on career development theory and vocational maturity. Despite the latter efforts, little work has been done in career development theory and research in France, partly because of the strength of the tradition of differential psychology, partly because of Ministerial misgivings about professional counseling psychologists ("conseillers psychologues"), and partly for funding reasons.

In Sweden, Husen (1969) and Magnusson, Duner, & Zetterblom, (1975) carried out longitudinal studies of career development at the same time that the National Labor Board and the Ministry worked together in developing and implementing programs of education and work experience designed to promote vocational maturity. It is not clear to what degree career development understanding (if not theory) contributed to the programs, which appear to have been derived largely from pragmatic common sense.

In the Netherlands, Wiegersma (1967) was a pioneer introducer of career development theory in a Dutch text, drawing heavily on Ginzberg and on my work but also on relevant European sources such as Naville in Belgium and keeping a nice balance between environmental forces and personal dynamics. Despite Wiegersma's eminence in his country as a developmentalist interested in careers and in vocational guidance and the contemporary interests of colleagues like Johan C. Helbing who are actively carrying on research in self-concept theory (itself capable of being viewed either differentially or developmentally) the differential theory and methods still prevail, perhaps because of the visibility of short-term matching methods and the short time span needed for differential research and matching assessment.

Career development theory has had impact, too, in other countries such as Spain (there is a Spanish edition of the *Psychology of Careers*), Portugal (through J. H. Ferreira Marques of the University of Lisbon), Czechoslovakia under Josef Koščo of Bratislava who has directed replications of some American studies with an approach that stresses self-actualization in a culture rather than self-subordination to the culture, and in Japan, where relevant U.S. studies and texts have been translated and Japanese studies of career maturity have been launched under the stimulus of exchanges and the leadership of Kihachi Fujimoto.

The total product overseas of developmental research is still not great. In few countries, Great Britain and Sweden being possible exceptions, has theory been implemented to any significant degree in career education and still less in counseling. But the trend has been started and will no doubt gather momentum as indigenous theory, methods, and programs develop.

Vocational Psychology in Practice

Just as this chapter aims to provide not a treatise on theories but one active person's perspective on the history of theories and applications, it aims not to describe practical applications in detail but to give a participant's eye view of the development of methods and programs. This account will therefore duplicate at points or refer to the sections on differential and developmental theories, especially when theory was visible only in its methods and instruments.

Vocational counseling. The original approach to formal vocational counseling is usually traced back to Frank Parsons (1909), a Boston lawyer–engineer–social reformer who became interested in unemployed school leavers and set up a counseling service in the Boston Civic House, a social settlement. In 1909 he published a book incorporating the three steps of vocational counseling as he saw them in practice and on reflection: self-analysis, occupational analysis, and "true reasoning" or counseling to relate personal to occupational information. At that time psychometric methods were in their infancy, Munsterberg's applications to personnel selection were unknown to those interested in helping unemployed youth, and assessment, like counseling, was done by interviewing.

Vocational tests soon became available, as we have seen. The result was that organizations such as the Vocational Service for Juniors in New York, the YMCA Vocational Services in Boston, New York, Chicago, Toronto, and elsewhere, sharing these concerns for the unemployed and for school leavers who might flounder in the labor force, began to use them early in the 1920s. The impetus given this work by the Minnesota studies, bearing full fruit in the U.S. Employment Service's and Bureau of Labor Statistics' DOT, GATB, and *Occupational Outlook Handbook,* together with the large-scale funding of counseling and placement work of the 1930s, made the matching method the eminently usable method of vocational counseling, whether directive as advocated by Edmund Williamson and John Darley (1936) and by H. M. Bell (1940), or nondirective as advocated by the Bixlers (1945). It led to the use of matching methods in occupational choice courses taught in high schools and colleges, where Parsons' methods were used with the aid of modern technology (Bennett, 1964). Even when computers were harnessed for use in counseling (Super, 1970) the first attempts (e.g., the Computerized Vocational Information System [CVIS], or the Educational and Career Exploration System [ECES]) used matching methods as easiest to computerize; it was only later that Bowlsbey, author of CVIS and influenced by Tiedeman and me, sought to introduce career development concepts and methods such as life-stages, developmental tasks, career maturity, and the Life–Career Rainbow into her second system, DISCOVER (Rayman & Bowlsbey, 1977). Similarly, the course on career exploration (Super & Bowlsbey, 1981) was innovative in that it, too, used the concepts of life stages and developmental tasks and of changing multiple roles.

The older models of counseling services with intake, testing, occupational libraries, and vocational counselors to help clients use all of these resources served as models for services launched by the Jewish Welfare Agencies, the National Youth Administration, high schools, colleges, and, with the approaching end of World War II, the Veterans Administration (VA).

Leaders in the early stage after World War I were Mary Hayes of the Vocational Service for Juniors in New York, Leona Buchwald, Susan Ginn, Richard Allen, and Helen Wooley, respectively, of the Baltimore, Boston, Providence, and Cincinnati public schools. In colleges, it was Donald Paterson of Minnesota, ably assisted and soon succeeded in that role by Williamson and Darley (1936), who established the model of college student counseling. It was widely copied elsewhere, a matching model that proliferated after World War II when thousands of veterans going to college on the GI Bill used the services of Veterans Administration Vocational Counseling Centers either under college auspices or in VA regional offices. It was Harold McCully and then Joseph Samler in the VA Central Office, with an advisory committee consisting of Daniel D. Feder of Iowa and San Francisco State, Williamson, and myself, with William Gellman added when more expertise in vocational rehabilitation became a greater need, who supported, more than guided, the enormous expansion of college counseling services that soon became integral to the colleges.

The U.S. Employment Service, with the return of control to the states after the war, lost much of its momentum for professional vocational counseling services. In a period of prosperity adult needs, other than those of the disabled, were less noticeable and the latter were served either by the VA or by the State Rehabilitation Services. These State Rehabilitation Services did expand and, with the private agencies especially, greatly raise their professional standards and services, still relying heavily on matching models but also recognizing the great assessment and developmental value of training and workshop experiences. The VA and the Federal Vocational Rehabilitation Service (under a confusing succession of ever-changing names) provided funds and leadership in the training, at the universities, of counseling psychologists and rehabilitation counselors in vocational counseling; they also stimulated and financed a considerable amount of relevant research.

Scholars of vocational counseling also contributed to the understanding of methods and instruments. Leona Tyler (1953/1969) wrote with unusual clarity and use of research on the work of the counselor, not just as assessment specialist but as counseling interviewer. Williamson (1950) produced more on directive counseling. Darley and Hagenah (1955) greatly illuminated the use of the Strong Vocational Interest Blank. My own texts (Super, 1949/1962, 1957) met real needs, as did Anne Roe's (1956) quite different work on occupations.

Guiding career exploration and planning. With the trends described above there began to be a distinct movement toward developmental counseling. Psychoanalytic theory and practice had made it clear that matching is often not enough. Nondirective theory had shown that helping people did not require choosing between three directive contacts and 3 years of in-depth exploration of the self, but that a good deal could be done to promote growth as well as a suitable placement if time were given to several interviews of self and interpersonal exploration without any predetermined number of appointments. And life-stage theory, as espoused by Pressey, Ginzberg, Tiedeman, and myself, had begun to add to the conviction that vocational guidance and counseling should begin early for exploratory purposes and progress through a series of learning experiences so that choices would emerge from experience as maturing required that they be made. Choice came to be seen as a process, not as an event. Models developed by Gelatt (1962) and Hilton (1962) and materials Gelatt devised for the College Entrance Examination Board helped to implement the theory in courses in career development and in career decision making.

Personnel selection, placement, and development at work. We have seen how the development of personnel selection procedures in World War I led to the expansion of business and industrial personnel work. V. V. Anderson (1929) led a pioneer program in Macy's Department Store in New York. Consulting organizations founded by Walter Bingham, Walter Scott, and J. McK. Cattell worked with corporate staff in many companies in the applications of matching methods. The limitations of such methods were too often underplayed, and they were for some time discredited despite the rebound and improvements of instruments of the 1930s. Again, World War II demonstrated the possibilities, and consulting firms blossomed and companies employed their own personnel psychologists.

This is when Douglas Bray et al. (1974) pioneered assessment methods at AT&T, Herbert Meyer did pioneer work at General Electric, Brent Baxter followed in the path of earlier pioneers in personnel selection for life insurance sales at Prudential, and Edwin Henry developed a widely heralded program at Standard Oil of New Jersey, to name just a few. Consulting firms like the McKinsey Company, Rohrer, Hibler, Replogle, and the Psychological Corporation worked on the selection of top management personnel and on employee selection systems for banks and other businesses.

Career development also came in for attention once selection procedures had been established and management could see that initial selection was not enough. Training was again recognized as important. Training now, however, was for more than the next assignment: training and development for the enhancement of promotion potential with the ultimate goal often uncertain, but with knowledge that an employee provided with opportunities to grow would often be ready for unanticipated assignments and to cope with unforeseen needs. The General Electric Company, at its Management Development Institute and with the leadership of Walter Storey, devised methods of including career development counseling its assessment center work, and related training needs to training offerings at the Institute. It went beyond that and aided by consultants devised methods and materials to take career development to staff members in the field who could not be accommodated at the Institute.

General Electric was not alone. IBM, AT&T, other giants, and even lesser companies prepared and carried out career development plans. They were not all in-house programs but often took advantage of the many assessment services and development or training activities carried on by consulting firms and by university professors of psychology, industrial engineering, or business administration. The National Training Laboratories started a movement of sensitization and personal development that became, for a time, something of a fad.

The life-long educational movement added another kind of impetus to this trend: If education had to go on throughout life in an ever-changing society, that education had to have a rationale, a purpose, a plan. Career development programs were a necessary consequence. Meetings of the American Society of Training Directors now reflect the trend. The U.S. Government, in its General Services Administration, has provided a model with its own career development program for its employees, and universities such as Virginia Polytechnic are pioneering with career development for not only maintenance and clerical staff but for hitherto training-exempt faculty members.

Envoi

The past still lives.   Matching people and jobs is as important as ever, and our methods and instruments are far better than they were 1, 2, 3, or 4 decades ago, inconceivable 60 years ago save perhaps to a Clark Hull (1928).

The present persists.   Career development has proved to be more than a fad and has found a permanent place in education and in industry while even the U.S. Army is developing, with Roger A. Myers of Columbia and JoAnn Bowlsbey of the Discover Center, computerized career development systems not only for officers but also for enlisted personnel.

The future cometh.   Not clearly, not as quickly to those of us who watch as the futurists would have us believe, but nonetheless inevitably. The past and the present are now producing something new in vocational psychology. Perhaps it will be something like the concept portrayed by my Life–Career Rainbow (Super, 1980) and used in several computer and paper-and-pencil career guidance systems, a concept that places the work role, or vocation, in the context of other life roles, some of which may be more important than that of worker.

Bray (1982) has come to see, in his longitudinal studies of managers, that career development is indeed a function of manifold roles, and the International Work Importance Study (Super et al., 1982) should soon provide tools for the assessment of the salience of the work, homemaking, civic, leisure, and study roles together with insights into the values sought by various types of people in these roles. The result should be a broadening and enrichment of our concepts and methods in vocational psychology.

Vocational psychology may thus indeed become career psychology and provide us with a theory for self-actualization in a combination of roles that change as the individual and society change.

REFERENCES

American Psychological Association. *Thesaurus of psychological index terms.* Washington, D.C.: Author, 1977.

Anderson, V. V. *Psychiatry in industry.* New York: Harper, 1929.

Astin, A. W., & Panos, R. J. *The educational and vocational development of college students.* Washington, D.C.: American Council on Education, 1969.

Bachman, J. G., Kahn, R. L., McCormick, M. T., Davidson, T. N., & Johnston, L. D. *Youth in transition.* Ann Arbor, Mich.: Institute for Social Research, 1967.

Baltes, P. B., & Brim, O. G. (Eds.) *Life-span development and behavior.* New York: Academic Press, 1979.

Baltes, P. B., & Schaie, K. W. (Eds.) *Life-span developmental psychology: Personality and socialization.* New York: Academic Press, 1973.

Bell, H. M. *Matching youth and jobs.* Washington, D.C.: American Council on Education, 1940.

Bennett, M. E. Strategies of vocational guidance in groups. In H. Borow (Ed.), *Man in a world at work.* Boston: Houghton Mifflin, 1964.

Bixler, R. H., & Bixler, V. H. Clinical counseling in vocational guidance. *Journal of Clinical Psychology,* 1945, *1,* 186–192.

Bray, D. W. The Assessment Center and the study of lives. *American Psychologist,* 1982, *37,* 180–189.

Bray, D. W., Campbell, R. J., & Grant, D. L. *The formative years in business.* New York: Wiley, 1974.

Brewer, J. M. *History of vocational guidance.* New York: Harper, 1942.

Brim, O. G., & Wheeler, S. *Socialization after childhood.* New York: Wiley, 1966.

Buehler, C. *Der menschliche lebenslauf als psychologisches Problem.* Leipzig: Hirzel, 1959. (Originally published, 1933.)

Card, J. J., Goodstadt, B. E., Gross, B. E., & Shanner, W. M. *Development of a ROTC/Army career commitment model.* Palo Alto, California: American Institutes for Research, 1975.

Claparède, E. *Problems and methods of vocational guidance.* Geneva: International Labor Office, 1922.

Crites, J. O. Measurement of vocational maturity in adolescence. *Psychological Monographs,* 1965, *79* (2, Whole No. 595).

Crites, J. O. *Vocational psychology.* New York: McGraw-Hill, 1969.

Crites, J. O. *The Career Maturity Inventory.* Monterey, Calif.: CTB/McGraw-Hill, 1978.

Darley, J. G., & Hageneh, T. *Vocational interest measurement.* Minneapolis: University of Minnesota Press, 1955.

34   SUPER

Davidson, P. E., & Anderson, H. D. *Occupational mobility in an American community.* Stanford, Calif.: Stanford University Press, 1937.

Davis, J. A. *Great aspirations.* Chicago: Aldine, 1964.

Davis, J. A., & Levinsohn, J. R. The National Longitudinal Study of the High School Class of 1972. In J. A. Mulholland (Ed.), *New Directions in testing and measurement.* San Francisco: Jossey-Bass, 1979.

Drapela, V. J. (Ed.). *Guidance and counseling around the world.* Washington, D.C.: University Press of America, 1979.

Dvorak, B. J. The new U.S.E.S. General Aptitude Test Battery. *Journal of Applied Psychology,* 1947, *31,* 372–376.

Earle, F. M. *Methods of choosing a career.* London: Harrap, 1931.

Eckert, R. E., & Marshall, T. O. *When youth leave school.* New York: McGraw-Hill, 1938.

Elder, G. H. Adolescent socialization and development. In E. F. Borgatta & W. W. Lambert (Eds.), *Handbook of personality theory and research.* Chicago: Rand McNally, 1968.

English, H. B., & English, A. C. *A comprehensive dictionary of psychological and psychoanalytic terms.* New York: Longmans Green, 1958.

Flanagan, J. C. *The Aviation Psychology Program of the Army Air Forces.* Washington, D.C.: U.S. Government Printing Office, 1948.

Flanagan, J. C., Dailey, J. J., Shaycroft, M. F., Gorham, W. A., Orr, D. B., & Goldberg, I. *Design for a study of American youth.* Boston: Houghton Mifflin, 1962.

Flanagan, J. C., Shaycroft, M. F., Richards, J. M., Jr., & Claudy, J. G. *Project Talent: Five years after high school.* Palto Alto, Calif.: American Institute for Research, 1971.

Flanagan, J. C., Tiedeman, D. V., & Willis, M. B. *Career data book.* Palo Alto, Calif.: American Institute for Research, 1973.

Foster, R. G., & Wilson, P. O. *Women after college.* New York: Columbia University Press, 1942.

Fryer, D. Occupational intelligence standards. *School and Society,* 1922, *16,* 273–277.

Gelatt, H. B. Decision making: a conceptual frame of reference for counseling. *Journal of Counseling Psychology,* 1962, *9,* 240–245.

Ghiselli, E. E. *The validity of occupational aptitude tests.* New York: Wiley, 1966.

Ginzberg, E., Ginsburg, S. W., Axelrod, J., & Herma, J. *Occupational choice.* New York: Columbia University Press, 1951.

Ginzberg, E., et al. *Life styles of educated women.* New York: Columbia University Press, 1966.

Gough, H. G. *The Adjective Checklist.* Palo Alto, Calif.: Consulting Psychologists Press, 1952.

Guilford, J. P. *Psychometric methods.* New York: McGraw-Hill, 1954. (Originally published, 1936.)

Hall, D. T. *Careers in organizations.* Pacific Palisades, Calif.: Goodyear, 1976.

Harrell, T. W. AGCT results for Air Force specialists. *Educational and Psychological Measurement,* 1946, *6,* 341–350.

Hilton, T. L. Career decision making. *Journal of Counseling Psychology,* 1962, *9,* 291–298.

Hilton, T. L. *The base year of the National Longitudinal Study of the High School Class of 1972.* Final Report to Dept. of Health, Education, and Welfare, National Center for Educational Statistics. Princeton, N.J.: Educational Testing Service, 1973.

Holland, J. L. *Making vocational choices.* Englewood Cliffs, N.J.: Prentice-Hall, 1973.

Hopson, B., & Hayes, J. (Eds.). *Theory and practice of vocational guidance.* Oxford, England: Pergamon, 1968.

Hull, C. L. *Aptitude testing.* Yonkers, N.Y.: World Book, 1928.

Husen, T. *Talent, opportunity, and career.* Stockholm: Almqvist & Wiksell, 1969.

Jordaan, J. P., & Heyde, M. B. *Vocational maturity during the high school years.* New York: Teachers College Press, 1979.

Keller, F. J., & Viteles, M. S. *Vocational guidance around the world.* New York: Norton, 1937.

Koščo, J. *Teoria a prax poradenskej psychologie.* (Theory and practice of counseling psychology.) Bratislava: Slovenske Pedagogicke Nakladatelstvo, 1980.

Krumbolz, J. D. A social learning theory of career decision-making. In A Mitchell, G. Jones, & J. D. Krumboltz (Eds.), *Social learning and career decision-making.* Cranston, R.I.: Carroll, 1979.

Kuder, G. F. *Manual to the Kuder Preference Record.* Chicago: Science Research Associates, 1939.

Lazarsfeld, P. *Jugend and Beruf.* Iena, Germany: Fischer, 1931.

Levinson, D. J. *The seasons of a man's life.* New York: Ballantine, 1978.

Lowenthal, M. F., Thurner, M., & Chiriboga, D. *Four stages of life.* San Francisco: Jossey-Bass, 1975.

Magnusson, D., Duner, A., & Zetterblom, G. *Adjustment: A longitudinal study.* Stockholm: Almqvist & Wiksell, 1975.

McClelland, D. C., Atkinson, J. W., Clark, R. A., & Lowell, E. L. *The achievement motive.* New York: Appleton-Century, 1953.

Memoirs. Washington: The National Academy of Sciences, 1921, *15,* Ch. 15.

Miller, D. C., & Form, W. H. *Industrial sociology.* New York: Harper, 1951.

Morton, N. W. *Occupational abilities.* New York: Oxford University Press, 1935.

Munsterberg, H. *Psychology and industrial efficiency.* Boston: Houghton Mifflin, 1913.

Murray, H. *Explorations in personality.* New York: Oxford University Press, 1938.

Murray, H., & the OSS Assessment Staff. *Assessment of men.* New York: Rinehart, 1948.

Nesselroade, J. R., & Baltes, P. B. *Longitudinal research in the study of behavior and development.* New York: Academic Press, 1979.

Osipow, S. H. *Theories of career development.* (2nd ed.). Englewood Cliffs, N.J.: Prentice-Hall, 1973.

Oxford. *The concise Oxford dictionary of current English.* Oxford: Clarendon Press, 1976.

Parsons, F. *Choosing a vocation.* Boston: Houghton Mifflin, 1909.

Paterson, D. G., & Darley, J. G. *Men, women, and jobs.* Minneapolis: University of Minnesota Press, 1936.

Paterson, D. G., Elliott, R. M., Anderson, L. D., Toops, H. A., & Heidbreder, E. *The Minnesota mechanical abilities tests.* Minneapolis: University of Minnesota Press, 1930.

Piéron, H. *La psychologie différentielle.* Paris: Presses Universitaires de France, 1949.

Pintner, R. *Intelligence testing.* New York: Henry Holt, 1923, 1931.

Pressey, S. L., Janney, J. E., & Kuhlen, R. G. *Life: A psychological survey.* New York: Harper, 1939.

Rayman, J. R., & Bowlsbey, J. A. H. DISCOVER: a model for a systematic career guidance program. *Vocational Guidance Quarterly,* 1977, *26,* 3–12.

Reuchlin, M. *L'orientation pendant la période scolaire: Idées et problèmes.* Strasbourg: Conseil de la Coopération Culturelle, 1964.

Rodger, A. *The seven-point plan.* London: National Institute of Industrial Psychology, 1952.

Roe, A. The personality of artists. *Educational and Psychological Measurement,* 1946, *6,* 401–408.

Roe, A. A psychological study of eminent physical scientists. *Genetic Psychology Monographs,* 1951a, *43,* 121–239.

Roe, A. A psychological study of eminent biologists. *Psychological Monographs,* 1951b, Whole No. 331.

Roe, A. A psychological study of eminent psychologists and anthropologists. *Psychological Monographs*, 1953, Whole No. 352.

Roe, A. *The psychology of occupations*. New York: Wiley, 1956.

Roe, A. Early determinents of vocational choice. *Journal of Consulting Psychology*, 1957, *4*, 212-217.

Roe, A., & Siegelman, M. The origin of interests. *The APGA Inquiry Series*, No. 1. Washington, D.C.: American Personnel and Guidance Association, 1964.

Sanctis, S. de Psicologia della vocazione. *Revista di Psicologia,* 1919.

Schein, E. H. *Career dynamics*. Reading, Mass.: Addison–Wesley, 1978.

Sewell, W. H., & Hauser, R. M. *Education, occupation, and earnings*. New York: Academic Press, 1975.

Shartle, C. L. *Occupational information: Its development and application*. Englewood Cliffs, N.J.: Prentice-Hall, 1946, rev. 1952, rev. 1959.

Stead, W. H., & Shartle, C. L. *Occupational counseling techniques*. New York: American Book, 1940.

Strong, E. K. Vocational guidance of executives. *Journal of Applied Psychology*, 1927, *11*, 331-347.

Strong, E. K. *Vocational interests of men and women*. Stanford, Calif.: Stanford University Press, 1943.

Strong, E. K. *Vocational interests 18 years after college*. Minneapolis: University of Minnesota Press, 1955.

Stuit, D. B. *Personnel research and test development in the Bureau of Naval Personnel*. Princeton, N.J.: Princeton University Press, 1947.

Super, D. E. *Dynamics of vocational adjustment*. New York: Harper, 1942.

Super, D. E. *Psychology of careers*. New York: Harper, 1957.

Super, D. E. *Appraising vocational fitness*. New York: Harper, 1949, rev. with Crites, J. O., 1962.

Super, D. E. (Ed.). *Computer-assisted counseling*. New York: Teachers College Press, 1970.

Super, D. E. *Career education and the meanings of work*. Washington, D.C.: U.S. Office of Education, 1976.

Super, D. E. A life-span, life-space approach to career development. *Journal of Vocational Behavior*, 1980, *16*, 282-298.

Super, D. E. Approaches to occupational choice and career development. In A. G. Watts, D. E. Super, & J. M. Kidd (Eds.), *Career development in Britain*. Cambridge, England: Hobson's Press, 1981.

Super, D. E. *Educational and vocational guidance as means of increasing mobility in the educational system*. Paris: UNESCO, 1982.

Super, D. E., Ferreira-Marques, J., Romeo, J., Casserly, C., Lokan, J., Srerko, B., Nevill, D., & Krau, E. *The relative importance of work: Reports from eight countries*. Symposium at the International Congress of Applied Psychology, Edinburgh, Scotland, July 27, 1982.

Super, D. E., & Bachrach, P. *Scientific careers and career development theory*. New York: Teachers College Press, 1957.

Super, D. E., & Bowlsbey, J. A. *Guided career exploration: Teachers manual*. New York: Psychological Corporation, 1981.

Super, D. E., Crites, J. O., Hummel, R. C., Moser, H. P., Overstreet, P. L., & Warnath, C. F. *Vocational development: A framework for research*. New York: Teachers College Press, 1957.

Super, D. E., & Overstreet, P. L. *Vocational maturity of ninth-grade boys*. New York: Teachers College Press, 1960.

Super, D. E., Thompson, A. S., Lindeman, R. H., Jordaan, J. P., & Myers, R. A. *The Career Development Inventory*. Palo Alto, Calif.: Consulting Psychologists Press, 1981.

Terman, L. M. *Genetic studies of genius*, (Vol. 1). Stanford, Calif.: Stanford University Press, 1925.

Terman, L. M., & Oden, M. H. *The gifted child grows up*. Stanford, Calif.: Stanford University Press, 1947.

Thorndike, E. L. *Prediction of vocational success*. New York: Commonwealth Fund, 1931.

Thorndike, R. L., & Hagen, E. *Ten thousand careers*. New York: Wiley, 1959.

Tolbert, E. L. *Counseling for career development*. Boston: Houghton Mifflin, 1974.

Trabue, M. R. Occupational ability patterns. *Personnel Journal,* 1933, *11,* 344–351.

Trent, J. M., & Medsker, L. L. *Beyond high school*. Center for Research in Higher Education, University of California, Berkeley, 1967.

Tyler, L. E. *The work of the counselor*. New York: Appleton-Century-Crofts, 1969. (Originally published, 1953.)

United States Department of Labor. *Dictionary of occupational titles*. Washington, D.C.: U.S. Government Printing Office, 1940, (revised periodically since).

United States Department of Labor. *Occupational outlook handbook*. Washington, D.C.: U.S. Government Printing Office, 1949 (revised periodically since).

Vaillant, G. E. *Adaptation to life*. Boston: Little, Brown, 1977.

van Geffen, L. *De keuze van werk*. (The choice of work). Culemborg, Holland: Scholpers, B. V., 1977.

Viteles, M. S. *Industrial psychology*. New York: Norton, 1932.

Vroom, V. H. *Work and motivation*. New York: Wiley, 1964.

Watts, A. G., Super, D. E., & Kidd, J. M. (Eds.). *Career development in Britain*. Cambridge, England: Hobson's Press, 1981.

White, R. W. *Lives in progress*. New York: Dryden, 1954.

White, R. W. (Ed.). *The study of lives*. New York: Atherton, 1963.

Wiegersma, S. *Psychologie van beroep en beroepskeuze* (Psychology of occupation and occupational choice). Groningen, Holland: Walters, 1967.

Williamson, E. G. *Counseling adolescents*. New York: McGraw-Hill, 1950.

Williamson, E. G., & Darley, J. G. *Student personnel work*. New York: McGraw-Hill, 1936.

2 Current Theoretical Issues in Vocational Psychology*

Lenore W. Harmon
Helen S. Farmer
University of Illinois

Introduction

There are those who believe that theory building in psychology is a pretentious attempt to emulate the physical sciences that results in adapting inappropriate strategies and models. Although we are sure that there is room in psychology for strategies that are not strictly experimental we believe that the psychologist, whether operating as scientist, practitioner, or in some combination of the two roles, should operate as a theory builder. The vocational counselor/practitioner who operates without a knowledge of accrued theory (whatever its level of explanatory power) and who operates without constructing microtheories that guide practice in specific cases, has little more to offer the client, or society as a whole, than the local palm reader. On the other hand, the vocational psychologist who builds theory without a firm basis in the reality of people's lives and needs, will at best be simply lucky or wrong, and at worst, squander resources and influence lives in a negative way.

It is possible to operate unethically in either the scientist or practitioner mode by ignoring the process by which good theory is built. This process seems to us to involve alternating and interacting cycles of inductive and deductive reasoning (Gibbs, 1979) with (if we are lucky) a few creative and revolutionary ideas that change the field drastically and irreversibly, occur-

---

*We enjoyed writing this chapter together. Much of it could have been written by either of us. However, the sections on achievement motivation are a special contribution of Helen Farmer, whereas the sections on sociology and economics are a special contribution of Lenore Harmon.

ring as a result of a unique confluence of knowledge and persons (Kuhn, 1970). We do not, however, believe following Kuhn that all counseling psychologists (scientists and practitioners) will or must ascribe to one paradigm. Reality can be viewed from more than one perspective and different paradigms may be required based on one's vantage point. For example, two individuals who have revolutionized vocational psychology by their contributions to theory building are John Holland and Donald Super. Holland's theory concerns itself primarily with vocational choices whereas Super's concerns itself primarily with the individual developmental state in which choices occur. It is not necessary that we choose between these theorists and their vantage points. What we do need is a creative and revolutionary theorist who will help us to understand when it is most useful to look at a situation from Holland's vantage point (here we use Holland as a proxy for all those vocational psychologists who are primarily concerned with vocational choice, realizing that we detract from the uniqueness of both Holland and those for whom he stands proxy) or from Super's vantage point (using Super as a general proxy for all those vocational psychologists who are primarily concerned with vocational development). Super himself (1980) has outlined the general topography of such a synthesis, but it remains for some theorist to hypothesize the rules by which we understand when to operate from theories of choice and when to operate from theories of developoment. When that revolution occurs, it is our belief that we will not as Kuhn (1970) suggests be united by one paradigm but that new apparent disjunctures will quickly appear or become more salient, only to be resolved by further creative theoretical ideas.

In this chapter we address several issues in vocational psychology that should be important both to researchers and practitioners. Most of these issues reflect the unfinished task of establishing increasingly comprehensive, parsimonious, and valid theory for the field. Our fragmented theories presently guide both research and practice but leave many unresolved issues for both practitioners and researchers to contend with. We have tried to avoid the temptation to review the evidence for one theory or to logically derive the next relationships to be tested within the confines of a given theory. Instead we have set ourselves the task of exploring among theories, in an attempt to suggest some issues that are not evident from the vantage point of a particular theory. It is our hope that the issues addressed here will help to illuminate the areas not covered by current theories and ultimately lead to research that will help to expand and integrate current theories.

The hallmarks of a good theory have been variously defined. Osipow (1973) suggested six such hallmarks for vocational theory: (1) the evidence available supports the predictions that arise from the theory; (2) the theory is elegant in that it encompasses a broad range of phenomena; (3) the explanations provided by the theory lead to a better understanding of certain events; (4) the theory is testable by empirical means; (5) the theory is logically consistent; and (6) the theory is parsimonious; that is, it attends to a broad range of phenomena with the least possible number of postulates.

In this chapter we address at least three of these hallmarks. In our effort to strengthen vocational psychological theory it seems important to increase the range of phenomena it addresses, hallmark (2), and at the same time increase parsimony, hallmark (6). One means of doing this is to incorporate within vocational psychology elements of other theoretical systems that relate to our field. Examples are the achievement motivation literature and the cognitive, personal, and moral development literature. In our effort to strengthen vocational psychological theory it seems important, too, that our explanations related to career choice and career development encompass the experience of persons from minority groups, females as well as males, and a full range of social classes, hallmark (3).

We discuss issues that arise in relation to theories that have developed outside the field of vocational psychology. Specifically, the relationship between theory growing out of the fields of sociology and labor economics to theory growing out of the field of vocational psychology is of interest. Within psychology, the relation of the work of the career development theorists to the work of persons who study ego development in general, cognitive development, and moral development has not been fully explored or exploited. Neither has the career motivation literature been well-related to the achievement motivation literature. Although there are other areas we could have addressed, we have limited ourselves to these broad areas outside vocational psychology in order to explore in some depth possible heuristic links between them and our field both for future research and for practice.

Within the field of vocational psychology there are several theoretical issues that could be addressed, but we have not attempted to be exhaustive. We have raised a number of illustrative issues related to different age groups, spanning children through mature adults. We have chosen issues that are of interest to us, more as a model of how we should think about current theories than as a definitive statement of which issues are most important. In relation to children we discuss the relative vacuum in vocational psychology and we raise the issue of the effect of this vacuum on career education programs in the elementary school years. An issue related to adolescence has to do with the theory and measurement of vocational maturity. The issue is whether vocational maturity is primarily cognitive, both cognitive and affective, or a more holistic concept encompassing cognitive, affective and behavioral aspects. A related issue is sex differences and vocational maturity. We discuss the research evidence indicating that girls are more mature than boys. The issue is whether this evidence is an artifact of measures used or actual sex differences in maturity. Several issues are discussed related to vocational choice. One revolves around theories that assume freedom to choose and theories that view choice as limited or ascribed by situational determinants such as social class, race, or sex. Other such issues have to do with whether or not it is useful to counsel adolescents in order to improve their career choice, and how vocational assessment affects career choice. Once the person has entered the job market several issues related to the sources of job satisfaction arise. Finally, we discuss issues of emphasis in the study of vocational behavior. Whether we study the most convenient or the most theoretically interesting groups and problems is discussed.

ISSUES RELATED TO NONPSYCHOLOGICAL THEORIES

Vocational Behavior and Occupational Sociology

Occupational sociology is a field that complements vocational psychology and has much to offer in building comprehensive theory in vocational psychology. Occupational sociologists have been interested in three areas of particular interest to vocational psychologists: (1) work roles and socialization into work roles; (2) the variables that effect social stratification; and (3) worker alienation.

Occupational roles are social roles. Different occupations require that workers display different behaviors, for instance in terms of the clothing, speech, social relationships, and values that the worker is expected to espouse. Psychologists have looked primarily at the abilities, physical skills, and interests associated with various occupations. Because psychologists are skilled in psychological measurement, they have tended to investigate variables that can be measured. Sociologists, in attempting to understand the roles played in various occupations have taken a more ethnographic descriptive approach in some of their research. For example, studies such as the one describing the roles of hockey players (Faulkner, 1974) have a richness that few psychological studies of occupations possess. In an attempt to be scientific, researchers in vocational psychology seem to have neglected methods such as case studies and participant observation that might be more fruitful heuristically than the type of descriptive studies that they usually do.

Studies by occupational sociologists are especially interesting in their analyses of the use of power within and between roles. A more sophisticated understanding of role theory, role socialization, and power might have helped vocational psychologists to understand sex segregation in occupations long before the assumption that women's innate psychological characteristics fitted them for "women's work" was challenged by members of the women's movement. At any rate, some occupational sociologists have taken a much more detailed look at people in occupations than vocational psychologists usually do. We must ask ourselves if this type of analysis might enhance our theories of vocational behavior.

On the other hand, some occupational sociologists have concerned themselves with intergenerational status attainment. For these sociologists the prediction of occupational level, as measured by indexes of income and education (Duncan, 1961; Nam & Powers, 1968) or prestige (Treiman, 1977) is of major interest. The predictive variables they have used, such as father's attainment and education, race, sex, and urban–rural residence have included, for the most part, things that are immutable. The usual form of analysis is path analysis performed on data from very large samples. None of these studies accounts for all of the variance in occupational attainment. This subunit of occupational sociology poses some interesting issues for vocational psychologists as follows.

One issue is the relative importance of occupational level and occupational type. Sociologists are interested in level because of their interest in social strata and mobility between social strata. Vocational psychologists have been less interested in level, probably because it is seen as closely related to *individual* ability, and more interested in type of occupation. Gottfredson and Becker (1981) have presented data that suggest that the general level of future occupational attainment is relatively fixed quite early by socioeconomic level and that attainment of various types of occupations takes place within the boundaries of a prespecified range of values on the level continuum. Warnath (1975) has cautioned vocational psychologists and counselors against promising attainments that society cannot deliver. Greater attention to the prediction of level in addition to type of occupational attainment seems to be in order within vocational psychology because level seems to be a more potent variable.

A second issue proposed by the status attainment research is whether the method of path analysis can be used to explore variables that are more amenable to change or intervention than those traditionally studied by occupational sociologists. We suggest that the method may be used to attempt to account for additional amounts of variance in status attainment by utilizing other types of predictor variables. The models presented by Farmer (1978) and O'Neil, Meeker, and Borgers (1978) for explaining career attainment in women each contain sets of self-concept variables and environmental or context variables, both of which are open to change, in addition to variables measuring background such as social class that are not open to change. Within the self-concept set in the Farmer model are such modifiable variables as self-esteem, achievement style (i.e., cooperative and competitive) and sex role orientation. Within the context set in this model are such potentially modifiable variables as support for achievement from parents, teachers, and important others. If these can be shown to influence career attainment as much as the background variables in the status attainment model by using a method such as path analysis, we may be able to use the model to determine how to change career attainment. Some preliminary path analyses by Farmer with her model indicate that long-range career commitment is more influenced by self-concept and context variables than by static background variables. However, research is still needed to determine the relationship of these types of variables to actual career attainment. We would encourage vocational psychologists to apply path analyses in their research for its potential to identify complex relationships among variables.

A final area in which we might learn from occupational sociology is the study of worker alienation. Occupational sociologists have paid attention to philosophers such as Marx (1964), who talked about workers whose only commitment to their work was to earn a living because they have no sense of control or relationship with the work they do, which may be boring, uncomfortable, and/or dangerous. Vocational psychologists have taken as a starting point the assumption that people are motivated to work by something other than necessity. Consequently, our theories do not deal very well with individuals who do not see mature vocational choices (as usually defined by vocational psychologists) as the means to any type of satisfaction. Industrial psychologists have done some work on the effects of redesigning jobs but these efforts are usually directed at workers in relatively high level jobs who are not usually defined as alienated. Little effort is expended within vocational psychology to understand the alienation of the young, unskilled workers or minority group members. The issue is whether we have any theories or concepts that help explain alienation.

In sum, theories of vocational psychology might be enhanced by including some traditionally sociological variables such as roles, power, alienation, and level of attainment as well as by considering the use of some research methods, such as direct observation, description, and path analysis, more often used by sociologists than by psychologists.

Labor Economics and Vocational Behavior

Vocational psychologists are interested in processes and decisions that result in life-long career patterns for individuals. Accordingly they focus on variables such as abilities, skills, values, and interests. Labor economists, on the other hand, are interested in supply and demand in the labor market. Their interests converge with those of vocational psychologists at the point where they are interested in long-run decisions of individuals to supply their labor in the market place, and in the decisions they make that affect their wage rates and other types of return from their labor. Labor economists are interested in workers as human capital, and in the factors that cause individuals and families to invest in human capital in the form of schooling and/or on-the-job training. Such factors include the cost in deferred income and interest as well as expected earnings on the investment (for example, people with more ability learn more from schooling than those with less ability, other things being equal). Likewise firms invest in workers through on-the-job training. Fleisher and Kniesner (1980) conclude

> the human capital approach is an extremely powerful and flexible tool of economic analysis that has yielded insights into a broad spectrum of social behavior and institutions which had not previously been viewed as within the province of economic analysis. Thus, health, child-rearing activities, and family size as well as occupational choice and schooling are all seen to require the investment of scarce resources that yield both pecuniary and nonpecuniary future returns [p. 304].

Labor economists are interested in how individuals are distributed in the labor market, which is, of course, related to wages offered. Although they studied different populations, Mincer (1962) found that schooling and experience (investments in human capital) accounted for 29% of the variation in earnings and Griliches (1977) found that schooling and age accounted for 29% of the variation in earnings. Although there are effects on wages related to both occupation and industry (Hanoch, 1965) they are much smaller than the effects of schooling and experience. No causal relationships can be implied from these studies that employed regression analyses but they raise some interesting questions for vocational psychologists.

One question has to do with how individuals use wage and labor market information in their career decision making. A review of the College Placement Annuals for several years will show that the number of graduates from a given educational program is related to previous demand and wages for graduates with similar education. Ekehammar (1977) discussed the application of three types of cost-benefit models in career decision making. He rejected the economic cost-benefit model as requiring an unrealistic level of sophistication on the part of the decision maker. His psychological-economic cost-benefit model utilized individuals perceptions of economic cost-benefits as opposed to factual data. Finally he proposed a psychological cost-benefit model that incorporates a broader range of psychological costs and benefits than the purely monetary. He showed that psychological profit (psychological benefit minus psychological cost) was positively related to educational aspiration level (years of post-high school education the individual was willing to undertake) and career choice (to go to work or to school after high school graduation). In a later analysis, Ekehammar (1978) tested a model for predicting career choice (as defined above) from background variables of intelligence and family background and intervening variables of psychological profit and educational aspiration. For boys, the model was efficient and psychological profit had direct and indirect effects on career choice. For girls, the model was much less predictive and psychological profit affected career choice only through educational aspiration. Ekehammar's work suggests that perceived costs and benefits including the economic, affect certain gross decisions about investing in human capital. His introduction of psychological and perceptual modifiers into the evaluation of costs and benefits is extremely important. There has been, as yet, no test between the psychological-economic cost-benefit model and the purely psychological cost-benefit model. Such a test would help illuminate the relationship between economic and psychological factors in career decision making.

Another related question that is suggested by economic analysis is whether choices about level of occupation or type of occupation or some combination of the two are effected by the economic perceptions of the choice maker. Gottfredson (1981) suggests that the boundaries of choices among occupational levels are set quite early in life. Labor economists would attribute this phenomenon, in part, to differing availabilities of resources (money for schooling, parental attention, and encouragement) for human resource development in different families. If it can be documented that economic forces affect investment in human capital and eventual occupational level, how does that effect the choice of occupational field? Gottfredson and Becker (1981) have shown that the choice of field and level are not independent. That is, some fields offer few opportunities at some levels. Will vocational interests in a field offering only low-level economic returns be ignored, or are vocational interests prepotent over economic interests? The same question might be asked concerning the effect of values and abilities utilization on overall levels of occupation.

The consequences for vocational behavior theory are clear. We need to determine how our favorite variables fare in combination with the variables stressed by labor economists. We need to be much clearer about when and for whom economic factors are dominant in influencing vocational behavior and when and for whom they are not.

ISSUES RELATED TO OTHER PSYCHOLOGICAL THEORIES

Within psychology itself we have chosen to explore developmental psychology and theories of achievement motivation. Other areas could have been selected but we chose to raise issues related to two areas in some depth rather than cover all possible psychological theories related to vocational psychology. These two areas were chosen because of their potential contribution to a study of vocational behavior and because they were of interest to the authors.

Ego Development and Vocational Behavior

Super's early understanding (Super, 1953) that career choice involves implementing a vocational self-concept should lead directly to the conclusion that the development of the self may be of primary importance in early career development. To avoid a complex discussion of the definitions of self and ego and their interrelationships, we have chosen here to focus on what theories of ego development, as exemplified by Loevinger, Erikson, Knefelkamp, and adult developmental theorists, have to suggest to career development theories.

Loevinger (1976) has reviewed the developmental stages and types proposed by many theorists and concluded, "When many people operating from different assumptions and different kinds of data have convergent conceptions, that convergence confirms the common elements [p. 68]." She shows the relationship among the stages proposed by various theorists (Ausubel, 1952; Erikson, 1963; Ferenczi, 1916), the ego types proposed by other theorists (Fromm, 1941; Graves, 1966; Riesman, Glazer, & Denney, 1954) and the ego stage types proposed by still another set of theorists (Kohlberg, 1964; Perry, 1970). She shows how each is related to her own set of ego stages that are designed to be developmental without being strictly age related.

Loevinger proposes several stages and levels but only those most relevant to vocational behavior are reviewed here. Because her stages are not strictly age-related they are described in ascending order.

Loevinger's Self-Protective stage is characterized by anticipating short-term rewards and punishments as a means of impulse control. Work is perceived as unpleasant. Adults at this stage are concerned with power and advantage and act in manipulative ways. This stage is related to Erikson's stage of Autonomy versus Shame and Doubt and Perry's stage of Duality.

Loevinger's Conformist stage is characterized by identification with the group rather than protection against it and a rather simplistic approach to right and wrong (based on group norms). This stage is related to Erikson's (1963) stages of Initiative versus Guilt and Industry versus Inferiority, as well as Perry's (1970) stage of Multiplicity–Prelegitimate.

Loevinger's Conscientious stage (1976) is characterized by "long-term self-evaluated goals and ideals, differentiated self-criticism, and a sense of responsibility [p. 20]." The individual has a sense of choice and achievement that is "measured primarily by *his* own standards rather than mainly by recognition or by competitive advantage [p. 21]." This stage is related to Erikson's stage of Identity versus Role Diffusion and to Perry's stage of Relativism.

Loevinger's Autonomous stage is characterized by an ability to recognize and cope with inner conflict and to integrate complex ideas and roles. Self-fulfillment is a goal that may be more important than achievement. This stage is related to Erikson's stage of Intimacy versus Isolation and to Perry's stage of Commitment.

Loevinger points out that the stages can be seen as developmental or as evidences of individual differences within cohorts. We may well ask ourselves if the vocational fantasies of childhood (Ginzberg, Ginsburg, Axelrod, & Herma, 1951) are related to the short-term rewards of the Self Protective ego stage, whether the sex stereotypic vocational choices of some young people (Harmon, 1971) are related to the Conformist stage, whether the level of an individual's career maturity and the realism and suitability of their career choices are related to attainment of the Conscientious stage, and whether the mid-life changes of adult males or the multiple roles currently being played successfully by many persons, especially women, are dependent on having reached the Autonomous stage.

Alternatively we can hypothesize that adults in the Self Protective stage, being concerned with power and advantage, may be Enterprising in Holland's sense (1973), that those in the Conformist stage, being concerned with right and wrong, may be Conventional, and that those in the Conscientious and Autonomous stages will be more widely distributed over Holland types or occupations than those in the Self Protective and Conformist stages. Obviously applying Loevinger's ego stages to vocational behavior may help us to explain in a richer way why certain vocational choices are made at various times in the life of the individual in response to differing conceptions of the self.

Erikson (1963) attempted to relate his work to the vocational sphere. It is interesting to note, however, that few vocational researchers have attempted to relate Erikson's work to the field of vocational behavior. However, Munley (1977) did review the implications of Erikson's theory for career development theory and did do some research relating Erikson's developmental theory to career development. Munley's own work (1975) showed that college students who had career choices that were consistent with their measured abilities and interests showed more successful resolution of Erikson's first six stages than those whose vocational choices were inconsistent with their measured abilities and interests. Although Munley (1977) concluded, "this area should be a productive one for career development research [p. 268]," little research has built upon his 1977 formulation. Fannin (1979), an exception, explored the relationship between ego-identity status as defined by Erikson and several other variables among college women. She found that women in the Foreclosure status (representing a premature commitment as a resolution to the identity crisis [Marcia & Friedman, 1970]) were in more typical majors, were less work role salient, and were more traditional in sex-role attitude than those in other statuses.

Some who have attempted to relate concepts from developmental theory to career development concepts have apparently been successful. Knefel-kamp and her co-workers have adapted Perry's developmental scheme to career development in general and to the career development of women in particular (Knefelkamp & Slepitza, 1976; Knefelkamp, Widick, & Stroad, 1976). This important theoretical application of developmental theory to career development seems currently to be sidetracked into issues of how to measure the developmental constructs of the Perry theory adequately. This step is inevitable in any application of developmental theory to career development. It may explain why more such adaptations are not made. Theory building is not easy and the field of vocational behavior will only advance when careful studies of such applications are made.

It is important to determine whether students' cognitive capabilities are related to their vocational behavior. Knefelkamp's adaptation suggests that students who make vocational choices while they are in the stage of Duality would make less satisfactory choices than those choosing after they have reached the Commitment within Relativism stage. It also suggests that some types of indecisive students should be best helped by being moved beyond the Relativism stage of cognitive development.

Recently, there has been increasing interest in adult development. These developmental approaches may emphasize stages. Erikson and Loevinger extended their stages into adulthood. Perry's stages seem to apply only to college students and adults. Levinson (Levinson, Darrow, Klein, Levinson, & McKee, 1978) postulates stages that apply to adult men only. Others, like Neugarten (1976) and Lowenthal (Lowenthal, Thurner, & Chiribogo, 1975), are more interested in studying adult transitions as responses to a set of roles and events faced by groups of individuals than stages.

These adult stages and transitions have some rather obvious applications to vocational behavior, but most of them are not even well-established let alone integrated in theories of vocational behavior. For instance Rush, Peacock, and Milkovich (1980) found that only 37% of 759 managerial, professional, and technical employees went through career stages in the order that Levinson's theory would predict and that the age-stage relationships suggested by Levinson did not occur. Career satisfaction, education, career commitment, job performance and productivity, and job commitment were also explored by Rush et al. as predictors of career stage with mixed results. The authors acknowledged the possibility that more sophisticated techniques than those they used may be needed to test the theory.

The adult development literature does suggest some interesting hypotheses about the vocational behavior of adults. For example, how does the process of mentoring effect either member of the dyad? How does the ability to cope with normal adult transitions, in family roles and relationships, in physical functioning, in social roles and relationships, relate to various aspects of vocational behavior such as creativity, productivity, and satisfaction? Under what conditions are these variables positively or negatively related?

Cognitive Developmental Theory and Vocational Decision-Making Skill

The relationship of cognitive developmental theory to vocational psychology may be illustrated with respect to career decision-making theory. Cognitive developmental theorists such as Piaget (1965) have found that cognitive capacity develops through a series of sequential stages and that the higher level cognitive skills cannot occur before a person has mastered the lower level skills in preceding stages. Certain cognitive skills associated with decision making are found to be age-related by Piaget. For example, the ability to engage in abstract formal thinking is a prerequisite to evaluative skill involved in decision making. The vocational psychologist would do well to know what the typical cognitive capacities of different age students are in order to encourage teaching these skills when students are cognitively ready.

There is considerable agreement about the skills involved in decision making. Jepson and Dilley (1974) summarized the various approaches to vocational decision making, indicating that most include the ability to: focus the problem/goal; generate a list of alternatives (i.e., brainstorming), seek out and obtain relevant information about alternatives (i.e., information processing skill); relate information to goals (i.e., means–ends thinking); evaluate among alternative solutions (i.e., evaluative skill, social cognition, time perspective); select from among alternatives; develop a plan for implementing the alternative; and act to implement the plan.

In middle school vocational educators/counselors might focus more on teaching means–ends thinking and brainstorming than on a full range of decision-making skills. Spivak, Platt, and Shure (1976) present evidence that one of the most important problem-solving skills is means–ends thinking. This skill involves the ability to orient oneself to and conceptualize the step-by-step process of moving toward a goal. It contains a number of elements, among them careful planning and the insight and forethought to forestall or circumvent potential obstacles. It also involves the recognition that a time perspective must be taken into account in successful planning. Spivak has found that middle school children are developmentally able to engage in this type of means–ends thinking. He and his associates have also found that middle school students vary in their level of expertise in this skill and that training can increase the capacity of those who have poor skill in means–ends thinking. The training programs developed by Spivak and his associates are typically a semester long and involve students in solving their own real life problems. Vocational psychologists might investigate the usefulness of such training for improving career decision-making skills at various ages.

Vocational psychologists who study career decision making, such as Katz (1966), Harren (1979), and Super and Bowlsbey (1979), have raised questions about the timing of counseling interventions aimed at teaching persons decision-making skills. It is possible that the theory and research of Piaget, and Spivak, et al. (1976) shed some light on this question. It appears that aspects of decision-making skill can be learned very early in life, for example brainstorming (Spivak, et al.). However, other aspects, would be more appropriately taught after the person has developed cognitively to the point where he or she has the capacity to demonstrate these skills.

Work Values and Moral Development Theory

Work values have been thought to play an important role in the career choice process, especially by Super (1970) and Katz and Kroll (1975). Both Super and Katz (1966) have identified particular values with certain occupational titles. In Katz's System of Interactive Guidance Information (SIGI), participants are invited to rank order their values. They are then presented with a list of occupational titles that are found to satisfy their highest ranked values. Later the participant is confronted with a value dilemma in which their top ranked values cannot be satisfied by the same occupation. Through this process of ranking and conflict resolution, Katz indicated, the student is led to clarify his/her values and their career development may thus be enhanced. In a similar vein, Super suggests that counselors and educators use a student's scores on the Work Values Inventory to discuss with the student what is important to them and how these values might be satisfied through particular occupations.

Overlap would seem to occur between the crystallization of some work values and the crystallization of moral values. Two examples of such overlap are the values of altruism and autonomy. Both of these values are prominent in moral development (Gilligan, 1977; Hogan, 1973; Kohlberg, 1981) and appear also on lists of work values (Katz, 1966; Super, 1970). Moral development theory suggests that these values mature rather late, if at all, and are found among college-aged students but less commonly among adolescents (Kohlberg, 1981). What does it mean for a high school student to rank altruism or autonomy at the top of his or her work values list? The student may be making a judgment about his or her values that is more a reflection of social desirability than personal choice. Kohlberg's moral development levels would place most adolescents at the Conventional level where reference to peers and family ultimately gives way to reference to community norms and socially accepted morality. Thus, a high rank for altruism by a high school student may simply reflect family or peer influences. It is only at the Postconventional or Principled level in Kohlberg's developmental schema that persons choose because they believe in a value for its own sake. If Kohlberg is correct it may be premature to counsel adolescents using their work values as a basis for occupational exploration. It would be interesting to investigate whether it might be developmentally more enhancing to challenge the student to think about why they rated a particular value so high (or low). This type of challenge might enhance the process of moving the person from a Conventional morality stage to an Autonomous stage in which work values are endorsed because they are valued independent of external social sanctions.

The value altruism has been associated by some authors (Bakan, 1966; Bernard, 1971; Gilligan, 1977; Parsons & Goff, 1980) with feminine characteristics. In contrast these authors associate autonomous, individualistic characteristics with male development. If these theorists are correct, that altruism is a feminine value and autonomy is a masculine value, the implications for vocational psychology are interesting. Super (1970) reported that his Altruism work value scale on the Work Values Inventory was endorsed more highly by females than by males at the twelfth grade. However, this difference was not significant at the seventh grade, although females at that grade, too, scored somewhat higher. Persons in occupations such as priest, social worker, and teacher also scored higher on this work value. Holland's (1973) Social interest scale, which measures interest in working with and helping people, is also endorsed more by females than by males. More recent data from high school populations indicates that males are scoring higher on the Social scale than in previous decades, although still not as high as females (Holland, 1980).

The development of altruistic and autonomous values is traced by Gilligan (1977), a colleague of Kohlberg's, back to early experiences in the family that may differ for males and females when they receive their primary parenting from the mother. When this parenting pattern holds males are required to develop a sense of discontinuity with the mother in order to develop a sense of their own identity, whereas females do not have to dissociate themselves from their mother in order to acquire a sense of their own identity. For females, Gilligan argued, relationships with others are continuous with a sense of their own identity and permit an earlier appearance of the helping ethic. For boys, the ethic of individualism necessarily precedes their experiencing and valuing of relationships and the helping ethic. Gilligan's argument suggests that vocational psychologists might investigate the effects of other parenting practices on the development of these values, for example the effect of encouraging the development of autonomy and altruism in both males and females by parents.

Because some values are not fully defined until adulthood, the role of moral development in mid-life career changes would be another interesting area for exploration.

This section has reviewed some of the work of moral development theorists such as Kohlberg and Gilligan at Harvard. We suggested that their work might be useful to vocational psychologists in better understanding age-related aspects of the development of values and the role of values in career choice and vocational satisfaction.

Developmental Approaches: General Issues

Most of the developmental approaches, implicitly or explicitly, leave us with a sense of order among the levels and the possibility that individuals will reach some maximum stage that is lower than the highest possible level. One of the most interesting issues arising from developmental theories is whether it is desirable to attempt to facilitate the highest level of development in everyone. This issue can be approached from an economic viewpoint once we have established how to facilitate the highest possible levels of ego development, cognitive development, and moral development among various groups or individuals. Alternatively, it can be approached from the viewpoint of social planning once we have established how various levels of ego, cognitive, and moral development interact with career choice and vocational behavior in the world of work. For instance, if it were possible to create the total work force of individuals who had reached Loevinger's Autonomous stage, Perry's stage of Commitment and Kohlberg's level of Individual Principles of Conscience, how would the world of work change? What jobs would not be done? Would the concepts of leadership, power, and subordinate position change? Would the process of producing goods and services change? Perhaps our failure to take these questions seriously is indicative of our lack of confidence in the power of scientific theory to lead to behavioral control.

Within the field of vocational psychology we are probably guilty of developing our theories from too narrow a base as well as of setting our goals for behavioral change so high that we would be frightened by the effects of success. As psychologists, we tend to conceptualize solutions in individual terms. It is quite obvious to us that it is healthy psychologically to be autonomous, committed, and highly principled. We tend not to think of the collective social consequences of such solutions. The authors submit that serious contemplation of the social consequences of these "good" psychological developments might lead to scenarios of social change that are frightening in their difference from what is now known and familiar. It seems to us that we can choose our puzzles as scientists. To choose to solve puzzles when we do not wish to contemplate the consequences of the sought-after solution may lead us to the remorse of the early atomic scientists (Stern, 1969). If we are not willing to look at the consequences then we should choose other puzzles with solutions that have more predictable social consequences. Good application of psychological theory, like good research, requires that one start the project with some forethought, some contemplation of the results, whether the hypotheses of the project are accepted or rejected.

Achievement Motivation Theory and Vocational Behavior

Achievement motivation theorists have distinguished between several concepts that could have an important bearing on vocational psychological theory. For example, achievement motivation theorists have distinguished between the concepts of long- and short-term achievement motivation. The former is typically associated with career motivation, whereas the latter is related to motivation to master a particular task. The concept of challenge or risk taking is related in different ways to both long- and short-term motivation by these theorists. The concepts of intrinsic and extrinsic values and of their satisfaction through achievement and work is also addressed by achievement motivation theorists.

These distinctions could have useful implications for vocational psychologists. Achievement motivation theory and research has seldom attempted to integrate or articulate with career motivation theory and research. For example, in the early work of achievement motivation theorists (Atkinson, 1958; McClelland, 1958, 1971), there is no reference in the indexes to career or vocation. In Super and Holland's numerous publications, achievement motivation research is rarely referenced. However, the dominant career development model represented by the work of Super (1957, 1980) defines the highly career motivated person in terms not unlike those of the achievement motivation model (i.e., persistence, independence, intrinsic motivation, self-esteem, etc.). It seems to us that career motivation is an important dimension of achievement motivation and relates not only to postschooling employment motivation but also to the development throughout life of a range of work-related interests, values, and skills that contribute to cumulative achievement in a career.

In their recent book Atkinson and Raynor (1978) devote their two final chapters to a discussion of career motivation and its relationship to achievement motivation. They view achievement motivation as the drive behind individual accomplishments whereas the cumulative accomplishments of an individual result, in their view, from career motivation. The measurement of the two types of achievement may be illustrated by a student's grade on a midterm and his or her cumulative grade point average (GPA). Students who score high on measures of short-term achievement such as a midterm may or may not score high on measures of long-term achievement such as their cumulative grade point average. The difference in scores depends in part on motivational factors affecting future orientation, persistence, fear of success, anxiety level, opportunities, and number of activities competing for the attention of the person. Important in this model is the view that persons who achieve well on individual achievement tasks may or may not achieve at a high level in a career. Atkinson describes the student whose test anxiety level is moderate as achieving optimally on individual achievement tasks, whereas the same student may not achieve optimally over time (i.e., GPA, career) if other activities distract or compete for his or her time.

One of the differences between achievement motivation and career motivation is the striving for excellence in self-selected areas in the former (Atkinson, 1978) whereas there is a striving for self-fulfillment in the latter (Holland, 1973; Super, 1980). Career motivation has a lifetime, long-term dimension made up of a series of satisfying experiences, but ultimately ceasing only at the termination of life itself. Achievement motivation may be targeted to specific areas (i.e., grades in school or sports) and continually be transferred to new areas as accomplishments in one area no longer challenge the person. Knowledge of differences in long- and short-term motivation may be useful in counseling an adult involved in changing occupations. Such a person may be strongly motivated to find self-fulfillment and it may be more important to them to select an occupation that he/she feels will be satisfying than one he/she performs best in. These possibilities could be investigated by vocational psychologists.

A limitation within achievement motivation theory is the view held concerning the types of goals or values satisfied by a career. Raynor's (1978) view of the goal of cumulative achievement (career motivation) is limited to extrinsic rewards such as salary increases, promotions, status, fame, and power. Career motivation theorists such as Super (1957, 1980) have stressed intrinsic rewards or goals as well as extrinsic rewards. Examples of intrinsic rewards include self-fulfillment, autonomy and creativity. Super's (1980) concept of work salience includes several intrinsic and extrinsic dimensions: work for leisure, security, economic gain, intrinsic meaning, and commitment to long-term goals.

The element of challenge in the choice of a career or an achievement task is of interest to both the career motivation theorists and achievement motivation theorists. The way a person responds to challenge is typically referred to as their risk-taking style or preference (Atkinson & Raynor, 1978). Research on risk-taking style is relatively neglected in vocational psychology. Atkinson's (1978) quarter-century of research on achievement motivation has led him to conclude that persons who exhibit a moderate risk-taking style are those who are most highly motivated to achieve. Atkinson (1978) has found that risk takers at both extremes of the continuum, that is, those who choose either very easy or very difficult achievement tasks, are less achievement motivated than those who choose tasks of intermediate difficulty, those for which there is a 50/50 risk of succeeding or failing.

Raynor (1978) has added a dimension to the Atkinson conceptualization of risk preference that appears relevant for vocational psychology. The distinction Raynor makes is between contingent tasks, (those that affect long-range career or achievement goals), and noncontingent tasks (such as solving an interesting puzzle). Raynor conducted studies and reviewed those of others, especially the work of Wish and Hasazi (1972), which found that highly motivated students choose college majors (i.e., a contingent task) that are judged to be "easy" in terms of the likelihood that the student will receive a degree. The Atkinson view of the role of risk taking in making choices is not as helpful as Raynor's because it predicts that highly motivated students would choose a risky major that has a 50/50 likelihood of success, one that would lead a person to expect good students to choose highly demanding majors rather than choose ones at which they are likely to succeed. The Raynor distinction between contingent and noncontingent tasks avoids this interpretation and may be more useful to the vocational psychologist in understanding the vocational choice process. The Raynor distinction might be investigated further by vocational psychologists with college students, or high school students for that matter, as it relates to their career development. The issue here is whether or not the type of choice (i.e., contingent or noncontingent) presented the subject will make a difference in their risk-taking behavior and in their vocational choices.

In summarizing this section we point out again that the issue for vocational psychologists is whether or not to continue to ignore the contribution of achievement motivation theory to vocational psychology. We have argued in favor of the latter. The distinction between long- and short-range achievement motivation was presented as a contribution of achievement motivation theory useful to vocational psychologists. One implication of this distinction, it was pointed out, is that one cannot assume that a student who does well on school tests will automatically do well in a career. A second distinction between long- and short-range achievement motivation is in the kind of values satisfied by each. Short-term achievements satisfy values such as recognition and a sense of competence whereas long-term achievements such as those in a career satisfy self-fulfillment values that may or may not be related to recognition and a sense of personal competence or mastery. We pointed to an important point of intersection between vocational psychology and achievement motivation theory. Both fields posit an element of challenge or risk taking in the choice of an occupation, a career, or a particular achievement task. We also pointed to a potentially useful contribution of achievement motivation theory related to the distinction between contingent and noncontingent tasks and the different risk-taking behavior associated with each. Vocational psychologists may continue to avoid the achievement motivation literature, but if they do it will be at a cost. The costs would be, first, to miss the distinction between achievement on selected tasks and achievement in a career and, second, to miss the contribution of the achievement research to understanding the role of risk taking in career development.

Childhood Determinants of Achievement Motivation

A critical issue for vocational psychologists is whether or not to begin to fill the vacuum in vocational development theory related to childhood. One place to begin might be to build on what achievement motivation theorists have already identified as behaviors that parents and teachers use with children. Those behaviors found to be related to later adult achievement behavior could then be encouraged. In addition, vocational psychologists could extend knowledge of what factors facilitate vocational development during the childhood period by investing research efforts in this area.

Vocational psychologists in general have not focused their research on children. Holland (1973) devotes a page or two to a description of theory related to the childhood determinants of career choice. Super (1957) devotes one chapter to theory related to the childhood "growth stage" of career development. Roe (1956) has the best articulated theory of the childhood determinants of career development, but the empirical evidence supporting her theory is weak (Osipow, 1973).

Before providing evidence that the achievement motivation theorists have a contribution to make here, we would like to pause briefly to reflect on the significance of theory related to childhood determinants for vocational psychologists. If vocational psychologists are concerned primarily with understanding phenomena that they in turn can influence through training school counselors for the nation's high schools and colleges, then childhood determinants are not very relevant to the field of vocational psychology. If, however, vocational psychologists are concerned about optimizing the career/vocational development of persons and view their role as one that includes interventions aimed at parents and at the elementary school experiences of children, as well as those of adolescents and adults, then a better understanding of the childhood determinants of career choice is relevant.

In recent years, particularly since legislation was passed (Hoyt, 1974) enabling career education to be fostered in schools from kindergarten through adult levels, the vocational psychologist has had the opportunity to play an increasingly important role in the career development of the nation's youth. Opportunities to shape policy at the national, state, and district level have led vocational psychologists to design, evaluate, and introduce career education programming for use in the public schools. Such programs frequently include special sections for parents.

It would seem useful, therefore, for vocational psychologists to review the contributions of achievement motivation researchers to a better understanding of the childhood determinants of the level of achievement striving in persons and how this striving in turn influences the level of career choice at later times.

The Fels Research Institute in Yellow Springs, Ohio has produced a series of studies on the childhood determinants of achievement motivation. Prominant among these studies are those of Crandall (1965, 1966) and Crandall and Battle (1970). In this latter work the authors describe the findings of a longitudinal study, of 38 men and 27 women from birth to age 26, on the adult correlates of academic and intellectual achievement effort. Subjects were studied at 6-month intervals from birth to 6 years, annually from age 6 to 10, once during adolescence, and once at age 26. They all grew up within a 30-mile radius from the Institute. The socioeconomic status of their subject's parents ranged across four of Hollingshead's (1957) five classes. None were in the lowest class. The IQ (Weschler–Bellevue) of subjects in early adolescence had a mean of 110. Crandall and Battle noted that although subjects were not gifted they came from families with more education than is true for the general American population.

A point of interest in the Crandall and Battle study was their definition of academic achievement. It was defined by several behavioral indicators: number of hours spent studying each week, taking more than average credit hours each semester, choosing more difficult courses (e.g., physics versus personal hygiene), and choosing an honors program when eligible. Their male subjects, high on this type of academic achievement, chose occupations at higher levels than those of their parents, valued excelling in their job, and exerted a good deal of effort in that direction. These men also valued independence and power in their jobs and were rated as holding positions of leadership in community groups. Crandall and Battle indicated that these high academic achievement men, when compared to men with low achievement motivation, had mothers who made deliberate attempts to train them in cognitive, motor, language, social, and personal skills during the years 3 through 10. In the years 0–3 these boys chose difficult rather than easy achievement tasks, provided nurturance and help to siblings and peers in the years 3–6, and persisted at achievement activities in the years 6–10.

For females high on academic achievement behaviors, the correlates for occupational level were quite similar to that found for males. One difference was that mothers of these high-achieving women had less education and lower intelligence test scores than mothers of the less-achieving women. The former placed an especially high value on academic accomplishment for their daughters. During the years 3–6 these daughters asked for more instrumental help on achievement tasks. Another interesting finding was that these girls, during the years 6–10 played more with opposite sex toys. By adolescence they had internal orientations; that is, they perceived their successes to be a result of their own instrumental behaviors, rather than awarded at the discretion of others in their environment.

Crandall and Battle's longitudinal study has provided evidence that parents of achieving adults vary their behaviors toward their children at different time periods. For example, for sons independence was encouraged in the years 0–6 and then dependence was encouraged in the years 6–10. For daughters independent behavior was not found to be related to higher academic effort in adulthood. These findings suggest caution concerning any blanket efforts to increase independent behavior in childhood as a means of facilitating achievement behavior in adulthood.

The research of achievement motivation theorists provides some interesting information on the childhood determinants of adult achievement behavior. The research identified more parental correlates for high-achieving adults than those related to in school experience. Some of the findings identify several behaviors in children related to later adult achieving behavior. These behaviors could be studied by vocational psychologists as they relate to career development. In other words, vocational psychologists might use this literature to design research that directly addresses the question of the childhood determinants of adult career choice and development.

ISSUES RELATED TO
THEORIES OF VOCATIONAL BEHAVIOR

In looking directly at theories of vocational behavior, we divide our discussion into three broad categories: issues of early career development, issues of vocational choice, and issues of postchoice development. These correspond roughly to childhood and early adolescence, late adolescence and early adulthood, and adulthood.

Issues of Early Career Development

Early childhood. Within vocational psychology there is a lack of attention to the childhood determinants of career choice and development. What little theory and research has to say about the childhood determinants is used to guide career education programs in the elementary school systems. There is a danger, in this practice, of misguided efforts stemming from theory that is not well-grounded in empirical evidence.

Three vocational theorists are identified in this section as having contributed to our understanding of the childhood determinants of later vocational behavior. These are Super (1957, 1980), Holland (1973), and Roe (1956). We review briefly what each suggests about these childhood determinants with related implications for educational practice. A recent entry in the area of theory on the childhood determinants of vocational behavior is Gottfredson (1981). Her work is also discussed.

In the writings of Super, (1957, 1980) a discussion of the childhood growth stage (ages 0–14) is provided. This stage is characterized by Super (1975) as an "interaction between the child and the home, neighborhood, and school environment, resulting in the active development of some abilities, interests and values, and in the neglect and atrophy of other potentials which, given a certain glandular and neural make-up, might have become important [p. 21]." It is these same abilities, interests, and values that later influence the person's choice of a particular vocational field. Implications from Super's work on the growth stage for career educators is for them to foster and encourage the development of a child's growing interests, values, competencies, and self-concepts through a broad range of experiences, both curricular and extracurricular.

Holland (1973) provides some evidence that children are likely to choose career fields similar to those of their parents partly as a result of being exposed to experiences and an environment consistent with that career field and partly as a result of not being exposed to other alternative fields. Each parental career type (i.e., Holland's Realistic, Conventional, Artistic, Investigative, Social or Enterprising) provides opportunities to the child related more to the parental career type than to other types. Thus a child's special heredity and experience is assumed to lead to preferences for some kinds of activities and aversions to others. Later these preferences become well-defined interests from which the person gains satisfaction as well as social rewards. Still later, the pursuit of these interests leads to the development of more specialized competencies as well as to the neglect of others.

Holland has encouraged career educators in the schools to provide children with opportunities to experience a broader range of work-related environments in order to increase the career fields considered by a student.

Roe (1956) examined the childhood experiences of some successful adults in scientific and social service fields and found that scientists tended to come from families that emphasized working with things and ideas and had parents who were not very warm or people-oriented. In contrast, Roe found persons in social service fields came from families who were warm and people-oriented. Several research studies have attempted to verify Roe's theory with other individuals and groups but have not been very successful (Osipow, 1973). In spite of this lack of success, counselors are often taught to obtain a family history from their clients on Roe's dimensions of people vs ideas and to conclude that the client is destined to be less interested in scientific or social service fields based on this kind of evidence. Such conclusions seem unwarranted because there is no strong evidence to support Roe's theory. However, the lack of alternative theories supported by evidence makes Roe's theory attractive to counselors and underlines the issue of a vacuum in vocational psychology as far as the childhood determinants of vocational behavior are concerned.

Career education and vocational counseling programs growing out of these theories assume that children will be free to choose from a full range of occupations and that the likelihood of a wise choice will be increased if they are provided with a broad range of experiences. The possibility that choice may be limited for some because of realistic constraints in the environment related to race, sex, or social class (see discussion on page 64 and Gottfredson, 1981) is ignored. The consequences of providing a broader range of experiences to elementary school children are not adequately considered in relation to the economic, social, and political realities in the United States. Research is needed to determine the consequences of such career education programs for racial minorities, the lower social classes, and females to determine if, in fact, their choices are broadened and, more importantly, if they are able to implement such choices.

Gottfredson (1981) has proposed a developmental theory of vocational choice using extant research to support her model. She traces the development of occupational stereotypes, the sex-role appropriateness of occupations, prestige strivings, and vocational interests from age 3 to adult. Gottfredson places the development of these dimensions in a time frame suggesting that occupational sex-type develops first between the ages of 6 and 8, prestige strivings develop next between the ages of 9 and 13, and interest in a particular career field develops last after the age of 14. She also argues that a persons' view of occupations as sex appropriate or inappropriate is more influential in their ultimate vocational choice than either prestige or field of interest.

Implications of Gottfredson's theory are far-reaching and would require a reconceptualization of vocational theory and related interventions in elementary, high school, and college populations. Instead of focusing on career interests as a prime determinant of career choice, vocational psychologists would focus first on the sex-role socialization process as it limits the vocational choices considered by young people. Gottfredson's review suggests that this process matures early (ages 6–8) and, if future research confirms this finding, interventions to expand options might well begin in the elementary school years and earlier. Elsewhere in this chapter we have pointed to the contributions of occupational sociologists and achievement motivation researchers to a better understanding of how achievement strivings develop and affect the level of career choice. Gottfredson has added to this discussion by describing the effect of prestige level on the career choice process. Her conceptualization places this effect prior to that of and prepotent over that of career interests and other self-concept variables. Such implications from Gottfredson's theory merit research and hopefully will be investigated in future studies by vocational psychologists.

Career maturity: Is its' present assessment adequate? Vocational psychologists beginning with Super (1955) have been concerned to assess career maturity in adolescents as a means of identifying those students who might benefit from programs aimed at preparing them to make wise vocational choices. Several measures have been developed for this assessment effort (Crites, 1978; Super, Thompson, Lindeman, Jordaan, & Myers, 1981; Westbrook & Mastie, 1974). However, those most frequently used have been found to assess primarily cognitive aspects of readiness and give less attention to attitudinal and behavioral aspects (Harmon, 1974; Richardson, 1974; Westbrook, Cutts, Madison, & Arcia, 1980). Because there is general agreement that the construct of career maturity includes attitudinal, behavioral, and cognitive dimensions (Fitzgerald & Crites, 1980; Super, 1974; Westbrook & Mastie, 1974) it appears that the present assessment may be inadequate.

Vocational maturity behaviors such as exploratory activity, information seeking activity, and decision-making behaviors and skills are typically assessed by means of self-report inventories (Crites, 1978; Super et al. 1981). The question as to whether or not persons with high scores on these dimensions have actually engaged in these behaviors and have better decision-making skills remains to be tested.

There is a tendency within vocational psychology to view rational decision making as superior to intuitive decision-making (Harren, Kass, Tinsley, & Moreland, 1978). In contrast, some recent work by Rubinton (1980) found that both an intuitive and a rational decision-making style were effective approaches to facilitating the career decision-making process. What Rubinton did was to provide career-undecided students with two types of treatment, one intuitive and the other rational. Students who were previously identified as having primarily an intuitive or a rational decision-making style were assigned equally to treatments. In this way Rubinton determined that persons who preferred an intuitive decision-making style benefited more from an intuitive approach to teaching decision-making skills. As expected, students who preferred a rational decision-making style benefited most from a rational approach to teaching decision-making skills. Rubinton's findings are consistent with those of McKenney and Keen (1976) of the Harvard Business School, who found that intuitive and rational decision-making styles complement each other. For example, in business these authors have found that management teams made up of persons some of whom are primarily intuitive decision makers and others primarily rational decision makers are more effective than teams made up solely of rational decision makers. It appears from both the evidence of McKenney and Keen and that of Rubinton that attention to and respect for individual differences in decision making would be important in the assessment of this skill, and in efforts made to improve it.

The assessment of the affective components of career maturity relies primarily on reported involvement in career planning and exploration activities (Super et al., 1981) and on dimensions that assess orientation toward (valuing) work, independence in decision making, preference for different vocational choice factors, and attitudes about how choices are made (Crites, 1974).

We repeat a theme, well-articulated in the Super (1974) monograph, that the relative importance of the employed work role to a person is an important dimension of vocational maturity. Attention should be paid to the salience of work for the individual especially those coming from different subcultures. LoCascio (1974), Harmon (1974) and Richardson (1974) argued that persons from minority races, from lower social class families, and females may work primarily to earn a living and/or value other life roles more. Harmon (1974) and Richardson (1974) suggested further that work salience may vary at different time points for females because they value home and family roles and need to consider the relative salience of such roles in relation to work when planning for a career. Super's recent work (1980) has expanded on the view that life roles and their relative salience vary for individuals. In a similar vein Gottfredson (1981) has suggested that life plans are the organizing framework for career choices. In the Guided Career Exploration Program (Super & Bowlsbey, 1979) adolescents are taught the concept of life stages and the interactive nature of a range of life roles constituting a broader conception of career.

Girls in high school have been found by several researchers to obtain higher scores on measures of vocational maturity compared to boys (Lunneborg, 1978; Rathburn, 1973; Smith & Herr, 1972). The evidence that these measures correlate highly with student's grades (Westbrook et al., 1980) combined with evidence that girls in high school obtain higher grades in verbal courses (Maccoby & Jacklin, 1974) compared to high school boys may provide a partial answer to the fact that girls appear to be more vocationally mature. Fitzgerald and Crites (1980) point out that many girls' aspirations in high school are unrealistically low. Because high career-maturity scores are based in part on realism of career choice, the finding that girls are both high in career maturity and low in realism is a puzzle. The explanation of the puzzle may lie in the fact that current measures of career maturity ignore the role conflict experienced by females that has been found to dampen their career aspirations (Farmer & Bohn, 1970; Richardson,

1974). Tittle (1981) has gathered data on eleventh grade boys and girls comparing their parenting, marriage, and work values. She found that girls' marriage values were different from those held by boys, whether or not the girls had high, low, or average career aspirations. The same was not true for the boys whose values differed for different levels of aspiration. It might be concluded that marriage values are similar for girls regardless of their career commitment. Again the issue appears to be whether or not career maturity assessment takes such values into account or not.

Issues of Career Choice: The Adolescent and Young Adult Years

Most vocational psychologists are interested in vocational choice because they assume that individuals can be helped to make "good" vocational choices. For some individuals, vocational counseling can lead to a better choice than the individual would make without such help. Over the years vocational psychologists have become fairly adept at creating psychological instruments designed to help the individual assess his or her traits in relationship to others who have made specific educational or vocational choices.

Career choice salience. The evidence for the efficacy of vocational counseling (e.g. Campbell, 1965) suggests that vocational counseling using psychometric data is helpful in academic achievement and eventual success and satisfaction. Evidence for the efficacy of psychometric interventions such as the Strong Vocational Interest Blank (SVIB), (Dolliver, Irvin, & Bigley, 1972; Strong, 1955) suggests that they do predict future behavior. The use of vocational choice theory and psychological measurement requires some additional assumptions that are not often noted or investigated. One is that career choice is salient for all individuals in this developmental stage under all conditions. We take the position that career choice will be salient only for individuals who believe that their choices are or can be effective (thus self-esteem, locus of control, and attributional concepts are all important), who live in an environment in which their choices truly can be effective, and who are free from survival needs for food, shelter, and safety (Maslow, 1970). Several writers (Harmon, 1977; Richardson, 1974; Warnath, 1975) have taken the position that there are large subgroups within our society, women, minority group members, and the poor, for whom these conditions are not met. Several studies have suggested relationships between these variables and career development (Smith, 1976).

It seems to us, then, that our theories of choice might pay more attention to the psychological and ecological variables that make career choice salient for an individual or not salient. Having developed a more sophisticated understanding of when career counseling is appropriate, we might move on to a consideration of the career problems of those for whom it is inappropriate. Shall we ignore the problems of young black unemployed males (whose unemployment rate is the highest of all groups) whose major vocational concern may be to find any job rather than to choose the "right" career? Surely part of the solution must come from areas outside of vocational behavior but problems of how to foster a sense of internal locus of control in career planning in the face of external barriers are of social significance. Perhaps we will find that career planning competencies for this group will be best learned from the vantage point of employment of some type. If so, the designing of jobs that foster the development of internal locus of control and concern for achievement will be very important.

Measurement and choice.   Much has been written of late about increasing exploratory validity (Holland, Takai, Gottfredson, & Hanau, 1978; Tittle, 1978) of the interest inventories we use in the choice process. The American College Testing Program has chosen to norm interest inventory scores by sex (Lamb & Prediger, 1979) explicitly so that exploratory behavior will be increased. Zytowski (1977) has suggested that there may be individuals for whom information from interest inventories is not salient. However, among those for whom exploratory validity is demonstrated, it is important to determine the long term effects upon behavior. It seems to us that a new rationale for interest inventories has become popular in response to the issues raised about whether interest inventories incorporate assumptions that make them biased. Clearly, inventories that do not depend on demonstrating concurrent or predictive validity in an occupational structure that is largely segregated by sex and race have some advantages. However, exploration is not choice but a preliminary operation. Whether wider exploration is related to nontraditional choices or mature choices remains to be demonstrated.

Osipow, Carney, Winer, Yanico, and Koschier (Osipow, Carney, & Barak, 1976) and Holland and Holland (1977) have developed relatively new measures of career indecision. These instruments appear to have acceptable reliability and validity. They demonstrate a concern for an important human problem. Osipow, Carney, and Barak (1976) showed that students had lower scores on indecision after an intervention. What remains to be demonstrated now is that the various components of indecision as originally conceived by Osipow, Winer, Koschir, and Yanico (1975) to be related to specific types of interventions can be influenced by those interventions. Often, it seems to us, vocational psychologists have been excellent describers of individual differences but not as adept at altering them.

We sometimes seem to believe that if we describe people to themselves, that the right action will be apparent. This is not true because not all behavior is rational. We have not even demonstrated in many cases that our descriptions (although psychometrically sophisticated) are any better than the individuals own self-descriptions (Rose & Elton, 1970).

Choice and social roles.   Career choice has clearly been influenced in the past by the social role occupied by the chooser. The clearest example of this phenomenon is sex role. An understanding of the interaction of social sex roles, occupational segregation, and personal characteristics such as androgyny (sex-balanced behavior), ego strength, locus of control, and self-esteem in effecting career behavior has been sought by many (Gable, Thompson, & Glanstein, 1976; Lokan, Boss, & Patsula, 1982; Stake, 1979; Yanico & Hardin, 1981). It seems to us that the differentiation between choices as traditional or nontraditional, pioneering or not (Tangri, 1972) has been a useful distinction in research of this type. However, it is important to note that these categories shift over time in how their boundaries cover occupations. Ultimately this research will need to focus on specific choices or types of choices if the results are to make sense over time. Yanico and Hardin (1981) have taken this approach. As with much research in new areas, some time must be devoted to resolving methodological issues such as how to represent occupations that are traditional or socially desirable. Psychologists have looked at choice as a product of personal characteristics in the past. Research related to the effect of social roles on choice should help us to delineate a broader understanding of what effects career choice.

Summary.   Ultimately, however, the issue of whether we *can* influence adolescent and young adult career choice arises and, if so, under what conditions and through what processes they can be influenced. Can specific type of choice, level of choice, or only the quality of the choice (appropriateness and realism) be influenced? If type and/or level of choice can be influenced rather serious ethical issues arise, and we might do well to consider them before we answer the latter question rather than after.

In summary, there are important questions of career choice salience to be resolved, questions of how intervening behaviors such as exploration relate to career choice, questions of how theoretical variables such as traditionality of career choice should be measured, and questions of whether these variables can be applied to practice.

Issues of Postchoice Career Development: Adult Vocational Behavior

In the last few years increased attention has been addressed to adult career development among vocational psychologists and industrial organizational psychologists as well (Dalton, Thompson, & Price, 1977; Hall, 1976; Super, 1980; Super & Kidd, 1979). There is certainly room for more understanding of vocational behavior in adulthood.

The emphasis vocational psychologists place on early career development, career maturity and career decision making in early adulthood is based on the assumption that there are early vocational behaviors that foster adult success and satisfaction. However, testing this assumption requires longitudinal study and few longitudinal studies have been conducted. Those that have been done (Project TALENT, the Career Patterns Study, Campbell's 25-year follow-up of Williamson & Bordin's subjects) yield mixed results. For instance, Campbell's data (1965) suggest that individuals who sought career counseling (supposedly a mature behavior) were ultimately more successful but less satisfied than those who did not. They were also more anxious as college students. Campbell reports no results related to Williamson and Bordin's (1940) earlier evaluation of the quality of vocational behavior of the counseled group, so it seems safe to assume there were no significant findings in this area.

Without clear-cut longitudinal evidence that early career maturity or realistic career decisions are related to desirable outcomes, there is little basis for a practice based on theories of vocational behavior. Career counseling may be like one of the medical fads of yesteryear—which were practiced for a while and then dropped as ineffective or when something new came along. It seems strange that this concern, "What is the longitudinal evidence that early vocational behavior is related to later success and satisfaction," should be first on our list of current theoretical issues related to adults. It is a basic question that has been around for a long time. Most of us have found it easier to assume the answer than to engage in difficult longitudinal studies.

A second issue concerns how adults move through their careers and the personal effects of various career patterns on individuals. The most basic question here is how job mobility occurs across levels and fields of occupations and across and within various industries in our society.

An interesting assumption of theories dealing with career mobility is that upward mobility (in terms of SES, prestige, and responsibility) is good. Thus, we are interested in the process through which one moves up on one of these dimensions. Several theorists (Hall, 1976; Dalton, Thompson, & Price, 1977) have proposed models that suggest how individuals progress in business and the professions. Not completely tested empirically, these models can be used not only to study mobility but the lack of mobility of individuals in organizations. Because many businesses and professions have a pyramid structure, there are fewer people at the top than at the bottom. What means do individuals who have reached the highest level they can reach use to accommodate themselves to that fact? Do they devote more energy to other arenas of life (Sheehy, 1974; Super, 1980) such as family and leisure time pursuits? Do they change fields of work? What personal and socioeconomic factors are related to the chosen solution?

There has also been some interesting work (Gottfredson & Becker, 1981; Gottfredson & Brown, 1981) that suggests that men in early adulthood adjust their aspirations to fit the jobs available to them and that their distribution into the work force is basically completed by the late twenties. Based on large national probability samples, these studies call the idea of mobility for the average male worker into question. Here again there is a need for longitudinal research evidence regarding movements of workers over the lifespan, to insure that our theories do not rest on faulty assumptions.

In the face of lack of mobility, industrial and organizational psychology has turned to job redesign and enrichment in an attempt to influence workers attitudes and behaviors. In a recent review, Bartol (1981) has concluded that there is "considerable recent research support for the idea that individual variables moderate the job characteristics—job satisfaction relationship [p. 137]." Studies by O'Reilly, Parlette, and Bloom (1980) and James and Jones (1980) suggest that individual perceptions of job characteristics such as the amount of challenge offered, the amount of autonomy afforded by the job, and the importance of the job are related to satisfaction in complex ways. These relationships can be spelled out in more detail by further research. The interesting related issue is whether perceptions and ultimately satisfactions can be manipulated, and whether they should be. Alternatively, the old idea of matching individuals and jobs may also be applied to the matching of individuals' need for growth and enrichment with the career's ability to meet such needs. Any attempts to resolve this issue are brought up against the fact that we don't seem to know much about the development of what have been termed high growth needs. If an individual has low growth needs at one point in time, will they be correlated with growth needs in the future? If not, what stimulates a change in level of the need for growth? Maslow's theory posits a hierarchical arrangement of needs that suggests some ways in which a high need for growth might be fostered or developed. Finally, regarding this issue, can we develop a society in which a large proportion of the available jobs are designed to meet needs for growth?

As indicated earlier, adult career satisfaction and success are the criteria by which interventions based as vocational development theory should be judged. There is a considerable amount of cross-sectional or correlational evidence that career satisfaction and success are related to life satisfactions (Schmitt & Mellon, 1980; Staines, 1980). The Schmitt and Mellon study supported the idea that life satisfaction causes job satisfaction. If this is the case, it seems possible that the earlier components of the causal chain may be more general personality variables such as internal locus of control, ego strength, and general adjustment rather than specific career-related variables such as career maturity and career choice realism. Again there is a need for more longitudinal research.

As in other areas considered here, there are problems in measurement. Clearly it is important to understand the importance of work in the life of the adult. Heath (1977) has cited evidence to show that in some cases work may effect other life roles adversely. However, there is little agreement on how to define those other life roles or to measure the importance of each to an individual (Near, Rice, & Hunt, 1980).

Our conclusion regarding issues of adult vocational behavior is that there are major problems in the realm of theoretical assumptions and definitions. Carefully planned longitudinal research is needed.

ISSUES OF EMPHASIS

Holcomb and Anderson (1977) reviewed the vocational articles printed in the *Journal of Counseling Psychology,* the *Journal of Vocational Behavior,* and the *Journal of Employment Counseling* from 1971 to 1975. They concluded that populations such as ethnic minorities or the poor were rarely studied. College students were overrepresented. Gottfredson (1980) analyzed the articles printed in the *Journal of Vocational Behavior* and the *Vocational Guidance Quarterly* between 1976 and 1980. Fifty-seven percent of the subjects were students and 35% of the subjects were clearly not students—usually workers. In 67% of the articles the race of the subjects was not clearly specified. Among those in which race was specified only 2.6% were black, and 5.7% were multiracial with the race well-specified. In 64% of the articles SES was not clearly specified. Among those in which SES was specified, only 5.2% specified low-SES and 6.4% dealt with two or more well-specified classes.

Holcomb and Anderson (1977) found 58% of the articles in their study dealt with individual differences and 11% with employment relations. Gottfredson (1980) found 49% and 23%, respectively. The conclusion we can draw from these findings is that research in vocational behavior has emphasized students of majority ethnic status and relative affluence. One might conlude that this pattern of research is reasonable because theory is most easily built from the most general case. On the other hand, we might evaluate our theory-building efforts from the perspective of what they reveal about individual and collective priorities. Among the articles tallied by Gottfredson, 50% were devoted to high school and/or college subjects. Presumably this betrays an interest in the career development processes of these age groups and a commitment to resolving problems presented by these age groups. Gottfredson also noted that researchers (among the authors of the articles she analyzed) responded to a questionnaire item about the priority they would give to obtaining information about various age groups by giving high priority to ages 25–34 (75% of the respondents), 19–24 (69%), and 35–54 (66%). All other ages were considered of high priority by less than 38% of respondents. This suggests an increasing interest in the vocational behavior of individuals beyond college age. Her data also reveals that vocational psychologists place low priority on understanding the very young, ethnic minority group members and the poor. Sex is a variable that has been more closely studied over recent years.

The relevant question for theory builders seems to be "theory for what"? The history of technology suggests that questions that are perceived as important are answered. Yet few pressing social problems are even addressed by vocational psychologists. There are, of course, exceptions to these generalizations. The work of Azrin and his colleagues (Azrin, Flores, & Kaplan, 1975) on finding employment for the unemployed through the Job Club Program is a notable one. It has been translated into practice and shows promise of producing economic as well as psychological and social benefits (Azrin, Philip, Thienes-Hontos, & Besalel, 1980).

It is common in review articles for authors to conclude that "the research evidence is mixed." If we had chosen to writen this chapter as a series of mini-reviews, each section would probably have ended with that statement. When we ask ourselves why this happens, the usual answers about different populations and instruments are not very satisfying. It appears to us that researchers have often begun their work without asking themselves what theoretical and practical applications might be made as a result of their potential findings. The result is a fragmented literature where not much is clear-cut. We conclude that we have placed too much emphasis on design and analyses and not enough on problem definition and logic.

Vocational psychology does have problems of emphasis. The literature suggests that we have emphasized doing research over both theory building and practice, we have concentrated on theories for relatively privileged groups, and we have concentrated primarily on variables of individual difference.

It is possible that our commitments to certain types of service delivery (individual over group) and certain settings (colleges and businesses over technical schools and government agencies) also cause us to place emphasis on certain populations and problems over others.

SUMMARY AND IMPLICATIONS

We have attempted to illustrate that research is the cornerstone of both theory and practice. We have argued that a broader perspective, looking at the interface between vocational psychology and other social sciences, between vocational psychology and other fields within psychology, and between theories in vocational psychology may help in theory building. We have looked at some (certainly not all) of these interfaces and suggested interesting and, to us, important questions. Finally, we have examined the emphases the literature of vocational behavior reveals and questioned whether we are addressing important questions or in fact whether most research is carefully addressed to either theory building or practice. A greater emphasis on problem definition and the philosophy of science and on a broad interdisciplinary outlook are recommended.

Practical implications growing out of the theoretical issues rasied in this chapter are mostly in the form of cautionary caveats. Theoretical gaps in our understanding of the process of career development in childhood suggest caution related to career education programs in the schools. Lack of longitudinal data providing evidence on the effectiveness of our vocational counseling efforts in high school and college for long-term adult vocational satisfaction and productivity suggest caution in these counseling efforts as well. We are particularly unprepared theoretically to counsel adults who are in the process of making career changes. We are also unprepared to counsel minorities, the poor, and the unskilled because of our relative lack of research with these populations.

Some ethical considerations were raised that have practical import. Developmental theories by their nature seem to imply a ''good, better, best'' schema whereby moving persons from lower stages to higher stages is seen as desirable. It was suggested that we take a hard look at the implications if we were to succeed in moving everyone up the developmental ladder to the highest level. Setting our counseling goals within a framework that we are willing to live with would be a responsible move within our discipline. Other ethical issues relate to using techniques developed for one population on other populations. Also, we cannot assume that everyone has the freedom to choose whatever occupation appeals to him/her.

Among the implications for research is the need for longitudinal studies that trace developmental changes from childhood through adulthood. Other research needs include the study of various patterns of coping with transitions as these relate to vocational maturity, the study of effectiveness of differing types of vocational counseling, and the study of the stability of career choices with respect not only to field, but to level and type (i.e., traditional, nontraditional, etc.). Without such research we are counseling in ways that may be harmful rather than helpful, or at least may be ineffective for the long-term. We also suggested that research methodology used in vocational psychology might well borrow from other disciplines. PATH analyses, used extensively by occupational sociologists, might be particularly useful in our theory-building efforts and has already been applied by some within our field. Research, we pointed out, within our field has focussed too narrowly on college-bound and student populations, the affluent rather than the poor. We need to include the young adult worker as well as the college student, and to make the effort necessary to include racial minorities in our studies. Other neglected populations include young children and older adults. Theory building requires theory testing. Research should continue to test vocational theory and in addition to test the relevance of theory from other disciplines (i.e., developmental, achievement motivation, labor economics) to career choice and career development.

REFERENCES

Atkinson, J. (Ed.). *Motives in fantasy, action, and society.* Princeton, N.J.: Nostrand, 1958.

Atkinson, J. The mainsprings of achievement-oriented activity. In J. Atkinson & J. Raynor (Eds.), *Personality, motivation and achievement.* New York: Halsted, 1978.

Atkinson, J., & Raynor, J. (Eds.). *Personality, motivation and achievement.* New York: Halsted, 1978.

Ausubel, D. P. *Ego development and personality disorders.* New York: Grune & Stratton, 1952.

Azrin, N. H., Flores, T., & Kaplan, S. J. Job-finding club: A group assisted program for obtaining employment. *Behavior Research & Therapy,* 1975, *13,* 17–27.

Azrin, N. H., Philip, R. A., Thienes-Hontos, P., & Besalel, V. A. Comparative evaluation of the Job Club program with welfare recipients. *Journal of Vocational Behavior,* 1980, *16,* 133–145.

Bakan, D. *The duality of human existence.* Chicago: Rand McNally, 1966.

Bartol, K. M. Vocational behavior and career development, 1980: A review. *Journal of Vocational Behavior,* 1981, *19,* 123–162.

Bernard, J. *Women and public interest.* Chicago: Aldine–Atherton, 1971.

Campbell, D. P. *The results of counseling: Twenty-Five years later.* Philadelphia: Saunders, 1965.

Crandall, V. *Parents' influences on children's achievement behavior.* Progress report, NIMH Grant No. MH-02238. Fels Institute, Yellow Springs, Ohio, 1965.

Crandall, V. Personality characteristics and social and achievement behaviors associated with children's social desirability response tendencies. *Journal of Personality and Social Psychology,* 1966, *4,* 477–486.

Crandall, V., & Battle, E. The antecedents and adult correlates of academic and intellectual achievement effort. In J. Hill (Ed.), *Minnesota Symposium on Child Psychology* (Vol. 4). Minneapolis: University of Minnesota Press, 1970.

Crites, J. The Career Maturity Inventory. In D. Super (Ed.), *Measuring vocational maturity for counseling and evaluation.* Washington, D.C.: American Personnel and Guidance Association, 1974.

Crites, J. Theory and research handbook for the *Career Maturity Inventory* (2nd ed.). Monterey, Calif.: CTB/McGraw-Hill, 1978.

Dalton, G. W., Thompson, P. H., & Price, R. L. The four stages of professional careers— A new look at performance by professionals. *Organizational Dynamics,* 1977, summer, 19–42.

Dolliver, R. H., Irvin, J. A., & Bigley, S. E. Twelve year follow-up of the Strong Vocational Interest Blank. *Journal of Counseling Psychology,* 1972, *19,* 212–217.

Duncan, O. D. A socio-economic index for all occasions. In A. J. Reiss, Jr. (Ed.), *Occupations and social status.* New York: Free Press, 1961.

Ekehammar, B. Test of a psychological cost-benefit model for career choice. *Journal of Vocational Behavior,* 1977, *10,* 245-260.

Ekehammar, B. Psychological cost-benefit as an intervening construct in career choice models. *Journal of Vocational Behavior,* 1978, *12,* 279-289.

Erikson, E. H. *Child and society* (2nd ed.). New York: Norton, 1963.

Fannin, P. M. The relation between ego-identity status and sex-role attitude, work-role salience, atypicality of major and self-esteem in college women. *Journal of Vocational Behavior,* 1979, *14,* 12-22.

Farmer, H. S. What inhibits achievement and career motivation in women? In L. W. Harmon, J. M. Birk, L. E. Fitzgerald, & M. F. Tanney (Eds.), *Counseling Women.* Belmont, Calif.; Brooks/Cole, 1978.

Farmer, H., & Bohn, M. Home–Career conflict reduction and the level of career interest in women. *Journal of Counseling Psychology,* 1970, *17,* 228-232.

Faulkner, R. R. Making violence by doing work: Selves, situations, and the world of professional hockey. *Sociology of Work & Occupations,* 1974, *1,* 288-312.

Ferenczi, S. Stages in the development of the sense of reality. In S. Ferenczi (Ed.), *Sex in psychoanalysis.* Boston: Gorham Press, 1916.

Fitzgerald, L., & Crites, J. Toward a career psychology of women: What do we know? What do we need to know? *Journal of Counseling Psychology,* 1980, *27,* 44-62.

Fleisher, B. M., & Kniesner, T. J. *Labor economics: Theory, evidence, and policy* (2nd ed.). Englewood Cliffs, N.J.; Prentice-Hall, 1980.

Fromm, E. *Escape from freedom.* New York: Farrer, Strauss, & Giroux, 1941.

Gable, R. K., Thompson, D. L., & Glanstein, P. J. Perceptions of personal control and conformity of vocational choice as correlates of vocational development. *Journal of Vocational Behavior,* 1976, *8,* 259-267.

Gibbs, J. C. The meaning of ecologically oriented inquiry in contemporary psychology. *American Psychologist,* 1979, *34,* 127-140.

Gilligan, C. In a different voice: Women's conception of the self and of morality. *Harvard Educational Review,* 1977, *47,* 481-517.

Ginzberg, E., Ginsburg, S. W., Axelrod, S., & Herma, J. L. *Occupational choice: An approach to a general theory.* New York: Columbia University Press, 1951.

Gottfredson, L. Circumscription and compromise: A developmental theory of occupational aspirations. *Journal of Counseling Psychology,* 1981, *28,* 545-579.

Gottfredson, L. S. *An outsider's view of vocational research priorities.* Unpublished manuscript, Center for Social Organization of Schools, Johns Hopkins University, 1980.

Gottfredson, L. S., & Becker, H. J. A challenge to vocational psychology: How important are aspirations in determining male career development? *Journal of Vocational Behavior,* 1981, *18,* 121-137.

Gottfredson, L. S., & Brown, V. C. Occupational differentiation among white men in the first decade after high school. *Journal of Vocational Behavior,* 1981, *19,* 251-289.

Graves, C. W. Deterioration of work standards. *Harvard Business Review,* 1966, *44,* 117-128.

Griliches, Z. Estimating the returns of schooling: Some econometric problems. *Econometrica,* 1977, *45,* 1-22.

Hall, D. T. *Careers in organizations.* Pacific Palisades, Calif.: Goodyear Publishing, 1976.

Hanoch, G. *Personal earnings and investment in schooling.* Unpublished doctoral dissertation, University of Chicago, 1965.

Harmon, L. Problems in measuring vocational maturity: A counseling perspective. In D. Super (Ed.), *Measuring vocational maturity for counseling evaluation.* Washington, D.C.: American Personnel and Guidance Association, 1974.

Harmon, L. W. The childhood and adolescent career plans of college women. *Journal of Vocational Behavior,* 1971, *1,* 45–56.

Harmon, L. W. Career counseling for women. In E. Rawlings & D. Carter (Eds.), *Psychotherapy for women: Treatment toward equality.* Springfield, Ill.: Charles C. Thomas, 1977.

Harren, V. A model of career decision making for college students. *Journal of Vocational Behavior,* 1979, *14,* 119–133.

Harren, V., Kass, R., Tinsley, H., & Moreland, J. Influence of sex role attitudes and cognitive styles on career decision-making. *Journal of Counseling Psychology,* 1978, *25,* 390–398.

Heath, D. H. Some possible effects of occupation on the maturing of professional men. *Journal of Vocational Behavior,* 1977, *11,* 263–281.

Hogan, R. Moral conduct and moral character: A psychological perspective. *Psychological Bulletin,* 1973, *79*(4), 217–232.

Holcomb, W. R., & Anderson, W. P. Vocational guidance research: A five year overview. *Journal of Vocational Behavior,* 1977, *10,* 341–346.

Holland, J. *Making vocational choices: A theory of careers.* Englewood Cliffs, N.J.: Prentice-Hall, 1973.

Holland, J. Johns Hopkins University, Baltimore. Personal communication, 1980.

Holland, J. L., & Holland, J. E. Vocational indecision: More evidence & speculation. *Journal of Counseling Psychology,* 1977, *24,* 404–414.

Holland, J. L., Takai, R., Gottfredson, G. D., & Hanau, C. A multivariate analysis of the effects of the self-directed search on high school girls. *Journal of Counseling Psychology,* 1978, *25,* 384–389.

Hollingshead, A. *The two factor index of social position.* New Haven, Conn.: The author, 1957.

Hoyt, K. *Career education, vocational education and occupational education: An approach to defining differences.* Columbus, O.: Center for Vocational and Technical Education, Ohio State University, 1974.

James, L. R., & Jones, A. P. Perceived job characteristics and job satisfaction: An examination of reciprocal causation. *Personnel Psychology,* 1980, *33,* 97–135.

Jepson, D., & Dilley, J. Vocational decision making models. *Review of Educational Research,* 1974, *44,* 331–349.

Katz, M. A model of guidance for career decision-making. *Vocational Guidance Quarterly,* 1966, *15,* 2–10.

Katz, M., & Kroll, A. Evaluating a computer-based guidance system. *Findings,* 1975, *2*(3), 5–8.

Knefelkamp, L. L., & Slepitza, R. A. Cognitive developmental model of career development and adaptation of the Perry scheme. *The Counseling Psychologist,* 1976, *6*(3), 53–58.

Knefelkamp, L. L., Widick, C. C., & Stroad, B. Cognitive-developmental theory: A guide to counseling women. *The Counseling Psychologist,* 1976, *6*(2), 15–19.

Kohlberg, L. Development of moral character and moral ideology. In M. L. Hoffman & L. W. Hoffman (Eds.), *Review of child development research* (Vol. 1). New York: Russell Sage Foundation, 1964.

Kohlberg, L. *The philosophy of moral development.* New York: Harper & Row, 1981.

Kuhn, T. S. *The structure of scientific revolutions* (2nd ed.). Chicago: University of Chicago Press, 1970.

Lamb, R. R., & Prediger, D. J. Criterion-related validity of sex-restrictive and unisex interest scales: A comparison. *Journal of Vocational Behavior,* 1979, *15,* 231–246.

Levinson, D. J., Darrow, C. N., Klein, E. B., Levinson, M. H., & McKee, B. *The seasons of a man's life.* New York: Ballantine, 1978.

LoCascio, R. The vocational maturity of diverse groups: Theory and measurement. In D. Super (Ed.), *Measuring vocational maturity for counseling evaluation.* Washington, D.C.: American Personnel and Guidance Association, 1974.

Loevinger, J. with the assistance of Blasi, A. *Ego development.* San Francisco: Jossey-Bass, 1976.

Lokan, J. J., Boss, M. W., & Patsula, P. T. A study of vocational maturity during adolescence and locus of control. *Journal of Vocational Behavior,* 1982, *20,* 331–342.

Lowenthal, M. F., Thurnher, M., Chiriboga, D., & Associates. *Four stages of life. A comparative study of women and men facing transitions.* San Francisco: Jossey-Bass, 1975.

Lunneborg, P. Sex and career decision-making styles. *Journal of Counseling Psychology,* 1978, *25,* 299–305.

Maccoby, E., & Jacklin, C. *The psychology of sex differences.* Stanford, Calif.: Stanford University Press, 1974.

Marcia, J. E., & Friedman, M. L. Ego identity status in college women. *Journal of Personality,* 1970, *38,* 249–263.

Marx, K. Marx–Engels Gesamtaugabe. In T. B. Bottomore & M. Rubel (Eds.), *Karl Marx: Selected writings in sociology and social philosophy.* New York: McGraw-Hill, 1964.

Maslow, A. H. *Motivation and personality* (2nd ed.). New York: Harper & Row, 1970.

McClelland, D. The importance of learning in the formation of motives. In J. Atkinson (Ed.), *Motives in fantasy, action and society.* Princeton, N.J.: Van Nostrand, 1958.

McClelland, D. *Assessing human motivation.* New York: General Learning Press, 1971.

McKenney, J., & Keen, P. How managers' minds work. *Harvard Business Review,* 1976, *52.*

Mincer, J. On-the-job training: Costs, returns, and some implications. *Journal of Political Economy,* 1962, *70,* 50–79.

Munley, P. H. Erik Erikson's theory of psychosocial development and career development. *Journal of Counseling Psychology,* 1975, *22,* 314–319.

Munley, P. H. Erikson's theory of psychosocial development an career development. *Journal of Vocational Behavior,* 1977, *10,* 261–269.

Nam, C. B., & Powers, M. G. Changes in the relative status level of workers in the United States, 1950–1960. *Social Forces,* 1968, *47,* 158–170.

Near, T. P., Rice, R. W., & Hunt, R. G. The relationship between work and nonwork domains: A review of empirical research. *Academy of Management Review,* 1980, *5,* 415–429.

Neugarten, B. L. Adaptation and the life cycle. *The Counseling Psychologist,* 1976, *6*(1), 16–20.

O'Neil, J. M., Meeker, C. H., & Borgers, S. G. The developmental, preventive, and consultative model to reduce sexism in the career planning of women. JSAS *Catalog of Selected Documents,* 1978, *8,* (No. 1684).

O'Reilly, C. A., Parlette, G. N., & Bloom, J. R. Perceptual measures of task characteristics: The biasing effects of differing frames of reference and job attitudes. *Academy of Management Journal,* 1980, *23,* 118–131.

Osipow, S. *Theories of career development* (2nd ed.). Englewood Cliffs, N.J.: Prentice-Hall, 1973.

Osipow, S. H., Winer, J. L., Koschir, M. & Yanico, B. A modular approach to self-counseling for vocational indecision using audiocassettes: A prototype. In L. Simpson (Ed.), *Audio-Visual media in career development.* Bethlehem, Pa.; College Placement Council, 1975, 34–38.

Osipow, S. H., Carney, C. G., & Barak, A. A scale of educational-vocational undecidedness: A typological approach. *Journal of Vocational Behavior,* 1976, *9,* 233–243.

Parsons, J., & Goff, S. Achievement motivation and values: An alternative perspective. In L. Fyans (Ed.), *Achievement motivation: Recent trends in theory and research.* New York: Plenum, 1980.

Perry, W. *Forms of intellectual and ethical development in the college years.* New York: Holt, Rinehart & Winston, 1970.

Piaget, J. *The moral judgment of the child.* New York: Free Press, 1965.

Rathburn, C. *Developmental trends in the career choice attitudes of male and female adolescents.* Unpublished manuscript, University of Maryland, 1973.

Raynor, J. Motivation and career striving. In J. Atkinson & J. Raynor (Eds.), *Personality, motivation and achievement.* New York: Halsted, 1978.

Riesman, D., Glazer, N., & Denney, R. *The lonely crowd.* Garden City, N.Y.: Doubleday, 1954.

Richardson, M. Vocational maturity in counseling girls and women. In D. Super (Ed.), *Measuring vocational maturity for counseling and evaluation.* Washington, D.C.: American Personnel and Guidance Association, 1974.

Roe, A. *The psychology of occupations.* New York: Wiley, 1956.

Rose, H. A., & Elton, C. F. Ask him or test him? *Vocational Guidance Quarterly,* 1970, *19,* 28–32.

Rubinton, N. Instruction in career decision making and decision-making styles. *Journal of Counseling Psychology,* 1980, *27,* 581–588.

Rush, J. C., Peacock, A. C., & Milkovich, G. T. Career stages: A partial test of Levinson's model of life/career stages. *Journal of Vocational Behavior,* 1980, *16,* 347–359.

Schmitt, N., & Mellon, P. M. Life and job satisfaction: Is the job central? *Journal of Vocational Behavior,* 1980, *16,* 51–58.

Sheehy, G. *Passages: Predictable crisis of adult life.* New York: Dutton, 1974.

Smith, E. J. Reference group perspectives and the vocational maturity of lower socioeconomic black youth. *Journal of Vocational Behavior,* 1976, *8,* 321–336.

Smith, E., & Herr, E. Sex differences in the mutation of vocational attitudes among adolescents. *Vocational Guidance Quarterly,* 1972, *21,* 177–182.

Spivak, G., Platt, J., & Shure, M. *The problem-solving approach to adjustment.* San Francisco: Jossey-Bass, 1976.

Staines, G. L. Spillover vs. compensation: A review of the literature on the relationship between work and nonwork. *Human Relations,* 1980, *33,* 111–129.

Stake, J. E. Women's self-estimates of competence and the resolution of the career/home conflict. *Journal of Vocational Behavior,* 1979, *14,* 33–42.

Stern, P. M. *The Oppenheimer case: Security on trial.* New York: Harper & Row, 1969.

Strong, E. J., Jr. *Vocational interests 18 years after college.* Minneapolis: University of Minnesota Press, 1955.

Super, D. E. A theory of vocational development. *American Psychologist,* 1953, *8,* 185–190.

Super, D. The dimensions and measurement of vocational maturity. *Teachers College Record,* 1955, *57,* 151–163.

Super, D. *The psychology of careers.* New York: Harper & Row, 1957.

Super, D. *Manual: Work Values Inventory.* New York: Houghton Mifflin, 1970.

Super, D. Vocational Maturity Theory: Toward implementing a psychology of careers in career education and guidance. In D. Super (Ed.), *Measuring vocational maturity for counseling and evaluation.* Washington, D.C.: American Personnel and Guidance Association, 1974.

Super, D. *Career education and meanings of work.* Paper available from the Office of Career Education, Office of Education, U.S. Department of Health, Education and Welfare, Washington, D.C., 1975.

Super, D. A life-span, life-space approach to career development. *Journal of Vocational Behavior,* 1980, *16,* 282–298.

Super, D., & Bowlsbey, J. *Guided career exploration.* New York: Psychological Corporation, 1979.

Super, D. E., & Kidd, J. M. Vocational maturity in adulthood: Toward turning a model into a measure. *Journal of Vocational Behavior,* 1979, *14,* 255–270.

Super, D., Thompson, A., Lindeman, R., Jordaan, J., & Myers, R. *Career development inventory.* Palo Alto, Calif.: Consulting Psychologists Press, 1981.

Tangri, S. S. Determinants of occupational role innovation among college women. *Journal of Social Issues,* 1972, *28,* 177–200.

Tittle, C. K. Implications of recent developments for future research in career interest measurement. In C. K. Tittle & D. G. Zytowski (Eds.), *Sex fair interest measurement: Research and implications.* National Institute of Education, Department of Health, Education and Welfare; Washington, D.C., 1978, 123–128.

Tittle, C. *Careers and family: Sex roles and adolescent life plans.* Beverly Hills, Calif.: Sage, 1981.

Treiman, D. J. *Occupational Prestige in Comparative Perspective.* New York: Academic Press, 1977.

Warnath, C. F. Vocational theories: Direction to nowhere. *Personnel and Guidance Journal,* 1975, *53,* 422–428.

Westbrook, B., & Mastie, M. The Cognitive Vocational Maturity Test. In D. Super (Ed.), *Measuring vocational maturity for counseling and evaluation.* Washington, D.C.: American Personnel and Guidance Association, 1974.

Westbrook, B., Cutts, C., Madison, S., & Arcia, M. The validity of the Crites model of career maturity. *Journal of Vocational Behavior,* 1980, *16,* 249–281.

Williamson, E. G., & Bordin, E. G. Evaluating counseling by means of a control-group experiment. *School and Society,* 1940, *52,* 434–440.

Wish, P., & Hasazi, J. *Motivational determinants of curricular choice behavior in college males.* Paper presented at the Eastern Psychological Association, Boston, April 1972.

Yanico, B. J., & Hardin, S. I. Sex-role self-concept and persistence in a traditional vs. non-traditional college major for women. *Journal of Vocational Behavior,* 1981, *18,* 219–227.

Zytowski, D. G. The effects of being interest-inventoried. *Journal of Vocational Behavior,* 1977, *11,* 153–157.

II
VOCATIONAL PSYCHOLOGY AND SPECIAL GROUPS

This part of the handbook consists of three chapters: a chapter on gender issues in vocational psychology by Louise Fitzgerald and Nancy Betz; a chapter on issues in minority vocational behavior by Elsie Smith; and a chapter on vocational behavior in adults by Robert Campbell and James Heffernan.

The chapter by Louise Fitzgerald and Nancy Betz thoroughly reviews what is known about the career choices, entry, and adjustment of women. This body of literature has grown large in a relatively short period of time but there continues to be a strong need for conceptual refinement and theoretical expansion. Fitzgerald and Betz note that since its inception the career psychology of women has been largely the study of sex differences. For almost 20 years, researchers have examined differences in women's and men's interests, abilities, and personalities. In the main, these investigations are based on the assumption that behavior can more reliably be predicted and explained when the sex of the subject is known. While studies of sex differences have been useful in many ways, this mode of research is essentially applied in nature in that no theoretical explanation is attempted. Given the inadequacies of gender per se as an explanatory variable, Fitzgerald and

Betz suggest that the concept of sex role may provide a more useful framework on which to base further studies of the career psychology of women. Differences as a function of sex role rather than gender itself are abundant in the literature, and the concept of sex role provides an improved basis for theoretical explanation and understanding than does that of sex alone. In addition, Fitzgerald and Betz suggest the adoption of Unger's (1979) proposition that gender itself can most usefully be considered a stimulus variable. The effect of gender on career adjustment can profitably be understood in terms of a stimulus variable that elicits reactions from others in the environment. The nature of this reaction is thought to be mediated by the sex-role orientation of the respondent. Related to suggested changes in the emphasis on sex versus sex role as explanatory concepts is the more general need as noted by Fitzgerald and Betz for increased attention to theory construction and explication in the area of women's career behavior. Theories are not only essential in guiding the directions and facilitating the understanding of research, but the lack of theory may lead to arbitrary interpretations of data.

The chapter by Fitzgerald and Betz has reviewed available literature concerning the career psychology of women and offered a preliminary theoretical framework from which to guide and organize research. The Fitzgerald and Betz call for increased attention to theoretical issues is not intended to minimize the importance of empirical research. Rather, the authors suggest that research will be enhanced by adherence to the functional mode of theory construction, in which one moves from the theory level to the data level and back again, constantly testing and revising hypotheses in the light of empirical findings. This interaction of theory and research seems to be the most viable model available to use in the construction of career psychology of women.

In the chapter on issues in minority vocational behavior, Elsie Smith notes that since the mid-1970s a number of studies have investigated the career behavior of ethnic American minorities. Investigators have examined the career development of black Americans, Asian Americans, Hispanics, and Native Americans. Black Americans have been the most highly studied group and it has only been relatively recently that the career behavior of other racial minorities have been studied as distinct groups in American society. Thus, the chapter on issues in minority vocational behavior by Elsie Smith examines the career behavior of four groups of racial and/or ethnic minorities: black Americans, Asian Americans, Hispanics, and native Americans. A primary goal of the chapter is to analyze the diverse factors that tend to influence career behavior. Some of these variables include work attitudes, career aspirations, interests, choices, and vocational maturity. A second goal of the chapter is to codify what is known about the career development of members of these various groups.

In pursuing this goal, demographic data are provided on each of the four groups, and an overall review of vocational research as it pertains to these groups is conducted. A final purpose of the chapter is to suggest future directions for research that may help to clarify the career behavior of American racial minorities.

Overall, Smith notes that the evidence suggests rather clearly that ethnic minorities have made progress in the careers within the past 2 decades. However, the progress has not been uniform across the various ethnic groups. The degree of progress a particular ethnic group makes appears to be dependent on a number of factors, including the history of the group within this country, the cultural factors that clash or mesh with the dominant American value system, the social distance majority Americans feel toward a given ethnic group, and the educational achievement and career behavior of the respective groups. However, Smith indicates that the prospects for the 1980s do not look very encouraging for those individuals who are both poor and members of ethnic minority groups. Currently, American society appears to be facing a future of shrinking job opportunities, increased credential requirements, and increased competition in job entry. Furthermore, there is reason to believe that as the American economy becomes increasingly internationally rather than nationally focused as it is now, labor market competition will likewise become international in scope. Thus, Smith suggests that the probability of a permanent underclass of ethnic minority Americans from lower socioeconomic backgrounds seems to be increasing rather than decreasing.

The third chapter in this section by Robert Campbell and James Heffernan deals with adult vocational behavior. Campbell and Heffernan note that for approximately 60 years research and practice in vocational psychology has been preoccupied with the adolescent and young adult and has appeared to assume that very little of interest happens after an adolescent selects and enters an occupation. However, the belief that a static occupational existence occurs beyond age 25 has rapidly changed. Steadily, awareness of the many key transitions and corresponding critical decisions throughout the adult life cycle has grown. People are discovering that there is a life after 40, even after 70. Many people have at least two careers if not three or more. There are 126 million adults 25 years of age and older and approximately one-third of them are seeking career changes according to Campbell and Heffernan. As a result, the past 10 years have seen interest in adult vocational behavior flourish. Obviously the growing numbers of adults in society reflecting the aging of the post-World War II baby boom have accounted for the increased interest in adult vocational behavior, but a number of other variables are also significantly related. As noted by Campbell and Heffernan, these include such factors as high divorce rates, the instability of the economy, changing job opportunities, changing family patterns, the proliferation of educational opportunities, new life styles, and the rise of women in the labor force.

The chapter on adult vocational behavior by Campbell and Heffernan is divided into two major sections. The first section describes theories of adult career development as espoused by Super, Levinson, Schein, Erikson, Havighurst, and Miller and Form. Most of these theorists specify that individual development proceeds through a series of stages, each of which requires the mastery of developmental tasks and/or the resolution of developmental issues unique to that stage. Movement to subsequent stages is viewed as contingent upon the satisfactory completion or resolution of previous stages. This section also discusses a diagnostic taxonomy developed by Campbell and Cellini as a means of identifying career development adjustment problems. The taxonomy is based on the assumption that problems arise when an individual experiences difficulty in coping with a career development task, when a task is only partially mastered, or when a task is not even attempted. The second major section of this chapter describes career and educational counseling services for adults. In that section it is noted that in 1980 some 465 programs and agencies were providing counseling information and support services to adults. Because most agencies have multiple sites (the median is between three and four), this means that there were nearly 700 such counseling centers in the United States in 1980. The chapter is concluded with the presentation of seven interesting and heuristic recommendations.

3 Issues in the Vocational Psychology of Women

Louise F. Fitzgerald
Kent State University

Nancy E. Betz
Ohio State University

Introduction

Although the field of vocational psychology itself is over 70 years old, the interest in the effects of gender on career choice and vocational adjustment, in particular interest in women's career development, is a relatively recent phenomenon. Only in the last 20 years or so have scholars begun to view women's career development as an important and in many respects unique area of study.

Although a comparatively new field of inquiry, then, the career development of women has been the subject of extensive and continuing interest and empirical investigation in the last two decades. This chapter will begin by addressing the need for theory and research focused specifically on women's career development. In subsequent sections, concepts and empirical research pertinent to the description and explanation of the processes of vocational choice, occupational entry, and vocational adjustment in women will be reviewed. Finally, implications of the research and recommendations concerning further directions for theory and research in this area will be presented.

Need for the Study of Women's Career Development

The lack of attention to women's career development during vocational psychology's first 50 years probably derived from one or both of two previously accepted assumptions. The first of these assumptions was that the primary roles of women were those of housewife and mother; women's "work" revolved around domestic and childcare responsibilities. When women did work outside the home they were observed to occupy primarily low-level, low-status positions providing little or no opportunity for advancement or societal recognition. The concept of career applied neither to those women whose "place" was in the home nor to the women workers who were viewed as working only until they could afford not to work. As stated by Vetter (1973), women workers were perceived as "individually transient and collectively insignificant due to the type and level of jobs available to them," (p. 54) as holding jobs rather than as building careers. Thus, the belief that women's place was in the home and that women themselves preferred that place made women an unsuitable and uninteresting population for psychologists interested in career development.

A second possible basis for the lack of attention to women's career development involved implicit assumptions that the theories and concepts developed to describe and explain male career development would generalize to the description and explanation of women's career development. The field of psychology as a whole has been characterized by this assumption (Hyde & Rosenberg, 1980), so it is not surprising to find it existing among vocational psychologists in particular.

Although assumptions concerning women's place in the home and the applicability to women of existing theories of career development were widely held, awareness of their lack of validity and the consequent need for specific attention to women's career development have dramatically increased in recent years.

Regarding the first assumption, "women's place" is clearly no longer exclusively in the home. Women work outside the home in ever-increasing numbers and are a significant, indeed critical, part of the labor force. For example, in 1979, 60% of all women 18 to 64 were working outside the home; these women constituted more than 40% of all workers (U.S. Department of Labor, 1980). The odds that any given woman would work outside the home at some time in her life were over 9 out of 10, and the average woman could expect to spend 27.6 years in the labor force compared with 38.3 years for the average man. About half of currently married women work, and the number of working mothers has increased tenfold since the period immediately preceding World War II; 55% of mothers with children under 18 are now working, as are 45% of mothers with preschool children (U.S. Department of Labor, 1980). Whereas about one-third of working women are married and have husbands making adequate incomes, the other two-thirds are women who are single, widowed, divorced, or separated or have husbands whose incomes were less than $10,000 in 1979 (U.S. Department of Labor, 1980). In summary, women whose adult lives will not include work outside the home are increasingly becoming the exception rather than the norm.

Not only will most women work outside the home, but the majority of young women now prefer to combine marriage and career pursuits in their adult lives. Since Matthews and Tiedeman's (1964) findings that 60%–75% of women aged 11 to 26 planned to be married and not working 10 years from the time of the study, research has shown a consistent decrease in women preferring marriage-only lifestyles. Rand and Miller (1972) described what they termed a new "cultural imperative," marriage *and* a career, in their finding that 95% of their sample of women of junior high through college age expected to both marry and work. Recent data support the trend described by Rand and Miller. For example, 50%–90% of Blaska's (1978) and a large majority of Altman and Grossman's (1977) college seniors were career oriented. Zuckerman (1980), in a study of women in coeducational "seven sisters" colleges, found that 92% were planning to complete education beyond the B.A. degree. Harmon (1980), in a follow-up of women 6 years after college entry, found that 46% wanted to work most of their lives (versus 27% in 1968) and that only 2% wanted minimal employment (versus 16% in 1968). Farmer (1980b) found no differences in the career commitment of ninth- and twelfth-grade boys and girls.

Thus, trends over the past 15 years and recent data strongly suggest the importance of occupational pursuits in the plans and lives of women. It is clear that most women will work outside the home at some time in their adult lives and that work will play an increasingly important role in their lives. Thus, women's place is in the work force, and women's work and careers deserve theoretical and empirical attention.

The second assumption, that is, that women's career development is capable of being described, explained, and predicted using existing theories of career development, is also untenable. The lack of applicability of theories developed on men to women's vocational behavior has been frequently discussed (Osipow, 1973, 1975a, 1975b) and can probably best be illustrated by discussion of some clearly evident sex differences relevant to vocational choices and patterns.

A first major sex difference concerns the relatively restricted range of occupational alternatives pursued by women in comparison to the much larger range pursued by men. Even though women constitute 40% of the labor force, they continue to be concentrated in a small number of "traditionally female" jobs and professions. A majority of women workers are in "pink collar" (Howe, 1977) jobs, such as clerical work, retail sales, waitress, beautician, and housekeeping services (U.S. Department of Labor, 1980). Women professionals are concentrated in professions of lower pay and status than the male-dominated professions; the vast majority of nurses, elementary school teachers, librarians, and social workers are female, whereas the majority of physicians, lawyers, scientists, and engineers are male (Prediger & Cole, 1975). Even within the same occupation or occupational field, women tend to be concentrated at the lower levels, whereas men predominate at the upper levels (Gottfredson, 1978). For example, 83% of workers in low-level conventional occupations are women, in contrast to only 25% in high-level conventional occupations; women constitute 44% of workers in low-level enterprising occupations but only 8% in the high-level occupations (Gottfredson, 1978). Within the teaching profession the percentage of women decreases as the level increases. For example 86% of elementary school teachers but only 26% of school administrators are women. Women constitute 51% of instructors in universities but only 5% of full professors (Chronicle of Higher Education; U.S. Department of Labor, 1977). Thus not only are women found primarily in traditionally female occupations, but they are clearly overrepresented in lower-level, lower-status, and lower-paying occupations and positions.

Not only are women actually employed in traditionally female fields, but the career aspirations of young women continue to focus on stereotypically female occupations. Almost all of the 95% of women planning both career and marriage in Rand and Miller's (1972) sample were planning to pursue traditionally female occupations. Occupations in the educational and social services, nursing, and clerical work were selected by 60% of the high school girls studied by Brito and Jusenius (1978) and Falk and Salter (1978), 50% of those studied by Prediger, Roth, and Noeth (1974), and the large majority of Fottler and Bain's (1980) high school girls. Harmon's (1980) study of women in their early 20s also supports the continued orientation toward traditionally female careers. Although there does seem to be a small proportionate increase in the number of women pursuing nontraditional careers, such as medicine (AMA, 1977), dentistry, and engineering (Farmer, 1980b; Zuckerman, 1980), the predominant pattern among women continues to suggest a limited and sex-stereotypic range of female occupational pursuits.

Related to women's concentration in traditionally female and frequently low-level occupations is the finding that, in contrast to men in general, women's intellectual capacities and talents are not reflected in their educational and occupational achievements; women's career aspirations and choices are frequently far lower than are the aspirations of males with comparable levels of ability (Fitzgerald & Crites, 1980).

Probably the most dramatic illustration of the failure of intellectually gifted women to utilize their talents in career pursuits was provided by the Terman and Oden (1959) follow-up studies of a large sample of gifted California children. Terman's sample, originally obtained in 1921–1922, consisted of 1528 children having measured IQs equal to or greater than 135. Of the sample, 671 were girls, and 847 were boys. The oldest and most durable model of vocational choice, the "matching" or trait-factor model (Parsons, 1909; Williamson, 1939), would yield the prediction that the intellectual capabilities of these children would lead to high educational and occupational achievement and productivity in adulthood.

The follow-up study of the gifted group at midlife indicated that, as expected, the great majority of men had achieved prominence in professional and managerial occupations. They had, by their mid-40s, been exceptionally productive scientists, made literary and artistic contributions, and become prominent lawyers, physicians, and psychologists. In contrast to the men, the women were primarily housewives or were employed in the traditionally female occupations. About 50% of the women, in their mid-40s, were full-time housewives. Of those who were working full time, 21% were teachers in elementary or secondary school, 8% were social workers, 20% were secretaries, and 8% were either librarians or nurses. Only 7% of those working were academicians, 5% were physicians, lawyers, or psychologists, 8% were executives, and 9% were writers, artists, or musicians. As children, these women had been as intellectually gifted as their male counterparts, but their achievements in adulthood were clearly in contrast to their early intellectual promise. Their sex was a better predictor of their occupational pursuits in adulthood than were their capabilities as individuals.

Bem and Bem (1970) described the phenomenon illustrated by the Terman study as indicative of the "homogenization" of American women. In other words, women are socialized to pursue the same role regardless of their individual capabilities and talents. A woman's life roles and vocational choices are predictable not on the basis of her characteristics as an individual but on the basis of her sex. Such homogenization results in losses both to individuals and to society when women's talents are so poorly utilized. In terms of vocational theory, then, sex has been a far more powerful predictor of vocational role choices in women than have the other individual factors postulated as important in vocational theories focusing, either explicitly or implicitly, on male career development.

Finally, women's career development has involved one more step than that of men. As stated by Kriger (1972), women's career development is actually the product of two sequential decisions. Before women decide what occupation or career to pursue, they must decide whether or not they want to make outside employment a focus of their life. Men, in contrast, are rarely allowed to consider whether or not to work and begin instead with considerations of what they would like to pursue. Men in this society grow up assuming that they will need to support themselves and their families, and, thus, begin with the choice of an occupation rather than with the choice of whether or not to work.

In summary, women's restricted range of career options, their disadvantaged position in the labor market, the underutilization of their capabilities, and the need for decisions concerning the role of career involvement in their lives are some of the major areas in which women's career development differs from that of men. Vocational psychologists have now recognized the need for theory and research focused specifically on women's career development. In subsequent sections, available literature concerning the processes by which women make vocational choices and the factors influencing women's vocational adjustment are reviewed.

VOCATIONAL CHOICE

One of the major areas of interest of vocational psychologists over the years has been the explanation and prediction of patterns of vocational choice. Investigations of and theories concerning the individual and environmental factors related to individuals' vocational choices have greatly contributed to both theoretical understanding and the practice of career counseling. Because research and theories have focused primarily on male career development, however, they have until recently neglected to consider the possible differential influence of major explanatory variables on the career choices of women versus those of men and the unique variables related to and dimensions descriptive of women's career development.

Although theoretically based research has focused on the applicability of existing theories of career development (Holland, 1973; Super, 1957) to women rather than on the development and explication of theories focused on women's career development per se, there have been several conceptual advances related specifically to the description and explanation of that development. The first section below will review these concepts, beginning with variables used to differentially describe women's career choice behavior (i.e., dependent variables) and proceeding with a review of variables considered uniquely important to the understanding and prediction of that behavior. The second section will review research concerning the correlates of women's career choices.

Concepts in the Study of Women's Career Choices: Dependent Variables

The study of women's career development necessitated the utilization of dependent variables not relevant to the study of male career development. In addition to dependent variables describing the content of career choices (e.g., occupational field and level), the study of women's career development added variables describing the degree to which a woman intended to work at all and the importance, if any, of career pursuits in her life. The following section reviews the major dependent variables used in the study of women's career choices.

Homemaking versus career orientation.   The earliest studies of women's career development focused on women's vocational or career orientation.

In other words, studies investigating the kinds of vocational choices made by women were less important than was the issue of whether or not and *why* women pursued careers at all (Kriger, 1972). Thus, the earliest body of research attempted to differentiate and to study the characteristics of homemaking versus career oriented women.

The first study attempting to differentiate and describe homemaking-oriented versus career-oriented women was that of Hoyt and Kennedy (1958). The two groups of women were differentiated on the basis of their responses to a questionnaire concerning the relative importance of marital versus career roles. Using the SVIB-W as a descriptive measure, career-oriented subjects were found to obtain higher scores on six scales, including artist, lawyer, psychologist, physician, and physical education teacher, whereas homemaking-oriented subjects scored higher on eight scales, including housewife, secretary, home economics teachers, and dietician.

The research paradigm developed by Hoyt and Kennedy (1965) was utilized in several subsequent studies also using the SVIB-W as the independent variable of interest. In these later studies, Hoyt and Kennedy's findings that career-oriented women tended to obtain higher scores on occupations traditionally dominated by men whereas homemaking-oriented women obtained higher scores on the housewife scale and on nonprofessional or traditionally female occupational scales were essentially replicated (Munley, 1974; Vetter & Lewis, 1964; Wagman, 1966).

Based on the consistency with which the SVIB-W differentiated homemaking-oriented from career-oriented women, other studies used the SVIB-W to differentiate the groups and then examined background, ability, personality, and value differences between home-oriented and career-oriented women. Studies of group differences in family background characteristics (Gysbers, Johnston, & Gust, 1968), in achievement motivation (Oliver, 1974; Rand, 1968; Tyler, 1964), personality characteristics (Rand, 1968), ability (Rand, 1968; Watley & Kaplan, 1971), and values (Goldsen, Rosenberg, Williams, & Suchman, 1960; Simpson & Simpson, 1961; Wagman, 1966), to be described in later sections, characterized early research on women's career development.

Although the variable of homemaker versus career orientation has been used occasionally in more recent research (Tinsley & Faunce, 1978), its predominance as a dependent variable decreased following criticism of its usefulness (Levitt, 1972; Oliver, 1974). Concepts describing the nature and degree of career orientation replaced the dichotomous variable of career-versus home-orientation.

Variables describing career orientation.   Whereas studies done in the 1960s suggested that the majority of young women did not plan to work outside the home (Matthews & Tiedeman, 1964), studies in the early 1970s strongly suggested that the majority of young women planned to combine marriage and career (Rand & Miller, 1972; Watley & Kaplan, 1971). Rand and Miller (1972) suggested that a new cultural imperative to combine marriage and career had replaced the previous stress on the centrality of marital and motherhood roles in the lives of women. Because of the growing numbers of young women planning to combine career and marriage, the homemaking-orientation versus career-orientation distinction decreased in usefulness (Levitt, 1972; Oliver, 1974). Rather, it was necessary to describe the nature and degree of career orientation itself to understand women's career choice behavior.

The major approach to describing the *nature* of women's career choices involved the classification of preferences or choices according to the degree to which they were traditional versus nontraditional for women. Rossi (1965) was among the first to suggest the utility of differentiating career-oriented women into those pursuing traditionally female careers (i.e., occupations in which women predominate) and those pursuing "pioneer" careers (i.e., occupations in which men have predominated). Women pursuing nontraditional or pioneer occupations have also been defined as "role innovators" (Almquist, 1974; Tangri, 1972). Thus, the terms *pioneer, innovator,* and *nontraditional* have been used interchangeably to differentiate women pursuing male-dominated fields, which are assumed to require stronger and more consistent career commitment and involvement, from "traditionals" (i.e., those pursuing traditionally female occupations). Studies of characteristics differentiating pioneers from traditionals dominated research in the early 1970s and, as described in later sections, documented numerous important differences between the two types of women (Astin & Myint, 1971; Nagely, 1971; Standley & Soule, 1974; Tangri, 1972).

In addition to comparisons of women in traditional versus pioneer fields, the concept of career orientation was extended and refined beginning with the work of Eyde (1962). Rather than conceiving of career orientation as a single undifferentiated state defined in opposition to homemaker orientation, career orientation began to be conceptualized as a continuous variable reflecting degree of preferred work involvement with or without concurrent involvement in the homemaker role. Eyde's (1962) Desire to Work scale represented the first systematic attempt to assess career orientation as a continuous variable. Eyde's scale, which requested respondents to rate their desire to work under varying conditions of marital status, number and ages of children, and perceived adequacy of husband's income, defined stronger career orientation in terms of the extent to which a woman wished to work even if also married and a mother.

Almquist and Angrist (1970, 1971; Angrist, 1972) adapted Eyde's Desire to Work scale for the assessment of "career salience," defined in 1971 as "aspiration for work as a central feature of adult life, regardless of financial necessity and under conditions of free choice [p. 263]." Their Life Style Index contained items pertaining to motivation to work under various family conditions and items concerning adult role aspirations and preferences.

Other approaches to the definition and measurement of the concept of career salience were those of Masih (1967) and Greenhaus (1971). Masih defined career salience as: (1) the degree to which a person is career motivated; (2) the degree to which an occupation is an important source of satisfaction; and (3) the priority ascribed to career among other sources of satisfaction. Greenhaus (1971) developed a 27-item measure of career salience and a twenty-eighth item requesting subjects to rank order six life areas, including career and family, in terms of their importance in the respondent's life.

A final conceptual advance was represented by Richardson's (1974) distinction between "work motivation" and "career orientation." Richardson defined work motivation as the desire to pursue work outside the home although not prioritizing work roles. Career orientation, on the other hand, was defined as the desire to pursue work as a primary life focus with homemaking interests viewed as secondary.

Most studies of women's career development have utilized then either the home–career or traditional–nontraditional distinction or a measure of career orientation or salience as the dependent variable. However, the failure of a single distinction or variable to adequately describe women's career development has been noted (Osipow, 1973). For example, a woman pursuing a traditionally female occupation such as nurse or elementary school teacher could be as strongly career oriented as a woman pursuing a nontraditional occupation (e.g., medicine or law). Conversely, female role innovators (e.g., physicians) undoubtedly differ in the extent to which marital and family roles are salient in their life plans. Thus, Osipow (1973) has suggested the necessity of research designs that utilize the various possible combinations of such variables in describing women's career development.

Career patterns. The third major approach to the description of women's career development utilizes the concept of career patterns, originally developed by Super (1957) and first used in the study of male career development.

In 1957, Super, noting both the centrality of homemaking in a woman's life and the trend for increased labor force participation among women, described seven career patterns of women:

1. The *stable homemaking* pattern, characterizing women who marry while in or shortly after leaving school and who have no significant work experience.

2. The *conventional* career pattern, characterizing women who work outside the home only until marriage.
3. The *stable working* pattern (i.e., women who work continuously over the life span and for whom work is their "career").
4. The *double-track* career pattern, characterizing women who combine home and work roles continuously.
5. The *interrupted* career pattern, characterized by a return to the work world later on in life.
6. The *unstable* career pattern, describing an irregular and repeated cycle of home versus work involvement.
7. The *multiple-trial* career pattern that, similar to the same male pattern, consists of an unstable job history.

In a study of the frequency of occurrence of these patterns, Vetter (1973) found the following percentages in a national cross-sectional sample of women: stable homemaking, 22%; conventional, 27%; stable working, 3%; double track, 14%; interrupted, 16%; and unstable, 18%. Multiple trial was not used because of overlap with other categories.

Whereas Super attempted to extend his theory's usefulness for women, a more heuristically useful model of women's career patterns was formulated by Zytowski (1969), who offered nine postulates that attempted to characterize female patterns of occupational participation. His central proposition was that the modal life role for women is that of homemaker, although this role was not static and may ultimately bear no distinction from that of men. A second major postulate was that vocational and homemaker participation are largely mutually exclusive and that consequently vocational participation constitutes departure from the homemaker role. Zytowski further postulated that vocational participation patterns could be characterized based on three dimensions of participation: age of entry, span (length) of participation, and degree of participation (i.e., the traditionality versus nontraditionality of the occupation for women). Based on these three dimensions, Zytowski described three resulting patterns: (1) the *mild* vocational pattern, characterized by early or late entry and brief and low-degree participation; (2) the *moderate* pattern, characterized by early entry and lengthy span but low-degree participation; and (3) the *unusual* career pattern, characterized by early entry, lengthy or uninterrupted span, and a high degree of participation. Thus, Zytowski's model attempts to combine a notion similar to that of career orientation (i.e., span of participation) with the traditional versus pioneer distinction (i.e., degree of participation). Unfortunately, however, this model is inadequate in terms of many women who enter male-dominated occupations; unless she enters early and works continuously, a female scientist, for example, would be unclassifiable in this framework.

A study by Wolfson (1976) was designed to investigate differences among groups of women characterized according to Zytowski's (1969) vocational patterns. She found, however, five rather than three distinguishable vocational patterns: in addition to the three formulated by Zytowski, Wolfson added a "never worked" pattern and a "high-moderate" pattern, including women whose span of participation was 18 years or more. Wolfson found that college graduation, attendance in graduate school, and unmarried status were predictive of membership in the "high-moderate" or "unusual" groups. All women in the "never-worked", "mild", and "moderate" groups were or had been married, whereas half of those in the "high-moderate" and "unusual" groups were single. The largest number of women were characterized by the "mild" pattern (49%), whereas the fewest (.05%) were characterized by the "unusual" pattern.

Finally, Harmon (1967), in a 25-year follow-up study of University of Minnesota students, classified women's career patterns into five categories: (1) no job experience; (2) work experience only until marriage or the arrival of the first child; (3) combined work with marriage and children; (4) reentered the labor force when children were older; and (5) the single career woman.

Summary.   The study of women's career choices, then, has involved the use of several variables that attempt to take into account what is probably the major difference in the career development of women versus that of men (i.e., the expectation that women's lives will usually include, if not revolve around, the roles of homemaking and childrearing). Because the assumption of competing roles was not previously considered relevant to the study of male career development, research on men could proceed more directly toward examination of the content of career choice. Thus, the study of women's career development is inherently more complex.

Concepts in the Study of Women's Career Choices: Independent Variables

Although the independent variables utilized in the study of women's career choices have included those emphasized in the study of men (e.g., abilities, interests, socioeconomic and family background factors), the study of women's career development has utilized several additional independent variables and systems of classification emphasizing environmental as well as individual facilitators of and barriers to women's career development.

The variables of marital/familial status, sex-role attitudes, and role conflict are the major independent variables considered uniquely pertinent to women's career choices and pursuits. The first attempt to include these variables was that of Sobol (1963), who proposed a classification of variables influencing the decisions of married women with children to work outside the home. This classification included: (1) "enabling" conditions (i.e., family characteristics including spouse's salary and satisfaction with the marriage); (2) facilitating conditions (e.g., educational level and previous work experience); and (3) precipitating conditions (i.e., individual attitudes, including self-concept and sex-role attitudes). As would be true in subsequent work, Sobol's classification included both situational (e.g., marital) and individual (e.g., attitudinal) factors.

Psathas (1968) suggested several factors influencing women's occupational participation. Emphasizing cultural, situational, and chance elements of the environment, Psathas cited intention to marry, time of marriage, the husband's economic situation and attitude toward his wife's working, and the woman's sex-role preferences as influential determinants of women's decisions to work.

Other writers focused specifically on barriers to women's career development. These approaches more than those of, for example, Sobol (1963) and Psathas (1968) were based on a concern with women's lack of vocational achievements and failure to utilize their abilities and talents and, thus, sought to elucidate the barriers to women's vocational participation and achievement. Matthews and Tiedeman (1964), for example, specified four conflicts unique to females: (1) the female's concern that career aspirations and achievements would necessitate the sacrifice of marriage; (2) sex-typed family roles qualifying women for homemaker but not breadwinner roles; (3) home–career conflict; and (4) the concurrence of desired age of marriage with the need to emphasize educational pursuits and goals necessary to career achievement.

Farmer (1976) suggested six internal or self-concept barriers to women, including fear of success, sex-role orientation, risk-taking behavior, home–career conflict, and low academic self-esteem, and three environmental barriers, that is, discrimination, family socialization and availability of resources (e.g., child care). Similarly, Harmon (1977) proposed that women's career development is affected by both internal/psychological and external/sociological constraints.

Falk and Cosby (1978) detailed several problems both unique and disruptive to the career development of females. These included the female's socialization into the traditional role, the sex-typing of occupations, the perceived conflict between marital and occupational success, and the influence and pressure of significant others toward traditional role pursuits and away from nontraditional, (i.e., educational and vocational) achievements.

Finally, both Senesh and Osipow (Osipow, 1975; Senesh, 1973) and O'Neil, Meeker and Borgers (1978) present comprehensive frameworks of factors influencing career development that they propose as useful for the study of women's career development. The framework proposed by Osipow and Senesh (Osipow, 1975a; Senesh, 1973) includes individual factors (e.g., abilities, interests, attitudes), social factors (e.g., family, significant others, sex role and occupational stereotypes), and moderating factors (e.g., fear of success, role conflict, discrimination [Osipow, 1975a, p. 5]). O'Neil et al. (1978) propose that individual, familial, societal, psychosocial, socioeconomic, and situational factors importantly influence the extent and nature of women's sex-role socialization and attitudes and, consequently, their career choice processes.

In summary, although there is as yet no comprehensive theory of women's career development, the formulation of several new variables both dependent and independent, the focus on unique barriers to women's career development, and the development of approaches to the classification of influential factors in that development are important steps toward theoretical understanding. The next section reviews available research concerning the roles of environmental and individual variables in women's career choices.

FACTORS INFLUENCING WOMEN'S CAREER CHOICES

Stimulus Variables: Culture

Societal sex-role stereotypes.   Our society has traditionally specified different life roles, personality characteristics, and acceptable behaviors for males and females. Norms governing the approved masculine or feminine image are clearly defined and consensually endorsed (Broverman, Vogel, Broverman, Clarkson, & Rosenkrantz, 1970; Mischel, 1970; Steinman & Fox, 1966) and become a powerful force in the socialization of children.

In terms of adult roles, men are expected to work and to be the family provider. Women are expected to be the nurturant wife and mother who stays at home. In terms of personality characteristics, men are expected to develop those associated with competency, instrumentality, and achievement, whereas women are to develop those comprising a "warmth-expressiveness" cluster, including nurturance, sensitivity, warmth, and emotional expressiveness.

The psychological mechanisms by which children learn sex-role stereotypes, normative expectations for the sexes, and develop sex-typed characteristics include reinforcement and punishment, modeling, and the adoption of rules, schemas, or generalizations based on observation of others or as they are taught by others (Hyde & Rosenberg, 1980; Williams, 1977). These mechanisms operate through the influence of parents, teachers, and the media, including literature and television (Maccoby & Jacklin, 1975; Williams, 1977).

Thus, culturally based sex-role socialization operates from early childhood to prepare young girls for the roles of wife and mother and to encourage in them the development of personality characteristics and behavioral competencies that will facilitate the performance of those roles. Young girls are usually not socialized to prepare for career pursuits or to develop the characteristics and competencies necessary to such pursuits.

Occupational sex stereotypes.   Related to sex-role stereotypes are occupational stereotypes or normative views of the appropriateness of various occupations for males and females. Occupational stereotypes are consistent and durable in adult populations (Albrecht, Bahr, & Chadwick, 1977; Panek, Rush, & Greenwalt, 1977; Shinar, 1975).

Not only do adults stereotype occupations as appropriate for males or females, but children appear to learn these stereotypes very early. For example, Gettys and Cann (1981) found that children as young as 2 1/2 were able to distinguish masculine and feminine occupations, whereas Tremaine and Schau (1979) found the preschoolers identified and agreed with adult job stereotypes. Occupational stereotypes are consistently found in elementary school children (Frost & Diamond, 1979; Gettys & Cann, 1981; Schlossberg & Goodman, 1972; Tremaine & Schau, 1979). Further, children's occupational preferences tend to be consistent with the occupational stereotypes they hold in that both boys and girls tend to choose sex-typed occupations (Frost & Diamond, 1979; Looft, 1971; Teglasi, 1981; Tremaine & Schau, 1979).

Although children of both sexes select sex-stereotypic occupational choices, the smaller number and more limited range of traditionally female occupations results in the limitation of girls' perceived options at very early ages. In Looft's (1971) sample of first- and second-graders, Siegel's (1973) sample of second-graders, and Nelson's (1978) third-graders, boys were found to indicate a wide variety of occupational preferences, almost all of them male dominated. Girls, on the other hand, listed a smaller number of occupations, and their choices were dominated by two occupations—nurse and teacher. In Siegel's sample, for example, 70% of second-grade girls selected either nurse or teacher, whereas the 32 boys chose 20 different occupations. Finally, Kriedberg, Butcher, and White (1978) found that although some second-grade girls expressed interest in male-dominated occupations, almost all sixth-grade girls were choosing traditionally female occupations. It is unfortunate indeed that occupational stereotypes have limited girls' perceived career options before they finish elementary school.

Not only do durable occupational stereotypes exist in both children and adults, but occupational informational materials designed for use at the high school and adult levels have been documented to perpetuate occupational stereotypes in both text and illustrative material (Birk, Tanney, &

Cooper, 1979; Lauver, Gastellum, & Sheehey, 1975; Yanico, 1978). Thus, materials that should serve to facilitate exploration of career options serve instead to reinforce the restrictions in women's options that result from occupational sex stereotypes in the culture.

Summary. In summary, cultural attitudes and beliefs concerning women's roles and capabilities, through the mechanisms of sex-role socialization and occupational stereotyping, operate to encourage the development of sex-typed psychological characteristics and to perpetuate sex-typed adult roles. Young women and girls learn not only that their appropriate adult roles are those of wife and mother but that if they do work there is a set of female-appropriate occupations from which they should choose. Thus, society influences girls and young women to limit their life roles and occupational options on the basis of gender alone, without regard for or interest in their unique individual capabilities and potentials for development.

Stimulus Variables: Subculture

In addition to the overall culture in the development and experiences of females and males, the subculture in which he/she develops affects career development. Major variables describing that subculture include socioeconomic status and race.

Socioeconomic status. The concept of socioeconomic status (SES) has been variously defined and measured; indices of SES have included the occupational or educational levels of the primary breadwinner (usually the father) and family income. Although occupational level is the most commonly used index, studies vary in the indices used and, unfortunately, often fail to specify how the index of SES was obtained. An additional problem for interpretive clarity is that indices of SES are not only highly correlated with each other but are strongly related to such variables as intelligence and race (Tyler, 1965). Thus, the effect of SES per se on occupational attainments may be difficult to disentangle from the effects of other variables covarying with SES.

In spite of definitional variation, socioeconomic status is one of the most consistent predictors of the occupational level achieved by males; higher family SES is related to higher achieved occupational levels in sons, whereas sons of lower-class backgrounds achieve lower occupational levels (Brown, 1970; Hollingshead, 1949; Sewell, Haller, & Strauss, 1957). As pointed out by Goodale and Hall (1976), sons are likely to "inherit" their fathers' occupational levels.

In contrast, data regarding the influence of parental SES on women's career development yield an inconsistent pattern of results. In some studies, higher SES was related to stronger career orientation and/or innovation in women (Astin, 1968; Astin & Myint, 1971; Burlin, 1976b; Werts, 1965). Several studies have found that women pursuing male-dominated professions (e.g., physicians, academics) are significantly more likely than women in general to have fathers who are professionals (Cartwright, 1972; Helson, 1971; Russo & O'Connell, 1980; Standley & Soule, 1974).

Other studies, however, have reported negative relationships between career orientation and SES (Del Vento Bielby, 1978; Eyde, 1962; White, 1967), and still others have found no relationships between the two variables (Card, Steel, & Abeles, 1980; Crawford, 1978; Falk & Salter, 1978; Ridgeway, 1978). Marini (1978) suggests that although family SES is associated with higher educational aspirations in daughters, the relationship of family SES to girls' occupational aspirations is far less clear.

Although studies based on father's occupational level provide a somewhat inconsistent pattern of findings, data regarding father's educational level provide a more consistent pattern of findings and suggest that more highly educated fathers tend to have more career-oriented and innovative daughters. Higher paternal education for women compared to men in the same occupations was noted by Astin (1969) and Constantini and Craik (1972) among others. Women in pioneer career fields had more highly educated fathers than did women in traditional fields in studies by Burlin (1976), Greenfield, Greiner and Wood (1980), Harmon (1977), and Russo and O'Connell (1980), among others. Father's educational level has been found to be positively related to daughter's educational aspirations (Falk & Salter, 1978) and career orientation (Gysbers et al., 1968; Patrick, 1973).

Thus, there is some evidence that women's career choices are influenced by the occupational level and, particularly, the educational level of their fathers. Having a highly educated professional father appears especially facilitative of women's pursuit of male-dominated professions. The failure of SES variables to be as predictive of women's career choices as they are of men's may at least in part be explained by differential expectations of the sexes in this society. While high-SES families are very likely to encourage and facilitate achievement-related behaviors in their sons, the extent to which they do so in their daughters is probably a function of parental attitudes and beliefs with regard to women's roles in society and, possibly, the presence or absence of sons in the family. Thus, Goodale and Hall's (1976) suggestion that parental interest and support moderate the relationship of SES to career achievements seems essential to and, as will be discussed in a subsequent section, particularly valid for the understanding of women's vocational aspirations.

Race. Most studies of race differences in American women's career choices have examined black versus white women; few studies have examined Hispanics, American Indians, or Asian–Americans, for example.

Thus, this section focuses on studies comparing black and white women.

One of the most consistent findings regarding black women is that, in comparison to their white counterparts, the majority expects to work part or all of their adult lives (Gump & Rivers, 1975; Turner & McCaffrey, 1974). This greater expectation of work is, in fact, actualized in black women's greater labor force participation in comparison to white women (Gump & Rivers, 1975; Jeffries, 1976; U. S. Department of Labor, 1977).

But whereas black women's expected and actual labor force participation exceeds that of white women, black women are even more disadvantaged than are white women in the nature of that participation. Black women, first of all, earn less money than women or men of any ethnic group and earn substantially less than do black men (Gump & Rivers, 1975; U.S. Department of Labor, 1977). And whereas proportionately more black women than black men are in professional level occupations, proportionately fewer black women than white women are professionally employed (Gottfredson, 1978; U.S. Department of Labor, 1977). In 1977, 13% and 7% of black women and men, respectively, were in professional occupations in comparison to 16% of white women and men. Even among black women professionals, the range of occupations is narrow; 54% of black women versus 39% of white women professionals are in teaching (Sorkin, 1972). In comparison to white women, black women are even more greatly concentrated in traditionally female occupations (Brito & Jusenius, 1978; Frost & Diamond, 1979; Murray & Mednick, 1977), particularly in domestic and service jobs (U.S. Department of Labor, 1977).

Black women's consistently greater expected and actual labor force participation may in part be a function of the fact that they are also more likely than white women to be the sole support of themselves and/or their families. Black women are far more likely than white women to be heads of households (Clay, 1975; U.S. Department of Labor, 1980) and to be single, divorced, or widowed (Epstein, 1973; Jackson, 1971). The incidence of divorce is higher for blacks and whites at every level of education, occupation, and income (Norton & Glick, 1976), and the ratio of males to females is more disproportionate among blacks than whites. Whereas the gender ratio among white adults is about 98 men to 100 women, estimates of that among blacks have ranged from 85 to 100 (Rosow & Rose, 1972) to 91 to 100 (Jackson, 1973). Highly educated black women in particular face a disparity of black men equally well educated and very high rates of marital disruption, e.g., divorce (Houseknecht & Spanier, 1980); thus, the capability of financial self-support is especially important.

Thus, black women differ from white women in that work is especially likely to play a major role in their lives and in the more frequent necessity of supporting themselves and their families. However, black women are similar to white women in that they are employed primarily in traditionally female and often low-paying, low-status occupations. And black women, of course, are affected by racial as well as sexual discrimination. In summary, although black women are, in general, more work oriented than white women, barriers to the full development and utilization of black women's potential for achievement exist just as they do for white women.

Stimulus Variables: Immediate Environment

Several aspects of the more immediate environment have been found to influence the career development of women. These include family background characteristics, variables related to marital and familial status as an adult, the availability of role models and supportive figures in the immediate environment, the educational system, and counseling services.

Family background factors. In addition to studies of the family's socioeconomic status, typically utilizing father's educational and/or occupational level as indices of that status, considerable research has investigated the impact of mothers' educational level and occupational status on women's career development. A focus on the influence of mothers is found in studying women's career development versus that of men because of the assumed importance of the same-sex parent in influencing development.

The influence of maternal employment on women's career development has been extensively studied. Theoretically, working mothers are postulated to facilitate daughters' career achievements because they provide a female model of career pursuits (Douvan, 1976) and a model of the successful integration of family and work roles (DiSabatino, 1976; Hoffman & Nye, 1974). Generally, research has suggested that, in fact, working mothers are an important and positive influence on their daughters' career development.

Numerous studies have found that daughters of working mothers are more career oriented (versus home oriented) than are the daughters of homemakers (Almquist & Angrist, 1970, 1971; Altman & Grossman, 1977; Huth, 1978). Other studies have suggested that daughters of working mothers are more likely to pursue nontraditional occupations in comparison to daughters of homemakers (Almquist, 1974; Astin, 1967; Crawford, 1978; Ginzberg et al., 1966; Haber, 1980; Tangri, 1972). Eyde (1962) found that the longer a mother worked after marriage, the greater the career involvement of her daughter.

Although maternal employment may influence women's career development through its provision of a model of female employment and role integration, it is also related to other variables facilitative of women's career development. Studies have suggested that the daughters of working mothers develop generally more liberal sex-role ideologies (Hoffman, 1974; Hoffman & Nye, 1974), are less stereotypically feminine themselves (Altman &

Grossman, 1977; Hansson, Chernovetz, & Jones, 1977; Vogel, Broverman, Broverman, Clarkson, & Rosenkrantz, 1970), and show greater self-esteem and more positive evaluations of female competence (Hoffman, 1974) in comparison to the daughters of homemakers.

Whereas maternal employment seems in general to facilitate women's career development, some research has suggested that daughters of homemakers who have positive attitudes toward career pursuits and/or who express dissatisfaction with the homemaker role are also more strongly career oriented (Altman & Grossman, 1977; Baruch, 1972; Parsons, Frieze, & Ruble, 1978). In contrast, daughters of working mothers who experience considerable difficulty and/or conflict in role integration may develop ambivalent attitudes toward their own future employment (Baruch, 1972; Sorenson & Winters, 1975). Although studies of these latter relationships are few in number, it seems reasonable to conclude that maternal attitudes and role satisfaction, as well as maternal life roles, affect the kinds of career decisions made by daughters.

In addition to maternal employment, maternal level of education, like paternal level of education, appears to be positively related to women's career orientation and choice of nontraditional careers. Mothers' level of education was found to be related to greater career orientation in their daughters in several studies (Almquist & Angrist, 1971; Del Vento Bielby, 1978; Patrick, 1973). Highly educated mothers have been consistently overrepresented in samples of women pursuing nontraditional professions (Astin, 1969; Haber, 1980; Harmon, 1977; O'Donnell & Anderson, 1978; Russo & O'Connell, 1980).

In summary, the data generally suggest that women's career development is influenced by variables related to maternal employment and by the educational levels of both parents. In addition to demographic aspects of family background, however, research has consistently suggested the importance of parental encouragement and support in facilitating daughters' career development.

Family encouragement was reported as a major facilitator by high school girls planning careers in science (McLure & Piel, 1978), by female medical students (Cartwright, 1972), and by samples of women pursuing male-dominated occupations (Haber, 1980; Standley & Soule, 1974). For example, 72% of Standley and Soule's architects, lawyers, physicians, and psychologists reported being the child of whom their parents had been proudest, and 60% reported being their father's favorite child. The extent of encouragement from the father has been found to differentiate pioneers from traditionals in several studies (Astin & Myint, 1971; Katz, 1969; Nagely, 1971; Turner & McCaffrey, 1974). Nontraditional women have also reported higher expectations from their parents in terms of educational attainments and occupational involvement (O'Donnell & Anderson, 1978;

Patrick, 1973), whereas traditional women perceived their parents as less supportive of career pursuits than did pioneers in the study of Trigg and Perlman (1976).

Possibly as important as parental encouragement of daughters' achievements is a concommitant lack of pressure toward the traditional female role. Parents who exert less pressure on their daughters to date, marry, and have children have been found to have more career-oriented daughters (Haber, 1980; Matthews & Tiedeman, 1964), as do parents who place less emphasis on the development of stereotypically feminine qualities (Turner & McCaffrey, 1974).

Although parental variables, then, appear to be importantly related to women's career development, a major limitation of this research is the assumption that both parents are present while the girl is growing up. Research on father-absent children has focused primarily on boys (Bannon & Southern, 1980) and little is known about women raised in single-parent or adoptive homes or with relatives or nonfamily members. Dramatic increases in the number of single-parent homes (Hoffman, 1977; VanDusen & Sheldon, 1975) suggest that research based on nuclear family assumptions will be increasingly irrelevant to an understanding of the career development of many women and men.

A final family background variable is birth order. Numerous researchers have noted the predominence of first-borns (including "only" children) among high achievers (Eysenck & Cookson, 1970; Helmreich, Spence, Beane, Lucker, & Matthews, 1980; Sampson; 1965; Schachter, 1963). Compared to the percentage of first-borns in the general population, first-borns were significantly overrepresented in Astin's (1969) and Helmreich et al.'s (1980) samples of female Ph.D.'s, in Standley and Soule's (1974) sample of female professionals, and in Patrick's (1973) sample of female graduates of highly competitive colleges. Other studies, however, have not found birth order to differentiate pioneers from traditionals (Crawford, 1978; Greenfield, Greiner, & Wood, 1980), and the importance of this variable in women's career development is not yet firmly established.

The influence of marriage and children. As stated by Osipow (1973), Matthews & Tiedeman (1964), and others, the major difficulty in women's career development is the certainty of marriage and motherhood to the future plans of most women. And, indeed, the most consistent predictor of women's career orientation and innovation is their adult marital/familial status or, among girls and young women, their plans for marriage and children.

Numerous studies have found that career-oriented and/or employed women are less likely than home-oriented women to be married (Gysbers et al., 1968; Harmon, 1970; Stake, 1979b, Tinsley & Faunce, 1980; Yuen,

Tinsely, & Tinsley, 1980). Career-oriented women are more likely than home-oriented women to plan to defer marriage (Houseknecht, 1978; Parsons et al., 1978; Tangri, 1972; Watley & Kaplan, 1971) and, when studied as adults, married at later ages than their home-oriented counterparts (Card et al., 1980; Harmon, 1970).

In comparison to women who marry, women who remain single achieve higher levels of education (Gigy, 1980; Houseknecht & Spanier, 1980) and are substantially more likely to pursue male-dominated occupations (Astin & Myint, 1971; Card et al., 1980; Del Vento Bielby, 1980; Gigy, 1980). Not only are professional women more often single than other women, they are more likely than male professionals to be single (Bailey & Burrell, 1981; Helmreich et al., 1980). Thus, although marital status has little bearing on men's career development, it is an important variable influencing the career development of women.

Career-oriented women also tend to have and/or want fewer, if any, children (Card et al., 1980; Greenfield et al., 1980; Harmon, 1970; Tickamyer, 1979; Tinsley & Faunce, 1980), and the presence and number of children are negatively related to the pursuit of nontraditional occupations (Astin & Myint, 1971; Greenfield et al., 1980). Just as female professionals are less likely than male professionals to be married, female professionals are less likely to have children and, if they do have children, tend to have fewer than do male professionals (Bailey & Burrell, 1981; Helmreich et al., 1980). Studies of voluntary childlessness, which is increasing in frequency (Hoffman, 1977; Kearney, 1979), tend to corroborate the above pattern of findings in that voluntarily childless women are likely to be strongly career oriented, highly educated, and disproportionately employed (Houseknecht, 1978, 1979).

In early research on women's career development, the strong association between singleness and career orientation led to questions concerning the direction of causality. That is, did failure in or inadequacy with regard to heterosexual relationships lead to forced singlehood that, in turn, led to career orientation as compensation for lack of marital roles? Or did high achievement motivation and strong career orientation lead to reduced heterosexual affiliation and/or a decision that remaining single or deferring marriage would most facilitate career achievements? The former explanation, known as the deviance hypothesis (Almquist & Angrist, 1971) or the compensation model (Sedney & Turner, 1975) has not been supported by research. In contrast the latter explanation, known as the enrichment model (Almquist & Angrist, 1971; Sedney & Turner, 1975) has received considerable empirical support (Lemkau, 1979; Tangri, 1972).

That career-oriented women are not heterosexually deficient has been supported by Almquist's (1974) findings of equivalent frequencies of dating and extracurricular activities in girls planning nontraditional and traditional careers, Tangri's (1972) findings that role innovators did not differ from other women in their reported number of romantic relationships, and Colwill and Ross' (1978) finding that the scores of female medical students on the EPPS Heterosexuality scale were higher than were those obtained in the normative group of female college students. On the basis of their research, Sedney and Turner (1975) conclude that career orientation develops in the context of normal heterosexual affiliation, and that dating frequency begins to decrease only in college when serious pursuit of career goals increases in saliency.

Although there is little support for a compensatory or deviance model, several studies suggest that high achievement motivation and career orientation follow from enriching experiences that lead young women to have broadened conceptions of the female role and of their own potential achievements. In addition to research indicating that career-oriented and/or pioneer women are more likely to have well-educated parents and working mothers, research has also suggested that pioneer women had more work experience in high school and college (Almquist, 1974) and come from home environments fostering achievement, independence, and active exploration of the environment (Lemkau, 1979). Lemkau (1979) concludes that "it takes unusual but positive circumstances to foster the androgynous individuation which manifests itself in an atypical career choice [p. 237]."

Influence of role models.   The literature regarding the selection of occupational role models indicates that males almost always report other males (e.g., fathers, male professors) as their significant models and influences (Brown, Aldrich, & Hall, 1978; Weishaar, Green, & Craighead, 1981). Females, on the other hand, are likely to report both male and female models (Andberg, Follett, & Hendel, 1979; Basow & Howe, 1978; 1980; Brown et al., 1978; Weishaar et al., 1981). Thus, whereas males follow a pattern of same-sex modeling, the lack of female occupational role models (Douvan, 1976; O'Connell & Russo, 1980) necessitates opposite-sex as well as same-sex modeling in the facilitation of females' career development (Douvan, 1976). As stated by Weishaar et al. (1981), in the absence of female models women rely on male models.

The literature suggests the importance of such models, male and female, in women's career development. Some studies have suggested that choice of a pioneer occupation is related to having a male model (Weishaar et al., 1981). Handley and Hickson (1978) found that mathematically talented women who had chosen traditionally female math-related occupations (e.g., secondary school teaching) usually cited female models, whereas two-thirds of those majoring in engineering, accounting, or mathematics cited male role models as most influential. Other research supports the importance of female role models. For example, Andberg et al.'s (1979) study of female veterinary students suggested the important role of female veterinarians as occupational role models; Tidball (1980) found that colleges employing a greater proportion of female faculty members had proportionately more highly achieving female students. Support from teachers and professors was important in the selection of pioneer occupations in the studies of Andberg et al. (1979), Almquist (1974), McLure and Piel (1978), and Tangri (1972) and in the development of high career salience (Almquist & Angrist, 1970, 1971; Simpson & Simpson, 1961; Stake & Levitz, 1979). Farmer (1980a) found that the support of teachers, parents, and peers was essential to the career motivation of tenth grade girls.

Although role models and encouragement and support from significant others appear to facilitate women's career development relative to that of other women, it should be noted that there has been a serious lack of female models of educational and occupational achievement for girls and young women to observe and emulate (Douvan, 1976) and that girls and women in general receive less support for achievement-related behavior than do men (Goodale & Hall, 1976; McLure & Piel, 1978). Thus, whereas the availability of environmental supports assists in the explanation of women's career orientation and innovation, the lack of such supports is a major barrier to the career development of most women.

Education.   Educational level is one of the most powerful predictors of the career achievements of both women and men and, at the same time, the educational system itself is far more facilitative of male than female educational attainment because blatant and subtle discriminatory practices operate to discourage or, at best, fail to encourage the educational achievements of many women students. The existence of discrimination against women in higher education has been amply documented (Furniss & Graham, 1974; Kutner & Brogan, 1976; Lockheed & Ekstrom, 1977; Merritt, 1976; Roby, 1975). Forms of discrimination include practices pertaining to student admission and the granting of financial aid, sexual harassment of women students, and sexist comments in letters of recommendation (Lunneborg & Lillie, 1973; Roby, 1975). Lunneborg & Lillie (1973), for example, found two major types of sexist comments in letters of recommendation for graduate work in psychology; one category described comments pertaining to the applicant's physical attractiveness, whereas the other described comments implying that although the applicant's record was good for a woman, she was being evaluated by lower standards than those applied to males. Although sexist comments appeared in letters written for 1 of 85 male applicants, they appeared in those of 11 of 38 female applicants.

Whereas discrimination and sexual harassment, for example, are examples of blatant practices, a number of other more subtle influences operate to the detriment of women's educational achievements. Bernard

(1976) cites the "avoidance syndrome" (i.e., the lack of mentoring of, interest in, and support of women students) and the "putdown" (i.e., derogatory comments to or about women) as types of more subtle yet still discriminatory practices affecting women. Similarly, research has documented females' lesser likelihood of being chosen as protégés and their consequent loss, both educationally and in terms of later job opportunities, of the benefits of close working relationships with professors (Epstein, 1970; Feldman, 1974; Goldstein, 1979; Young, McKenzie, & Sherif, 1980). The existence of negative attitudes of faculty members toward women, including a failure to take women students seriously, has also been found (Bernard, 1976; Carnegie Commission on Higher Education, 1973; Holahan, 1979; Joyce & Hall, 1977).

Although discrimination against and negative attitudes toward women students are clearly a barrier to their educational attainments, an equally serious concern is the lack of support and encouragement women students receive (Goldstein, 1979; Holahan, 1979; Widom & Burke, 1978). For Freeman (1975), a "null academic environment" (i.e., one lacking in support and encouragement) has effects on women similar to those of overt discrimination. According to Freeman, "an academic environment that neither encourages or discourages students of either sex is inherently discriminatory against women because it fails to take into account the differentiating external environments from which women and men students come [p. 198]." In other words, professors do not have to discourage female students because society has already done that. For male students, the support of parents, relatives, friends, and societal norms is available even when faculty support is minimal. Career-oriented female students, in contrast, often must survive and persist with very little encouragement from others in the environment.

The effects of such overt and subtle discriminatory practices are not completely known, but it is likely that such findings as the consistently higher attrition rates among women at all levels of higher education (Carnegie Commission on Higher Education, 1973; Merritt, 1976; Patterson & Sells, 1973), the decreasing proportions of women students with increasing level of the educational program (e.g., graduate school versus college [Thomas, 1980], and the lower status, prestige, and visibility of the job placements of women Ph.D.'s (Astin & Bayer, 1972; Epstein, 1970; Helmreich et al., 1980; Robinson, 1973) are due in part to such practices and to what for many women students are null academic environments.

Even though the educational system may provide a null or discriminatory environment for women, women's attained educational level is strongly related to the type and extent of their vocational participation. Higher attained education is related to greater labor force participation among women whether married or not (Blaska, 1978; Houseknecht & Spanier,

1980; Huth, 1978), to stronger career orientation and career salience (Astin & Myint, 1971; Gysbers et al., 1968; Harmon, 1970; Tinsley & Faunce, 1980; Watley & Kaplan, 1971; Wolfson, 1976), and to the choice of pioneer versus traditional occupations (Almquist, 1974; Astin, 1968; Greenfield et al., 1980; Lemkau, 1979; Peng & Jaffe, 1979).

The influence of educational level on the pursuit of nontraditional occupations is even stronger for graduates of women's colleges (Astin, 1977; Brown et al., 1978; Douvan, 1976). Women's colleges may provide a larger number of female faculty role models (Douvan, 1976) and/or lead to less tendency among young women to yield leadership roles to men (Astin, 1977) and to avoid unfeminine behaviors (Brown et al., 1978). Interestingly, Finn (1980) reported that children in sex-segregated schools in the United States, England, and Sweden had higher educational aspirations than did their counterparts in coeducational schools.

In summary, although the educational environment may prove an unsupportive or even negative and discriminatory environment for many women students, the pursuit and completion of higher education are major facilitators of women's career development. However, in considering the influence of higher education on women's career development, its other correlates should also be noted. Higher education in women is related to a greater tendency to remain single, to higher rates of marital disruption, and to lower fertility rates (Houseknecht & Spanier, 1980). Higher education in women is related to more liberal attitudes toward women's roles (Mason, Czajka, & Arber, 1976), and to such characteristics as autonomy and the desire for direct, versus vicarious, achievement (Ginzberg et al., 1966). Thus, educational level is related to other major variables positively related to women's career development. Because few studies have controlled some of these variables while varying others, it is difficult to make conclusions concerning the variables most directly related to women's career involvement. Level of attained education, however, is most certainly an important, if not a key, variable in women's vocational achievements.

Career counseling.   One final aspect of the environment that may serve as a barrier to women's career development concerns possible stereotypes and biases on the part of career counselors. The existence of biased attitudes on the part of counselors has been documented by numerous studies summarized recently by Fitzgerald and Crites (1980). Generally, the data suggest that many career counselors of both sexes hold traditional attitudes toward women's roles and stereotypic views of the appropriateness of various occupations for males and females. Studies have suggested counselor disapproval of women's attempts to combine career roles with marital and family roles (Ahrons, 1976; Bingham & House, 1973; Kaley, 1971) and of women's desire to pursue nontraditional career fields

(Bingham & House, 1973; Donahue & Costar, 1977; Medvene & Collins, 1976; Rohfeld, 1977; Thomas & Stewart, 1971).

Although some (Smith, 1979) have questioned the extent to which biased attitudes are actually reflected in discriminatory practices, it seems illogical to assume that attitudes are not reflected in counseling practice. Even if biased counselors are not overt in their disapproval of women's atypical ambitions, a neutral stance on their part further contributes to the existence of a "null" environment. As Bem and Bem (1976) conclude, society has spent thirty or more years marking the woman's ballot in the direction of traditional female roles, so the failure of teachers and counselors to attempt to "upend" (Fitzgerald & Crites, 1980) those socialized expectations serves instead to reinforce and perpetuate traditional sex-role stereotypes.

Summary.   The preceding section has reviewed stimulus or environmental variables influencing women's career choices. Some of these variables (e.g., occupational sex typing and biased career counseling) serve primarily to limit women's career options. Others (e.g., the educational system and the availability of role models and/or support for achievement) serve as barriers to many women but, at the same time, appear to be important aspects of the career achievements of women. Finally, several family background factors (e.g., parental education and maternal employment) are related to women's career choices and achievements. All of these environmental variables, however, interact with the characteristics of the individual herself to affect career choice and development. The next section reviews major individual difference variables studied in relationship to women's career development.

Response Variables: Aptitudes

Aptitudes have long been viewed as important variables in the prediction of the career development of both women and men. In men, the level of intelligence has been consistently found to predict attained occupational levels (Crites, 1969; Tyler, 1965) and extent of achievement and contribution in career-related activities (Terman & Oden, 1959). Among women, level of intelligence is related to educational and occupational attainments, but the relationship is far less consistent than that among men. Generally it may be said that although women who have achieved educationally and occupationally are of higher ability than women in general, women's educational and occupational achivements are on the average less than those of a man of equal ability. As was illustrated previously in the follow-up study of gifted children (Terman & Oden, 1959), the occupational achievements of women often represent an underutilization of their intellectual abilities (Fitzgerald & Crites, 1980). Thus, the relationship of aptitudes to women's career development is a complex question.

Research does suggest that higher academic aptitude is associated with stronger career orientation in girls and women. Higher aptitude and/or achievement test scores have been found to differentiate career-oriented from home-oriented women in several studies (Astin, 1968; Rand, 1968; Tinsley & Faunce, 1978; Tyler, 1964; Watley & Kaplan, 1971).

Whereas high ability in general appears to be associated with career orientation, ability in mathematics and science appears to be an important variable differentiating women who pursue male-dominated occupations from those who pursue traditionally female occupations (Astin & Myint, 1971; Peng & Jaffe, 1979). Mathematics has, more generally, been viewed as a "critical filter" in women's career development (Sells, 1973). Math background is essential to an ever-increasing range of college majors and careers and to adequate performance on the quantitative portions of the aptitude tests required for admission to graduate and professional schools. Because of women's lack of preparation in comparison to that of men, they may be prevented from pursuing many otherwise attractive occupational possibilities. Thus, mathematics training serves as a filter through which many young women cannot pass.

For example, in a study of freshmen at the University of California at Berkeley, Sells (1973) found that only 8% of the women versus 57% of the men had taken 4 years of high school math. Because 4 years of high school math were prerequisite to entering the calculus or intermediate statistics courses required in three-fourths of the possible major areas, the major and career options of 92% of the freshman women were severely restricted at the beginning of their college educations. Goldman and Hewitt's (1976) study also illustrated the determining character of mathematics performance. Using a five-level science–nonscience continuum to describe college majors, Goldman and Hewitt found that SAT mathematics scores were the predominant predictor of choice of a science versus nonscience major. They concluded that the major reason for females' avoidance of science-based majors was their poorer performance on tests of mathematics aptitude.

Given the critical nature of mathematics to women's potential range of career options, various hypotheses concerning the basis for poorer math performance among females than among males should be noted. The first hypothesis concerns the existence of sex differences in mathematical ability. The most widely cited review of the research on sex-related differences in cognitive abilities (Maccoby & Jacklin, 1975) concludes that although the sexes do not differ in general intelligence, females generally obtain higher mean scores on measures of verbal ability whereas males generally obtain higher mean scores on measures of mathematical reasoning and spatial visualization abilities. However, Maccoby and Jacklin (1975) offer several interpretive cautions in conjunction with this review. First, consistent sex differences in these abilities do not appear until adolescence, by which time children have had ample opportunity to learn sex-role appropriate characteristics and the cultural expectations for females versus males. Second, although the majority of studies suggest this pattern of sex differences, many studies have failed to show these differences or have found differences in the opposite direction. Third, and probably most importantly, it is essential to note that an observed "sex difference" refers to a significant difference in the *mean* scores obtained by males and females. However, the magnitude of these mean differences is relatively small, ranging from .1 SD to .5 SD for verbal ability and from .2 SD to .66 SD for mathematical ability. Further, the great variability of members of each sex around the mean score for their sex and the relatively small numerical differences between the male and female means leads to distributions characterized by substantial or near total overlap of the scores of males and females. In other words, a sex difference in favor of males does not preclude findings of females who score higher than the majority of males and of males whose scores are below those of most females. Conversely, similar statements about males accompany findings of a sex difference in favor of females. Thus, an observed sex difference is of almost no utility in the prediction of the capabilities of individuals of either sex and is an insufficient explanation for females' poorer math achievement.

A second set of hypotheses concerns the influence of sociocultural beliefs and expectations on female achievement in mathematics. Societal stereotypes and attitudes convey the beliefs that math is a "male domain" (Osen, 1974), that girls do not need to study math (Fennema & Sherman, 1977), and that females are incompetent in mathematics (Osen, 1974). Osen (1974) summarizes societal attitudes as perpetuating the notion that females cannot and should not succeed in math. That girls and their parents and teachers internalize these societal beliefs is well-documented. For example, girls may avoid high achievement in math because they fear social disapproval (Benbow & Stanley, 1980) and are less likely than boys to view math as useful to them (Fennema & Sherman, 1977; Hilton & Berglund, 1974). Girls are less confident than boys of their math abilities at ages prior to the appearance of sex differences (Fennema & Sherman, 1977), and when their mathematics performance is equal or superior to that of boys (Fennema & Sherman, 1977; Frieze, Fisher, Hanusa, McHugh, & Valle, 1981). Boys report more positive attitudes toward them as math learners from parents (Fennema & Sherman, 1977).

In addition to acquiring negative attitudes toward math, girls take fewer math courses than boys beginning in high school and continuing throughout college (Ernest, 1976; Fennema & Sherman, 1977). The importance of math background to performance on mathematics aptitude and achievement tests is well-documented (Ernest, 1976; Green, 1974) and, in practice, aptitude and achievement are not easily distinguishable (Green, 1974).

In summary, although aptitudes, particularly those in science and mathematics, are important variables in women's career development, societal attitudes and stereotypes lead many women to fail to fully develop, not to mention utilize, their intellectual capabilities. Until girls are helped to overcome the societal and internal barriers to the development of their intellectual potentials, the relationship of aptitudes to female career development will remain complex.

Response Variables: Vocational Interests

Early studies of women's vocational interests focused on factor analytic studies and on comparisons of the interests of homemaking versus career-oriented women. As early as 1939, Crissy and Daniel compared the factor structure of the SVIB-W and the SVIB-M. Three of the four resulting factors corresponded to factors in the men's scales—interest in people, interest in language, and interest in science. The fourth factor, on which the office worker, housewife, and stenographer/secretary scales loaded strongly, was labeled "interest in male association" and had no counterpart in the men's scales. Darley (1941) grouped these three scales under the factorial label of "nonprofessional interests," whereas Layton (1958) suggested that these three scales and the elementary-teacher scale were indicative of "premarital patterns of interest."

The first study using the SVIB-W to differentiate the interests of homemaking versus career-oriented women was that of Hoyt and Kennedy (1958). In this study, homemaker and career groups were specified on the basis of responses to a questionnaire concerning the relative importance to subjects of marital versus career roles. Career-oriented subjects obtained higher scores on six SVIB-W scales, including artist, lawyer, psychologist, physician, and physical education teacher scales, whereas homemaking-oriented subjects scored higher on eight scales, including housewife, secretary, home economics teacher, and dietician.

Later studies utilizing the research paradigm developed by Hoyt and Kennedy essentially duplicated these results. For example, Wagman (1966) found that career-oriented girls scored higher on the lawyer, physician, and psychologist scales, whereas homemaking-oriented girls scored higher on the housewife, home economics teacher, and dietician scales. Subsequent studies (Parker, 1966; Vetter & Lewis, 1964; Wagman, 1966) revealed similar differential SVIB-W patterns for career-oriented and homemaking-oriented young women. Thus, a pattern of interest in culturally stereotyped "feminine" stopgap occupations was observed in marriage-oriented subjects (Levitt, 1972). Munley (1974), whose findings based on the revised SVIB-W (Form TW398) essentially duplicated those of previous studies, summarized the trend for career-oriented women to obtain high interest similarity ratings for occupations traditionally dominated by males and for homemaking-oriented women to obtain higher scores on occupations traditionally dominated by women, including several nonprofessional occupations. Interests in scientific and technical activities were also frequently found to differentiate career-oriented women from home-oriented women (Tinsley & Faunce, 1978; Tyler, 1964) and pioneers from traditionals (Goldman, Kaplan, & Platt, 1973; Rezler, 1967). Thus, interests in nontraditional occupations and activities appear to be related to career orientation in women.

Whereas nontraditional interests do appear more characteristic of career-oriented than noncareer-oriented women, the vocational interests of women in general have been strongly influenced by traditional sex-role socialization. This influence, in turn, has led to a restriction in the range of women's expressed and measured interests and, consequently, has contributed to the limited range of career options both pursued by and suggested to women.

Historically, the vocational interests of the two sexes have been measured separately (Campbell, 1977). The construction of separate forms of the Strong Vocational Interest Blank for men (in 1927) and for women (in 1933) was based on the different item responses of men and women and on the marked differences between men and women in the extent and nature of their employment (Campbell, 1977). For decades this system was generally accepted, although career-oriented women were frequently administered the SVIB-M rather than the SVIB-W because of the former's greater utility in suggesting professional-level careers (Campbell, 1977). Although the more recent criticisms of sex bias and restrictiveness in interest inventories have largely eliminated the use of separate forms for males and females, males and females continue to respond differentially to many interest inventory items. Generally, women are more likely than men to indicate interests in social and artistic activities, whereas men are more likely than women to indicate interest in scientific, technical, and mechanical activities.

The existence of sex differences at the item level has resulted in different overall score patterns for the two sexes (Cole & Hanson, 1975; Prediger & Hanson, 1976). For example, on measures of the Holland themes using raw scores or combined-sex normative scores, females obtain higher mean scores on the Social, Artistic, and Conventional themes, while males obtain higher means on the Realistic, Investigative, and Enterprising themes (Gottfredson, Holland, & Gottfredson, 1975; Holland, 1972; Prediger & Hanson, 1976). Similar findings have resulted using the Vocational Interest Inventory (VII, Lunneborg, 1977), a measure of Roe's eight fields of occupational interest. Findings of sex differences on basic dimensions of vocational interest are more evident and durable for Social and Realistic (technical) interests. Social interests are far more predominant among females, whereas Realistic interests are found far more frequently among males (Lunneborg, 1979, 1980; Prediger, 1980).

One major implication of differential raw score patterns among males and females is that the resulting occupational suggestions tend to be correspondent with beliefs concerning traditionally female and traditionally male occupations. High scores on the Social and Conventional themes suggest traditionally female educational, social welfare, office, and clerical occupations (Holland, 1973). In contrast, females' lower scores on the Realistic, Investigative, and Enterprising themes result in infrequent suggestion of traditionally male professions (e.g., medicine, engineering, science) and of occupations in management and the skilled trades (Holland, 1973). Thus, socialized patterns of interest lead to interest inventory results that perpetuate females' overrepresentation in traditionally female occupations and their underrepresentation in occupations traditionally dominated by males.

Such divergent and sex-stereotypic suggestions of occupational alternatives to males and females were the basis for the criticisms of sex bias and sex restrictiveness in interest inventories, extensively documented and discussed in a report funded by the National Institute of Education (Diamond, 1975). According to this and other discussions of sex bias, the use of separate forms for men and women, sexist language in occupational titles (e.g., policeman versus police officer), and raw scores or combined-sex normative scores, among other things, contributed to the failure of interest inventories to result in fairness in the suggestion of occupational alternatives to males and females. In other words, interest inventories served to maintain and perpetuate the limited range of occupations considered appropriate for and usually pursued by women.

In response to the criticisms of sex bias, many test developers have addressed these issues by combining the men's and women's forms (e.g., the SCII), by eliminating sexist language, and by discussing issues of sex-role socialization in interpretive materials (AMEG Commission on Sex Bias in Measurement, 1977). Other test developers have focused on reducing the sex restrictiveness of the resulting scores.

The two major approaches to reducing sex restrictiveness in the scores provided for basic dimensions of vocational interest are the use of same-sex normative scores and the use of sex-balanced items (i.e., items endorsed approximately equally by males and females). The SCII, for example, provides same-sex normative scores for both the General Occupational (i.e., Holland) Themes and the Basic Interest Scales. The Unisex Edition of the ACT-IV (UNIACT, Hanson, Prediger, & Schussel, 1977) and the revised version of the Vocational Interest Inventory (VII, Lunneborg, 1980) are based on the principle that if sex-balanced items are utilized, the sexes will obtain a more equivalent distribution of scores across the six Holland themes (UNIACT) or Roe's eight fields (VII). Thus, on the UNIACT for example, the Realistic scale contains items pertaining to sewing and cooking (i.e., *content* areas more familiar to females) in addition to items more reflective of males' socialization experiences (e.g., the kinds of things learned in high school shop courses). The use of same-sex normative scores and sex-balanced interest inventories is intended to increase the probability that females who could potentially be interested in Realistic, Investigative, or Enterprising occupations will obtain interest inventory profiles suggesting those areas. Thus, such methods of constructing and scoring interest inventories are designed to facilitate females' exploration of the full range of occupational alternatives, and to minimize the extent to which women continue to be directed toward traditionally female occupations.

Although attempts to remove sex restrictiveness from interest inventories are important and useful, the more direct solution to the problem of sex-stereotypic vocational interests involves increasing the range of experiences relevant to the development of those interests. Until girls and women have the opportunity to engage in activities relevant to, for example, Realistic and Investigative as well as Social and Artistic interest areas, interests in nontraditional areas will not develop in the majority of women. Encouraging a wider variety of activities and experiences for young girls and, for women, encouraging involvement in jobs or job-related experiences beyond the limits of socialized interests and experiences is necessary; women's vocational interests and, consequently, their career choices should derive from a rich background of experience and knowledge rather than from a background exposing them only to stereotypically female areas of activity and interest.

In conclusion, it appears that women who do develop scientific and technical interests often utilize these in the pursuit of nontraditional careers. However, the failure of many women to develop interests beyond the bounds of traditional female socialization continues to be a major barrier to their career development and seriously limits their vocational options.

Response Variables: Personality

A variety of personality characteristics has been found to be associated with the career orientation and innovation of women. In general, characteristics positively associated with women's career development are those more often associated with males or masculinity, whereas those negatively related to women's career development are stereotypically feminine traits.

Self-concept. Although the self-concepts of females in this society have generally been found to be less positive than those of males (O'Connor, Mann, & Bardwick, 1978; Stake, 1979a) career-oriented women have consistently been found to have more positive self-concepts and higher levels of self-esteem than other women. In studies comparing home-oriented versus career-oriented women, the latter have been found to have stronger intellectual self-concepts (Rand, 1968; Tinsley & Faunce, 1980) and stronger personal self-concepts (Tinsley & Faunce, 1980). Greater self-confidence and self-esteem have been found to be associated with stronger career orientation in women (Baruch, 1976; Ridgeway & Jacobson, 1979; Stake, 1979a, 1979b) and, in particular, to characterize women in male-dominated professions (Bachtold, 1976; Bachtold & Werner, 1970; Lemkau, 1979). The correspondence of ideal and real choices was greater for high self-esteem women in the study of Greenhaus and Simon (1976). Stake (1979b) found that high self-esteem women were more consistent in their choices between home and career (i.e., if career-oriented, high self-esteem women were more likely to be single, childless, and employed in pioneer fields). Among low self-esteem women, however, career orientation was not associated with the presence or absence of children or with work status.

Thus, women with positive views of themselves are not only more likely to be career-oriented and innovative in their choices of careers but may also be more likely to make actual choices consistent with their early aspirations and leading to consistent and manageable lifestyles.

Instrumental characteristics. A constellation of characteristics best summarized as instrumentality or competency-related is also strongly facilitative of women's career development. Often associated with traditional masculinity (Spence & Helmreich, 1980), instrumentality refers to such characteristics as the capability of actively and effectively dealing with the environment, competency, self-directedness, assertiveness, independence, and self-sufficiency (Spence & Helmreich, 1980). Generally, characteristics related to instrumentality appear both essential to women's career development and descriptive of career-oriented and innovative women. As stated by Spence and Helmreich (1980), "entry into and successful attainment in highly demanding, male-dominated occupations may require a high level of instrumentality in both sexes [p. 158]." Thus, instrumentality, although less often developed in females than in males because of traditional sex-role socialization practices, appears to be an important, if not essential, factor in women's career development.

Several studies have shown that career-oriented women, particularly those pursuing male-dominated occupations, are more likely to possess the instrumentality and competency-related characteristics of the traditional masculine sex-role stereotype. The prevalence of such characteristics in women in male-dominated occupations have been noted in numerous studies (Bachtold, 1976; Bachtold & Werner, 1970, 1973; Helson, 1971; O'Leary & Braun, 1972). Bachtold and Werner (1970), for example, found that the personality characteristics of women psychologists were more similar to those of male psychologists than they were to women in general.

Helmreich et al. (1980), in a study of male and female academic psycholgists, found no sex differences on instrumentality characteristics that, in the general population, would be found to a greater degree in males. Thus, women pursuing traditionally male occupations appear to possess the same degree of instrumentality and competency related characteristics as do their male colleagues.

Other characteristics associated with traditional masculinity have been found to characterize career-oriented women. Handley and Hickson (1978) found that engineering, math, and accounting majors scored higher on measures of creativity and independence than did women majoring in math education; the two groups, however, did not differ in extraversion or poise. Greater autonomy and independence in pioneer women were also reported by Cartwright (1972), Tangri (1972), and Rand (1968), among others. In comparison to women low in career orientation, career-oriented women have been reported to be more self-directed and more likely to emphasize their own needs (Cartwright, 1972; Gysbers et al., 1968; Tangri, 1972) and to perceive themselves as more internally versus externally controlled (Burlin, 1976a; Maracek & Frasch, 1977; Tangri, 1972). Burlin (1976a) found that internally oriented women more often both aspired to and expected innovative career choices than did externally oriented women and that the correspondence of ideal and real choices was considerably greater for internally versus externally oriented women.

In summary, a pattern of instrumentality, independence, assertiveness, high self-esteem and self-confidence, competence, and internal bases of both self-evaluation and control seems to characterize career-oriented women, particularly those pursuing male-dominated careers. It should be noted, however, that inferences regarding causality are unjustified at this stage in research. Although it is possible that these personality characteristics lead women to broader conceptions of the female role and of their own potential educational and career achievements, it is also possible, as suggested by Spence and Helmreich (1980), that women lacking such characteristics lack confidence in their ability to pursue careers and, consequently, elect to pursue the traditional roles for which their socialization has prepared them. Because female socialization often fails to equip women with skills beyond those necessary for traditional expressive and nurturant roles, the lack of career orientation among women is not surprising.

Thus, it is suggested that attention to sex-role–related characteristics is essential for both the understanding and modification of women's vocationally related behaviors (Kutner & Brogan, 1976; O'Neil et al., 1978). Greater possession of traditionally masculine characteristics (e.g., competence, instrumentality, self-confidence, independence, and assertiveness) would serve to broaden women's perceived and actual career options and thus lead to lifestyle choices made other than by default.

Theoretical Variables

Hypothetical constructs.   Crites (1969) has defined hypothetical constructs generally as concepts that summarize the relationships between two or more response variables, noting that such a construct need not imply a nonobservable entity (although such interpretations are often made) but, rather, may refer only to the empirical relationship between behaviors. Two such general constructs that are of importance to the career development of women are *achievement motivation* (including *fear of success*) and *career maturity.*

Achievement refers to the evaluation of performance against some standard of excellence (Unger & Denmark, 1975). Given this requirement of agreed-upon performance standards, it is possible at this time to gather achievement data only in the occupational and academic spheres (Unger, 1979). It is relatively clear that whatever measures of achievement are employed, women achieve less than men. Despite the large amount of data that suggests that institutional processes such as selection and compensation discrimination account for much of the sex difference in achievement, psychology has focused on personality variables as the major explanation of these differences.

Chief among such variables has been the concept of *achievement motivation.* The most widely known work in this area is the expectancy-value theory articulated by McClelland and his associates (McClelland, Atkinson, Clark, & Lowell, 1953) that assumes that achievement behavior is determined by the interaction of the tendency to achieve success, the tendency to avoid failure, and extrinsic motivation. The tendency to achieve success is itself comprised of the motive to achieve success, assumed to be a relatively stable personality characteristic, in combination with the situational variables of the perceived probability of success and the incentive value of the success. O'Leary (1977) noted that although situational variables are considered important in theoretical conceptualizations of achievement behavior, most of the research has focused on the motivational components ordinarily measured by means of projective devices such as the Thematic Apperception Test. When female subjects did not respond to experimental instructions designed to arouse their motive to achieve, this finding was interpreted as evidence that women are not as motivated to achieve as men (Veroff, Wilcox, & Atkinson, 1953). Thus, one early explanation for women's lower levels of achievement was that women were simply less motivated than men. (It is interesting to note that discussions of the Veroff et al. study never address the concurrent finding that women's achievement-need scores under relaxed conditions were higher than those of men. Rather, such discussions have focused on the fact that under arousal conditions, women's scores did not increase).

Recently, the research in this area has been criticized as based on a "male model" of achievement and, therefore, as unsuitable for explaining female behavior. Women were not *less* achievement oriented than men, according to this argument; rather, their achievement motivation was somehow *different*. For example, Hoffman (1972) suggested that rather than being motivated by mastery strivings and desire for excellence, as are males, females are conditioned by their upbringing to strive for love, approval, and social approbation. Stein and Bailey (1973) argued that many women strive for excellence in the social arena, which has been defined as an appropriate sphere for female endeavor. Tangri (1972) reported data supporting the hypothesis that women with traditional role orientations appeared to have projected their achievement needs onto their husbands. A full discussion of these, and other, approaches to achievement behavior in women is available in Mednick, Tangri and Hoffman (1975).

Fitzgerald and Crites (1980) have criticized these theoretical positions, noting that they do not account for the behaviors of high achieving women who do display the modal masculine pattern. They argue that the notion that female achievement motivation is a fundamentally different phenomenon from male motivation is therefore demonstrably inaccurate and suggest that it is more parsimonious to consider such behavior as *inhibited* by the effects of sex role socialization. Supportive evidence is provided by Stake (1976), who reported that subjects of both sexes set higher goals for themselves when told that members of their sex typically outperformed those of the opposite sex on the experimental task.

Consistent with the idea that female achievement motivation is inhibited by the sex-role socialization process is the work of Horner (1968; 1972), who has extended expectancy-value theory (McClelland et al., 1953) to include a tendency to avoid success. Widely popularized as "fear of success", this concept suggests that women who have high achievement aspirations often deny such aspirations because they see femininity and achievement as incompatible. Using traditional projective methodology but a nontraditional cue ("After first-term finals, Anne finds herself at the top of her medical school class"), Horner found that 65.5% of her female subjects gave "fear of success" responses, including hostility, denial, and social and professional failure. She also found that those females high in fear of success demonstrated poorer performance in a competitive situation, whereas their low fear-of-success peers, like males, improved their performance under conditions of competition.

Unger (1979) noted that over 200 studies on fear of success have been reported since Horner's original work appeared. Despite the popularity of the concept, it has become increasingly apparent that it does not have the comprehensive explanatory power that was originally supposed (Tresemer,

1977). Unger (1979) discusses several variables that appear to interact with the motive, such as sex-role orientation, age or developmental stage, the sex-role context of the experimental cue, and the living environment of the subjects (e.g., subjects from all-female colleges versus subjects from coeducational institutions). She also suggests that the focus on intrapsychic variables as explanations for inhibited achievement by females has the effect of "blaming the victim," suggesting that it is women and not society that need to change. In this context, it should be noted that high-ability women who fear that achievement, particularly in a masculine field, will bring negative as well as positive consequences may be demonstrating not "fear of success" but, rather, accurate perceptions of reality.

The second construct to be considered here is that of *career maturity*. Defined by Super in 1955 as the "place reached (by the individual) on the continuum of vocational development from exploration to decline [p. 153]," this construct was introduced in the Career Pattern Study (Super, 1955; Super, Crites, Hummel, Moser, Overstreet, & Warnath, 1957; Super & Overstreet, 1960), a 20-year longitudinal study of the career development of a selected sample of young men. The vocational maturity of women was not systematically investigated until Crites (1973b) included female subjects in his standardization of the Career Maturity Inventory (CMI), a standardized paper-and-pencil measure that is today widely used in studies of career development. Interestingly, whereas Crites (1965) reported no sex differences at the item response level (that is, males and females do not systematically differ in their responses to any particular item), Smith and Herr (1972) found that females were significantly more career mature than males when total score was used as the dependent variable. Further, Rathbun (1973) analyzed longitudinal data and reported that, although the sexes did not differ up to grade 7, females demonstrated significantly greater career maturity by grade 8, and maintained this difference in each subsequent year, implying a developmental difference favoring females.

Fitzgerald and Crites (1980) noted that this greater degree of career maturity on the part of females represents an interesting anomaly. Because career maturity predicts realism of choice, and because females demonstrate greater career maturity than males, we would expect females to make earlier and more realistic career choices than males. Instead, the reverse is actually true (L. Patterson, 1973); females consistently select occupations that are unrealistically low in terms of their interests and ability. Thus, they most often appear to fall in that diagnostic category that Crites has labeled "unfulfilled" (Crites, 1981). Fitzgerald and Crites (1980) suggest that this diagnosis, combined with high career maturity scores is indicative of sex-role, or home–career, conflict in women and that counselors should be alert to this highly prevalent condition. Interventions designed to facilitate career maturity in women are now being designed to include components dealing with sex-role stereotypes, and initial results are quite promising (Rathburn, 1973).

Intervening variables. Intervening variables can be defined as concepts that summarize the relationships between two or more stimulus and/or response variables (Crites, 1969). In the following section, two variables postulated to influence the degree to which women's response characteristics (e.g., abilities, interests) are manifested in vocationally related behavior are discussed. These two variables are math anxiety and self-efficacy expectations.

Although studies have suggested male superiority on measures of math ability, observed sex differences are simply inadequate to explain the much greater discrepancies between males and females in their pursuit of math-related coursework, curricula, and careers. Rather, differences in male and female sex-role socialization and consequent differences in attitudes toward mathematics are being examined as possible causes of sex differences in mathematics performance (Fennema & Sherman, 1976).

Based on Aiken's (1970, 1976) reviews of literature suggesting that attitudes toward math influence mathematics performance, several investigators have studied one aspect of such attitudes, that is, math anxiety (Betz, 1978; Hendel, 1980; Tobias, 1978). Math anxiety, defined by Richardson and Suinn (1972) as "feelings of tension and anxiety that interfere with the manipulation of numbers and the solving of mathematical problems in a wide variety of ordinary life and academic situations" (p. 551) is postulated to underlie both avoidance of and poor performance in math courses and math-related majors and careers.

Although math anxiety is assumed to affect both males and females, there are several bases for the postulate that math anxiety is more frequent and more severe in women than in men (Betz, 1978; Tobias, 1978). For example, competence in math and science is associated with males, whereas females are presumed to be less competent (Bem, 1974). Even if a young woman has high mathematical aptitude she may internalize the societal beliefs of female incompetence. As stated by Tobias (1978), math anxiety stems from "a culture that makes mathematics ability a masculine attribute, that punishes women for doing well in mathematics, and that soothes the slower math learner by telling her that she does not have a 'mathematical mind' [p. 57]." Further, the relative lack of female models of competence in math and science and low expectations on the part of parents and teachers would also seem to prevent females from developing attitudes of competency in mathematics.

The small body of research to date on math anxiety suggests that it may be more predominant among females (Betz, 1978), that it is strongly associated with a lack of math background (Betz, 1978; Hendel, 1980), and that it is related to lower self-estimates of math ability (Hendel, 1980) and to higher levels of test anxiety (Betz, 1978; Hendel, 1980) and trait anxiety (Betz, 1978).

Although measures of math anxiety have not yet been demonstrated to add considerably to what can be predicted on the basis of test anxiety, previous math background, and other attitudes toward math (e.g., confidence in one's math abilities [Rounds & Hendel, 1980]), mathematics does seem to be a subject matter often avoided by otherwise competent and achieving women. It is likely that perceived abilities, anxiety, math background, and math performance are related in an interactive manner. Although further study of women's attitudes toward and beliefs with regard to mathematics competence both as antecedents to and consequences of mathematics performance and pursuit versus avoidance of math coursework is necessary, the fact of traditional female socialization and its impact on females' attitudes and beliefs necessitates continued consideration of attitudes and cognitions in understanding female achievement in mathematics.

A final variable postulated to explain the effects of socialization experience on achievement-related behavior is that of expectations of self-efficacy. According to Bandura (1977), behavior and behavior change are mediated primarily by expectations of personal efficacy (i.e., expectations or beliefs that one can successfully perform a given behavior). Expectations of personal efficacy influence not only the kinds of behaviors in which an individual engages, but her or his persistence in behavior when obstacles or disconfirming experiences are confronted.

Hackett and Betz (1981) have suggested that female socialization is less likely than male socialization to facilitate the development of expectations of self-efficacy with regard to educational and occupational pursuits. Male socialization is more likely to include the experiences necessary for development of strong career-related self-efficacy expectations (i.e., opportunities for performance accomplishments) and vicarious learning (i.e., modeling) relevant to future vocational behaviors and, as discussed previously herein, encouragement and support for achievement-related behaviors. Thus, Hackett and Betz postulate that the failure of women's career pursuits and achievements to fully reflect their capabilities and talents may in part be due to a lack of strong expectations of personal efficacy with regard to career-related behaviors. Higher expectations of self-efficacy in women would therefore be expected to not only increase the range of women's perceived career options but the persistence of career pursuits in the face of such external barriers as discrimination or lack of support. Thus, self-efficacy expectations are postulated as important mediators between an individual's abilities and talents and the extent to which she actually uses and further develops those abilities and talents.

Available research to date has supported the postulated utility of the concept of self-efficacy expectations in the understanding of women's career development. Betz and Hackett (1981) found significant differences in the self-efficacy expectations of college students with regard to their ability to pursue traditionally female versus traditionally male careers. Whereas males perceived themselves as equally capable of pursuing traditional versus nontraditional careers, females' perceived capability with regard to male-dominated careers was significantly less than their perceptions of capability with regard to traditionally female careers. In addition, the self-efficacy expectations of females in relationship to male-dominated careers were significantly lower than the expectations of males of comparable levels of academic ability. Ayres-Gerhart (1981) found that females' self-efficacy expectations with regard to behaviors requiring performance in math and science were significantly lower than those of males.

Summary

The preceding sections have reviewed research concerning factors influencing the career orientation and choices of women. A variety of factors, both environmental and individual, have been found to influence women's career development. Several points regarding the research findings should, however, be noted. First, the findings describe groups of women and do not necessarily describe the factors that have influenced any particular woman. In other words, family background characteristics (or any other variables) obviously do not characterize all such women. Second, the manner in which these numerous factors interact to affect women's career development and the relative importance of their effects are poorly understood and in need of further investigation. This review has for practical reasons examined each factor separately but, in reality, the factors occur concurrently and in interaction with each other. And, finally, the factors influencing women's career development may change as societal attitudes and norms change and as increasing numbers of women enter the work force. If girls and women, like boys and men, begin to assume that career pursuits will be an integral part of their lives, we may see changes in the nature of and influences on women's career choices. Thus, the study of these choices will be a continuing and challenging endeavor.

WOMEN'S OCCUPATIONAL ENTRY

Discrimination in Selection

Sex discrimination in occupational practices (e.g, selection, promotion) has been illegal since the passage of the Civil Rights Act of 1964. In 1968, the Equal Employment Opportunity Commission issued a ruling forbidding sex

discrimination in help wanted advertisements and outlawed classified advertisements that were segregated by sex. Despite such congressional legislation
and agency regulation, the probability remains high that much of the inequity between the occupational attainment of males and females can be accounted for by outright discrimination.

Discrimination can take any of three forms: *formal, informal,* and *in-advertent.* Formal discrimination can be said to exist when an occupation or
job is formally closed to one sex or the other, and when sex is not a bonafide
occupational qualification (BFQ) for successful performance of that job.
Although such discrimination was an integral part of the world of work
only 20 years ago (for example, men were not considered for positions as
flight attendants, nor were women accepted as candidates for training as
pilots, and this policy was both public and acceptable), today it is relatively
rare. Although a few jobs still exist where sex is considered a BFQ (e.g.,
only males are hired as prison guards in a male prison, and vice versa), such
instances arise from other considerations such as a prisoner's right to
privacy and not from social norms concerning the supposedly appropriate
role for males and females. It is the rare employer who is foolhardy enough
to proclaim, "No women (or men) need apply."

However, if formal discrimination has all but disappeared, informal
discrimination is still widespread in selection, promotion, and compensation as well as in other areas of occupational treatment that are more difficult to measure. Informal sex discrimination can be defined as any
systematically differential treatment of one sex or the other based on
membership in that gender rather than on objective work-related characteristics or performance. Such differential treatment, although it may be infor-
mally sanctioned by the organization, is not formal organizational policy. A
great deal of research has been conducted in this area, and the results are
fairly consistent in their support for the hypothesis that women are
discriminated against in selection. Dipboye, Arvey, and Terpstra (1977);
Dipboye, Fromkin, and Wiback (1975); Haefner (1977); and Zikmund,
Hitt, and Pickens (1978) have reported significantly higher ratings and/or
stronger hiring recommendations for male candidates than for female candidates having resumes identical except for sex. Arvey (1979a) points out
that, although applicant sex accounted for only a small part of the variance
where evaluators are only allowed one or two hiring choices, these choices
are highly related to applicant sex. In other words, given only one position
to fill, evaluators overwhelmingly select a male candidate.

In addition to finding a simple main effect favoring males, the research
on informal discrimination has also focused on other variables that might
be expected to interact with gender to affect recommendations for selection.
The most prominent of these is the sex-typing of the job under study, the
hypothesis being that men will be underrated for feminine-typed positions,
and that females will be underrated for masculine-typed positions. Arvey

(1979b) termed this the sex-congruency notion, and relevant research appears to confirm it (Cash, Gillen, & Burns, 1977; Cohen & Bunker, 1975; Shaw, 1972). In a particularly creative field experiment, Levinson (1975) had pairs of male and female experimenters make telephone inquiries concerning 265 positions that had been selected from the classified advertisements of two metropolitan newspapers in a major Southeastern city. The positions were classified as male or female on the basis of their current sex composition. In each case, one partner made a telephone inquiry to a sex-inappropriate job, followed a short time later by a matched call from the other partner, a sex-appropriate situation. Employer responses were carefully recorded, and 35% of the calls resulted in clear-cut discrimination (e.g., the sex-inappropriate caller was told the job was filled, whereas the sex-appropriate caller was invited to fill out an application or come for an interview). An additional 27% of the calls were classified as cases of "ambiguous" discrimination; for example, sex-inappropriate callers were discouraged from applying, and/or employers displayed surprise or dismay at the calls. Although plagued by the usual imprecision of field experimentation, this study provides powerful data in support of the sex-congruency notion.

Another variable that has been hypothesized to interact with sex to influence the selection decision is that of physical attractiveness. Physical attractiveness has long been seen as an advantage for the persons possessing it; this has been particularly true for females. Because females have traditionally been defined by their biological functions of mating and motherhood, it follows that physical attractiveness (which presumably facilitates these functions, either directly or indirectly) has been seen as a more salient characteristic in their lives than in the lives of men, who have other criteria on which they are evaluated (Bar-Tal & Saxe, 1976; Miller, 1970). Recent research in career psychology strongly suggests that this may also hold true in the world of work. Early studies supported the validity of a general "what is beautiful is good" hypothesis—that is, that physically attractive persons are assumed to possess more socially desirable traits, as well as being more successful than unattractive persons (Berscheid & Walster, 1974; Cash, Begley, McCown, & Weise, 1975; Cash, Kehr, Polyson, & Freeman, 1977; Dermer & Theil, 1975; Dion, Berscheid, & Walster, 1972).

In addition to the "general goodness" that is attributed to attractive persons, Gillen (1975) has presented evidence for a "sex-typed goodness". In his research, attributions of masculinity on the Bem (1974) scales increased with the attractiveness of the male stimulus persons. A similar phenomenon was observed for female stimulus persons on the feminine scales. Thus, attractive persons were seen as *more* sex-role stereotyped than unattractive persons.

Dipboye, Fromkin, and Wiback (1975) found that male college recruiters were more willing to hire a physically attractive candidate than an equally qualified unattractive candidate. Although male candidates were preferred to female candidates, attractive candidates were preferred to unattractive candidates, regardless of their sex. These findings were replicated by Dipboye, Arvey, and Terpstra (1977). Cash, Gillen, and Burns (1977) investigated the effect of candidates' sex and attractiveness on personnel consultants' judgements of qualifications, predictions of success, hiring recommendations, attributions of success and failure, and suggestions for occupational alternatives for candidates for masculine, feminine, and neutral jobs. Most of their major hypotheses were supported in that male candidates received more favorable personnel evaluations than females for masculine jobs, and females for feminine jobs. In particular, highly attractive male candidates for masculine jobs received the highest rating on all variables, followed by a "control" male of unknown attractiveness, and then an unattractive male. Interestingly enough, for the masculine job, the *unattractive* female candidate was more favorably evaluated on all variables than her attractive or "control" colleagues. This finding, which the authors do not directly address, is consistent with earlier results reported by Dipboye et al. (1977) that indicated that whereas raters most often chose a highly qualified attractive male for a sex-neutral managerial position, *the next most highly chosen candidate was the highly qualified unattractive female.*

Reviewing these findings, Heilman and Saruwatari (1979) suggested that physical attractiveness might not always be an advantage in the work world, particularly for females. Drawing on the earlier work of Gillen (1975), which suggested that attractiveness exacerbates sex-role stereotyping and noted that sex-typed feminine characteristics are not those judged appropriate or necessary for success in managerial occupations (Schein, 1973, 1975), these researchers hypothesized that females' attractiveness would prove advantageous only for a nonmangerial lower-level position. For an upper-level managerial position, an attractive female candidate was hypothesized to be at a disadvantage. The data clearly supported the hypothesis for all dependent measures, including evaluation of qualifications, hiring recommendation, and suggested starting salary. For male candidates, on the other hand, attractiveness produced higher ratings regardless of the type and level of the position for which they were applying.

Other variables that have been suggested to interact with applicant sex have included sex of rater (Muchinsky & Harris, 1977; Rose & Adiappan, 1978), sex of subordinates in the job (Rose & Adiappan, 1978), level of applicant competence (Haefner, 1977; Heneman, 1977), and rater authoritarianism (Simas & McCarrey, 1979). This research has produced mixed results; however, whereas competent candidates are generally preferred to incompetent ones, highly competent males are preferred over highly competent females.

The final form of selection discrimination to be discussed is that which can be termed "inadvertent." By this we are referring to the effect of certain selection devices on the selection ratio for women. The Uniform Guidelines on Employee Selection Procedures (EEOC, 1978) prohibit the use of any test or device that has an adverse impact on the selection rate of a protected group (i.e., women, blacks, etc.) and that cannot clearly be shown to be job-related. The classic legal case in this area is *Griggs vs. Duke Power Company,* in which the Supreme Court ruled that the use of a general intelligence test, a mechanical aptitude test, and the requirement of possession of a high school diploma were illegal in the selection of common laborers, as they resulted in the selection of far fewer blacks than whites and were not job related.

Although paper-and-pencil tests most often result in adverse impact on blacks, performance tests, such as those required for selection into the police and fire services, more often affect female candidates adversely. Such tests often contain what amount to hidden requirements for height and strength that exceed established minimum qualifications (MQ's), are not job related, and are illegal. Obviously, any test that uses height as a factor will have a negative effect on women. For example, in a now famous New York State Police case, the court found that a requirement that applicants be able to sight and fire over the roof of a police car had the effect of imposing an excessive height requirement. This requirement, rather than being job related, was actually contrary to established police procedure. A discussion of adverse impact and inadvertent discrimination involves highly complex legal and psychological issues that cannot be articulated at length there. However, the salient point is that selection devices of questionable validity may effectively close certain jobs to women even when employers are not consciously intending to discriminate against women. Combined with the underevaluation by employers and other forms of informal discrimination, adverse impact is thus one more factor creating barriers to occupational entry for women.

WOMEN'S VOCATIONAL ADJUSTMENT

External Barriers

The progress of women along the career path continues to be problematic even after the process of career entry has been successful. The existence of both internal and external barriers operates to complicate women's vocational adjustment, that is, their attainment of success and satisfaction (Crites, 1969). The following discussion focuses on the external barriers to women's career adjustment: (1) the attitudes of men (and women) towards women, particularly towards those working in a nontraditional occupation; (2) sexual harassment; and (3) discrimination in compensation. Much of the following review will focus on women in managerial or other nontraditional occupations.

Attitudes of men (and women) toward women.   Although not explicitly stated, early research appeared to support the notion that women were underrepresented in the occupational world, particularly in the masculine-oriented managerial ranks, because they lacked the drive, aggressiveness, and leadership ability required for success (Bond & Vinache, 1961; Maier, 1970). If this assumption were accurate, then negative attitudes towards women would be rationally justifiable on the basis that women are actually less capable than men. A study illustrative of early research in this area is that of Megargee (1969), who paired high-dominance subjects with low-dominance subjects in a laboratory study of leadership. He found that high-dominance women were equally as likely as high-dominance men to assume the leadership role when the experimental pairs were of the same sex. Women were, however, far less likely to assume the leadership position when paired with a low-dominance male. Interestingly enough, these women often actually made the leadership *decision,* but made it in such a way that it did not threaten their appropriate sex-role.

In contrast to these early studies, more recent research suggests that women are similar to men in ways important to managerial success (e.g., leadership behavior [Day & Stogdill, 1972; Hansen, 1974]) and decision accuracy (Muldrow & Bayton, 1979). Thus, it seems inappropriate to offer a completely "person-centered" explanation (Riger & Galligan, 1980) of women's scarcity in the middle and upper echelons of management. Other evidence supporting this view is provided in a study by Bowman, Worthy, and Greyser (1965) who found that women were not perceived as desirable for management even when they were judged to be capable. In this study of male executives, the majority of the subjects believed that men are not comfortable with a female supervisor; many felt that placing women in managerial positions would have a negative effect on employee morale.

Closely related to the notion that women lack the requisite managerial behavioral repertoire is the idea that they also lack appropriate personality characteristics. In a pair of studies reminiscent of the Broverman et al. (1970) investigations of stereotypes of mental health, Schein (1973) requested managerial personnel to rate the concepts "men in general," "women in general" and "successful middle managers." In a sample of 300 male middle managers, successful middle managers were described as possessing characteristics more commonly ascribed to men in general than women in general (1973). Schein (1975) later replicated these results with 167 female middle managers. More recently, Powell and Butterfield (1979) required 684 business students to describe the concept "good manager" using the Bem Sex Role Inventory (Bem, 1974). Contrary to their hypothesis that the good manager would be seen as androgynous, the authors found that their subjects of both sexes rated the concept as overwhelmingly masculine.

Whereas studies such as those of Schein (1973, 1975) and Powell and Butterfield (1979) assess sex-role stereotypes and then postulate that such stereotypes will result in differential treatment of men and women, other studies investigate differential treatment and postulate sex-role stereotypes as the causal factor. For example, Rosen and Jerdee (1973), postulating that stereotypes would lead to differential treatment of women on the job, found that bank supervisors were more willing to promote a male than a female candidate, were more likely to select a male employee to attend a conference, and were more willing to approve a male supervisor's request to terminate a problem employee. Interestingly enough, Rosen and Jerdee (1973) also reported the first evidence that sex role discrimination operates to the disadvantage of males as well as females; they found that their subjects judged a leave of absence to care for small children as significantly less appropriate when it came from a male employee than from a female employee. In a further study (Rosen & Jerdee, 1974) 235 male business majors rated a hypothetical female applicant as having less potential for the technical aspects of the job and for long service to the organization, and as less likely to fit in well in the organization.

Whereas studies such as those reported above provide indirect evidence for the effects of stereotyping on the evaluation and treatment of women and men in organizations, direct evidence is provided by studies assessing both stereotypes toward and evaluations of females in leadership positions. For example, Rice, Bender, and Villers (1980) reported that West Point cadets having traditional sex-role attitudes reacted very negatively to a female leader. Terborg and Ilgen (1975) found that subjects with unfavorable views toward women would be more likely than those with favorable attitudes toward women to engage in discriminatory hiring practices but that attitudes toward women were unrelated to the likelihood of engaging in discriminatory treatment practices (e.g., promotion and salary decisions). Finally, Stevens and DeNisi (1980) administered the Women as Managers Scale (Peters, Terborg, & Taynor, 1974) to 143 male and 383 female subjects and found that subjects with positive attitudes were more likely than those with negative attitudes to attribute a hypothetical female manager's success to ability and effort and her failure to bad luck and a difficult job. This effect was particularly strong for the male subjects.

Although the research results do, then, support the existence of stereotypic biases toward women and the relationship of these to discriminatory attitudes and/or behaviors, some writers have urged that they be interpreted with caution. Brown (1979), in his review of male and female leadership studies, notes that although "trait" studies consistently support the existence of the traditional attitude that women lack adequate leadership characteristics, there is a sharp division in the attitudes of managers and nonmanagers. That is, studies using students as subjects support the traditional female stereotype, whereas studies of practicing managers were not supportive. He suggests the possibility of a socialization process that modifies the attitudes of persons actually in the world of work. If this is so, the negative studies would be less damaging to women's career development than had been thought. Terborg and Ilgen (1975) support this view when they suggest that:

> At the time of hiring when little is known about the job applicant, it is relatively easy to categorize the female applicant as an undifferentiated member of the subgroup of women. However, once the female is actually placed on the job and more information is obtained concerning her performance, it becomes more difficult to stereotype her. Thus, these findings suggest that stereotypes influence sex discrimination most when little is known about the female's potential (e.g., hiring decision) and that the effect of sex role stereotypes diminishes as more information about the female worker is obtained [p. 373].

Obviously, determination of the validity of this view will require longitudinal field research in which prior measurement of stereotypes is obtained. Bass, Krusell, and Alexander (1971) present data that suggest that a "socialization" hypothesis may be overly optimistic; in their study of 1974 lower-, middle-, and upper-level male managers, they found that men who did not work with women had a higher regard for them than men who did.

Closely related to the literature on attitudes towards women is the body of research on women and leadership behavior, or leadership style. Even though this literature is much too voluminous to be adequately summarized in the space available, it is possible to identify significant themes that have emerged and to articulate questions for further research. The work on women and leadership has addressed itself to the following set of progressively more complex and sophisticated questions. The first question to be addressed was the simplistic one, "Are women as capable of leadership as men?" More sophisticated studies contemplated *styles* of leadership (e.g., "consideration" vs. "initiating structure"). Noting that these styles bore a marked resemblance to approved sex role behaviors, these investigations raised the following question(s):

1. Are their sex differences in leadership style?
2. Is one style more effective for one sex than the other?
3. Is one style perceived as more appropriate for one sex than the other?

It is not clear from the literature that there are, indeed, clear-cut and reliable sex differences in leadership style. Chapman (1975) reported that, contrary to popular opinion, female leaders are not more task-oriented or consideration-oriented than male leaders. Similarly, Day & Stogdill (1972) found that male and female leaders who occupy parallel positions and perform similar functions exhibit similar patterns of leader behavior. However, Denmark and Diggory (1966) indicated that men used power much more often than women to maintain work group conformity, and Eskilson and Wiley (1976) found that male leaders in their role-playing task groups concentrated significantly more on recognizable leadership behavior. Maier (1970) noted that when information is absent female leaders are less assertive than male leaders, but when tasks were more structured no differences between male and female leaders were found.

In contrast to this body of research that reports no clear sex differences in leadership style is literature that assesses the reactions of observers (e.g., subordinates) to women leaders. Terborg (1977) wrote, "Some evidence suggests that behavior that is consistent with accepted sex-role behavior is evaluated more positively than where it is out of role; that is, women leaders are perceived better than men if they are high on consideration behaviors rather than initiating structure behaviors [p. 658]." Hagen and Kahn (1975) reported that, under conditions of *competition* (and out-of-role behavior) competent women were evaluated negatively; this effect did not appear under conditions of *cooperation*. Haccoun, Haccoun, and Sallay (1978) had 30 male and 30 female nonmanagement personnel rate the effectiveness of three different supervisory styles (directive, rational or friendly) portrayed by male or female supervisors. The directive style was rated least favorably when it was displayed by female versus male supervisors, thus providing further support for the "out-of-role" hypothesis. Similarly, Rosen and Jerdee (1973) reported that male supervisors were evaluated more favorably than females where they utilized a *reward* style, whereas both males and females received higher evaluations where they employed a *friendly–dependent* style toward opposite-sex subordinates. The authors noted "both males and females probably are expected to react more favorably to intimations of dependency coming from the opposite sex [p. 46]."

It appears, then, that although there are no clear-cut sex differences in management style, both superiors and subordinates may believe that there *should* be such differences. That is, female leaders who exhibit a "masculine" style (e.g., initiating structure, directive) may be negatively evaluated for employing out-of-role behaviors. These beliefs can be detrimental to women's career adjustment because they may affect both evaluations and effectiveness of women's leadership efforts. Indeed, subordinate's perceptions that a leader's behavior is inappropriate may, in fact, be all that is required to make it ineffective.

Although subordinates may in general react negatively to out-of-role behavior, other variables such as sex of subordinate (Haccoun, Haccoun, & Sallay, 1978), the conservatism versus liberality of subordinates, and the particular occupation or work setting (Terborg, 1977) may influence these reactions. For example, female leaders in an engineering or aerospace firm may well be in a situation quite different than those in educational or social service settings where there have traditionally been more females in leadership positions.

A related but as yet unsubstantiated type of attitudinal bias toward women is that described as the "Queen Bee Syndrome" (i.e., successful women who are hostile toward and unsupportive of other women's attempts to achieve and advance in the organization). Research has failed to establish the Queen Bee Syndrome as a common phenomenon, Terborg; Peters, Ilgen, & Smith (1977), for example, found that women with higher levels of education (and thus potential Queen Bees) reported more favorable attitudes toward women as managers than did those with lower levels of education.

A final area in which attitudes have been hypothesized to operate to the detriment of women's career adjustment is that of socialization into collegial networks. Although little if any empirical research has appeared in this area, several writers have discussed the potential difficulties of women in this regard. For example, Epstein (1970) speculated that the sponsor-protégé relationship may inhibit feminine advancement in that the sponsor (most likely a man) may have mixed feelings about accepting a woman as protégé. Females may be viewed as less likely than males to fulfill the functions of the protégé (e.g., to carry on the work of the mentor, to provide him with a sense of the continuity of his work, and to ease the transition to retirement [Hall, 1948; Hughes, 1945]). In terms of collegial networks, Terborg (1977) speculates that the "solo" or "token" status of many women serves to exclude them from formal and informal work contacts, elicits extreme evaluations from group members, and serves to promote turnover. Support for this final notion comes from Mattingly (1981) who reports that when males and females are placed in a nontraditional training program, the failure rate is 100% when the student is the only male or female in the group. The addition of only one more same-sexed student reduces this rate dramatically.

In summary, several types of attitudinal bias on the part of others in the organization may serve to inhibit the achievements, advancement, and satisfaction of women. Negative and discriminatory attitudes are a major and serious barrier to women's career adjustment.

Sexual harassment. Another serious barrier to the career adjustment of women is that complex of behaviors that has come to be known as sexual harassment. There is less than complete agreement on what constitutes sexual harassment, with almost as many definitions as there are writers on the subject. Harragan (1977) offers the terms sexual molestation, sexual exploitation, and civil rape (within the employment situation) but does not explicitly define the behaviors to which these terms refer. She does note, however, that most typically the behavior is verbal, including comments on the female worker's physical characteristics and invitations to sexual contact. Physical molestation, though perhaps less common, can be even more destructive. Harragan suggests that the typical victim is a woman who is financially vulnerable and that the perpetrator is necessarily a male supervisor or employer who wields economic power over her. If the woman refuses a sexual relationship, she may be fired or her performance evaluation downgraded, suggesting that she is incompetent. Because Harragan's discussion implies that harassment is possible only when the perpetrator is superior in position to the victim, she minimizes the potentially serious effects of persistent, offensive, and unwelcome sexual advances by peers; thus, her definition appears unnecessarily and inappropriately limited in scope.

A broader definition of sexual harassment is provided by Farley (1978), who writes:

> Sexual harassment is best described as unsolicited nonreciprocal male behavior that asserts a woman's sex role over her function as worker. It can be any or all of the following: staring at, commenting upon, or touching a woman's body; requests for acquiesence in sexual behavior; repeated nonreciprocated propositions for dates; demands for sexual intercourse; and rape [pp. 14–15].

Whereas Farley acknowledges that sexual harassment may involve inequities in the positions of the perpetrator versus the victim, she also points out that males have inherently higher societal status by virtue of being male, usually outnumber females in the organizational setting, and can penalize noncooperative females even when positions are equal in status (e.g., through noncooperation or verbal denigration). Farley's definition obviously encompasses a much wider range of behaviors and, in fact, could be criticized on the grounds that almost *any* social approach made by a male to a female co-worker or subordinate could be construed as sexual harassment.

The most explicit, and probably most important, definition of sexual harassment was set forth in 1980 by the Equal Employment Opportunity Commission (EEOC), the federal agency responsible for enforcement of Title VII of the Civil Rights Act; Title VII is that portion of the Act that prohibits discrimination in the employment situation. The EEOC (1980) states:

"Unwelcome sexual advances, requests for sexual favors, and other verbal or physical conduct of a sexual nature constitute sexual harassment when: (1) submission to such conduct is made either explicitly or implicitly a term or condition of an individual's employment; (2) submission to or rejection of such conduct by an individual is used as the basis for employment decisions affecting such individual; or (3) such conduct has the purpose or effect of substantially interfering with an individual's performance, or creating an intimidating, hostile, or offensive working environment."

This definition is precise enough to be workable, and has the added advantage of not being sex specific; that is, under the EEOC Guidelines, sexual harassment is behavior that is legally prohibited for both men and women. Given the power structure of organizations, as well as societal norms about sexual behavior, it may seem ludicrous to suggest that females may also be guilty of sexual harassment. However, there is nothing to suggest that this is not a possibility in and of itself, and for any law to be nondiscriminatory it should be equally applicable to both sexes.

Although sexual harassment undoubtedly has serious negative effects on women's career adjustment, data regarding the prevalence of the phenomenon are scarce. Harragan (1977) suggested the magnitude of the problem in her statement that more women are refused employment, fired, or forced to quit salaried jobs as the result of sexual demands than for any other single cause. She did not, however, cite data to support this statement but referred instead to Farley (1978). Farley cited two systematic studies that were conducted on working women in the private sector. In May of 1975, the Women's Section of the Human Affairs Program at Cornell University queried a sample of New York women concerning sexual harassment, which they defined as any repeated or unwanted sexual comments, looks, suggestions, or physical contact that were found to be objectionable or offensive and caused discomfort on the job. Of the 155 respondents, 92% described sexual harassment as a serious problem, 70% had personally experienced some form of harassment and, of these, 56% reported physical harassment. Farley noted that the incidents occurred among all job categories, ages, marital statuses, and pay ranges.

Farley also cited the results of a survey conducted by *Redbook* magazine (*Redbook,* 1976), in which responses from over 9000 women were obtained. Of these women, 92% reported sexual harassment as a problem and 90% reported that they had personally experienced one or more forms of unwanted sexual attentions on the job. In addition, the Ad Hoc Group on Equal Rights for Women conducted a study among members of the United Nations Secretariat. Although the questionnaire was designed to obtain information about sex discrimination in general, a question about sexual pressures (overt or subtle) was included. Eight hundred seventy-five staff members of the United Nations responded; 73% were women, of whom more than 50% reported that they had personally experienced or were aware that such pressures existed in the United Nations. According to the report that was issued, the job situations involved were promotion (62%), recruitment (13%), obtaining a permanent contract (11%), and transfer and going on missions (7% each). Obviously, these data do not meet the strict standards of scientific acceptability; the samples are not random, total N's are not reported, and distinctions between personal experience of harassment versus knowledge of harassment of others are not clearly made. Just as obviously, the percentages reporting the behavior in question in three widely distinct (and one national) sample(s) lead to the inescapable conclusion that sexual harassment is a phenomenon of perhaps overwhelming proportions, and that it constitutes what may be the most serious problem that women currently face in securing success and satisfaction on the job.

Discrimination in compensation: The comparable worth controversy. Although legislation prohibiting discrimination in compensation is almost 20 years old, the gap between male and female workers has widened rather than narrowed (U.S. Department of Labor, 1975). One of the major reasons for the failure of legislation to improve women's earning power is the fact that the guideline of "equal pay for equal work" fails to take into account the differential distribution of males and females across occupations and within specific job categories. As was detailed earlier in this chapter, women workers continue to be concentrated in a small number of low-paying, "traditionally female" jobs. Traditionally female occupations may require as much or more knowledge, skill, or training as male-dominated occupations, but the fact that they are held primarily by females renders them lower in apparent value, at least in terms of compensation, in comparison to occupations and jobs in which males predominate. For example, registered nurses, most of whom have baccalaureate degrees, earn less than do drivers of city buses; most of the former are female whereas most of the latter are male.

It seems, therefore, that the level of financial compensation often has more relationship to the sex of the average worker than to the nature of the work performed. Reviewing the body of research that indicates that female performance is consistently less valued than identical male performance, Blumrosen (1979) notes a study by the National Academy of Science that concludes:

> the evidence for sex stereotyping in job related contexts is certainly strong enough to suggest the likelihood that sex stereotyping will pervade the evaluation of jobs strongly identified with one sex or the other. That is, it is likely

that predominately female jobs will be undervalued relative to predominately male jobs in the same way that women are undervalued relative to men.''

The combination of the fact that the sex segregation of the world of work ensures that women do not perform male jobs and the consistent under-compensation of female jobs results in the finding that a woman college graduate can expect to earn less than a male high school dropout (Unger, 1979). This also implies, of course, that legislation requiring equal pay for equal (i.e., identical) work will do little to ensure financial equity for women, as it is obvious that women do not *do* the same jobs that men do.

Given this finding, it has recently been argued that rather than "equal pay for equal work", which is meaningless for most women workers, the legal requirement should be "equal pay for work of equal value," a position that has come to be known as "comparable worth" theory. Under this system, any job would be systematically evaluated on the usual factors of knowledge, skill, ability, responsibility, etc.; points would be assigned for the level of each compensable factor that is required for the successful performance of the job. Thus, jobs that required equal levels of the relevant underlying factors would be compensated at an equal rate, regardless of whether or not the actual tasks performed were identical.

This position, most articulately stated by Blumrosen (1979), has been strongly opposed (Nelson, Opton, & Wilson, 1980) on the grounds that it lies beyond the power of present legislation to compel and because of the supposed burden it would lay on business and industry. Opponents suggest that such a system would result in a major reallocation of financial resources in this country; proponents reply "Exactly."

Internal Barriers

The foregoing discussion has focused on external barriers to women's career adjustment. Despite the seriousness and saliency of such obstacles as discriminatory attitudes, sexual harassment and discrimination in employment compensation, it seems clear that *internal* factors also play a critical role in preventing women from fulfilling their career potential and achieving vocational satisfaction. Two major types of internal barriers salient during the career adjustment stage are role conflict and overload and the management of dual career issues.

Role conflict and role overload.   Probably the most salient issue in the career development of the adult woman is the conflict that is experienced between her role as homemaker and her role as worker. Over the past 10 years, the scholarly journals concerned with vocational psychology have been filled with research attempting to distinguish between career-oriented and homemaking-oriented women. More recently, as this distinction has become less meaningful due to the heavy influx of women into the work world, the research focus has shifted to the nature and extent of women's work involvement (e.g., traditional versus pioneer occupations) and the effects of this work involvement on the roles traditionally held by women (i.e., domestic and childrearing). These roles are seen, by definition, to be in conflict with one another, leading to studies of role conflict, role overload, and coping styles (i.e.,, the methods employed by women to cope with their conflicting role demands).

It seems reasonable to assume that few, if any, employed married women have escaped completely the stress of role conflict and its resulting strain. O'Leary (1977) describes three types of role conflict. First, there is *intrarole* conflict, defined as the incompatibility of multiple demands within a single role. Many university professors faced with administrative requirements for teaching and service and professional requirements for research and writing are painfully familiar with this type of conflict.

The second type of conflict to be distinguished is *interrole* conflict, which occurs due to the incompatibility of the demands associated with two or more roles. This can be distinguished from *role overload,* or the inability to satisfy all role expectations in the time available, despite recognizing the legitimacy of all of the demands. Interrole conflict usually involves concerns that are psychological in nature, whereas role overload is a practical concern involving too little time to fulfill multiple role demands.

Gray (1980a) discussed three sources of psychological pressure leading to interrole conflict. The first source derives from the possible lack of support and/or outright disapproval on the part of significant others, primarily husbands, but also neighbors, husband's colleagues, and parents (Bailyn, 1970). Darley (1976) also underscores the psychological importance of societal support to employed married women. Secondly, the supposed incompatibility of career success, particularly in a nontraditional field, with the feminine role has led to the phenomenon of fear of success (Horner, 1972) discussed previously. Finally, the conflict and guilt associated with combining the role of worker with that of mother is particularly difficult for many women. Johnson and Johnson (1977) reported that each of the mothers in their study of dual career families mentioned major concerns over this issue. Supporting data are provided by Lopata (1966) who reports that satisfaction with management of competing roles decreases with the addition of each child but rises as the children begin to leave home. Hall and Gordon (1973) note that, in their sample, home pressures are the most salient factor in role conflict.

In contrast to the psychological pressures associated with interrole conflict, role overload is primarily related to a more concrete, mundane variable: the finite nature of time. Married career women are faced each day with the regrettable fact that Parkinson's Law does not have an inverse; time does *not* expand to encompass the work available. This "corollary" has more impact for women than for men for, typically, when women opt for careers, they are adding to their lives a new set of roles and role demands without a commensurate decrease in the old ones. Although the research is somewhat unclear as to exactly how much time employed married women spend on homemaking activities, two facts appear well established: (1) career women appear to spend somewhat less time on household responsibilities than their nonworking counterparts; and (2) they still spend considerably more time on these tasks than do men. Despite egalitarian attitudes, the actual division of labor within the family consistently relegates the bulk of the responsibility for housework and child care to the female (Bryson, Bryson, & Licht, 1975; Epstein, 1971; Wallston, Foster, & Berger, 1975). Thus, the research establishes that wives, even those with full-time careers, still perform the overwhelming majority of domestic tasks (Bird, 1979; Hall & Hall, 1980; Rapoport & Rapoport, 1969, 1971, 1976; Rice, 1979; Scanzoni, 1972, 1978; St. John-Parsons, 1978; Weingarten, 1978).

In particular, the working wife and mother retains almost sole responsibility for the care and well-being of children. Weingarten (1978) found that, although household chores were divided more equitably where a working couple possessed a similar employment history, the child care responsibilities were still relegated to the wife, supposedly as "reparation" for the time she spent away. Bird (1979) discusses this phenomena in terms of maternal guilt, which appears to be widespread despite solid evidence that maternal employment does not have a deleterious effect on children. The fact that women retain almost complete responsibility for child care, despite the presence of a husband and the demands of a full-time career, is probably the result of the societal prescription that children be raised by one person (i.e., the mother) despite the fact that this arrangement might well not be the optimal one for anyone, including the children (Washburn, 1981).

Bryson, Bryson, Licht, and Licht (1976), in their study of 200 husband and wife professional psychologist pairs, reported that these highly educated and professionally employed women had major responsibility for cooking, marketing, school-age child care, preschool child care, and laundry. Only in the area of housework did these wives not bear almost the total burden of responsibility, but this was not due to husbands' cooperation; rather, outside help was employed.

Haas (1978) studied egalitarian marriages, that is, marriages in which the husband and wife share equally in the roles and responsibilities traditionally assigned to one sex or the other, including the areas of breadwinning, decision making, and domestic chores and reported that most of the problems encountered lay in the area of the division of domestic chores. The couples reported four types of difficulties: first, a lack of skills on the part of one of the spouses; second, a lack of inclination on the part of one spouse (most often the husband) to do some of the nontraditional tasks for which she/he had skills or that required no special skill; third, many of the wives were reluctant to give up their traditional authority over many domestic chores; and, finally, a difference in standards that husbands and wives had for housekeeping. Over half the sample reported that wives generally advocated a higher standard of cleanliness than their husbands. Thus, role overload for working women appears to be a function of husbandly disinclination to perform household chores, or to perform them adequately, exacerbated by female guilt and inability to "let go" of their traditional responsibilties.

Given the pervasiveness of the problem of role overload for employed married women, several authors have discussed methods of coping with the conflicting demands of multiple roles. Epstein (1971) identified nine such methods:

1. The elimination of social relationships.   This involves reducing or eliminating contact with those persons whose expectations cause her strain, for example disapproving neighbors or colleagues who have negative attitudes towards married professional women. Conversely, she attempts to surround herself with those persons who share professional and family statuses—that is, other working mothers.

2. Reducing the total number of contacts involved in social relationships. A good example of this strategy is exhibited by the woman who limits the number of her children, friends, etc.

3. Reducing or controlling the number of statuses in the status set.   Given that possession of a large number of statuses can present a serious problem in terms of time demands, it is necessary for the woman to limit the number of obligations she takes on. Also, when the obligations associated with one status increase (e.g., the birth of a child), the woman may have to reduce the demands of another (for example, refusing elective or appointive office in a professional organization). Epstein (1971) aptly characterizes this as "playing a zero-sum game [p. 136]."

4. The mechanism of redefinition.   The strategy requires the woman to redefine her occupational status as adjunctive to her family statuses. For example, a woman who forms a professional partnership with her husband may define her work goal as "helping" her husband, thus reducing guilt about her career involvement.

5. Intermittent activation of statuses.   This is more characteristic of females whose professional status allows them flexibility in terms of time.

For example, the self-employed free-lance writer or the physician or psychologist in private practice can manipulate her schedule to emphasize the statuses more salient at the time (particularly that of mother versus professional).

6. *Compartmentalization by scheduling.* This involves such things as adopting a nine-to-five work schedule and/or avoiding evening or weekend work activities in order to avoid role overlap.

7. *The delegation of tasks and roles.* This involves the use of outside domestic help to perform many of the household chores that are part of the wife role.

8. *Increasing the observability of role demands.* Becoming well-known and visible in the community through organizational involvement (e.g., PTA) may result in the career woman's being excused from many responsibilities (including family) because people know "how busy she is."

9. *Reliance on rules (or appeals to "third parties") for legitimation of role behavior.* The appeal to outside demands, such as publisher's deadlines and class schedules may serve to legitimate the woman's lesser degree of participation in family or social activities.

A number of studies have appeared indicating that women do actually adopt these coping mechanisms identified by Epstein (1971). For example, Johnson and Johnson (1977) report that many of their subjects lowered their career aspirations while their children were young, and associated mainly with individuals possessing similar attitudes toward careers, marriage, and child rearing. Rapoport and Rapoport (1971) found three characteristic patterns of coping: (1) consciously setting aside leisure time for themselves, (2) delegating as many chores as possible to others; and (3) modifying their work involvement to fit in with their partner's career. These last two coping patterns appear to correspond with Epstein's mechanisms of *delegation* and *redefinition.* Van Dusen and Sheldon (1976) analyzed recent census data and reported that many women are reducing family size expectations (*reduction of the total number of role contacts*); they also found a rise in the number of women who are choosing not to bear children (*reduction of the number of statuses in the status set*).

Two studies have attempted to evaluate various methods of coping. Hall (1972) classified 16 common coping strategies into one of three types: (1) Type I, *structural role redefinition,* involves redefining roles in ways that more equitably distribute the burdens of time and responsibility across family members (e.g., husbands) or changing the expectations imposed on the woman by others (e.g., husband, children, employers, etc.); (2) Type II coping, or *personal role redefinition,* which involves the woman's changing her own behavior and expectations without attempting to change the environment; and (3) Type III coping, or *reactive role behavior,* which attempts to meet all role demands and thus please everyone (the "superwoman" syndrome). O'Leary (1977) speculated that Type I coping was probably the most effective means of dealing with role conflict, but also the most difficult to implement, as it involves obtaining the approval of others in the environment.

Hall (1972b) examined the relationship between these coping styles and satisfaction among women. He found that the association between Type I coping and satisfaction was positive, although it did not reach the usual standards of statistical significance. There was a negative relationship between Type III coping and satisfaction. Kroeker (1963) has suggested that attempts to respond to all the demands of multiple roles reflect defensiveness rather than coping, and Hall (1972b) and O'Leary (1977) view Type III coping as maladaptive even though it may be necessary.

Gray (1980b) suggested that Hall's categories were not mutually exclusive, and therefore investigated the linkages between individual coping strategies and satisfaction. She analyzed the results of a questionnaire completed by 232 married professional women and found strong positive associations between satisfaction and the strategies of having family members share household tasks (delegation), reducing standards within certain roles, and considering personal interests important. Gray (1980b) reports that certain strategies were negatively related to satisfaction, including overlapping roles, keeping roles totally separate, attempting to meet all expectations, eliminating entire roles, and lacking any conscious strategy for dealing with role conflict.

In summary, multiple approaches to dealing with the problem of role overload have been suggested. Further research on the effectiveness and practicality of various coping strategies would contribute to women's attempts to manage this barrier to career adjustment.

Dual-career couples.   The recent focus on the combination of work and family responsibilities for an increasingly large number of women has culminated in investigations of the phenomenon known as the "dual-career" family. Hall and Hall (1980) defined a dual-career couple as two people (not necessarily married) who share a life style that includes cohabitation, separate work roles for both partners, and a love relationship that supports and facilitates both persons. Similar definitions have been offered by Rapoport and Rapoport (1971) and by Rice (1979), although Rice limited his definition to those dual-career partners who are legally married.

Hall and Hall (1980) identify four types of dual-career couples: Type I couples, labeled *Accommodators,* are couples in which one partner is high in career involvement and low in home involvement, and the second partner displays the reverse pattern of involvement. They note that this pattern comes closest to that of the traditional family, although in their typology the career-involved person can be either partner. They suggest that this pattern minimizes conflict and allows each partner to achieve satisfaction without undue expense. Type II couples, termed *Adversaries,* are characterized by high career involvement and low home involvement in both partners. In this arrangement, the primary identity of each partner is defined by his/her career; yet emotional investment is maintained in having a well-ordered home and family life. Unfortunately, neither partner is willing to fulfill this role function. The Halls note that this is probably the most stressful structure for couples. Type III couples, termed *Allies,* consist of partners who are both highly involved in one aspect of their lives, with little investment in the other areas. Thus, both may be strongly family oriented, with little ego identification with their careers; the converse may also be true. This structure also minimizes conflict and facilitates the setting of priorities. Type IV, termed *Acrobats,* is one in which both partners are highly involved in all their roles—they are ego invested in, and receive satisfaction from, both home and career. Like Type II Adversaries, they are apt to experience conflict between career and other demands; the difference is that they are both committed to success in both areas. Their behavior is reminiscent of the Type III copers described by Hall (1972a, 1972b).

Although all writers on the subject agree that the dual-career pattern represents a high-stress life-style (see, particularly, Hall & Hall, 1980), there is disagreement concerning the desirability and feasibility of the life-style. Representative of pessimistic views are Hunt and Hunt (1977), who contend that the dual-career pattern is fundamentally incompatible with the nuclear family and may operate to the detriment of both career and family goals. Arguing that a full-time professional career requires the full-time support of a domestically based partner responsible for housework, child care, consumption, integrative and support functions, and maintenance of social networks, they suggest that the lack of such a partner puts any career person at a distinct disadvantage and is detrimental to the quality of family life. The Hunts argue that this life-style can only be maintained through the extensive use of domestic servants and increased day care and schooling for children, which they maintain is exploitive and oppressive for the two classes of persons involved, that is, servants and children. Hunt and Hunt therefore would propose structural changes in society and in the family rather than continued accommodation to what they believe is an inherently undesirable life-style.

In contrast, Haas (1978) describes the many possible advantages of the dual-career life-style. In her study of egalitarian marriages she found that, despite difficulties such as inflexible work hours and resistance to engaging in nontraditional domestic tasks, role sharing enhanced self-actualization and led to better family relationships. Thus, the stresses of the dual-career life-style may be accompanied by advantages stemming from the involvement of both partners in a greater variety of roles.

CONCLUSIONS AND COMMENTARY

This chapter has reviewed what is known about the career choices, entry, and adjustment of women. Although this body of literature has grown quite large in a relatively short period of time, there continues to be a need for conceptual refinement and theoretical expansion. The following discussion outlines conceptual and theoretical inadequacies in the available body of literature and provides recommendations for further increasing our understanding of women's career development.

Since its inception the career psychology of women, like the field of the psychology of women as a whole, has been largely the study of sex differences. For almost 20 years, researchers have examined differences in men's and women's interests, abilities, and personalities. Investigations have been conducted to determine which jobs they enter, what they are paid, differential selection and promotion rates, and how they demonstrate leadership behavior. Like all studies of psychological sex differences, these investigations are based on the assumption that behavior can more reliably be predicted and explained when the sex of the subject is known. Although studies of sex differences have been useful in many ways, Unger (1979) has pointed out that this mode of research, like most investigations of individual differences, is essentially *applied* in nature, in that no theoretical explanation is attempted. That is, research may demonstrate sex differences in achievement motivation, for example, but does not offer theoretical explanations for the existence of these differences. Unger further notes that sex has been "tacked on" to investigations of every conceivable variable, resulting in a confusing body of conflicting results that serves mostly to obscure the existence of sex similarities which are, in fact, much more prevalent.

Given the inadequacies of gender per se as an explanatory variable, it is suggested that the concept of *sex role* may provide a more useful and powerful framework on which to base further studies of the career psychology of women. Differences as a function of sex role rather than gender per se are abundant in the literature, and the concept of sex role provides a better basis for theoretical explanation and understanding than does that of sex alone. For example, differences in need for achievement among groups of women who are classified on the basis of their sex-role orientation will be more meaningful than differences between males and females alone. And, such comparisons can be made even more powerfully when such groupings are accomplished for both sexes. Such an approach has been advocated for some years by theorists concerned with the theoretical explanation of sex differences (Maccoby & Jacklin, 1975; Unger, 1979; Williams, 1977). Noting the very large overlap in the distributions of sex differences, these writers have suggested that examinations of differences between subjects who are high and low on the variable of interest, within each sex, offer greater explanatory power than simple investigations of gender differences. Thus it is suggested that the correlates of career choice are better predicted by sex-role orientation than by gender itself and that the predictive power of sex role holds for both males and females but is stronger for females.

In addition, we suggest the adoption of Unger's (1979) proposition that sex itself can most usefully be considered a *stimulus* variable. In practice, of course, this is already quite common. Most studies of attitudes and/or bias (Broverman, et al., 1970; Schein, 1975) implicitly define sex in this way. We suggest that the effect of sex on career adjustment can most meaningfully be understood in terms of a stimulus variable, which elicits reactions from others in the environment. The nature of this reaction is thought to be mediated by the sex role orientation of the respondent. Thus, regardless of sex, managers with traditional sex roles should respond more negatively to a female leader than to a male leader. In this paradigm, then, sex would be a stimulus, or independent, variable, subjects' sex-role orientation would be a blocking or classification variable, and the dependent variables would encompass any of a number of measures, depending on the purpose of the study.

It may be, as research progresses, that sex role will emerge as the most powerful explanation of career choice phenomena, whereas sex-as-a-stimulus-variable will interact with sex role to explain more of the career adjustment process. The research on internal and external barriers to women's career adjustment, reviewed above, suggests such an interaction.

Related to suggested changes in the emphasis on sex versus sex role as explanatory concepts is the more general need for increased attention to theory construction and explication in the area of women's career behavior. Theories are not only essential in guiding the directions and facilitating the understanding of research, but the lack of theory may lead to arbitrary, capricious, and/or value-laden interpretations of data (Cook & Campbell, 1979). If theoretical explanations of women's career behavior are not generated and tested, the data concerning such behavior may often be interpreted in ways that are detrimental to individual self-determination of both women and men. If science is to be a guide to rather than a servant of social policy, we must accept and implement its historical responsibility to explain, as well as to describe and predict, phenomena.

What is true for our science is even more true for our practice. It has been argued elsewhere that different theoretical explanations of women's career behavior have profoundly different implications for the practice of career counseling with women (Fitzgerald & Crites, 1980). To the extent that we accept purely empirical representations of reality (e.g., more women generate Holland codes in the social and conventional categories, whereas men more often are classified as investigative and enterprising) without attempting a theoretical explanation of such reality, we are at a loss to design interventions aimed at the alternation of such phenomena. The final historical responsibility with which science is charged (i.e., to control behavior) is interpreted here in the context of counseling; that is, we must look to science as a source of testable hypotheses regarding the values to be supported in the counseling process (Samler, 1960). Thus, the process of career counseling for women (and men) must rest on a body of testable theory; otherwise there is little to constrain the impact of counselor attitudes and bias.

In summary, this chapter has reviewed available literature concerning the career psychology of women and offered a preliminary theoretical framework from which to guide and organize research. Our call for increased attention to theoretical issues is not intended to minimize the importance of empirical research. Rather, we suggest that research will be stimulated and enhanced by adherence to what Marx (1963) has termed the functional mode of theory construction, in which one moves from the theory level to the data level and back again, constantly testing and revising hypotheses in the light of empirical findings. This interaction, constant and mutual, of theory and research seems to us the most viable model for the construction of a career psychology of women.

REFERENCES

Ahrons, C. R. Counselors' perceptions of career images of women. *Journal of Vocational Behavior,* 1976, *8,* 197–207.

Aiken, L. R. Attitudes toward mathematics. *Review of Educational Research,* 1970, *40,* 551–596.

Aiken, L. R., Jr. Update on attitudes and other affective variables in learning mathematics. *Review of Educational Research,* 1976, *46,* 293–311.

Albrecht, S. L., Bahr, H. M., & Chadwick, B. A. Public stereotyping of roles, personality characteristics, and occupations. *Sociology and Social Research,* 1977, *61,* 223–240.

Almquist, E. M. Sex stereotypes in occupational choice: The case for college women. *Journal of Vocational Behavior,* 1974, *5,* 13–21.

Almquist, E. M., & Angrist, S. S. Career salience and atypicality of occupational choice among college women. *Journal of Marriage and Family,* 1970, *32,* 242–249.

Almquist, E. M., & Angrist, S. S. Role model influences on college women's career aspirations. *Merrill-Palmer Quarterly,* 1971, *17,* 263–279.

Altman, S. L., & Grossman, F. K. Women's career plans and maternal employment. *Psychology of Women Quarterly,* 1977, *1,* 365–376.

AMEG Commission on Sex Bias in Measurement. A case history of change: A review of responses to the challenge of sex bias in interest inventories. *Measurement and Evaluation in Guidance,* 1977, *10,* 148–152.

American Medical Association. Undergraduate medical education. *Journal of the American Medical Association,* 1977, *238,* 2767–2780.

Andberg, W. I., Follett, C. V., & Hendel, D. D. Career influences, educational experiences, and professional attitudes of women and men in veterinary medicine. *Journal of College Student Personnel,* 1979, *20,* 158–165.

Angrist, S. S. Variations in women's adult aspirations during college. *Journal of Marriage and Family,* 1972, *34,* 465–468.

Arvey, R. D. Unfair discrimination in the employment interview: Legal and psychological aspects. *Psychological Bulletin,* 1979, *86,* 736–765.(a)

Arvey, R. D. *Fairness in selecting employees.* Reading, Mass.: Addison–Wesley, 1979.(b)

Astin, A. W. *Four critical years.* San Francisco: Jossey-Bass, 1977.

Astin, H. S. Factors associated with the participation of women doctorates in the labor force. *Personnel and Guidance Journal,* 1967, *46,* 240–246.

Astin, H. S. Career development of girls during the high school years. *Journal of Counseling Psychology,* 1968, *15,* 536–540.

Astin, H. S. *The woman doctorate in America.* New York: Russell Sage Foundation, 1969.

Astin, H. S., & Bayer, A. E. Sex discrimination in academe. *Educational Record,* 1972, *53,* 101–118.

Astin, H. S., & Myint, T. Career development of young women during the posthigh school years. *Journal of Counseling Psychology Monograph,* 1971, *18,* 369–393.

Ayres-Gerhart, A. *Self-efficacy expectations with respect to occupationally specific behaviors.* Paper presented at the annual convention of the American Psychological Association, Los Angeles, 1981.

Bachtold, L. M. Personality characteristics of women of distinction. *Psychology of Women Quarterly,* 1976, *1,* 70–78.

Bachtold, L. M., & Werner, E. E. Personality profiles of gifted women: Psychologists. *American Psychologist,* 1970, *25,* 234–243.

Bachtold, L. M., & Werner, E. E. Personality characteristics of women scientists. *Psychological Reports,* 1972, *36,* 391–396.

Bachtold, L. M., & Werner, E. E. Personality profiles of creative women. *Perceptual and Motor Skills,* 1973, *36,* 311–319.

Bailey, S., & Burrell, B. Harvard graduate women's unequal career development. *Second Century Radcliffe News,* January, 1981, p. 15–17.

Bailyn, L. Career and family orientations of husbands and wives in relation to marital happiness. *Human Relations,* 1970, *23,* 97–113.

Bandura, A. Self-efficacy: Toward a unifying theory of behavioral change. *Psychological Review,* 1977, *84,* 191–215.

Bannon, J. A., & Southern, M. L. Father-absent women: Self-concept and modes of relating to men. *Sex Roles,* 1980, *6,* 75–84.

Bar-Tal, D., & Saxe, L. Physical attractiveness and its relationship to sex-role stereotyping. *Sex-Roles,* 1976, *2,* 123–134.

Baruch, G. K. Maternal influences upon college women's attitudes toward women and work. *Developmental Psychology,* 1972, *6,* 32–37.

Baruch, G. K. Girls who perceive themselves as competent: Some antecedents and correlates. *Psychology of Women Quarterly,* 1976, *1,* 38–49.

Basow, S. A., & Howe, K. G. Model influences on career choices of college students. *Vocational Guidance Quarterly,* 1978, *27,* 239–243.

Basow, S. A., & Howe, K. G. Role model influence: Effects of sex and sex-role attitude in college students. *Psychology of Women Quarterly,* 1980, *4,* 558–572.

Bass, B. M., Krusell, J., & Alexander, R. A. Male manager's attitudes toward working women. *American Behavioral Scientist*, 1971, *15*, 221–236.

Bem, S. L. The measurement of psychological androgyny. *Journal of Consulting and Clinical Psychology*, 1974, *42*, 155–162.

Bem, S. L., & Bem, D. J. Case study of a nonconscious idealogy: Training the woman to know her place. In D. J. Bem (Ed.), *Beliefs, attitudes, and human affairs*. Monterey, Calif.: Brooks/Cole, 1970.

Benbow, C. P., & Stanley, J. C. Sex difference in mathematical ability: Fact or artifact? *Science*, 1980, *210*, 1262–1264.

Bernard, J. Where are we now? Some thoughts on the current scene. *Psychology of Women Quarterly*, 1976, *1*, 21–37.

Berscheid, E., & Walster, E. H. Physical attractiveness. In L. Berkowitz (Ed.), *Advances in experimental social psychology* (Vol. 7). New York: Academic Press, 1974.

Betz, N. E. Prevalance, distribution, and correlates of math anxiety in college students. *Journal of Counseling Psychology*, 1978, *25*, 441–448.

Betz, N. E., & Hackett, G. The relationship of career-related self-efficacy expectations to perceived career options in college women and men. *Journal of Counseling Psychology*, 1981, *28*, 399–410.

Bingham, W. C, & House, E. W. Counselor's attitudes towards women and work. *Vocational Guidance Quarterly*, 1973, *22*, 16–32.

Bird, C. *The two-paycheck marriage: How women at work are changing life in America*. New York: Pocket Books, 1979.

Birk, J. M., Tanney, M. F., & Cooper, J. F. A case of blurred vision: Stereotyping in career information illustrations. *Journal of Vocational Behavior*, 1979, *15*, 247–257.

Blaska, B. College women's career and marriage aspirations: A review of the literature. *Journal of College Student Personnel*, 1978, *19*, 302–306.

Blumrosen, R. G. Wage discrimination, job segregation, and Title VII of the Civil Rights Act of 1964. *University of Michigan Journal of Law Reform*, 1979, *12*, 399–502.

Bond, J. R., & Vinache, W. E. Coalitions in mixed-sex triads. *Sociometry*, 1961, *24*, 61–75.

Bowman, G. W., Worthy, N. B., & Greyser, S. A. Problems in review: Are women executives people? *Harvard Business Review*, 1965, *43*, 52–67.

Brito, P. K., & Jusenius, C. L. A note on women's occupational expectations for age 35. *Vocational Guidance Quarterly*, 1978, *27*, 165–175.

Broverman, I. K., Broverman, D. M., Clarkson, F. E., Rosenkrantz, P., & Vogel, S. R. Sex-role stereotypes and clinical judgements of mental health. *Journal of Consulting Psychology*, 1970, *34*, 1–7.

Brown, D. *Students' vocational choices: A review and critique*. Boston: Houghton Mifflin, 1970.

Brown, J. W., Aldrich, M. L., & Hall, P. Q. *Report on the participation of women in scientific research*. Washington, D.C.: National Science Foundation, 1978.

Brown, S. M. Male versus female leaders: A comparison of empirical studies. *Sex Roles*, 1979, *5*, 595–611.

Bryson, J., Bryson, R., & Licht, B. *Professional pairs: Relative career values of wives and husbands*. Paper presented at American Psychological Association Annual Meeting, 1975.

Bryson, R. B., Bryson, J. B., Licht, M. H., & Licht, B. G. The professional pair: Husband and wife psychologists. *American Psychologist*, 1976, *31*, 10–16.

Burlin, F. Locus of control and female occupational aspiration. *Journal of Counseling Psychology*, 1976, *23*, 126–129.(a)

Burlin, F. The relationship of parental education and maternal work and occupational status to occupational aspiration in adolescent females. *Journal of Vocational Behavior*, 1976, *9*, 99–106.(b)

Campbell, D. P. *Manual for the Strong-Campbell Interest Inventory* (2nd ed.). Stanford, Calif.: Stanford University Press, 1977.

Card, J. J., Steel, L., & Abeles, R. P. Sex differences in realization of individual potential for achievement. *Journal of Vocational Behavior,* 1980, *17,* 1-21.

Carnegie Commission on Higher Education. *Opportunities for women in higher education.* New York: McGraw-Hill, 1973.

Cartwright, L. K. Conscious factors entering the decisions of women who study medicine. *Journal of Social Issues,* 1972, *28,* 201-215.

Cash, T. F., Begley, P. J., McCown, D. A., & Weise, B. C. When counselors are heard but not seen: Initial impact of physical attractiveness. *Journal of Counseling Psychology,* 1975, *22,* 273-279.

Cash, T. F., Gillen, B., & Burns, D. S. Sexism and "beautyism" in personnel consultant decision-making. *Journal of Applied Psychology,* 1977, *62,* 301-310.

Cash, T. F., Kehr, J., Polyson, J., & Freeman, V. The role of physical attractiveness in peer attributions of psychological disturbance. *Journal of Consulting and Clinical Psychology,* 1977.

Chapman, J. B. Comparison of male and female leadership styles. *Academy of Management Journal,* 1975, *18,* 645-650.

Clay, W. L. The socioeconomic status of blacks. *Ebony,* 1975, *29,* p. 000.

Cohen, S. L., & Bunker, K. A. Subtle effects of sex role stereotypes on recruiters hiring decisions. *Journal of Applied Psychology,* 1975, *60,* 566-572.

Cole, N. S., & Hanson, G. R. Impact of interest inventories on career choice. In E. E. Diamond (Ed.), *Issues of sex bias and sex fairness in career interest measurement.* Washington: D.C.: National Institute of Education, 1975.

Colwill, N. L., & Ross, N. P. Debunking a stereotype: The female medical student. *Sex Roles,* 1978, *4,* 717-722.

Constantini, E., & Craik, K. H. Women as politicians: The social background, personality, and political careers of female party leaders. *Journal of Social Issues,* 1972, *28,* 217-236.

Cook, T. D., & Campbell, D. T. *Quasi-experimentation: Design and analysis issues for field settings.* Chicago: Rand McNally, 1979.

Crawford, J. D. Career development and career choice in pioneer and traditional women. *Journal of Vocational Behavior,* 1978, *12,* 129-139.

Crissy, W. J., & Daniel, W. J. Vocational interest factors in women. *Journal of Applied Psychology,* 1939, *34,* 488-494.

Crites, J. O. Measurement of vocational maturity in adolescence: I. Attitude Test of the Vocational Development Inventory. *Psychological Monographs,* 1965, *79* (2, Whole No. 595).

Crites, J. O. *Vocational psychology.* New York: McGraw-Hill, 1969.

Crites, J. O. *Career Maturity Inventory.* Monterey, Calif.: CTB/McGraw-Hill, 1973.(a)

Crites, J. O. *Theory and research handbook for the CMI.* Monterey, Calif.: CTB/McGraw-Hill, 1973.(b)

Crites, J. O. A comprehensive model of career development in early adulthood. *Journal of Vocational Behavior,* 1976, *9,* 105-118.

Crites, J. O. *Career counseling: Models, methods, and materials.* New York: McGraw-Hill, 1981.

Darley, J. G. *Clinical aspects and interpretation of the Strong Vocational Interest Blank.* New York: Psychological Corporation, 1941.

Darley, S. A. Big-time careers for the little woman: A dual-role dilemma. *Journal of Social Issues,* 1976, *75,* 37-40.

Day, D. R., & Stogdill, R. M. Leader behavior of male and female supervisors: A comparative study. *Personnel Psychology,* 1972, *25,* 353-360.

Del Vento Bielby, D. Maternal employment and socioeconomic status as factors in daughters' career salience: Some substantive refinements. *Sex Roles,* 1978, *4,* 249–266.

Denmark, F. L., & Diggory, J. C. Sex differences in attitudes toward leaders' display of authoritarian behavior. *Psychological Reports,* 1966, *18,* 863–872.

Dermer, M., & Thiel, D. L. When beauty may fail. *Journal of Personality and Social Psychology,* 1975, *31,* 1168–1176.

Diamond, E. E. Guidelines for the assessment of sex bias and sex fairness in career interest inventories. *Measurement and Evaluation in Guidance,* 1975, *8,* 7–11.

Dion, K. K., Berscheid, D., & Walster, F. What is beautiful is good. *Journal of Personality and Social Psychology,* 1972, *24,* 285–290.

Dipboye, R. L., Arvey, R. D., & Terpstra, D. E. Sex and physical attractiveness of raters and applicants as determinants of resume evaluations. *Journal of Applied Psychology,* 1977, *62,* 288–294.

Dipboye, R. L., Fromkin, H. L., & Wiback, K. Relative importance of applicant sex, attractiveness, and scholastic standing in evaluation of job applicant resumes. *Journal of Applied Psychology,* 1975, *60,* 39–43.

DiSabatino, M. Psychological factors inhibiting women's occupational aspirations and vocational choices. *Vocational Guidance Quarterly,* 1976, *25,* 43–49.

Donahue, T. J., & Costar, J. W. Counselor discrimination against young women in career selection. *Journal of Counseling Psychology,* 1977, *24,* 481–486.

Douvan, E. The role of models in women's professional development. *Psychology of Women Quarterly,* 1976, *1,* 5–20.

Epstein, C. F. Encountering the male establishment: Sex-status limits on womens' careers in the professions. *American Journal of Sociology,* 1970, *75,* 965–982.

Epstein, C. F. *Woman's place.* Berkeley, Calif.: University of California Press, 1971.

Epstein, C. F. Positive effects of the multiple negative. *American Journal of Sociology,* 1973, *78,* 912–935.

Equal Employment Opportunity Commission, Civil Service Commission, Department of Labor, and Department of Justice. Adoption by four agencies of uniform guidelines on employee selection procedures. *Federal Register,* 1978, *43,* 38290–38315.

Equal Employment Opportunity Commission. Discrimination because of sex under Title VII of the Civil Rights Act of 1964, as ammended: Adoption of interim interpretive guidelines—Sexual harassment. *Federal Register,* April 11, 1980, *45,* 25024–25025.

Ernest, J. Mathematics and sex. *The American Mathematical Monthly,* 1976, *83,* 595–614.

Eskilson, A., & Wiley, M. G. Sex composition and leadership in small groups. *Sociometry,* 1976, *39,* 183–194.

Eyde, L. D. *Work values and background factors as predictors of women's desire to work.* (Research Monograph No. 108.) Columbus, Ohio: Bureau of Business Research, The Ohio State University, 1962.

Eysenck, H. J., & Cookson, D. Personality in primary children: III—Family background. *British Journal of Educational Psychology,* 1970, *40,* 117–131.

Falk, W. W., & Cosby, A. G. Women's marital-familial statuses and work histories: Some conceptual considerations. *Journal of Vocational Behavior,* 1978, *13,* 126–140.

Falk, W. W., & Salter, N. J. The stability of status orientations among young white, rural women from three southern states. *Journal of Vocational Behavior,* 1978, *12,* 20–32.

Farley, L. *Sexual shakedown: The sexual harassment of women on the job.* New York: McGraw-Hill, 1978.

Farmer, H. S. What inhibits achievement and career motivation in women? *The Counseling Psychologist,* 1976, *6,* 12–14.

Farmer, H. S. Environmental, background, and psychological variables related to optimizing achievement and career motivation for high school girls. *Journal of Vocational Behavior,* 1980, *17,* 58–70.(a)

Farmer, H. S. The importance of family and career roles for high school youth. Paper presented at the annual meeting of the American Psychological Association, Montreal, 1980.(b)

Feldman, S. D. *Escape from the doll's house: Women in graduate and professional school education.* New York: McGraw–Hill, 1974.

Fennema, E., & Sherman, J. Sex-related differences in mathematics achievement, spatial visualization, and affective factors. *American Educational Research Association Journal,* 1977, *14,* 51–71.

Fennema, E., & Sherman, J. A. Fennema–Sherman Mathematics Attitudes Scales: Instruments designed to measure attitudes toward the learning of mathematics by males and females. *Catalog of Selected Documents in Psychology,* 1976, *6,* 31. (MS. 1225)

Finn, J. D. Sex differences in educational outcomes: A cross-national study, *Sex Roles,* 1980, *6,* 9–26.

Fitzgerald, L. F., & Crites, J. O. Toward a career psychology of women: What do we know? What do we need to know? *Journal of Counseling Psychology,* 1980, *27,* 44–62.

Fottler, M. D., & Bain, T. Managerial aspirations of high school seniors: A comparison of males and females. *Journal of Vocatonal Behavior,* 1980, *16,* 83–95.

Freeman, J. How to discriminate against women without really trying. In J. Freeman (Ed.), *Women: A feminist perspective.* Palo Alto, Calif.: Mayfield, 1975.

Frieze, I. R., Fisher, J., Hanusa, B., McHugh, M. C., & Valle, V. A. Attributions of the causes of success and failure as internal and external barriers to achievement in women. In J. Sherman & F. Denmark (Eds.), *Psychology of women: Future directions in research.* New York: Psychological Dimensions, 1981.

Frost, F., & Diamond, E. E. Ethnic and sex differences in occupational stereotyping by elementary school children. *Journal of Vocational Behavior,* 1979, *15,* 43–54.

Furniss, W. T., & Graham, P. A. *Women in higher education.* Washington, D.C.: American Council on Education, 1974.

Gettys, L. D., & Cann, A. Children's perceptions of occupational sex stereotypes. *Sex Roles,* 1981, *7,* 301–308.

Gigy, L. L. Self-concept in single women. *Psychology of Women Quarterly,* 1980, *5,* 321–340.

Gillen, B. *Physical attractiveness as a determinant of perceived sex-role appropriateness.* Paper presented at the meeting of the Southeastern Psychological Association, Atlanta, March 1975.

Ginzberg, E., Berg, I., Brown, C., Herma, L., Yohalem, A., & Gorelick, S. *Lifestyles of educated women.* New York: Columbia University Press, 1966.

Goldman, R. D., & Hewitt, B. N. The scholastic aptitude test "explains" why college men major in science more often than college women. *Journal of Counseling Psychology,* 1976, *23,* 50–54.

Goldman, R. D., Kaplan, R. M., & Platt, B. B. Sex differences in the relationship of attitudes toward technology to choice of field of study. *Journal of Counseling Psychology,* 1973, *20,* 412–418.

Goldsen, R. K., Rosenberg, M., Williams, R. M., & Suchman, E. A. *What college students think.* Princeton, N.J.: C. Van Nostrand, 1960.

Goldstein, E. Effects of same-sex and cross-sex role models on the subsequent academic productivity of scholars. *American Psychologist,* 1979, *34,* 407–410.

Goodale, J. G., & Hall, D. T. Inheriting a career: The influence of sex, values, and parents. *Journal of Vocational Behavior,* 1976, *8,* 19–30.

Gottfredson, G. D., Holland, J. L., & Gottfredson, L. S. The relation of vocational aspirations and assessments to employment reality. *Journal of Vocational Behavior,* 1975, *7,* 135–148.

Gottfredson, L. An analytical description of employment according to race, sex, prestige, and Holland-type of work. *Journal of Vocational Behavior,* 1978, *13,* 210–221.

Gray, J. D. Counseling women who want both a profession and a family. *Personnel and Guidance Journal,* 1980, *59,* 43–45.(a)

Gray, J. D. Role conflicts and coping strategies in married professional women. *Dissertation Abstracts International,* 1980, *40,* 3781–A.(b)

Green, D. R. *The aptitude-achievement distinction.* New York: McGraw–Hill, 1974.

Greenfield, S., Greiner, L., & Wood, M. M. The "Feminine Mystique" in male-dominanted jobs: A comparison of attitudes and background factors of women in male-dominated versus female-dominated jobs. *Journal of Vocational Behavior,* 1980, *17,* 291–309.

Greenhaus, J. H. An investigation of the role of career salience in vocational behavior. *Journal of Vocational Behavior,* 1971, *1,* 209–216.

Greenhaus, J. H., & Simon, W. E. Self-esteem, career salience, and the choice of an ideal occupation. *Journal of Vocational Behavior,* 1976, *8,* 51–58.

Gump, J., & Rivers, L. A consideration of race in efforts to end sex bias. In E. Diamond (Ed.), *Issues of sex bias and sex fairness in career interest measurement.* Washington, D.C.: National Institute of Education, 1975.

Gysbers, N. C., Johnston, J. A., & Gust, T. Characteristics of homemaker and career-oriented women. *Journal of Counseling Psychology,* 1968, *15,* 541–546.

Haas, L. *Benefits and problems of egalitarian marriage: A study of role sharing couples.* (ERIC Microfiche, ED 165052.) (1978).

Haber, S. Cognitive support for the career choices of college women. *Sex Roles,* 1980, *6,* 129–138.

Haccoun, C. M., Haccoun, R. R., & Sallay, G. Sex differences in the appropriateness of supervisory styles: A nonmanagement view. *Journal of Applied Psychology,* 1978, *63,* 124–127.

Hackett, G., & Betz, N. E. A self-efficacy approach to the career development of women. *Journal of Vocational Behavior,* 1981, *18,* 326–339.

Haefner, J. E. Sources of discrimination among employees: A survey investigation. *Journal of Applied Psychology,* 1977, *62,* 265–270.

Hagen, R. I., & Kahn, A. Discrimination against competent women. *Journal of Abnormal and Social Psychology,* 1975, *5,* 362–376.

Hall, D. T. A model of coping with role conflict: The role behavior of college educated women. *Administrative Science Quarterly,* 1972, *17,* 471–489.(a)

Hall, D. T. Role and identity processes in the lives of married women. Unpublished paper 1972(b). Quoted in V. E. O'Leary, *Toward understanding women.* Monterey, Calif.: Brooks/Cole, 1977.

Hall, D. T., & Gordon, F. E. Career choices of married women: Effects on conflict, role behavior, and satisfaction. *Journal of Applied Psychology,* 1973, *58,* 42–48.

Hall, D. T., & Hall, F. E. Stress and the two-career couple. In C. L. Cooper & R. Payne (Eds.), *Current concerns in occupational stress.* New York: Wiley, 1980.

Hall, O. The stages of a medical career. *American Journal of Sociology,* 1948, *53,* 327–336.

Handley, H. M., & Hickson, J. F. Background and career orientations of women with mathematical aptitude. *Journal of Vocational Behavior,* 1978, *13,* 255–262.

Hansen, D. Sex differences and supervision. Paper presented at the annual meetings of the American Psychological Association, 1974.

Hanson, G., Prediger, D., & Schussel, R. *Development and validation of sex-balanced interest inventory scales* (ACT Research Report No. 78). Iowa City, Iowa: American College Testing Program, 1977.

Hansson, R. O., Chernovetz, M. E., & Jones, W. H. Maternal employment and androgyny. *Psychology of Women Quarterly,* 1977, *2,* 76–78.

Harmon, L. W. Women's working patterns related to their SVIB housewife and "own" occupational scores. *Journal of Counseling Psychology,* 1967, *14,* 299–301.

Harmon, L. W. Anatomy of career commitment in women. *Journal of Counseling Psychology,* 1970, *17,* 77–80.

Harmon, L. W. Career counseling for women. In E. Rawlings & D. Carter (Eds.), *Psychotherapy for women*. Springfield, Ill.: Charles C. Thomas, 1977.

Harmon, L. W. Life and career plans of young adult college women: A follow-up study. Paper presented at the annual convention of the American Psychological Association, Montreal, August 1980.

Harragan, B. L. *Games mother never taught you: Corporate gamesmanship for women*. New York: Warner Books, 1977.

Heilman, M. E., & Saruwatari, L. R. When beauty is beastly: The effects of appearance and sex on evaluations of job applicants for managerial and nonmanagerial jobs. *Organizational Behavior and Human Performance*, 1979, *23*, 360-372.

Helmreich, R. L., Spence, J. T., Beane, W. E., Lucker, G. W., & Matthews, K. A. Making it in academic psychology: Demographic and personality correlates of attainment. *Journal of Personality and Social Psychology*, 1980, *39*, 896-908.

Helson, R. Women mathematicians and the creative personality. *Journal of Consulting and Clinical Psychology*, 1971, *36*, 210-221.

Hendel, D. D. Experiential and affective correlates of math anxiety in adult women. *Psychology of Women Quarterly*, 1980, *5*, 219-230.

Heneman, H. G. Impact of test information and applicant sex on applicant evaluation in a selection simulation. *Journal of Applied Psychology*, 1977, *62*, 524-526.

Hilton, T. L., & Berglund, G. W. Sex differences in mathematical achievement: A longitudinal study. *Journal of Educational Research*, 1974, *67*, 231-237.

Hoffman, L. W. Early childhood experiences and women's achievement motives. *Journal of Social Issues*, 1972, *28*, 129-156.

Hoffman, L. W. Effects of maternal employment on the child. *Developmental Psychology*, 1974, *10*, 204-228.

Hoffman, L. W. Changes in family roles, socialization, and sex differences. *American Psychologist*, 1977, *32*, 644-657.

Hoffman, L. W., & Nye, F. I. *Working mothers*. San Francisco: Jossey-Bass, 1974.

Holahan, C. K. Stress experienced by women doctoral students, need for support, and occupational sex typing. *Sex Roles*, 1979, *5*, 425-436.

Holland, J. *Professional manual for the Self-Directed Search*. Palo Alto, Calif.: Consulting Psychologists Press, 1972.

Holland, J. *Making vocational choices: A theory of careers*. Englewood Cliffs, N.J.: Prentice-Hall, 1973.

Hollingshead, A. *Elmtown's youth*. New York: Wiley, 1949.

Horner, M. A. *Sex differences in achievement motivation and performance in competitive and non-competitive situations*. Unpublished doctoral dissertation, University of Michigan, 1968.

Horner, M. S. Toward an understanding of achievement-related conflicts in women. *Journal of Social Issues*, 1972, *28*, 157-175.

Houseknecht, S. K. Voluntary childlessness: A social psychological model. *Alternative Lifestyles*, 1978, *1*, 379-402.

Houseknecht, S. K. Timing of the decision to remain voluntarily childless: Evidence for continuous socialization. *Psychology of Women Quarterly*, 1979, *4*, 81-96.

Houseknecht, S. K., & Spanier, G. B. Marital disruption and higher education among women in the United States. *The Sociological Quarterly*, 1980, *21*, 375-389.

Howe, L. K. *Pink collar workers*. New York: Putnam, 1977.

Hoyt, D. P., & Kennedy, C. E. Interest and personality correlates of career-motivated and homemaking-motivated college women. *Journal of Counseling Psychology*, 1958, *5*, 44-49.

Hughes, E. Dilemmas and contradictions of status. *American Journal of Sociology*, 1945, *50*, 353-359.

Hunt, J. T., & Hunt, L. L. Dilemmas and contradictions of status: The case of the dual-career family. *Social Problems,* 1977, *24,* 407–416.

Huth, C. M. Married women's work status: The influence of parents and husbands. *Journal of Vocational Behavior,* 1978, *13,* 255–262.

Hyde, J. S., & Rosenberg, B. G. *Half the human experience: The psychology of women.* (2nd Ed.). Lexington, Mass.: D. C. Heath, 1980.

Jackson, J. J. But where are the men? *The Black Scholar,* 1971, *3,* 30–41.

Jackson, J. J. Family organization and ideology. In K. S. Miller & R. M. Dreger (Eds.), *Comparative studies of blacks and whites in the United States.* New York: Seminar Press, 1973.

Jeffries, D. Counseling for the strengths of the black woman. *The Counseling Psychologist,* 1976, *6,* 20–22.

Johnson, C. L., & Johnson, F. A. Attitudes toward parenting in dual-career families. *American Journal of Psychiatry,* 1977, *134,* 391–395.

Joyce, N. C., & Hall, P. Q. Women researchers analyze education, job barriers. *Science,* 1977, *198,* 917–918.

Kaley, M. M. Attitudes toward the dual role of the married professional woman. *American Psychologist,* 1971, *26,* 301–306.

Katz, J. Career and autonomy in college women. In J. Katz (Ed.), *Class, character, and career.* Stanford, Calif.: Stanford University Press, 1969.

Kearney, H. R. Feminist challenges to the social structure and sex roles. *Psychology of Women Quarterly,* 1979, *4,* 16–31.

Kriedberg, G., Butcher, A. L., & White, K. M. Vocational role choice in 2nd and 6th grade children. *Sex Roles,* 1978, *4,* 175–182.

Kriger, S. F. Achievement and perceived parental childrearing attitudes of career women and homemakers. *Journal of Vocational Behavior,* 1972, *2,* 419–432.

Kroeker, T. Coping and defensive function of the ego. In R. W. White (Ed.), *A study of lives.* New York: Atherton, 1963.

Kutner, N. G., & Brogan, D. Sources of sex discrimination in educational systems: A conceptual model. *Psychology of Women Quarterly,* 1976, *1,* 50–69.

Lauver, P. J., Gastellum, R. M., & Sheehey, M. Bias in OOH illustrations? *Vocational Guidance Quarterly,* 1975, *23,* 335–340.

Layton, W. L. *Counseling use of the Strong Vocational Interest Blank.* Minneapolis: University of Minnesota Press, 1958.

Lemkau, J. P. Personality and background characteristics of women in male-dominated occupations: A review. *Psychology of Women Quarterly,* 1979, *4,* 221–240.

Levinson, R. M. Sex discrimination and employment practices: An experiment with unconventional job inquiries. *Social Problems,* 1975, *22,* 533–542.

Levitt, E. S. Vocational development of professional women: A review. *Journal of Vocational Behavior,* 1972, *1,* 375–385.

Lockheed, M. E., & Ekstrom, R. B. *Sex discrimination in education: A literature review and bibliography.* Princeton, N.J.: Educational Testing Service, 1977.

Looft, W. R. Sex differences in the expression of vocational aspirations by elementary school children. *Developmental Psychology,* 1971, *5,* 366.

Lopata, H. Z. The life cycle of the social role of the housewife. *Sociology and Social Research,* 1966, *51,* 5–22.

Lunneborg, P. W. Construct validity of the Strong-Campbell Interest Inventory and the Vocational Interest Inventory among college counseling clients. *Journal of Vocational Behavior,* 1977, *10,* 187–195.

Lunneborg, P. W. Service vs. technical interest—Biggest sex difference of all? *Vocational Guidance Quarterly,* 1979, *28,* 146–153.

Lunneborg, P. W. Reducing sex bias in interest measurement at the item level. *Journal of Vocational Behavior,* 1980, *16,* 226–234.

Lunneborg, P. W., & Lillie, C. Sexism in graduate admissions: The letter of recommendation. *American Psychologist,* 1973, *28,* 188–189.

Maccoby, E. E., & Jacklin, C. N. *The psychology of sex differences.* Stanford, Calif.: Stanford University Press, 1975.

Maier, N. R. Male versus female discussion leaders. *Personnel Psychology,* 1970, *23,* 455–461.

Maracek, J., & Frasch, C. Locus of control and college women's role expectations. *Journal of Counseling Psychology,* 1977, *24,* 132–136.

Marini, M. M. Sex differences in the determination of adolescent aspirations: A review of research. *Sex Roles,* 1978, *4,* 723–754.

Marx, M. H. *Theories in contemporary psychology.* New York: Macmillan, 1963.

Masih, L. R. Career saliency and its relation to certain needs, interests, and job values. *Personnel and Guidance Journal,* 1967, *45,* 653–658.

Mason, K. O., Czajka, J. L., & Arber, S. Change in U.S. women's sex-role attitudes, 1964–1974. *American Sociological Review,* 1976, *41,* 573–596.

Matthews, E., & Tiedeman, D. V. Attitudes toward career and marriage and the development of lifestyle in young women. *Journal of Counseling Psychology,* 1964, *11,* 374–383.

Mattingly, J. Personal communication, 1981.

McClelland, D. C., Atkinson, J. W., Clark, R. A., & Lowell, E. L. *The achievement motive.* New York: Appelton–Century–Crofts, 1953.

McLure, G. T., & Piel, E. College-bound girls and science careers: Perceptions of barriers and facilitating factors. *Journal of Vocational Behavior,* 1978, *12,* 172–183.

Mednick, M., Tangri, S. S., & Hoffman, L. W. *Women and achievement.* Washington, D.C.: Hemisphere, 1975.

Medvene, A. M., & Collins, A. M. Occupational prestige and appropriateness: The views of mental health specialists. *Journal of Vocational Behavior,* 1976, *9,* 63–71.

Megargee, E. E. Influence of sex roles on the manifestation of leadership. *Journal of Applied Psychology,* 1969, *53,* 377–382.

Merritt, K. Women and higher education: Voices from the sexual Siberia. In J. I. Roberts (Ed.), *Beyond intellectual sexism: A new woman, a new reality.* New York: D. McKay, 1976.

Miller, A. G. Role of physical attractiveness in impression formation. *Psychonomic Science,* 1970, *9,* 241–243.

Mischel, W. Sex typing and socialization. In P. H. Mussen (Ed.), *Carmichael's manual of child psychology.* New York: Wiley, 1970.

Muchinsky, P. M., & Harris, S. L. The effect of applicant sex and scholastic standing on the evaluation of job applicant resumes in sex-typed occupations. *Journal of Vocational Behavior,* 1977, *11,* 95–108.

Muldrow, T. W., & Bayton, J. A. Men and women executives and processes related to decision accuracy. *Journal of Applied Psychology,* 1979, *64,* 99–106.

Munley, P. H. Interests of career and homemaking-oriented women. *Journal of Vocational Behavior,* 1974, *4,* 43–48.

Murray, S. R., & Mednick, M. T. S. Black women's achievement orientation: Motivational and cognitive factors. *Psychology of Women Quarterly,* 1977, *1,* 247–259.

Nagely, D. Traditional and pioneer working mothers. *Journal of Vocational Behavior,* 1971, *1,* 331–341.

National Academy of Sciences. *Job evaluation: An analytic review.* Interim report to the Equal Employment Opportunity Commission, 1979. Washington, D.C.: Author.

Nelson, B. A., Opton, E. M., Jr., & Wilson, T. E. Wage discrimination and the "comparable worth" theory in perspective. *University of Michigan Journal of Law Reform,* 1980, *13,* 233–301.

Nelson, J. A. N. Age and sex differences in the development of children's occupational reasoning. *Journal of Vocational Behavior,* 1978, *13,* 287–297.

Norton, A. J., & Glick, P. C. Marital instability: Past, present, and future. *Journal of*

Social Issues, 1976, *32,* 5-19.

O'Connor, K., Mann, D. W., & Bardwick, J. M. Androgyny and self-esteem in the upper middle class: A replication of Spence. *Journal of Consulting and Clinical Psychology,* 1978, *46,* 1168-1169.

O'Donnell, J. A., & Anderson, D. G. Factors influencing choice of major and career of capable women. *Vocational Guidance Quarterly,* 1978, *26,* 214-221.

O'Leary, V. E. *Toward understanding women.* Monterey, Calif.: Brooks/Cole, 1977.

O'Leary, V. E., & Braun, J. S. *Antecedents and correlates of academic careerism in women.* Proceedings of the 80th Annual Convention of the American Psychological Association, 1972, *7,* 277. (Summary)

Oliver, L. W. Achievement and affiliation motivation in career-oriented and homemaking-oriented college women. *Journal of Vocational Behavior,* 1974, *4,* 275-281.

O'Neil, J. M., Meeker, C. H., & Borgers, S. B. A developmental, preventative, and consultative model to reduce sexism in the career planning of women. JSAS *Catalog of Selected Documents in Psychology,* 1978, *8,* 39. (Ms. 1684)

Osen, L. *Women in mathematics.* Cambridge, Mass.: MIT Press, 1974.

Osipow, S. H. *Theories of career development* (2nd ed.). Englewood Cliffs, N.J.: Prentice-Hall, 1973.

Osipow, S. H., (Ed.). *Emerging women: Career analysis and outlooks.* Columbus, Ohio: Charles E. Merrill Publishing, 1975.(a)

Osipow, S. H. The relevance of theories of career development to special groups: Problems, needed data, and implications. In S. Picou & R. E. Campbell (Eds.), *Career behavior of special groups.* Columbus, Ohio: Charles E. Merrill, 1975.(b)

Panek, P. E., Rush, M. C., & Greenwalt, J. P. Current sex stereotypes of 25 occupations. *Psychological Reports,* 1977, *40,* 212-214.

Parker, A. W. Career and marriage orientation in the vocational development of college women. *Journal of Applied Psychology,* 1966, *50,* 232-235.

Parsons, F. *Choosing a vocation.* Boston: Houghton Mifflin, 1909.

Parsons, J. E., Frieze, I. H., & Ruble, D. N. Intrapsychic factors influencing career aspirations in college women. *Sex Roles,* 1978, *4,* 337-348.

Patrick, T. *Personality and family background characteristics of women who enter male-dominated professions.* Unpublished Ph.D. dissertation, Columbia University, 1973.

Patterson, L. E. Girl's careers—Expression of identity. *Vocational Guidance Quarterly,* 1973, *21,* 268-275.

Patterson, M., & Sells, L. Women dropouts from higher education. In A. Rossi & A. Calderwood (Eds.), *Academic women on the move.* New York: Russell Sage Foundation, 1973.

Peng, S. S., & Jaffe, J. Women who enter male-dominated fields of study in higher education. *AERA Journal,* 1979, *16,* 285-293.

Peters, L. H., Terborg, J. R., & Taynor, J. Women as Managers Scale (WAMS): A measure of attitudes toward women in management positions. JSAS *Catalog of Selected Documents in Psychology,* 1974. (Ms. No. 585)

Powell, G. N., & Butterfield, D. A. The "good manager": Masculine or androgynous? *Academy of Management Journal,* 1979, *22,* 395-403.

Prediger, D. J. The determination of Holland types of characterizing occupational groups. *Journal of Vocational Behavior,* 1980, *16,* 33-42.

Prediger, D. J., & Hanson, G. R. Holland's theory of careers applied to men and women: Analysis of implicit assumptions. *Journal of Vocational Behavior,* 1976, *8,* 167-184.

Prediger, D. J., Roth, J. D., & Noeth, R. J. Career development of youth: A nationwide study. *Personnel and Guidance Journal,* 1974, *53,* 97-104.

Prediger, D. P., & Cole, N. S. Sex role socialization and employment realities: Implications for vocational interest measures. *Journal of Vocational Behavior,* 1975, *7,* 239-251.

Psathas, G. Toward a theory of occupational choice for women. *Sociology and Social Research,* 1968, *52*(2), 253–268.

Rand, L. Masculinity or femininity: Differentiating career-oriented and homemaking-oriented college freshman women. *Journal of Counseling Psychology,* 1968, *15,* 444–449.

Rand, L. M., & Miller, A. L. A developmental cross-sectioning of women's careers and marriage attitudes and life plans. *Journal of Vocational Behavior,* 1972, *2,* 317–331.

Rapoport, R., & Rapoport, R. N. The dual-career family: A variant pattern and social change. *Human Relations,* 1969, *22*(1), 3–30.

Rapoport, R., & Rapoport, R. N. *Dual-career families.* Great Britain: Penguin, 1971.

Rapoport, R., & Rapoport, R. N. *Dual-career families re-examined: New integrations of work and family.* London: Martin Robertson, 1976.

Rathburn, C. *Developmental trends in the career choice attitudes of male and female adolescents.* Unpublished M. A. thesis, University of Maryland, 1973.

Redbook Magazine, November 1976, p. 49.

Rezler, A. G. Characteristics of high school girls choosing traditional or pioneer vocations. *Personnel and Guidance Journal,* 1967, *45,* 659–665.

Rice, D. *Dual-career marriage: Conflict and treatment.* New York: Free Press, 1979.

Rice, R. W., Bender, L. R., & Villers, A. G. Leader sex, follower attitudes toward women, and leadership effectiveness: A laboratory experiment. *Organizational Behavior and Human Performance,* 1980, *25,* 46–78.

Richardson, F. C., & Suinn, R. M. The mathematics anxiety rating scale: Psychometric data. *Journal of Counseling Psychology,* 1972, *19,* 551–554.

Richardson, M. S. The dimensions of career and work orientation in college women. *Journal of Vocational Behavior,* 1974, *5,* 161–172.

Ridgeway, C. Parental identification and patterns of career orientation in college women. *Journal of Vocational Behavior,* 1978, *12,* 1–11.

Ridgeway, C. L., & Jacobson, C. K. The development of female role ideology: Impact of personal confidence during adolescence. *Youth and Society,* 1979, *10,* 297–315.

Riger, S., & Galligan, P. Women in management: An exploration of competing paradigms. *American Psychologist,* 1980, *35,* 902–910.

Robinson, L. H. Institutional variation ı the status of academic women. In A. Rossi & A. Calderwood (Eds.), *Academic Women on the Move.* New York: Russell Sage Foundation, 1973.

Roby, P. Structural and internalized barriers to women in higher education. In J. Freeman (Ed.), *Women: A feminist perspective.* (1st ed.) Palo Alto, Calif.: Mayfield, 1975.

Rohfeld, R. W. High school women's assessment of career planning resources. *Vocational Guidance Quarterly,* 1977, *26,* 79–84.

Rose, G. L., & Andiappan, P. Sex effects on managerial hiring decisions. *Academy of Management Journal,* 1978, *21,* 104–112.

Rosen, B., & Jerdee, T. H. The influence of sex-role stereotypes on evaluations of male and female supervisory behavior. *Journal of Applied Psychology,* 1973, *57,* 44–48.

Rosen, B., & Jerdee, T. H. Effects of applicant's sex and difficulty of job on evaluations of candidates for managerial positions. *Journal of Applied Psychology,* 1974, *59,* 511–512.

Rosow, I., & Rose, K. D. Divorce among doctors. *Journal of Marriage and the Family,* 1972, *34,* 587–598.

Rossi, A. S. Women in science: Why so few? *Science,* 1965, *148,* 1196–1202.

Rounds, J. B., Jr., & Hendel, D. D. Measurement and dimensionality of mathematics anxiety. *Journal of Counseling Psychology,* 1980, *27,* 138–149.

Russo, N. F., & O'Connell, A. N. Models from our past: Psychology's foremothers. *Psychology of Women Quarterly,* 1980, *5,* 11–53.

Samler, J. Change in values: A goal in counseling. *Journal of Counseling Psychology,* 1960, *7,* 32–39.

Sampson, E. The study of ordinal position: Antecedents and outcomes. In B. Maher (Ed.), *Progress in experimental personality research.* New York: Academic Press, 1965.

Scanzoni, J. H. *Sexual bargaining: Power politics in the American marriage.* Englewood Cliffs, N.J.: Prentice–Hall, 1972.

Scanzoni, J. H. *Sex roles, women's work, and marital conflict.* Lexington, Mass.: D. C. Heath, 1978.

Schachter, S. Birth order, eminence, and higher education. *American Sociological Review,* 1963, *28,* 757–768.

Schein, V. E. The relationship between sex role stereotypes and requisite management characteristics. *Journal of Applied Psychology,* 1973, *57,* 95–100.

Schein, V. E. Relationships between sex role stereotypes and requisite management characteristics among female managers. *Journal of Applied Psychology,* 1975, *60,* 340–344.

Schlossberg, N. K., & Goodman, J. A woman's place: Children's sex stereotyping of occupations. *Vocational Guidance Quarterly,* 1972, *20,* 266–270.

Scriven, M. *The values revolution.* Paper presented at the meeting of the American Psychological Association, San Francisco, August 1977.

Sedney, M. A., & Turner, B. F. A test of causal sequences in two models for the development of career orientation in women. *Journal of Vocational Behavior,* 1975, *6,* 281–291.

Sells, L. High school mathematics as the critical filter in the job market. In *Developing opportunities for minorities in graduate education.* Proceedings of the Conference on Minority Graduate Education, University of California, Berkeley, May 1973.

Senesh, L. *New paths in social science curriculum design.* Chicago: Science Research Associates, 1973.

Sewell, W. H., Haller, A. O., & Strauss, M. A. Social status and educational and occupational aspiration. *American Sociological Review,* 1957, *22,* 67–73.

Shaw, E. A. Differential impact of negative stereotyping in employee selection. *Personnel Psychology,* 1972, *25,* 333–338.

Shinar, E. H. Sexual stereotypes of occupations. *Journal of Vocational Behavior,* 1975, *7,* 99–111.

Siegel, C. L. E. Sex differences in the occupational choices of second graders. *Journal of Vocational Behavior,* 1973, *3,* 15–19.

Simas, K., & McCarrey, M. Impact of recruiter authoritarianism and applicant sex on evaluation and selection decisions in a recruitment interview analogue study. *Journal of Applied Psychology,* 1979, *64,* 483–491.

Simpson, R. L., & Simpson, I. H. Occupational choice among career-oriented college women. *Marriage and Family Living,* 1961, *23,* 377–383.

Smith, E. D., & Herr, E. L. Sex differences in the maturation of vocational attitudes among adolescents. *Vocational Guidance Quarterly,* 1972, *21,* 177–182.

Smith, M. L. Counselor "discrimination" based on client sex: Reply to Donahue and Costar. *Journal of Counseling Psychology,* 1979, *26,* 270–272.

Sobol, M. G. Commitment to work. In F. I. Nye & L. W. Hoffman (Eds.), *The employed mother in America.* Chicago: Rand–McNally, 1963.

Sorenson, J., & Winters, C. J. Parental influences on women's career development. In S. H. Osipow (Ed.), *Emerging woman.* Columbus, Ohio: Charles C. Merrill, 1975.

Sorkin, A. L. Education, occupation, and income of non-white women. *Journal of Negro Education,* 1972, *41,* 353–351.

Spence, J. T., & Helmreich, R. L. Masculine instrumentality and feminine expressiveness: Their relationships with sex role attitudes and behaviors. *Psychology of Women Quarterly,* 1980, *5,* 147–153.

Stake, J. E. The effect of information regarding group performance norms on goal setting in males and females. *Sex Roles,* 1976, *2,* 23–28.

Stake, J. E. The ability/performance dimension of self-esteem: Implications for women's achievement behavior. *Psychology of Women Quarterly,* 1979, *3,* 365–377.(a)

Stake, J. E. Women's self-estimates of competence and the resolution of the career/home conflict. *Journal of Vocational Behavior,* 1979, *14,* 33–42.(b)

Stake, J. E., & Levitz, E. Career goals of college women and perceived achievement-related encouragement. *Psychology of Women Quarterly,* 1979, *4,* 151–159.

Standley, K., & Soule, B. Women in male-dominated professions: Contrasts in their personal and vocational histories. *Journal of Vocational Behavior,* 1974, *4,* 245–258.

Stein, A. H., & Bailey, M. M. The socialization of achievement orientation in females. *Psychological Bulletin,* 1973, *80,* 345–366.

Steinman, H., & Fox, D. J. Male–female perceptions of the female role in the United States. *Journal of Psychology,* 1966, *64,* 265–276.

Stevens, G. E., & DeNisi, A. S. Women as managers: Attitudes and attributions for performance by men and women. *Academy of Management Journal,* 1980, *2,* 355–361.

St. John-Parsons, D. Continuous dual-career families: A case study. *Psychology of Women Quarterly,* 1978, *3,* 30–42.

Super, D. E. The dimensions and measurement of vocational maturity. *Teachers College Record,* 1955, *57,* 151–163.

Super, D. E. *The psychology of careers.* New York: Harper and Row, 1957.

Super, D. E., Crites, J. O., Hummel, R. C., Moser, H. P., Overstreet, P. L., & Warnath, C. E. *Vocational development: A framework for research.* New York: Teachers College Bureau of Publications, Columbia University, 1957.

Super, D. E., & Overstreet, P. L. *The vocational maturity of ninth grade boys.* New York: Teachers College Bureau of Publications, Columbia University, 1960.

Tangri, S. S. Determinants of occupational role innovation among college women. *Journal of Social Issues,* 1972, *28,* 177–199.

Taylor, S. E. Structural aspects of prejudice reduction: The case of token integration. In J. Sweeney (Ed.), *Psychology and politics.* New Haven, Conn.: Yale University Press, in press.

Teglasi, H. Children's choices of and value judgements about sex-typed toys and occupations. *Journal of Vocational Behavior,* 1981, *18,* 184–195.

Terborg, J. R. Women in Management: A research review. *Journal of Applied Psychology,* 1977, *62,* 647–664.

Terborg, J. R., & Ilgen, D. R. A theoretical approach to sex discrimination in traditionally masculine occupations. *Organizational Behavior and Human Performance,* 1975, *13,* 352–376.

Terborg, J. R., Peters, L. H., Ilgen, D. R., & Smith, F. Organizational and personal correlates of attitudes towards women as managers. *Academy of Management Journal,* 1977, *20,* 89–100.

Terman, L. M., & Oden, M. H. *Genetic studies of genius: V. The gifted group at midlife.* Stanford, Calif.: Stanford University Press, 1959.

Thomas, A. H., & Stewart, N. R. Counselor response to female clients with deviate and conforming career goals. *Journal of Counseling Psychology,* 1971, *18,* 352–357.

Thomas, G. E. Race and sex group inequity in higher education: Institutional and major field enrollment statuses. *American Educational Research Association Journal,* 1980, *17,* 171–181.

Tickamyer, A. R. Women's roles and fertility intentions. *Pacific Sociological Review,* 1979, *22,* 167–184.

Tidball, M. E. Women's colleges and women achievers revisited. *Signs,* 1980, *5,* 504–517.

Tinsley, D. J., & Faunce, P. S. Enabling, facilitating, and precipitating factors associated with women's career orientation. *Journal of Vocational Behavior,* 1980, *13,* 327–337.

Tobias, S. *Overcoming math anxiety*. New York: W. W. Norton, 1978.

Tremaine, L. S., & Schau, C. G. Sex-role aspects in the development of children's vocational knowledge. *Journal of Vocational Behavior,* 1979, *14,* 317–328.

Tresemer, D. *Fear of success*. New York: Plenum, 1977.

Trigg, L. J., & Perlman, D. Social influences on women's pursuit of a nontraditional career. *Psychology of Women Quarterly,* 1976, *1,* 138–150.

Turner, B. F., & McCaffrey, J. H. Socialization and career orientation among black and white college women. *Journal of Vocational Behavior,* 1974, *5,* 307–319.

Tyler, L. E. The antecedents of two varieties of vocational interests. *Genetic Psychology Monographs,* 1964, *70,* 177–227.

Tyler, L. E. *The psychology of human differences*. New York: Appleton–Century–Crofts, 1965.

Unger, R. K. *Female and male: Psychological perspectives*. New York: Harper & Row, 1979.

Unger, R. K., & Denmark, F. L. (Eds.). *Woman: Dependent or independent variable?* New York: Psychological Dimensions, 1975.

U.S. Department of Labor, Bureau of Labor Statistics. *U.S. working women: A data book*. Washington, D.C.: Bureau of Labor Statistics, 1977.

U.S. Department of Labor, Women's Bureau. *1975 Handbook on women workers*. Washington, D.C.: U.S. Government Printing Office, Bulletin 297, 1975.

U.S. Department of Labor, Women's Bureau. *Job options for women in the 80's*. Washington, D.C.: U.S. Department of Labor, 1980.

Van Dusen, R. A., & Sheldon, E. B. The changing status of American women. *American Psychologist,* 1976, *31,* 106–116.

Veroff, J., Wilcox, S., & Atkinson, J. W. The achievement motive in high-school and college age women. *Journal of Abnormal and Social Psychology,* 1953, *48,* 108–119.

Vetter, L. Career counseling for women. *Counseling Psychologist,* 1973, *4,* 54–67.

Vetter, L., & Lewis, E. C. Some correlates of homemaking versus career preference among college home economics students. *Personnel and Guidance Journal,* 1964, *42,* 593–598.

Wagman, M. Interests and values of career and homemaking-oriented women. *Personnel and Guidance Journal,* 1966, *44,* 794–801.

Wallston, B., Foster, M., & Berger, M. *I will follow him: Myth, Reality, Forced Choice*. Paper presented at American Psychological Association annual meeting, 1975.

Washburn, S. *Partners: How to have a loving relationship after liberation*. New York: Athenem, 1981.

Watley, D. J., & Kaplan, R. Career or marriage? Aspirations and achievements of able young college women. *Journal of Vocational Behavior,* 1971, *1,* 29–44.

Weingarten, K. The employment pattern of professional couples and their distribution of involvement in the family. *Psychology of Women Quarterly,* 1978, *3,* 43–52.

Weishaar, M. E., Green, B. J., & Craighead, L. W. Primary influences of initial vocational choices for college women. *Journal of Vocational Behavior,* 1981, *18,* 67–78.

Werts, C. E. Social class and career choice of college freshmen. National Merit Scholarship Corporation Research Reports, 1965, *1* (No. 8).

White, K. Social background variables related to career commitment of women teachers. *Personnel and Guidance Journal,* 1967, *45,* 648–653.

Widom, C. S., & Burke, B. W. Performance attitudes, and professional socialization of women in academia. *Sex Roles,* 1978, *4,* 549–562.

Williams, J. H. *Psychology of women: Behavior in a bio-social context*. New York: Norton, 1977.

Williamson, E. G. *How to counsel students*. New York: McGraw–Hill, 1939.

Wolfson, K. P. Career development patterns of college women. *Journal of Counseling Psychology,* 1976, *23*(2), 119–125.

Yanico, B. J. Sex-bias in career information: Effects of language on attitudes. *Journal of Vocational Behavior,* 1978, *13,* 26–34.

Young, C. J., Mackenzie, D. L., & Sherif, C. W. In search of token women in academia. *Psychology of Women Quarterly,* 1980, *4,* 508–525.

Yuen, R. K. W., Tinsley, D. J., & Tinsely, H. E. A. The vocational needs and background characteristics of homemaker-oriented women and career-oriented women. *Vocational Guidance Quarterly,* 1980, *28,* 250–256.

Zikmund, W. G., & Hitt, M. A., & Pickens, B. A. Influence of sex and scholastic performance on reactions to job applicant resumes. *Journal of Applied Psychology,* 1978, *63*(2), 252–254.

Zuckerman, D. M. Self-esteem, personal traits, and college women's life goals. *Journal of Vocational Behavior,* 1980, *17,* 310–319.

Zytowski, D. G. Toward a theory of career development of women. *Personnel and Guidance Journal,* 1969, *47,* 660–664.

4 Issues in Racial Minorities' Career Behavior

Elsie J. Smith
Michigan State University

Introduction

Over the past decade and a half, researchers have explored issues related to the career behavior of ethnic minorities. Prior to this time, few studies were conducted on members of racial minorities. Research in this area was largely neglected. As Crites (1975) has stated: "in attempting to codify what was known about special groups (ethnic minorities, women, the handicapped) with the extant subject matter of vocational psychology in the late 1960s, I reluctantly excluded it because the disparate nature of the literature on special groups precluded its organization according to any one scheme and there were many gaps in both research and theory [p. ix]."

Since the mid-1970s, a number of studies have investigated the career behavior of ethnic American minorities. Researchers have examined the career development of black Americans, Asian Americans, Hispanics, and Native Americans (Berry & Lopez, 1977; Osipow, 1973, 1975; Scott & Anadon, 1980; Smith, 1975, 1977; Sue, 1975). Black Americans, however, have been the most researched group. It has only been relatively recently that the career behavior of other racial minorities have been studied as distinct groups in American society.

Recent professional positions by the National Vocational Guidance Association and the American Vocational Association (NVGA/AVA, 1973) have emphasized the need for greater research and counselor skill in career counseling for ethnic minorities. According to the 1973 NVGA/AVA position statement, there is "increasing national concern with the need to develop all human talent, including the talents of women and minorities [p. 6]." On a similar note, the Association of Counselor Educators and Supervisors (ACES) proposed (Hansen, 1978) that counselors should have knowledge of and competencies in the "unique career development needs of special client groups (women, minorities, handicapped, disadvantaged, and adults) and the skills necessary to assist them in their development [p. 169]."

The interest in American ethnic minorities has been spurred on by a number of developments. Within the past decade and a half, Americans have become increasingly aware of the uneven distribution of the races and the sexes in the labor market (Miller & Oetting, 1977; Picou & Campbell, 1975). Awareness of the inequality and the underrepresentation of racial minorities and women in jobs has led to various strategies, inlcuding legislation to correct restricted job opportunities and expanded academic (usually college) and career training. Primarily, however, the emphasis has been on developing ways to reduce the educational, attitudinal, and employment handicaps that thwart minorities and women in their employment efforts.

In order for the American society to progress effectively, alleviating the unemployment of racial minorities has to improve significantly. The high unemployment rate for minority adults has become a major issue in the career literature. From 1975 to 1977, the jobless rates for blacks declined slightly from 14.7% to 13.9% in 1978. In contrast, the unemployment rate declined substantially for whites, dropping from 7.8% in 1975 to 6.2% in 1977 (Current Population Reports, 1978).

Since 1975, the jobless rate differentials between blacks and whites have widened. Whereas in 1975 the black jobless rate was 1.9 times the white rate (i.e., relative to the proportion of the labor force, 1.9 black workers were unemployed for every unemployed white worker), by 1977 the black jobless rate was 2.2 times the white rate—a substantial increase over the 1975 ratio. By mid-1978, the black-and-other-races unemployment rate was 2.4 times the white rate—marking the widest gap between the two groups since the Federal government began recording employment statistics by race (U.S. Bureau of the Census, 1978b). Overall statistics in 1982 have shown that both black and white unemployment is on the increase, 18.9% for blacks and 8.6% for whites.

Since 1975, the black, Hispanic, and Native American communities have remained in a state of economic crisis. Both in 1959 and 1974, the poverty rate for blacks was about three times that for whites. As Glasgow (1980) has stated: "These last two factors, namely the stabilization of a poverty population among black and white unemployment (and an ever-widening) gap between black and white unemployment, . . . highlight the economic crisis of the growing black underclass [p. 5]."

The high unemployment rate of minority youth has been another issue that has focused increased attention on the career behavior of racial minorities. According to recent reports, both minority and majority youth are having a difficult time finding employment, but the situation appears to be critical for minority youth, especially blacks and Hispanic youth (Hill, 1978). In 1978, the unemployment rate for white males in the 16–19 age group was 13.5% and 7.6% for the 20–24 age group. In contrast, the unemployment rate for black males in the 16–19 age group was 38.4% and 21.4% for the 20–24 age group (Freeman, 1980). The unemployment rate for Hispanics during 1978 was slightly less than that for black Americans (Newman, 1978).

The emphasis on reducing minority youth unemployment is based on several factors. First, there is reason to believe that many minority youth face an uncertain work future, one that has few chances for long-term job security or career mobility (National Commission on Manpower Policy, 1976). Second, there is the concern that the employment prospects for black and Hispanic youth are so bleak, especially in an era of job scarcity, that many will drop out permanently from the labor force (Bowers, 1979; Stafford, 1981). The third concern has focused on the fear that the high unemployment rate for minority youth will become a major cause of crime and delinquency, and that this could become a major disruptive force in society (Stafford, 1981; Trow, 1980). Fourth, concern has been expressed that without employment during the teenage years, many minority youth will not have the work experience that will assist them in their transition from adolescence to adulthood, from school to work. The high unemployment rates of minority youth constitute, then, an important issue in their career development.

In America, work or preparation for careers is a major undertaking. Most Americans will spend a large portion of their lives working. Yet, for some eight million or more individuals—many of whom are black, Hispanic, and Native Americans—a permanent job will never become an economic reality (*Time,* 1977). Many of these individuals are grouped in what has become known as the underclass—that large group of people who are so removed from the mainstream of America that they are no longer considered part of the traditional class structure. In contrast to immigrant majority populations who previously (1870s to 1940s) swelled the ranks of the needy poor, the underclass now consists of a significantly younger population. Its members come from the poor families of the 1950s and 1960s; their ranks are further increased by their children and offspring—from the 1960s and 1970s.

In many ways, members of the underclass, according to Glasgow (1980), are "already earmarked for failure—they are undereducated, jobless, without social skills or the social credentials to gain access to mainstream life. They are rendered obsolete before they even begin to pursue a meaningful role in society [p. vii]." As the *Time* (1977) article stated: The underclass has become a rather "common description of people who are seen to be stuck more or less permanently at the bottom, removed from the American dream. Though its members come from all races and live in many places, the underclass is made up mostly of impoverished urban blacks, who still suffer from the heritage of slavery and discrimination [p. 14]."

Despite the emphasis on unemployment statistics, escaping underclass status is not merely determined by one's having or not having a job. There are thousands of blacks, Hispanics, and Native Americans who hold jobs, who attempt to fulfill the American work ethic, but who are still members of the underclass. What seems to differentiate the "working members" of the underclass from other segments of American society is the type of job they hold. Generally speaking, working members of the underclass do not have jobs that provide for continuous full-time employment, upgrading, seniority protections, and provisions aiding mobility. Instead, they are members of the long-term poor, those who have been employed for most of their productive lives but who have never moved from the level of bare subsistence.

Other members of the underclass have refused to work or have simply given up on work as a means to deliver them from their low-class status. Instead, these individuals have sought other options for economic survival —ranging from hustling and welfare system to other illegitimate hustling schemes.

The emergence of the underclass as a permanent fixture of our nation's social structure represents one of the most significant class developments in the past two decades. Its existence challenges the cherished American belief that one can pull oneself up by the bootstraps, if only one has enough motivation, enough drive. Its existence also challenges many of the underlying assumptions of our current theories of career development and choice. As Hill (1978) has warned: "It is evident that a permanent black underclass has developed, that virtually an entire second generation of ghetto youth will never enter the labor force" [p. 668]."

Clearly, maintaining the underclass is an expensive enterprise— economically, socially, and politically. Maintenance of the underclass is supported by tax dollars from all classes of wage earners, but disproportionally and inequitably from middle-income workers. The entrapped poor constitute increasingly a permanent part of the welfare population; they fill our prisons and take their toll in expenditures for law enforcement. Equally important are the damaging effects of the underclass on the communities in which blacks, Hispanics, and Native Americans live.

There are, however, other factors to be taken into account when analyzing the employment and career behavior of minority individuals. Major issues include the entire concept of career development, the career maturity of youth, the types of intervention strategies used, and the measurement devices used to gauge their career progress, interests, and choices. What role does career information, family background, and culture assume in an individual's career behavior? Is there a symbiotic relationship among how we conceptualize a problem, what we measure, and how we go about correcting a situation? To what extent may patterns of employment be explained by occupational values and aspirations, by one's social class membership? How do we go about counseling members of the underclass for career development and mobility? How useful have our policies and programs been in changing patterns of occupational segregation for individuals from racial minority backgrounds?

Compensatory and intervention strategy programs in public schools have supplied the major programmatic thrust for assumed deficits in the traditional institutions of family, school, and church. Yet, the extent to which these programs and intervention strategies have been helpful has been the subject of much debate (Rivlin & Timpane, 1975). A major issue has been that the intervention strategies themselves were fragmented and directed toward only piecemeal results. As Oetting and Miller (1977) have observed: "The federal government has spent billions of dollars on training job placement and supportive services. (Yet) Almost every project has failed to really have an impact on unemployment . . . While we were helping with many of the problems that prevent successful employment, we were not providing the kind of help that would move the client upward, step-by-step on the hierarchy [p. 29]."

Moreover, increasingly researchers have challenged the relevance of vocational theories and traditional counseling approaches to racial minorities (Griffith, 1980; June & Pringle, 1977; Warnath, 1975). Osipow (1976) has noted that despite the criticisms regarding the inappropriateness of vocational theories to minorities, there exists some empirical evidence to suggest that Holland's instruments and concepts have relevance for black Americans. Osipow (1976) has observed: "There is likely to be increasing attention paid to this problem. The result will be to dispel myths about the relevance or irrelevance of theory and methods for blacks [p. 141]."

The potential importance of work in the life of each individual makes it imperative that educators and vocational psychologists examine both the process of career development and the factors that promote or impede its growth. This chapter examines the career behavior of four groups of racial and/or ethnic minorities: black Americans, Asian Americans, Hispanics, and Native Americans. A primary goal is to analyze the diverse factors that may influence their career behavior. Some of these variables include their work attitudes, career aspirations, interests, choices, and vocational maturity. Another goal is to codify what we do know about the career development of members of these various groups. Along such lines, demographic data are provided on each of the four groups, and an overall review of vocational research as it pertains to these groups is conducted. A third goal is to suggest future directions for research that may help to clarify the career behavior of American racial minorities.

RACE, ETHNICITY, AND INCOME: SOME PERSPECTIVES

It has become a truism that every person is like all persons, like some persons, and like no other persons. These three aspects of a person constitute the various levels of an individual's identity—the universal, the group specific, and the unique. The intertwining of universality aspects with group similarity and uniqueness is not easily untangled and presents many difficulties for research on the career behavior of racial and ethnic minorities. Reseachers may experience two types of pitfalls in conducting studies on racial minorities: one of being overly concerned with group and cultural differences and one of not being concerned enough.

The terms *race, ethnic,* and *minority* are often used interchangeably in the literature. There are, however, important distinctions between these terms as well as a great deal of overlap. For the purposes of this chapter, it is important to understand both the differences and similarities between these terms.

Race, ethnic group, and minority refer to group-level characteristics that a person shares more prominently with some people rather than others. According to Krogman (1945) race may be defined as " . . . a subgroup of peoples possessing a definite combination of physical characters, of genetic origin, the combination of which to varying degrees distinguishes the subgroup from other subgroups of mankind [p. 49]." Mack (1968) has maintained that race in the biological sense contains only the artificial trappings of human difference. According to her, it is not the factor of race that is so important as it is a case of what people choose to believe about different races. As Mack (1968) has stated: "Most of men's discussions about race are discussions about their beliefs, not about biological fact [p. 103]."

Ethnicity, on the other hand, refers to a group's sense of shared history and culture. As in the case of majority Americans, a number of different ethnic groups may be found in the same race. Although ethnic membership is important in majority American society, race is the more prepotent factor in determining one's status, income, and career development patterns. This situation occurs not because there are inherent differences among the various races in ability, subscription to success goals, or attitudes but rather because structural factors found in labor market dynamics, institutional practices, and the legacy of racism serve to perpetuate a differential career development among Americans of different racial backgrounds.

A major issue in career literature is untangling what is truly racial about an individual's career development. Thus far, a large part of the career literature has concentrated on the racial difference approach and suggested, perhaps unwittingly or unconsciously, that physiological differences among people rather than peoples' responses/beliefs or life circumstances were the most significant factor in their career behavior. This situation has been further perpetuated by the types of methodologies that have been used traditionally in research—that is, black–white comparisons in areas such as work attitudes, aspirations, or career maturity. Essentially, we need to ask: What are researchers actually measuring when they use race alone as a dependent variable in career-related studies? Are they measuring true racial differences among individuals, or are they measuring other factors?

The term *minority group,* although related to race and ethnicity, has slightly different connotations. According to Wirth (1945), a minority may be defined as "a group of people, who, because of physical or cultural characteristics are singled out from the others in the society in which they live for differential and unequal treatment, and who therefore regard themselves as objects of collective discrimination [p. 347]."

Wirth's definition has some meaningful implications for racial minorities as compared to majority Americans who are in the lower class. Clearly, ethnic American whites, especially those who are situated in the lower class face similar but strikingly different problems than the four racial minority groups designated for study in this chapter. Regardless of their humble or poor socioeconomic origins, lower-class whites do not face the barriers of structural and institutional racial prejudice that function to restrict their career development and opportunities. Lower-class majority Americans, because of their race, have higher status than black, Hispanic, or Native Americans.

Lower-class majority Americans, then, do not regard themselves as a group of people who may be singled out from others in American society for differential and unequal treatment based on their racial membership. The discrimination they encounter in the labor market is class rather than race bound. The same situation cannot be said to exist for racial American minorities. Most racial American minorities have a history of racial discrimination (Tauber & Tauber, 1965). Such a history of discrimination, regardless of racial minorities' objectively measured indicator of social class, has served to elevate the primacy of race in the labor market and occupational structure.

For racial minorities, especially black, Hispanic, and Native Americans, the economic and career consequences of racism may be clearly seen. Blacks, Hispanics, and Native Americans have lower incomes than whites, are more concentrated in the least desirable jobs, and have higher unemployment rates. Even when American racial minorities overcome the hurdles of poverty and race, they may not be able to capitalize on their educational and training investments. To quote from a government publication (U.S. Department HEW, 1969):

> Because most Americans can realize their highest ambitions through education, it is often assumed that Negroes [blacks] can similarly overcome the handicaps of poverty and race. But this has not been so in the past. To be sure, even in minority groups, better educated individuals tend to occupy more desirable occupational positions than do the less educated. Yet the returns on an investment in education are much lower for Negroes than for the general population. Indeed, for a Negro, educational attainment may simply mean exposure to more severe and visible discrimination than is experienced by the dropout or the unschooled.
>
> Thus, in addition to the handicap of being born in a family with few economic or other resources, the average Negro also appears to have less opportunity because of his race alone [p. 24].

In writing this chapter, I chose to exclude the many white ethnic Americans, not because they are not deserving of study, but rather because as a group they face consistently different types of career issues. It is true enough that many ethnic white Americans face high rates of unemployment, suffer from educational deficits, and restricted career opportunities. But the racial differences minorities experience in structural and institutional labor market inequalities are too numerous to overlook. For example, data show that even when comparisons are made among high school graduates, unemployment rates among blacks remain twice as high as those for white high school graduates. Although high school completion offers some advantages in reducing the unemployment rates for whites, the unemployment rates for black high school graduates were virtually similar to those of white high school dropouts. Although only 13.1% of white high school graduates were unemployed in 1977, about 23.7% of the white high school dropouts were unemployed. Among blacks, the unemployment rate for high school graduates was 41.8% and 41.6% for high school dropouts. Hence, in 1977, blacks between the ages of 16 and 24 who had achieved a high school diploma fared no better in the job market than did those blacks who were high school dropouts (U.S. Department of Labor, Bureau of Statistics, 1977, table 31).

Even more revealing, white youth who were high school dropouts had lower unemployment rates (22.3%) than black youth with college educations (27.2%) or black graduates from high school (1978).

According to Newman, Amidet, Carter, Day, Kruvant, & Russell (1978), blacks are disproportionately "learning without earning" and have lower employment opportunities not primarily because of deficient education and skills. In a well-documented work, Newman et al. stated:

> . . . one especially stubborn and widespread notion has persisted into the seventies and is as ill-founded for the present as it was for the past. This is the firm belief that blacks are more likely to be unemployed because they are not "qualified" for jobs in the American economy and, in particular, not "qualified" for those jobs resulting from changing technology . . .
>
> Today, with black and white Americans receiving about equal years of schooling, credentialism—fairly applied—would mean similar unemployment rates for white and black high school graduates and a lower unemployment rate for black graduates than for dropouts of either race. But the requirements have never been equally applied: young white dropouts have had consistently lower unemployment rates than young black graduates. Among employed male workers in the same age and education groups, having a high school diploma or better does not give black workers the same occupational status as whites . . .
>
> What has made a difference in working or not, at high-status jobs or not, has not been the possession of a high school diploma; it has been the color of the applicant's skin. It is difficult to review the evidence for every age and educational group since 1940 and come to any other conclusion [p. 71 and 86].

Lest one should think that the difficulty of translating educational achievement and credentials is solely a problem for black Americans, an examination of career-related issues facing other racial American minorities proves otherwise. For example, Asian Americans are often called the model minority; they are frequently mentioned as being unusually successful in using education as a vehicle for upward career mobility (Cheng, Brizendine, & Oakes, 1979). In general, this "model minority" image developed because Asian Americans have been able to achieve a higher level of education and greater upward mobility in comparison with other visible racial minority groups.

However, Suzuki's (1977) examination of the success of Asian Americans found that although this group is one of the most highly educated ethnic groups in the nation, education has not produced as much earning power for Asian males as it has for white males with the same educational background. As a result of his analysis of 1969 data from the U.S. Department of Labor, which compared the relative earnings of whites, blacks, and Chinese at different levels of education (high school graduate, college graduate, and postgraduate), Suzuki found that the percentage of Chinese males earning $10,000 or more was consistently below that of white males at the same educational levels, and below that of black males at the postgraduate level. Suzuki also examined data from the 1970 U.S. Census on median annual incomes of individuals, median years of schooling completed, and the median ages of whites, blacks, and three major Asian subgroups by sex. Again, he found that the median incomes of Chinese and Filipino males were only about 75% of the median income of white males. Although the median income of Japanese males was found to be approximately 10 percent above that of white males, Japanese males' median years of schooling and age were substantially greater than those of white males. Suzuki's (1977) findings led him to conclude that Asian Americans are generally "underemployed, underpaid or both . . . the celebration of their phenomenal 'success' as the model minority is at best premature, and at worst, a devious deception [p. 41]."

Suzuki's findings of lower earning power for Asian Americans even when they have attained an educational level comparable to whites would appear to contradict studies that indicate individual income is primarily dependent on educational level and family socioeconomic background. According to him, the earning discrepancy for Asian Americans is greatly influenced by stereotyping and racism.

Suzuki's (1977) statements on the influence of stereotyping and racism on Asian Americans' career development have been supported by Sue (1975). Sue has observed that Asian Americans may be encouraged to go into the sciences and math, presumably because of their past success in these areas and their perceived language difficulties. Stereotypes also exist of other racial minority groups, including the Native American high steelworker, the Hispanic migrant worker or farmer, and the black skycap. These stereotypes are frequently the perceptions of the reality of occupational segregation.

Recently, a number of Americans have begun to assume that the difficulties racial minorities experience in their career development are little different from those experienced by lower socioeconomic, ethnic majority Americans. This position is often supported by the belief that racial minorities have significant, if not phenomenal economic progress, and that racial discrimination exerts only a minor influence, if at all, on their career and economic progress (see the Louis & Harris Poll, 1977).

Data presented in the section, however, has challenged such a position. This section has pointed out that there are important differences among the terms race, ethnicity and minority. It is not just the definitions of these terms that is important, but rather the meaning they have for individual's career development. Race rather than ethnicity was found to have a more potent influence on an individual's employment and income, even when comparable levels of educational attainment existed. Both racism and stereotyping have been found to be significant factors in the career behavior of racial minorities. The four groups discussed in this chapter may be termed as racial ethnic minorities, because all three terms apply to them in some way or another.

RACIAL MINORITIES: SOME BASIC
DEMOGRAPHIC DATA

Demographic data indicate that vocational psychologists have an increasing likelihood of coming in contact with racial minorities. Currently, blacks, Hispanics, Asian Americans and Native Americans have been estimated to constitute approximately 17–19% of the American population. The high percentage of ethnic American minorities, plus their status in the labor market, increases the likelihood that many of them will need counseling if only to deal with their periodic entry into and exit from the labor force. In order to understand some of the career issues facing minorities, vocational counselors must become more aware of the overall situations of members from these various groups.

There are several ways of looking at minority groups. According to Kinloch (1979), minority groups may be differentiated into several types: (1) physiological types (nonwhites, women, young people, students and the aged); (2) cultural types (non-Anglo Europeans, blacks, Hispanics, Native Americans, and Asian Americans); (3) economic types (the poor, the lower classes without power); and (4) the behavioral types (the legal and social deviants including the mentally ill). Whereas some of the racial minorities discussed in this section may show prominent membership in several of these categories, others are typically seen to fit in only a couple of these categories or types.

Regardless of a racial minority's "typecasting," there is one common denominator among them and that is their lack of power when compared to the dominant, white male majority.

This section presents basic demographic data on four racial minorities: black Americans, Asian, Hispanic, and Native Americans. In some respects, the presentation and the type of information provided on each group is uneven. This situation can be largely attributed to the lack of availability of similar statistics and information on the various racial groups. For example, in contrast to the amount of research done on black Americans, relatively little sociological, historical, occupational, or statistical research has been completed on Asian, Hispanic, or Native Americans. Only a brief summary of each group is given.

Black Americans

Black Americans constitute the largest racial minority in the nation. Approximately 12% of the nation's population or 26 million people are black Americans (U.S. Bureau of the Census, 1979). The black population is largely an urban and a relatively young population. In 1975, the median age for the black population was 23.4 years, and in 1980, it was estimated to be approximately 28 years (U.S. Bureau of the Census, 1978b, 1979).

The experience of black Americans in the United States has been written about extensively. Historically, the prevalence of slavery had a major impact on their educational and career development. For example, in the latter part of the nineteenth century, the illiteracy rate for blacks was high. Most blacks lived in the South, with the majority of black men employed primarily as agricultural workers and black women in domestic and personal service occupations.

The twentieth century marked a number of developments for black Americans. During the 1940s, blacks began a primarily one-way stream of migration from the South to the North, and this movement remained fairly constant to the 1970 decade. From 1940 to 1970, the South lost close to 1.5 million blacks during each decade (U.S. Bureau of the Census, 1978b). A search for job opportunities in the industrialized North during World War II was a major factor contributing to the outward migration from the South. By 1970, 81% lived in urban areas, and only 53% lived in the South.

Considering the devastating influence of slavery, black Americans have made significant progress in their educational and career development. Most of this change has taken place since 1960. For example, in 1940 only 1 out of 10 blacks aged 25 to 34 years had completed high school; by 1960 the ratio was 3 out of 10; by 1970, the proportion had increased to 5 out of 10; and by 1975, the proportion had risen to 7 out of 10.

The proportion of blacks aged 25 to 34 who have completed a college education has also increased substantially, from 2 percent in 1940 to 11 percent in 1975. Despite this progress, the proportion of young black adults who are college graduates has still lagged behind that of whites. In 1975, whites were twice as likely as blacks to have attained a college education (U.S. Bureau of the Census, 1978b). The number of black students currently enrolled in college still reflects considerable growth and progress. The number of black college students increased from 522,000 in 1970 to about 1 million in 1980, with the bulk of this increase occurring between 1970 and 1976.

The distribution of black Americans in the work force also provides important information for the vocational psychologist. During the 1960s, black Americans achieved measurable gains in technical, managerial, and other white-collar jobs. In general, they left low-paying jobs in agriculture and household service. In the 1970s, however, the rate of increase slowed among blacks (and whites also) entering the professions. Overall, the black proportion of total employment in professional and technical fields rose from 6.7% in 1970 to 8.7% in 1978. The largest proportion of blacks are blue-collar workers (38%). Black men moved faster out of their previous lower-status occupations than did black women, and by 1970, one-fourth of the black men were in operative occupations.

Representation of blacks in selected professions has continued to be minimal over an 80 year span (from 1890 to 1970). For instance, in 1970, blacks comprised only 2% of all physicians and surgeons, 1% of all lawyers and judges, but 8% of all teachers (U.S. Bureau of the Census, 1978b).

The improved quality and quantity of education of black Americans have had an important effect on their earning capacity. In 1967, black high school graduates earned approximately 67% of white incomes. By 1978, that ratio had increased to 77%. Yet, once an age group has entered the labor force, the relative income of its members tends to remain fixed. For example, if an entering black generation earned 85% of white income, it will probably be earning that same 85% for the entire career lifetime, with individuals averaging below or above that average.

A review of the literature on black Americans in the United States also has revealed that, for the most part, blacks have been a wage-earning as opposed to a propertied or self-employed class (Jones, 1979). Traditionally, blacks have been workers rather than owners of production. Their predominant position as workers has contributed to their extreme vulnerability to changing economic conditions in American society. For example, according to Jones (1979), approximately 81% of all income going to black families came in the form of wages and salaries, whereas returns to wealth or poverty income accounted for less than 1% of black family income. As Jones (1979) has stated: "Thus, it is readily apparent that the single most important factor in assessing the state of the black economy is the status of Blacks as workers [p. 79]."

Data on the historical role of blacks as workers and their labor force participation rates have major implications for their career development. First, blacks of all ages must be made keenly aware of their historical role as workers rather than as owners of production. Such a realization should not be made to discourage blacks, but rather to encourage them to strive for and achieve an increased role in the ownership of production. Second, black Americans must become more knowledgeable about the trends in the labor force participation rates of all groups. They must recognize that the increased and continued high labor force participation of white women and mainly white teenagers constitutes one of the most significant developments in the American work world.

As Jones (1979) has indicated: "The trend in labor force participation rates has negative implications for incomes of black families . . . if white women and teenagers continue to increase their work rates relative to Blacks, a higher proportion of whites than Blacks will live in multiple earner families and enjoy the obvious economic advantages of the arrangement [p. 81]." The labor force participation rates of black Americans is now profoundly affected by the increased work participation of white women and white teenagers.

Overall, then, in the 100 or so years since slavery, black Americans have made considerable progress in their career development. Many of the career development handicaps that they currently face are historical in nature. Other factors are related to the current overall economic situation in the United States, racial discrimination, poor educational preparation in the elementary and high schools, an increasing rate of family instability and female-headed households that appears to be growing among the general American population, and the failure of this group to come to grips with a changing national and international economic and work situation.

Asian Americans

Asian Americans have been described as the forgotten minority, primarily because they are often viewed as the advantaged minority, a highly successful group that has "made it" in American society. As Sue (1981) has stated: "the belief that Asian Americans represent a 'model' minority has been played up by the popular press in such headlines as 'Success Story: Outwhiting the Whites,' and 'Success Story of One Minority Group in the U.S.' [p. 113]."

Asian Americans constitute a diverse group. They include Chinese, Japanese, Pilipinos[1] (Philippinos), Koreans, Hawaiian, and what has now been labeled the Indochina refugees. According to the 1970 census, there was a total of 1,539,412 Asian Americans (Sue, 1981). That figure has now changed. Currently, Tsu (1977) has estimated that Asian and Pacific Islanders number 3.5 million. The approximate breakdown of the largest group is as follows: Japanese Americans, 650,000; Chinese, 600,000; Pilipinos, 500,000; Koreans, 250,000; and Indo–Chinese, 150,000 (Tsu, 1977).

In terms of geographical location, most Asian Americans are concentrated on the West Coast and in Hawaii. According to the 1970 census report, 38% of the total Asian population lives in California and another 27% in Hawaii (Kitano & Matsushima, 1981). Asian Americans have generally been perceived as the "silent racial minority." Traditionally, they have been viewed as accommodating and adaptable to the dominant American society; they are also viewed as hard working, and skilled academically in math and in the sciences (Maykovich, 1976).

In many respects, the Asian American experience has been qualitatively different from that of blacks, American Indians, Chicanos, and Puerto Ricans. As Kitano and Matsushima (1981) have pointed out, much of the Asian migration was voluntary, even though there were instances of con-

---

[1]Just as ethnically conscious Asians find a perjorative association to the word *Oriental* so they find Phillipinos or Filippinos (white definitions). The preferred reference is now Pilipinos.

tract laborers, sojourners, and the recent refugees from Southeast Asia. Second, their cultures were not quickly destroyed or dismantled. The Japanese, however, were one notable exception to this. During the internment of Japanese Americans in World War II, acculturation was not only actively encouraged, but the repression of "Japanese ways" was strongly reinforced. According to Kitano and Matsushima (1981), "the cohesive ethnic communities of Chinese and Japanese aided in providing alternative social and economic opportunities when entrance into the mainstream was limited by discrimination and prejudice. Third, ties with a home country were strong . . . Finally, most of the Asian American groups were able to bypass a significant long-term dependency on the United States Government, although the new refugees from Southeast Asia may be an exception [pp. 168–169]."

The different circumstances that led to Asian Americans' coming to the United States, the fact that they were allowed to preserve their various cultures (and more important, were allowed to maintain their families as a unit), the fact that their language was not destroyed, that their communities provided alternative social and economic opportunities to the mainstream, that ties with their home countries were strong, and that they were not dependent on the Federal government for economic support has had a great deal to do with their more positive receptions from white majority American society and possibly to their greater economic success than the other racial minorities discussed in this section. For example, Sue (1981) has pointed out that Asian Americans and whites have been found to have relatively low social distance as measured by the Bogardus Social Distance Scale (1925). The Bogardus Social Distance Scale is presumably a measure of prejudice and/or discrimination against racial minority groups. A key question or issue on the Bogardus Social Distance Scale has to do with white Americans' feelings about intermarriage and forming intimate relationships with racial minorities.

There appears to be some support for Sue's (1981) statements on the relatively low social distance between Asian Americans and whites. Sue (1981) notes, for example: "The incidence of interracial marriages for Japanese Americans (mainly Japanese-white) in 1970 for areas like Los Angeles, San Francisco, and Fresno, California, has approached 50%. . . . This is in marked contrast to Black-white marriages for all married Blacks in 1970 that was well under 2% [p. 114]."

The Asian American experience in America has been a rich one, marked by both success and injustice. In order to understand this experience, one must have information about their respective cultures, the various reasons for their migration to the United States, and their reception by the majority American culture as well as other basic demographic data. Although an in-depth study of Asian Americans is beyond the scope of this chapter, information is provided on the migration patterns of major Asian American minorities. The immigration patterns of Asian Americans reflect their historical ties to American society.

Most textbook and historical publications on Asian Americans have observed that the Chinese were the first Asian immigrants to the United States (Kitano & Matsushima, 1981; Maykovich, 1976). Chinese immigration to the United States began effectively in 1847, when the news reached Hong Kong that gold had been discovered in California (Maykovich, 1976). From 1898 to 1877, the Chinese enjoyed more than 30 years of free immigration, with more than 130,000 Chinese arrivals to the United States. Two forces primarily pulled Chinese to the United States: the gold rush and the resulting demand for labor in California.

According to Maykovich (1976):

> For the first few years at least, the arrival of Chinese laborers was hailed, and they were warmly welcomed both by the people of California and by state and county officials. The Chinese laborers were seen to be reticent, industrious, thrifty, and adaptable to various kinds of employment—ready and willing to perform labor uncongenial to the Caucasian. They were satisfied with low wages and were cooperative with their employers. With the acute scarcity of unskilled labor and with the Chinese totaling about 25 percent of the foreign-born population of California (1960–1880), the Chinese soon filled in as general laborers, domestic servants, cooks, and gardeners. The majority went into the mines; several thousand went into the construction of the Central Pacific Railroad. Thus the contribution of the Chinese pioneers to the economic development of American society was significant [p. 72].

Gradually, majority Americans began to react against the Chinese as economic and labor invaders. In addition, the sociocultural behavior of Chinese came under attack from white Americans. Chinese were viewed as unassimulatable and immoral; their style of life was different from that of white Americans in that the Chinese wore different clothes, ate different food, lived in seclusion, were without wives, and used the services of prostitutes to make up for their lack of wives and feminine sexual contact. In essence, the Chinese were conceptualized by white Americans as the Yellow Peril. The white majority society's contact with the Chinese led to several developments: it led to the Chinese Exclusion Act of 1882 and the Immigration Act of 1924, which sought to restrict the flow of immigration of other Asian Americans—notably that of Japanese Americans. Despite the negative immigration acts, the arrival of the Chinese in the United States paved the way for other Asian American immigration.

The Japanese came to the United States during the late 1880s via Hawaii (Maykovich, 1976). Many of the problems of prejudice and racial discrimination the Japanese faced were similar to those of the Chinese. The discrimination against Japanese reached its greatest height during World War II. The majority of the early Japanese immigrants found employment on the railroad, canneries, and mining. As Sue (1981) has stated: "Since many of the Japanese had previously come from a farming class, their gravitation toward farming and gardening could be predicted . . . . The Japanese's knowledge of argriculture and perseverance made them highly successful in these fields, where they subsequently became economic competitors [p. 119]."

Maykovich (1976) has noted that the Japanese came from a society that emphasized education. Upon arrival in the United States, the Japanese maintained their belief in the importance of education but because of language and other handicaps, the Japanese immigrants were unable to attain a higher education but directed their children toward educational achievement. As Maykovich (1976) has stated: "The emphasis on educational achievement operated within the context of competing with the white majority. This became a pragmatic pursuit to demonstrate the superiority of the Japanese [p. 74]."

The Koreans did not come to this country in large numbers until after 1960 (Urban Associates, 1974). The first major immigration of Pilipinos came after the Spanish–American War when Spain ceded the Phillipines to the United States. In general, prior to 1964, immigration quotas for Eastern Hemipshere countries prevented large-scale Asian immigration to the United States. After the 1965 Immigration Act, Asian American migration increased. As a result, the Asian American group, although small in numbers, is now one of the fastest growing racial minority groups in the United States (Tsu, 1977). According to Maykovich (1976): "Postwar Asian immigrants are quite different from their pre-war counterparts. They are emigrating from independent and/or industrialized rather than subordinate and/or rural Asian countries of prewar days. . . . Present day Asian immigrants are more heterogeneous than their pre-war counterparts, including professionally trained people who are given preferential treatment under the new immigration law, and those who have illegally fled from communism [p. 77]."

Upon the United States' lifting of the immigration restrictions, the Japanese and Chinese began to show a remarkable economic upward mobility. Much of this upward mobility was tied to their achievement in education and in business. In 1940, the Japanese had surpassed whites in the median school year completed (8.8 median school year versus the white 8.1 median year). In contrast, the Chinese in 1940 ranked as low as blacks and other racial minority groups with a school completion level below the sixth grade. This situation can probably be attributed to the fact that many of the older Chinese immigrants had little or no education; 23.5% of males 25 years and older had no schooling in 1940 (Maykovich, 1976).

By 1950, the Japanese median school year was 12.3%, whereas the white median school year completed was 9.3, giving the Japanese a 3 years higher advantage. Also, by this time, more than half of the Japanese males 25 years and over had completed college, whereas whites in the same group had completed only a high school education. By 1970, the median school year completed for males 25 years old and over was 12.1 for whites, 9.4 for blacks, 12.5 + for Japanese, 12.4 + for Chinese and 12.2 + for Pilipino (Maykovich, 1976). Moreover, in 1970, more than half of the Japanese, Chinese, and Pilipino Americans 25 years old and over had attained above college level education, whereas the median school year completed by blacks, Hispanics, and Native Americans was still relatively low.

Asian Americans were able to use their educational attainments to move up the occupational ladder. By 1960, the Japanese and Chinese were more likely than any other group (including white Americans) to be found in professional and technical occupations (Maykovich, 1976). The 1970 census has shown that Japanese, Chinese, and Pilipinos were more likely to be found in the professional and technical occupations than were white or black Americans. Much of the improved status of the Pilipinos can be attributed to the fact that after the 1965 Immigration Law they entered the United States as doctors, lawyers, engineers, teachers, nurses, and other professionals who had very few opportunities for employment at home.

Asian Americans also experienced a gradual increase in their incomes. Despite the achievements of Japanese Americans in education, they did not achieve parity in income with white Americans. As Maykovich (1976) has stated: "Thus, until 1959 it was argued that Japanese and Chinese were still discriminated against since they were excluded from the top, high-paying positions monopolized by white Americans within each occupational category including professional work [p. 79]." By 1969, this situation was corrected, and the Japanese median income ($7472) was higher than that of any other group including white Americans ($6773). Despite the fact that the Chinese had attained a similar educational and occupational status to Japanese and white Americans, Chinese Americans' median income was $5120, the Pilipinos was $4989, and Black Americans' median income was $4069.

According to the U.S. Commission on Civil Rights (1978), Asian Americans have one of the lowest rates of unemployment. In 1960, the unemployment rate for Japanese Americans was 2.4%, 1.8% in 1970, and 2.9% in 1976. These figures may be compared with the unemployment rates for white males in these same years, which were 4.7% in 1960; 3.6% in 1970; and 5.9% in 1976. Only in 1976 was the unemployment rate of Chinese males higher than that for white males (7.2% and 5.9%, respectively). The unemployment rate for male Pilipinos was 4.9% in 1960; 5.4% in 1970; and 5.6% in 1976. Thus, in 1976, the Pilipino unemployment rate, like the Japanese unemployment rate, was lower than that for white males, blacks, Native Americans, Mexican Americans, and Puerto Ricans. In terms of all the major groups studied in the United States, Asian Americans have the lowest unemployment rates.

The career development of Asian Americans has been influenced by their culture. Asian Americans have a collective rather than an individual orientation. Their selection of career fields seems to reflect this orientation. Although many Asian Americans go to college, their degrees are almost never in the liberal arts, but rather in business administration, engineering, or science. Asian Americans tend to view eduation as a means of acquiring a saleable skills rather than a means of developing a critical mind (Maykovich, 1976). Other reasons have also been offered to explain Asian Americans concentration in selected fields. As Maykovich (1976) has stated:

First they (Asian Americans) went into low-level clerical and technical fields in order to avoid direct competition with white Americans. Once they performed well in these areas, the positive stereotype was created. These areas then became established as fields in which the Asian American was expected to excel naturally. Parents pushed their offspring into accounting, engineering, drafting, and clerical work until they became "math and science freaks, eating their meals with slide rules [p. 85]."

An additional reason cited by Maykovich (1976) for their concentration in science is that the jobs required less human interaction than other fields.

Asian Americans are not good at verbal skills and social interaction because of their cultural heritage and their subordinate position in America. Traditionally they have been taught not to express their feelings freely, which makes social interaction with white Americans difficult because the latter are used to more spontaneous express. . . . Asian Americans feel much more at ease dealing with numbers or machines than with people [p. 85].

However, stereotypes of the abilities of Asian Americans (good in science and math) and cultural characteristics such as restraint of strong feelings and difficulty with language facility may function to limit exploration of a wide variety of career options, notably those in the social sciences. Likewise, Sue (1981) has noted that while the term model minority has some advantages, it also has a functional value for those who hold power in society. The model minority American stereotype reasserts the "erroneous belief that any minority can succeed in a democratic society if the minority group members work hard enough . . . and the Asian American success story is seen as a divisive concept used by the Establishment to pit one minority group against another by holding one group up as an example to others [p. 117]."

Hispanic Americans

Hispanic Americans are the second largest minority group in the United States. Hispanic Americans are composed of several historically and culturally distinct ethnic groups linked together primarily by their share of Spanish heritage. They include Mexicans, Cubans, and Puerto Ricans. Each of these groups came to the United States for different reasons, at different points in time, and entered different parts of the country; and as a result show different labor force behavior patterns (Newman, 1978).

There are approximately 12 million persons of Hispanic descent living in the United States. Members of this group account for 5.6% of the population in the United States (Newman, 1978). Mexican Americans constitute the largest group, with approximately 7 million people. There are nearly 1.8 million Puerto Ricans (excluding Puerto Rico), .7 million Cubans, and another 2.4 million persons of other Hispanic origin or descent. In actual numbers, rather than percentages, Hispanic Americans constitute one of the fastest growing racial minority groups in the United States. For example, Newman (1978) has pointed out that during the 5-year period from 1973 to 1978, the Hispanic population grew by almost 14%, whereas the non-Hispanic population grew by only 3.3%. More specifically, the Mexican American population grew by about 14%, the Puerto Ricans by 18%, and other Hispanics by about 19%.

The Hispanic population is relatively younger than the non-Hispanic population (excluding Cubans who tend to be older). The median age for Puerto Ricans was 20 years, 21 years for Mexican Americans, and 23 years for other Hispanics (Newman, 1978). These different age distributions may be attributed to different migratory patterns and reasons for leaving their various places of origin. For example, Puerto Ricans, Mexicans, and other Hispanics have migrated principally for economic reasons; therefore, they tend to be young. Cubans, on the other hand, migrated mainly for political reasons, encountered age restrictions (men aged 15–26 were not allowed to leave their homeland for military reasons) and, therefore, were inclined to be older. The median age of Cubans was 37 years in 1977.

Overall, then, about 42% of all persons of Spanish origin were under 18 years in 1978, compared with about 29% of persons not of Spanish origin. Morever, the aged Spanish population is relatively small. About 4% of persons of Spanish origin were 65 years old and over, compared with 11% of persons of non-Spanish origin. The age distributions of Hispanics have had important influences on their labor force participation rates (U.S. Bureau of the Census, 1978a).

In general, Hispanics have a higher unemployment rate than that for whites but a lower rate than that for blacks. The unemployment rate for Hispanics was 10.1% in 1977 (compared to 6.7% for all white workers), whereas the overall rate for black workers was 13.1%. Among groups of

Spanish origin, Puerto Ricans had the highest rate of unemployment in 1977, 13.6%, compared with 10.1% for Mexicans, 8.8% for those of Cuban origin, and 8.6% for persons of other Hispanic origin (Newman, 1978). Variations in jobless rates among Hispanics stem from age group differences and differences in educational attainment.

Persons of Cuban descent generally migrated to the United States with higher levels of educational attainment than either Puerto Ricans or Mexicans. The Cubans who migrated during the 1960s and 1970s were of middle-class origin, had had extensive work experience, and had marketable skills. In contrast, Mexican and Puerto Rican migrants were younger, had less work experience, less educational attainment, and fewer marketable skills. Persons of Cuban and other Hispanic heritage have also been more successfully integrated into the American economic mainstream than either Mexicans or Puerto Ricans.

Despite the stereotypes of Hispanics working in farm occupations, only 5% of employed men of Spanish origin were working in farm occupations in 1978 (U.S. Bureau of the Census, 1978a). In 1978, approximately 58% of employed Spanish men were blue-collar workers, an additional 24% were white-collar workers, and 13% were employed as service workers.

Employed men of Spanish origin had lower median incomes in 1977 than did men who were not of Spanish origin ($7797 and $10,261, respectively). Nearly 21% of Spanish-origin families had incomes below the poverty level compared with 9% of families of non-Spanish origin. Among adults aged 25 to 29 years, 57% had completed at least a high school education.

The Hispanic population is a diverse one, and their career development needs should take into account the diversity of their migratory patterns, educational attainment levels, unemployment rates, and prior levels of work experience and skill development.

Native Americans

There are about 800,000 American Indians in the United States (Youngman & Sadongei, 1974), and most of them are concentrated in five states: Oklahoma, Arizona, California, North Carolina, and New York. According to Johnson (1975), Native Americans may be the most economically disadvantaged group in this country. Gerlach (1972) has observed that 50% of the Native Americans in the labor force who lived on reservations were unemployed. More recent data from the United States Commission on Civil Rights (1978), has noted that the unemployment rate for male American Indian and Alaskan Natives was 12.2% in 1976. Hence, in 1976, the American Indian and Alaskan Native male unemployment rate was 2.07 times as high as the rate of majority males (U.S. Commission on Civil Rights, 1978).

According to Johnson (1975), the American Indian population is experiencing a period of change—economically, socially, and culturally. Similar to the Hispanics, the American Indian population is young and becoming more urban. In 1970, for example, the median age for Indians was 20.4 years. Also, in 1970, the American Indians were the only minority group classified as predominantly rural. Between 1960 and 1970 the percentage of American Indians classified as rural declined from 70% to 55%. As Johnson (1975) has stated: "Many Indians, especially the young, have sought employment opportunity in urban areas during the decade. And this has brought about a change in lifestyle, occupation, and certain attitudes and customs [p. 3]."

According to Richardson (1981), the plight of the American Indian is one of hardships, incarcerations, and degradations. Richardson (1981) stated that: "One out of three Indians will be jailed at sometime during his/her lifetime. . . . The life expectancy of Indians is 44 years. . . . Approximately 25 to 35 percent of all Indian children are separated from their families and placed in foster homes, adoptive homes, or institutions. . . . Suicide is seven times the national rate, and 75 to 80 percent or more of all suicides among Indians are alcohol related [pp. 216–217]."

The career development problems of American Indians are severe, and isolation on the reservation from the mainstream of American culture delimits their knowledge of the world of work. Moreover, American Indians have a number of cultural traits that collide with the values of majority American society. For example, Youngman and Sadongei (1974) have noted that it is considered bad manners to speak of one's accomplishments. Career knowledge and experience of American Indians is often restricted to those occupations that are visible on the reservations.

Social psychological, economic, and educational attainment levels and labor force participation rates from the background for analyzing the career behavior of American ethnic minorities. The social and economic history of each group has had profound influences on their career development.

OCCUPATIONAL PRESTIGE, MOBILITY, AND SEGREGATION

Occupational Prestige and Racial Minorities

In addition to knowing some basic demographic information on racial minorities, it is important to examine the types of occupations in which minorities are represented. An important area here is occupational prestige. The term occupational prestige generally refers to the honor or social esteem usually accorded to individuals working in an occupation. To measure occupational prestige, members of a society are usually asked to evaluate occupational categories in terms of their relative standing or general desirability. In general, research has found that the esteem or social status that the general population gives occupations is an important factor affecting their occupational choice. Individuals tend to be drawn to occupations that have high social prestige and to move away from occupations with lower prestige rankings.

Moreover, the prestige rankings of occupations has remained fairly stable over a number of decades. For example, Kanzaki (1976) conducted a study investigating the prestige rankigns of a wide range of occupations from 1925 to 1975. Kanzaki (1976) found that there are clear-cut differences in the social status of occupation and that there is stability in the rankings of occupations from 1925 to 1975. He concluded that "the occupations that people select have a critical psychological and sociological impact, not only on them but also on their families [p. 104]."

The U.S. Commission on Civil Rights (1978) developed a mean occupational prestige value index in order to compare the prestige value of occupations held by racial minorities and majority males. The Commission found that blacks, American Indians/Alaskan Natives, Mexican Americans, and Puerto Ricans of both sexes typically have much less prestigious occupations than majority males. The Commission (1978) concluded:

> Despite more rapid movement toward more prestigious jobs, most minority male groups still have much lower prestige scores than majority males.
>
> The female groups show a far different pattern. Although each minority male group had its lowest indicator value in 1960 and the highest in 1976, among the female groups the following had their worst scores in 1976: Mexican American, Puerto Rican, and majority [p. 38].

Farley (1977) also used prestige scores to examine trends in the types of occupations held by nonwhites and white workers. He found that since the 1950s there has been a modest upgrading of the occupations pursued by white workers, but "among nonwhites there has been a more dramatic shift into higher status jobs and thus racial differences in occupational prestige have declined [p. 196]." Despite the improvements noted, Farley observed that these changes have not eliminated the very large gap pursued by whites and nonwhites. Farley (1977) concluded: "Despite three and one-half decades [from 1950 to 1975] of improvements, the average prestige score for nonwhite workers in 1975 was inferior to that of white workers in 1940 [p. 198]."

Concept of Occupational Segregation and Mobility

Two primary concerns expressed in the literature on racial American minorities have focused on the issues of occupational segregation and mobility. The concept of occupational segregation deals with the critical issue of whether individuals in different groups have different occupations.

According to the U.S. Commission on Civil Rights (1978), the "term segregation reflects the extreme degree of separation of races, ethnic groups, or sexes that can result from deliberate acts of channeling and restricting choices and opportunities [p. 39]." Employment segregation refers to those situations in which minorities and women have different employers than majority males, resulting in segregated work settings. In contrast, the term occupational segregation is used to describe the situation in which minorities have different occupations or types of jobs regardless of where or for whom they work (U.S. Commission on Civil Rights, 1978). For example, in a typical hospital setting, the white male is usually the doctor, the white female the nurse, the black female the nurses aid, and the black male the orderly.

The U.S. Commission on Civil Rights (1978) used the "index of similarity" to measure the occupational segregation of minorities. Basically, this index represents the percentage of a group who would have to change occupations in order for the group to have the identical occupational distribution as the comparison group, in this instance, white males. In 1976, for example, 37.9% of black males would have had to change their occupations in order for their group to be employed in the same occupations in the same proportions as majority males. Analyzing data from 1970 to 1976, the U.S. Commission on Civil Rights (1978) found two generalized patterns based on their index of occupational dissimilarity. First, occupational segregation had increased substantially for most groups, but especially for Asian Americans and Hispanics. Blacks had made some progress in the relative distribution in the occupational structure. Second, from two-thirds to three-fourths of the minority females would have to change occupations in order for their groups to have occupational distributions similar to the majority males.

Clearly, there has been some occupational mobility for minorities and women. The Commission (1978) noted, for example, that from 1965 to 1970, approximately 40% of the minority and female populations changed occupations, implying at least some possibility for improvement in the types of occupation for minorities and females in comparison to majority males. Although minorities were upwardly mobile, they were considerably less upwardly mobile than majority males. In fact, some changes in jobs for minorities meant a decrease in occupational prestige.

Not all occupational segregation has to be bad. Asian Americans, for example, are generally segregated into the technological areas, occupational areas that have a high likelihood of current and continued employment. Also, one has to examine carefully the data on occupational segregation for racial minoroities. To what extent does a self-selection process take place based on group members' perceptions of open or preferred occupations?

Black Americans who continue to choose majors in the social sciences may be only further helping to segregate themselves occupationally.

The distributions of both majority and racial minority groups in the occupational structure have important implications for the American society and the field of vocational psychology. By analyzing the occupational distribution of any group, one can obtain an idea of that group's prospects for further employment and the income of its workers.

ISSUES IN VOCATIONAL PSYCHOLOGY REGARDING AMERICAN RACIAL MINORITIES

A number of issues can be raised about the adequacy with which vocational psychology deals with the career development of racial minorities. These issues include: (1) the relevance of career theories for minorities; (2) the utility of major constructs in vocational psychology; (3) the validity of vocational testing; (4) the research methods used; and (5) the accuracy of our data on American ethnic minorities. Because other chapters deal with some of the issues outlined, for example, vocational maturity, assessment, and research methodologies, these issues are mentioned briefly. The primary focus is on the relevance of career theories and the utility of major constructs in vocational psychology. Because most of the major constructs for vocational psychology have been based on career theories, these two issues are combined.

CAREER THEORIES: RELEVANCE OR IRRELEVANCE FOR MINORITIES

Much has been written about the relevance or irrelevance of theories for American ethnic minorities (Griffith, 1980; June & Pringle, 1977; Osipow, 1975, 1976; Smith, 1975; Warnath, 1975). In general, two positions have appeared most frequently in the career literature: (1) one that has tended to dismiss career theories as irrelevant, or at the very least severely limited in application to racial minorities; and (2) another that has tended to acknowledge the shortcomings of career for special groups, although still pointing out their overall value for understanding vocational development. The question of just how applicable career theories are for racial minorities is an important one. Currently, career theories form the basis of how vocational psychologists conceptualize the work-related behavior of individuals. As Picou and Campbell (1975) have stated: "Theories provide the basis for classifying and organizing phenomena, explaining past events, predicting future events, and understanding how specified structures of relationships merge in a meaningful manner [p. 1]." Perhaps, equally as important, research based on theories of career behavior has often been used to make important policy decisions regarding funding of occupational programs for minority youth and adults.

Criticisms of career theories have been several: (1) they were developed from restricted or majority populations; (2) they are based on some faulty assumptions; (3) they are not the most meaningful for minority populations; (4) they tend to ignore the social psychological realities that shape racial minorities' lives; and (5) they tend to ignore the changing economic and social situation. For example, Warnath (1975), Griffith (1980), June and Pringle (1977), and Picou and Campbell (1975) have observed that existing theories of career behavior are based on limited samples of middle-class majority male Americans. Generally speaking, the Ginzberg, Ginsberg, Axelrad, & Herma (1951) theory of career development, Super's (1953) Middletown's study, Roe's theory of career choice, and Holland's (1959) theory of personality and work environments were developed primarily from research on white males. Most theories also tend to stress a career pattern that is continuous, uninterrupted, and progressive, wherein both psychological and economic resources are available to aid the individual's purposeful career development. Given these set of circumstances, there is the likelihood that a high correspondence will exist between a person's self-concept and vocational self-concept.

These conditions do not usually reflect the life circumstances of racial minorities, especially black Americans, Hispanics and Native Americans. For example, LoCasio (1967) has pointed out that the career development of black Americans may be delayed or impaired because of external constraints. Likewise, Osipow (1975) has stated:

> For poor black males, no real exploration period may ever occur. A job may be taken, often in the very early teens while other youngsters are still vicariously exploring the world of work. Following the initial job, a succession of unrelated jobs may occur, possibly extending over the next fifty years. These jobs may be interspersed with varying periods of unemployment or partial employment. In fact, the career pattern of poor, black males may not include stages in the usual sense of the term [p. 18].

Life-stage development as typically described by career theorists may have limited generalizability to racial minorities. External constraints, limited economic resources, and racial discrimination make the concept of life-stage development for racial minorities more of a dream than a reality for all but the most persistent, the most fortunate, and the group or mixture of individuals perceived as most socially desirable within a given racial group. For both minority and majority Americans, vocational psychologists must begin to reexamine the concept of life-stage development for its meaningfulness in the current work world. The concept of career development implies a life of planfulness that, given the survival orientation and catch-as-catch-can life of individuals from lower socioeconomic backgrounds, may not be possible or reasonably attained.

There are also other underlying assumptions that need to be called into question when examining the career behavior of racial ethnic minorities. Most career theories and current career education philosophy have assumed that dignity exists in all work (K. Hoyt, 1974; L. B. Hoyt, 1978). This concept, although attractive to vocational psychologists, neither reflects the reality of many individuals' work lives nor the career literature that shows there is in American society (and most societies in the world) a clear hierarchy by which jobs are ranked from very high to very low in desirability. Often when vocational psychologists speak about the dignity of all work they are confusing issues. People may have or experience dignity because they are able to work to provide for themselves economically; they may or may not believe that their occupation is rejected by society. Vocational psychologists need to reexamine the concept of the dignity of all work and its corollary that work is central to the lives of all individuals. For both minority and majority Americans, work may simply help to mark the passage of time. When one's job is desirable and respected, it makes that passage of time all the more desirable and central to an individual's psychological well-being; if the job is not desirable, it may not be central to that person's life. Put in an alternate way, vocational psychologists must begin to analyze the concept of work from the perspective of racial minorities rather than from that preconceived of middle-class white men.

Another assumption of most career theories is that there exists a free and open labor market (Warnath, 1975) and that people have an array of choices about their careers. For racial ethnic American minorities, the labor market may not be free or open. As Osipow (1975) has stated: "With respect to vocational behavior particularly, it is generally implicitly assumed that people possess an array of choices about their careers. This opportunity to choose has the consequence that people are required to consider those vocational alternatives actively and to implement what appears to them to be the most desirable of the alternatives [p. 9]."

Warnath (1975) has challenged the assumption that persons with sufficient motivation, information, and guidance can move through education and the labor force to satisfying jobs. From his perspective, this position represents the propaganda of the status quo. Moreover, such a position focuses too exclusively on the characteristics of individuals and their vocational decision making. Warnath (1975) has stated:

Vocational psychologists have centered their theories of vocational decision making on the individual. They have assumed an open market, the dignity of all work and, as Stubbins (1973) has put it, the persons "ability to operate free of environmental constraints" . . . As leading advocates of populism and romantic individualism, vocational theorists have concentrated their attention almost exclusively on those characteristics of the individual that can be exploited in the individual's search for self-realization [p. 425].

Warnath's (1975) comments have particular significance for ethnic minorities. All too often the career literature has left us with the impression that if we could only change the attitudes of minorities, all would be well with the world—more minorities would have self-fulfilling jobs, more minorities would have jobs at all. Economic facts, like recession and high unemployment rates are cast aside. Clearly, in encouraging ethnic minorities to search for the source of their job problems primarily in themselves rather than in the prevailing economic and social conditions, vocational psychologists are leading some ethnic minorities astray and perhaps discouraging them from dealing with other sources of their problems.

Likewise, Griffith (1980) has maintained that career theories must attempt to deal with the "issue of attribution of cause." That is, researchers must begin to analyze more carefully if the patterns observed in the career behavior of ethnic minorities should be attributed to minorities themselves or to the effects of a restricted opportunity structure. According to Griffith (1980), black Americans respond to three levels of the American opportunity structure: the ideal, perceived, and real. The ideal opportunity structure symbolizes the American ideal of equal access to employment opportunity, whereas the perceived opportunity structure "represents what is subjectively seen as the obtainable," as opposed to ideal choices. " . . . The perceived opportunity structure is less than the ideal and less than the real [pp. 303–304]." The career behavior of many poor ethnic minorities is likely to emphasize the perceived and real opportunity structure.

There are other more specific limitations of career theories for ethnic American minorities. Osipow (1975) has pointed out that career theories represent the ideal career development of individuals at the upper level professional and vocational activities, and that the occupational environments described by Holland may not be equally available to ethnic minorities because of level bias. For example, many poor black and Hispanic males may be channeled into lower-level Realistic and Conventional-type careers. A similar situation exists with Roe and Klos' (1969) conically shaped occupational classification system. Top-level jobs, where the cone is wide, have highly differentiated psychological environments whose access may be limited to ethnic minorities because of racial discrimination, social and economic factors, and personal skill characteristics (Osipow, 1975).

Moreover, Super's (1953) theory, which views career development as mainly a process of implementing one's self-concept, also has limitations in applications for racial minorities. For many of the reasons cited previously, ethnic minorities may not be able to implement their self-concept during their career course. In fact, the jobs that many minority individuals hold may constitue a direct challenge to their self-concept. To protect their sense of worth as individuals, members of racial minority groups may have to separate their personal self-concept from their work self-concept. Reference groups other than the work group may assume greater salience in the lives of racial minorities, not necessarily because of any inherent differences in values but out of survival needs.

Thus, as Osipow (1975) has suggested, many minorities who enter lower-entry-level jobs do not attempt to implement their self-concept in the traditional ways that vocational psychologists have theorized. Often times, such individuals are following the "path of least resistance." That is, they know ahead of time that the jobs they seek, the jobs that are open to them, or the jobs that they qualify for in terms of their skills will not allow them to implement their self-concept. Career development as a process of implementing one's self-concept is a fast eroding dream for many Americans, and not just racial minorities. One good example of this is the increasing number of underemployed majority college students.

Brief mention should also be made of Super's (1955, 1964) construct of vocational maturity, a construct that is used widely in the career literature. Theoretically, vocational maturity and the instruments that are based on it are supposed to measure the rate and progress of an individual in mastering vocational tasks. However, my own research (Smith, 1976) as well as that of others (Westbrook & Mastie, 1973) has raised some questions about this construct. For example, the concept of career maturity suggests: (1) that we truly understand the concept of career development; (2) that there is a career life-stage development that can be applied to all or most groups in American society; (3) that there are common vocational tasks that should be mastered, with little or no differentiation based on one's race, sex, or socioenonomic status; and (4) that the mastery of these tasks leads to healthy career development and increases one's likelihood of making good/satisfactory career choices.

These assumptions are problematic for majority Americans, let alone ethnic minority Americans. First, there is no clear consensus as to what career development actually entails. Theorists have conceptualized the process of career development differently. Second, there is some evidence that the life-stage development of women (Zytowski, 1969) and some racial minorities (especially lower socioeconomic blacks, Hispanics, and Native Americans) may be different from that of white males. Third, a person's minority status, whether racial or sexual, may add additional tasks not currently taken into account. For example, one career-related rask of racial minorities may be that they have to come to terms with the issue of race and what this means for their career development in American society. Racial minorities who have succeeded in climbing the occupational ladder to implement their career choices have often had to use various coping strategies and mechanisms to transcend societal limitations placed on their even considering certain careers, let alone their preparing for and entering their chosen careers.

The current concept of career maturity does not adequately take these factors into account. The concept of career maturity makes many of the previously noted assumptions that were assumed by vocational theories, namely that there exists an environment that encourages/supports an uninterrupted and progressive career development that allows for exploration and crystallization of career choice alternatives. Like the theories of career behavior, the construct of career maturity may represent the ideal rather than the real aspects of individuals' occupational development.

Fourth, there is some debate as to whether or not instruments of career maturity actually measure all the aspects of maturity that they purport to measure (Westbrook & Mastie, 1973). There is limited evidence to suggest, for example, that the Career Maturity Inventory (CMI) may be only measuring middle-class reference group perspectives or outlooks on work and life (Smith, 1976) or measuring only cognitive ability (Westbrook, Butts, Madison, & Arcia, 1980).

The Validity of Vocational Testing, Research Methods, and the Accuracy/Meaningfulness of Data on Ethnic American Minorities

As noted previously, only brief mention is made about the issue of vocational testing and its corollary issue involving the meaningfulness of the research that has been conducted. Much criticism has surrounded the issue of testing racial minorities, regardless if such testing has involved academic or career interest tests (Williams, 1975, 1978). Recent studies have shown however, that certain interest tests may have validity for racial minorities, although limitations have been noted (Borgen & Harper, 1973; Doughtie, Chang, Alston, Wakefield, & Yom, 1976; Harrington & O'Shea, 1980; Kimball, Sedlacek, & Brooks, 1973). An important task of the counselor is knowing which career tests are appropriate for racial minorities and how to counsel members of such groups about their test scores. For example, problems have been noted in the career maturity tests as to whether they are measuring career maturity or middle-class outlooks on life or cognitive reality.

Summary. Some of the underlying assumptions and theoretical constructs of career theories may have limited relevance to racial minorities, especially those from lower socioeconomic backgrounds. In analyzing the career behavior of ethnic minorities, we need to ask ourselves: What do we mean by career development? To what extent can this concept be applied to various racial groups? What are the significant variables in racial minorities' career behavior? Although many career theories have mentioned the importance of situational variables on individual's career development, they have done so in abstract terms and global terms, making it difficult to operationalize or, at the very least, measure the concepts presented. It seems clear, for example, that family history, peers, the community in which one is reared, the socioeconomic status, individuals' perceived view of the opportunity structure, their explosure to a variety of work role models, and the amount and level of accurate career information have an impact on individuals' career development. The central question is: how much of an influence, under what circumstances, when, and for whom? Although we continue to treat racial minorities as homogeneous groups, they are not. Equally important, we need to understand better if our methods of intervening, which are often based on existing career theories, are also culture-bound. We need to know, for example, when our career-oriented interventions should occur to have the maximum impact or benefit on individuals' progress.

Because much of our understanding of individuals' career behavior comes from studies that have used various measurement devices that have not typically included members from minority groups, we must be aware of the potential limitations of these instruments in assessing the career behavior of members from these groups. Career assessment inventories based on the vocational behavior of restricted samples may miss or exclude important material from culturally different racial groups. In addition, many of the generalizations made about ethnic minorities are based on such limited samples that one cannot feel at all confident that either the similarities or differences observed with majority Americans would hold true if larger, more broadly based samples were used.

SPECIFIC CAREER BEHAVIOR OF ETHNIC AMERICAN MINORITIES

Vocational psychologists have explored various dimensions of racial minorities' career behavior, for example, their work attitudes, knowledge of occupational information, career aspirations and expectations, interests and choices, vocational maturity, and in general, the social psychological factors that presumably affect their career growth. As noted previously, information about these various aspects of career development have not been investigated uniformly among the various minority groups.

Work Attitudes

The concept of work attitudes is an important one in vocational psychology, presumably because attitudes reveal individuals' motivation for work—what they are willing to sacrifice to achieve their occupational goals, and how they view work in relationship to other aspects of their lives. It has been assumed that individuals who have positive work attitudes will view work as central to their lives and as a basis for evaluating themselves and relative importance in life. Despite the challenges of researchers to the work ethic itself (Warnath, 1975), much of American society still ostensibly operates on the basis of the Protestant Work Ethic, the ethic that regards work as a virtue in and of itself. The idle person in American society has tended to be regarded as a parasite, and as a person who makes little meaningful contribution to the rest of the world. American society is essentially a work-oriented society, wherein workaholics (meaning those who are addicted to work) are both criticized and exalted (Machklowitz, 1980). Ethnic minority Americans who reject work on the basis that their work is a dead-end street or that they have little chance for occupational mobility receive little sympathy from majority Americans.

Few studies have been conducted on the work attitudes of Asian Americans, Hispanics, and Native Americans. One can only infer the work attitudes from research studies that describe these groups' cultural values. According to Sue (1975), Asian Americans appear to have strong work values. The strong work orientation of Asian Americans is based on three factors: (1) their opportunity to establish many of the independent work behaviors exhibited previously in their native lands; (2) the decreased social distance and more accepting attitudes of majority Americans toward them, hence their opportunity to participate more fully in the work than other racial minority groups; and (3) their willingness to adopt the work values and assimilate into the mainstream of American life.

The work attitudes of Native Americans are likely to be affected by their work experiences on the reservations and within the general American society. Spencer, Windham, and Peterson (1975) have pointed out the limited exposure of Native Americans to the full range of occupations within the United States and the impact that high unemployment rates may have on the work attitudes of Native Americans. Richardson (1981) has provided some insight regarding the value differences between Native Americans and majority Americans. According to him: "No two races could so grossly differ in value systems than the American Indian and white [p. 225]." Richardson (1981) has listed two work-related values of American Indians. These values are contrasted with those of whites. The American Indian value system states: "Work for a purpose—once you have enough then quit and enjoy life, even if for just a day." In contrast the Anglo perspective is seen as: "Work for retirement—plan your future and stick to a job, even if you don't like it." The American Indian adheres to the maxim: "Live with your hands—manual activity is sacred," compared with the Anglo value system that suggests: "Live with your mind . . . show the teacher how well you know the answers to questions he/she might ask of you [p. 226]." It can be hypothesized that these differences in value systems can influence the work attitudes and career behavior of Native Americans. Richardson (1981) has observed, however, that some of the Native American value systems are changing and that members of this racial group have come to realize that the only way to succeed is through education.

Cultural conflicts in attitudes toward work have also been noted for Hispanics, although membership in this group is so diverse that only the most general comments can be made. Chandler (1974) studied the value orientation of Mexican Americans in a southwestern city. Among the variables studied were emphasis on family relationships, education, and occupational primacy. Chandler (1974) found high levels of familism or emphasis on the family in all age groups of Mexican Americans and that the importance of occupational primacy was negatively associated with age; younger Mexican Americans demonstrated greater occupational primacy. Some of the questions that measured occupational primacy included: "The most important purpose of the public schools is to prepare people for occupational success; the best way to judge a man's worthiness is by his success in his occupation [p. 270]." A positive relationship existed between modernity or the adjustment to the dominant American value system and occupational primacy. Moreover, persons in the sample who were in higher level occupations were less familistic,and education was the most powerful influencer in the adoption of modern work values of Mexican Americans. It appears that a dominant issue for Hispanics may be the primacy that work should assume in comparison with traditional values regarding the family.

Much of the research on work attitudes and ethnic minorities has focused on black Americans. Because studies on the work attitudes of this group have been summarized elsewhere (Smith, 1975, 1977), only a brief overview of some of the issues and findings are presented here. Prior to 1975, the preponderance of studies on the work attitudes of black Americans tended to indicate that members of this racial group have negative work attitudes (Lefton, 1968; Lipsman, 1967; Murphy, 1973; Neff, 1967; Shlensky, 1972). It was generally hypothesized that black people view work more extrinsically than intrinsically and emphasize lower-order security needs more than toward their higher-order needs for self-fulfillment and self-actualizatiion (Lipsman, 1967).

The findings of many of the studies that showed negative attitudes of black people toward work were used to set important educational, counseling, and governmental funding policies for work programs for members of this racial group (Smith, 1977). For example, career educationalists designed programs to change the work attitudes of young black children; and some state and federal manpower training programs were also directed toward modifying disadvantaged black workers' job attitudes (Gottlieb, 1979). It was theorized that if the attitudes of these workers could be changed to reflect a positive orientation toward work, many of their work-related problems would be reduced substantially.

On the basis of Smith's (1977) review of the literature, several conclusions were reached. First, findings regarding the work attitudes of black Americans were conflicting. Whereas some studies found that blacks held negative attitudes toward work, other studies found just the opposite. In fact, in some instances, black workers not only held more positive attitudes toward work than did a comparable sample of whites, but also they viewed work as a more centralizing force in their lives than did whites. Second, most blacks subscribed to the common success goals of American society. This was a point that Merton (1968) had made earlier in his research.

Third, black Americans approached the world of work with both lower-order and higher-order needs regardless of their socioeconomic status, and the salience of either category of needs was an interaction of social psychological factors, racial discrimination, and employment circumstances. Fourth, race and socioeconomic status were confounded in many of the studies reviewed, thereby making it difficult to ascertain which was the more important variable in determining work attitudes. Fifth, studies did not demonstrate clearly the relationship of work attitudes to work behavior. Presumably, if work attitudes constitute a significant variable, one should be able to determine the relationship of attitudes to work behavior. Sixth, Smith (1977) concluded that more studies were needed to investigate the possible impact of racial discrimination on work attitudes.

More recent investigations of work attitudes and alienation have tended to support some of Smith's (1977) conclusions. For example, Gottlieb (1979) has challenged the belief that lower-socioeconomic black youth are alienated from both society in general and work. According to Gottlieb (1979), an important issue related to alienation is adjustment to limited prospects. From Gottlieb's (1979) perspective, there is little reason to believe that alienation is more characteristic of poor and minority youth than it is characteristic of majority, middle-class youth. In fact, the argument could be made that adjustment to limited employment prospects would "generate greater adjustment problems for the middle-class than lower-class young simply because more affluent youth hold higher expectations and are under greater social pressure to achieve [p. 100]."

In addition, research cited by Raspberry (1981) has raised serious questions regarding which is more important: the work attitudes of lower socioeconomic, primarily black youth or the attitudes of employers toward such youth. The data upon which Raspberry (1981) based his article were taken from a recent study conducted by the Manpower Demonstration Research Corporation of New York. Working under grants from the Rockefeller Foundation, the Rockefeller Brothers Fund, and the U.S. Department of Labor, this corporation investigated the extent to which private businesses were willing to hire disadvantaged youths and the reasons why. A total of 6000 private businesses were recruited as work sponsors with the prime sponsors, CETA agencies, subsidizing the workers' pay ranging up to 100%.

The findings regarding the willingness of private businesses to participate in the project and their views toward the youth who did so were instructive. According to Raspberry (1981), "only 18 percent of the employers who were offered a 100 percent wage subsidy agreed to participate in the project. When the subsidy was set at 75 percent, the participation rate fell to 10 percent. At a 50 percent subsidy, the participation rate was only 5 percent [p. 36]."

Although the most frequently cited reasons for nonparticipation were that the employer did not have enough work or that the work available required higher skills than high school students could offer, a closer analysis of the employers revealed other factors that were related to employers' attitudes toward the young, primarily disadvantaged workers. The employers simply did not want the young people around, even though these young peoples' work habits and attitudes were on a par or better than those of the typical, more traditionally employed workers. On the basis of his review of the study, Raspberry (1981) concluded:

> It seems clear that employers tended to see the youngsters as not worthwhile—even when no money was involved. On the other hand, 80 percent of those who did participate found the youth's work habits, attitudes and willingness to work average or better; three-fourths found their performance improving over time, and two-thirds said the young workers required no more supervision than they had originally anticipated [p. 30].

These data indicate that the work attitudes of employers, especially those in the private sector, may be of equal or perhaps even greater significance than the attitudes that have been attributed to low-income, minority youth. More studies are needed to assess the attitudes of employers.

Occupational Information

Occupational information is considered an important aspect of career development. It has been suggested that those individuals who have a good, broad-based knowledge of the work are better suited to make career-related decisions. Several dimensions of occupational information are usually mentioned as important; these include knowledge of self, knowledge of occupations and their current outlooks, and information about the education and training needed to obtain jobs. A major role of the counselor is to help young people and adults integrate educational, personal, and occupational information.

Studies that have researched the level and amount of occupational information young people possess have found that youth need greater occupational information than they currently possess. For example, Prediger, Roth, and Noeth (1973) collected occupational data from a nationally representative sample of 32,000 students in 200 schools in 1973. These investigators found that most students stated they could use better occupational information and greater assistance in making career decisions. Nearly 78% of the eleventh grade students sampled stated that they needed help in making career plans, and the expressed need for assistance in making career plans increased from the eighth to the eleventh grade. Students reported that they received less help than they needed and their limited tested knowledge of the world of work and the career planning process reinforced their statements.

Although the lack of adequate occupational information is an issue for both minority and majority American youth, the situation appears to be more dire for minority youth. Spencer, Windham, and Peterson (1975) have reported that occupational information of Choctaw youth was limited to eight occupations on or near their reservation. Kuvlesky and Juarez (1975) have observed similar problems in Mexican American youths' degree and level of occupational information.

Davidson (1980) has noted that black youth are severely hampered by the lack of information regarding job availability. Osterman (1978) found that compared to white youth, black youth depended on formal networks (employment agencies, placement offices) because the informal connections of parents, friends, and neighbors were insufficient to them. However, Mangum (1978) has reported that employers use informal contacts and closed systems before they use public agencies and placement offices. Thus, the black youth who depends on formal networks of employment agencies and placement offices is at a decided disadvantage.

Recent studies on black females have indicated that their knowledge of the occupational system falls far short of that of young white females. The Ohio State University's Center for Human Resource Research conducted a 5-year study of the work experience of a sample of over 5000 women who were 14 to 24 years of age when first surveyed in 1968 (U.S. Department of Labor, 1973). The results of the study revealed that young black women were less knowledgeable about the world of work than were young white women. Black females scored lower on the occupational information test than did white women. Females who scored high on the occupational information test were more likely to be employed than were those who scored low on the test. In addition, high scorers on the occupational information test were more often found in white-collar positions and in higher-paying jobs than the low scorers. These patterns existed for young women of both races; however, the differences were more pronounced for black than for young white females.

Gottfredson (1978) analyzed data from the 1973–1974 assessment of career and occupation development conducted by the National Assessment of Educational Progress (1977). This assessment was established to measure the development of occupational skills, knowledge, attitudes, and decision making in a nationally representative sample of 9-year-olds, 13-year-olds, 17-year-olds, and adults aged 26–35. Data for the 9-year-old age group were not reported by Gottfredson. The remaining three age groups were asked to list 10 things a person should consider when choosing a job. In the 13-year-old age group, black males and black females had higher percentages of people unable to name any things to be considered when choosing a job. The same general findings held true for the 17-year-olds and the adult group. At age 13, only 6.2% of the white males whose parents' education was less than 12 years were unable to name any things to be considered when choosing a job; for the other groups studied, the percentages were respectively 3.6% white females, 6.2% black males, and 28.2% black females. Among 13-year-olds, black females had the highest percentage of individuals who were unable to name any things to be considered when choosing a job.

Clearly, the amount, level, and type of occupational information a person has may have an important impact on his or her career behavior. Minority youth, especially black Americans, Hispanics, and Native Americans have been found to have less occupational information than majority Americans.

Career Aspirations and Expectations of Ethnic Minorities

Generally speaking, vocational psychologists have maintained that career aspirations and expectations constitute important aspects of a person's career development (Nafziger, Holland, Helms, & McPartland, 1974). A person's level of aspiration has been viewed as significant because it appears to affect curriculum choice and career choice. For example, Merton (1957, 1968) proposed that young people maintain a "frame of aspirational reference [pp. 132–133]" composed of personal goals for status attainment when they become adults. The greater congruency between aspirations and expectations, the more likely that the individual is vocationally mature

(Crites, 1969). Moreover, career aspirations and educational attainment goals are often related. Individuals who have high educational attainment goals often times have similarly high career goals.

As in the other areas discussed, differences exist in the amount of data on career aspirations for black Americans, Asian Americans, Hispanics, and Native Americans. There is considerably more information on black Americans and Hispanics than on the other two racial groups.

Vocational aspirations begin in early childhood; however, few researchers have investigated the aspirations of minority children. The research of Vondracek and Kirchner (1974) has provided some information regarding the vocational aspirations of minority children. Vondracek and Kirchner investigated the career aspirations of 282 children between the ages of 0–3 and 5–11 from 51 Pennsylvania day-care centers. The sample consisted of black and white, male and female children from large metropolitan and adjacent sururban areas. Vondracek and Kirchner (1974) found that career development begins in early childhood and involves "mastery of the task of projecting oneself into the future and conceiving of oneself as one day achieving adult status. Race comparisons indicated that urban blacks were less mature than urban whites in terms of mastery of the vocational projective task seen as characteristic of this developmental period [p. 251]." Although no significant sex differences were found in the rate of development, Vondracek and Kirchner found indications that the pattern of vocational projection differed for males and females, with females undergoing occupational foreclosure earlier than their male counterparts. Females had fewer fantasy responses than males, and urban black children were less able to project themselves into the vocational future than urban white children. Black children also evidenced a less highly differentiated conceptualization of adult role characteristics than did their white peers. From Vondracek and Kirchner's study, one could conclude that differences in the vocational aspirations of black and white children begin in early childhood and continues throughout their later development.

Frost and Diamond (1978) surveyed fourth-, fifth-, and sixth-grade public school black, Hispanic, and Anglo children regarding their career choices and perceptions of the appropriateness of selected occupations for male and female children and adults. The findings showed that Hispanic and Anglo girls chose more nontraditional, higher-status occupations than black girls; however, no significant relation was found between the career choices of boys and their ethnic group membership. Young black girls demonstrated the most stereotypic views of job appropriateness, whereas no clear trend was shown in the view of Hispanic girls. Overall, Frost and Diamond (1979) noted that subjects who "stereotyped child jobs tended also to stereotype adult occupations, suggesting a link between the child's current experience and the more remote world of adults [p. 43]."

A significant finding of the Frost and Diamond study is related to the interaction between sex and ethnicity/race and occupational aspirations. The finding that young black American girls may tend to choose more low-status and traditionally female occupations than Anglo or majority females suggests an area of concern previously unaddressed in most of the vocational literature. Although much of the career literature has tended to focus on the influence of sex-role stereotyping for majority females, greater attention may have to be devoted to the interaction of race and sex and the consequences of this interaction for black females. Much of this concern is supported by recent research on the career development of young black females (Smith, 1980).

Data on the career aspirations of minority adolescent youth have been more extensive than on young children. Zito and Bardon (1968) investigated the achievement imagery of black adolescents in terms of how they perceived the probabilities of their success and failure in school and work. Although these investigators found strong needs for achievement among blacks, they also found that school-related measurements of success tended to threaten black adolescents with failure, even though work-related materials elicited fantasies of their successful achievement of goals. Even though subjects in the Zito and Bardon study were discouraged with their present occupational (primary school) situation, they looked forward to and anticipated a more optimistic work situation.

In general, researchers have presented antithetical points of view regarding the vocational aspirations of black adolescents. Although some investigators have reported that black youth have similar aspirations as white youth, others have declared just the opposite (Antonovsky, 1967; Dreger and Miller, 1968; Rosen, 1959). Most researchers have agreed that a great deal of discrepancy exists between black adolescents' aspirations and occupational expectations. If one controls for socioeconomic status and ability, black aspirations are generally as high or higher than whites. The problem is the lack of controls for socioeconomic status and class.

MacMichael (1974) found a discrepancy between the high educational aspirations of black youth (92% of black high school students interviewed stated they were certain they would complete college and 80% believed their parents wanted them to finish) and their low career aspirations. Approximately 30% of black students who aspired to a college degree did not aspire to a job that required such a level of educational attainment.

In contrast, Haberman (1966) has explained black adolescents' incongruity of career aspirations and expectations by noting: "Disadvantaged youngsters often overcompensate for feelings of inadequacy by assuming superficially high aspirations." Sexton (1971) has also suggested that the recent gains of black people have contributed to soaring and unrealistically high ambitions.

Cosby (1974) studied occupational expectations and the hypothesis of increasing realism of choice among black and white students in 23 rural Texas schools. The sample consisted of tenth grade students tested in 1966 and again in 1968 in order to monitor change in occupational expectations. Cosby (1974) found that black youth tended to lower their levels of occupational expectations over time. He also noted that although "race appeared to have an effect, it was of low magnitude and explained only a small portion of the variation [p. xx]." Cosby also found that occupational expectations tended to vary with changes in occupational aspirations and educational expectations. "However, family socioeconomic index, perception of occupational goal blockage, three measures of self image and change in perception of occupational goal blockage, were not found to be associated with the dynamics of occupational expectation [p. 53]."

Several researchers have investigated the issue of black college students' aspirations to traditionally open and traditionally closed occupations to black Americans. Traditionally open occupations were defined as "protected" professions that relied on mainly black clientele, for example, doctor, lawyer, teachers, and social workers. In contrast, traditionally closed occupations were defined by Littig (1968) as those that were "unprotected, required black to compete directly with whites, and made them (meaning blacks) particularly vulnerable to discrimination". Traditionally closed occupations were nuclear physicist, airline pilot, architect, and engineering. Littig's data revealed that 49% of the male sample of black undergraduates at Howard University were in majors leading to the traditionally closed occupations (meaning occupations to which minorities believe access is denied) and that there was a significant positive association between strong achievement motive and occupational risk-taking. Middle class identification for blacks was negatively associated with occupational risk-taking.

Using Littig's (1968) study as a base, Glanz (1977) examined the relationship between locus of control and black college students' aspiration to traditionally open and traditionally closed occupations. Glanz (1977) found that there was a statistically significant relationship between black students' internal sense of control and their occupational risk-taking. Those individuals who had a high internal sense of control aspired to traditionally closed occupations and those who had evidenced an external sense of control aspired to traditionally open occupations for black Americans. Moreover, according to Glanz (1977) there was a negative association between high antisystem belief and aspiration to traditionally closed occupations, "a finding which suggests that system-blame can sometimes act as a psychological barrier between an aspiring youngster and the mainstream of society . . . . it seems that an individual who faults the system repeatedly may overlook or underestimate the larger opportunities which tend to come along [p. 286]."

Kuvlesky, Wright, and Juarez (1971) examined the black, Mexican American, and Anglo adolescents' occupational and educational status projections, levels of aspiration and expectation, intensity of aspiration, and certainty of expectation. The investigators found that the three ethnic groups were generally similar; however, black youth held higher-level expectations and Mexican American youth evidenced strong intensity of aspiration. In addition, Mexican American youth were least certain of attaining their expectations, and black youth held higher goals. Kuvlesky, Wright, and Juarez (1971) conjectured that the findings regarding Mexican American youth's low expectations may indicate that members of this group have not progressed as far as blacks in the process of "dissociation" from the negative status of their ethnic status in the larger society. The investigators hypothesized that Mexican American youth, as compared with blacks, were more willing to conform to their negative status position relative to Anglos or that more of them perceived greater restrictions to their desired mobility.

In contrast, Anderson and Johnson (1971) found that Mexican American children showed a significantly strong desire to succeed, and reported experiencing the same high degree of encouragement and aid at home as their Anglo peers.

Wright (1968) conducted a review of the literature on the occupational projections of Mexican American youth. He concluded that large proportions of Mexican American youth aspired to high-prestige jobs, few aspired to jobs of low occupational status, and that the expectations of these youth were similar to their aspirations but some were lower. In general, Mexican American youth held high aspirations for intergenerational occupational mobility.

Kuvelsky and Juarez (1975) have conducted the most comprehensive studies and most thorough review of the career aspirations and vocational behavior of Mexican Americans. Citing the findings of two studies they conducted in 1967 and in 1973, Kuvelsky and Juarez (1975) concluded that: (1) overall Mexican American youth held high educational aspirations, with the majority stating they desired posthigh school education or training; (2) although educational expectations were consistently lower than aspirations, the majority of youth still anticipated posthigh school education and training; (3) the majority evidenced strong desires to attain high-level jobs; however, their expectations of achieving such positions were lower, but still relatively high; and (4) most held congruent job aspirations and expectations.

On the basis of their studies and extensive review of the literature, Kuvlesky and Juarez stated that Mexican American youth have very high and strong aspirations for occupational attainment. Kuvlesky and Juarez (1975) noted that "we must move away from simple notions of heroic easy solutions or programs—'raising aspirations of disadvantaged kids,' 'building up their self-images,' 'teaching them American values,' 'creating compensatory education.' Too often such general cure-alls are based on unfounded stereotypes and do as much or more harm than they do good [p. 284].''

Summary. Literature on the career aspirations of minority youth, especially blacks and Hispanics, has been conflicting. What does seem clear is that minority youth start off having high career aspirations, although the study conducted by Vondracek and Kirchner (1974) that black children as early as age 3 may experience some measure of identity foreclosure is not encouraging.

Although some studies have compared racial differences in career aspirations among several racial minority groups, the majority of studies have focused on comparing one racial minority group with majority Americans. More studies are needed that compare the career aspirations among the various racial minority groups as well as majority Americans. Presently, we do not know if (as Kuvlesky, Wright, and Juarez (1971) suggested) we are measuring "true" career aspirations of minority groups or their relative stages in dealing with the majority power/work structure.

In addition, research must begin to focus not just on the fact that racial minorities aspire to high-status occupations, but rather on the type of occupations to which they aspire. Herein, the studies of Littig (1968) and Glanz (1977) may be useful. Greater numbers of minority youth may want to consider nontraditional occupations.

Currently, vocational literature has tended to emphasize the importance of congruency of individuals' aspirations and expectations. Yet, given the labor market projections, not all individuals will be able to realize their career aspirations, even though they may have the necessary skills and education. In some instances, the situation is simply a matter of having too many people wanting to go into a certain occupational area with too few job openings. The role of the counselor working with individuals who are not able to find jobs to match their aspirations is unclear. Also, counselors must consider what their roles are in helping young people come to terms with their aspirations and the future projections for job openings.

Career Interests and Choices of Ethnic Minority Groups

Studies on the career interests of ethnic minorities have focused on answering mainly two questions: (1) Are the career interests of ethnic minorities similar to or different from those of white people? (2) Do the present instruments measure accurately their career interests?

Validity of interest inventories for minority groups. Debate about the appropriateness or inappropriateness of interest inventories for ethnic minorities has led to a number of studies. Williams (1978) has maintained that most psychological tests, including interest tests, have little relevance or may be biased toward blacks. Although the findings regarding the validity of vocational interest of racial minorities have been mixed, the majority of the studies have tended to show interest testing is valid for members of ethnic minority groups.

Borgen and Harper (1973) examined the validity of the Strong Vocational Interest Blank (SVIB) for measuring the career interests of blacks and whites. The sample consisted of black males who were winners of National Achievement Scholarships and white males who were winners of National Merit Scholarships. Tests were administered to individuals before they entered college in 1966 and later when they were about to enter their senior year in 1969. The findings indicated that the Occupational and Basic Scales of the SVIB had a predictive validity for blacks that equaled if not surpassed that for whites. Borgen and Harper advised against generalizing the predictive validity of the Strong Vocational Interest Blank to blacks who come from disadvantaged economic and educational backgrounds.

Whetstone and Hayles (1975) examined the relative usefulness of the SVIB for black and white men at the University of Colorado. These investigators found that the SVIB could be relevant for black students without using different norms. Nearly two-thirds of the black and three-fourths of the white students were majoring in an area judged to be consistent with their SVIB primary and secondary occupational interest patterns.

Kimball, Sedlacek, and Brooks (1973) examined black and white students' vocational interests on Holland's Self-Directed Search (SDS). The sample consisted of 143 blacks and 143 nonblacks attending the University of Maryland. The investigators found that the Self-Directed Search was equally apropriate for blacks and whites, but that blacks tended to have more first choice Social Codes.

Doughtie, Chang, Alston, Wakefield, and Yom (1976) administered the Vocational Preference Inventory (VPI) to 115 black undergraduates attending a predominantly black state university and 122 white undergraduates at a predominantly white state university. The investigators found that the overall VPI profiles of the two groups were significantly different; seven of the 11 scales yielded differences between the two groups. Blacks tended to score higher on the Social, Conventional, and Enterprising scales, whereas no differences were found on the Realistic, Intellectual, or Artistic Scale. The pattern of differences lent support to other findings that showed that blacks chose social-type occupations more often than whites (Hager & Elton, 1971).

Wakefield, Yom, Doughtie, Chang, and Alston (1975) examined the geometric relationship between Holland's personality topology and the vocational preference inventory for blacks. These investigators found that the Vocational Preference Inventory scales for black subjects corresponded generally to Holland's model but not as well as they did for white subjects. Three weaknesses in the correspondence between the scales of black students and Holland's model were identified. Wakefield et al. (1975) stated: "As Holland developed his measurements of vocationally related constructs with predominantly white samples, it is not surprising that black subjects do not correspond to them as well as white subjects. What is surprising is they do approximate the model with only a few weaknesses [p. 60]"

Several studies have investigated the concurrent validity of Holland's theory for black women. Ward and Walsh (1981) used the Vocational Preference Inventory and Self-Directed Search to examine the concurrent validity of Holland's theory for employed noncollege-degreed black women. The sample consisted of 102 black women workers in occupational environments consistent with Holland's six vocational environments. The findings showed that four of the scales of the VPI and four of the SDS successfully differentiated the occupational groups consistently with Holland's theory.

These findings tend to support the earlier ones of Bingham and Walsh (1978) who found that the VPI and SDS successfully differentiated employed college-degreed black women. In addition, O'Brien and Walsh (1976) tested the concurrent validity of Holland's theory for noncollege-degreed black working men. The results tended to suggest that Holland's theory is meaningful for employed noncollege-degreed black men.

Anadon (1977) examined the usefulness and validity of the American College Testing Interest Inventory with 58 Native American freshmen college students for the years 1973 to 1974. The findings revealed that the American College Testing Interest Inventory was valid for Native Americans. Anadon concluded differences in cultural background of individuals does not necessarily mean that they will present different interest data than that of another cultural group. A later study by Scott and Anadon (1980) also found that the American College Test Interest Inventory produced profiles for Native American college students that were valid.

Lamb (1976) administered the American College Testing Interest Inventory to samples of black, Asian American, Hispanics, and white ethnic groups of college seniors. The findings showed that the basic interest structure for each of the minority samples generally corresponded to the configuration for the white sample of the same sex. Moreover, the configurations followed the expected hexagonal pattern proposed by Holland. Lamb concluded that the Holland structure of interests was generally valid for blacks and Hispanic males.

Harrington and O'Shea (1980) studied the applicability of Holland's model and the Career Decision-Making (CDM) instrument to 148 Mexican American, 64 Puerto Rican, 26 Cuban, and 29 South American Spanish-speaking individuals. Harrington and O'Shea found that the six Holland personality types as measured by the Harrington/O'Shea System for Career Decision Making were present in four different Hispanic cultures: Mexican American, Puerto Rican, Cuban, and South American. The Holland hexagon model was found to be applicable to Spanish-speaking high school and college students.

Chu (1975) used a sample of 3538 freshmen students, 2178 American students from the University of Wisconsin and 1360 Chinese students from the University of Fu Jen to conduct a cross-cultural study of vocational interests as measured by the Strong Campbell Interest Inventory. Chu concluded the following:

> 1. The response differences between American and Chinese college students to the Strong Campbell Interest Inventory items showed that a cultural factor assumed an important role in influencing vocational interests. 2. In its present form, the Strong Campbell Interest Inventory cannot be used to measure the vocational interests of non-American Chinese. 3. To follow the results of the SCII answer sheets scored with keys prepared by Americans can be misleading in counseling Chinese college students. 4. The SCII should be carefully revised and standardized according to Chinese norms for counseling purposes in China.

Chu's (1975) study is important because of the large number of subjects, especially Chinese students, (even though subjects were non-American Chinese) who constituted the sample, and the questions raised regarding the use of American scoring keys. Chu observed that before undertaking this research project, he believed confidently as did Campbell (1974) that "American norms have been found usable in other countries as representations of the interests of specific occupations [p. 3]." After the findings of his study, Chu (1975) stated: "On what grounds, can the American norms be applied to responses from people of other cultures or to what extent are American norms valid for other cultural groups? The argument is that, once the responses are scored with the American scoring keys, the original differences have already been bleared or twisted [p. 80]."

Clearly, the question "Do interest tests measure accurately the interests of American ethnic minorities?" has not been resolved. The samples of many of the studies reviewed were often small and blurred a number of factors, including sex differences and differences in socioeconomic background.

Career Choices

Studies have revealed that minority youth are not participating in the broad spectrum of careers (Gottfredson, 1978b; Sue, 1975). Instead, they have tended to be concentrated in a limited range of occupations. For example, Gottfredson (1978b) has pointed out that enterprising and investigative occupations tend to be financially rewarding and that enterprising occupations constitute a large proportion of all jobs. The percentage of ethnic minorities, especially blacks, holding enterprising jobs is quite small compared to their proportional numbers.

With the exception of Asian Americans, most members of minority groups have majored in and sought professional employment in the social sciences—especially teaching and social work (Smith, 1980). A disproportionate number of Asian Americans have tended to major in the hard sciences, math, and technological areas, whereas few are in the social sciences (Sue, 1975).

Bayer (1972) has observed that the tendency of black college freshmen to select majors in the social sciences, education, or business did not change between 1968 and 1971. During this same time span, however, whites and Asian Americans continued to more often choose majors in the physical sciences, biological sciences, engineering, and architecture. Research by Centra (1980) has also revealed that Asian Americans who apply to graduate schools are more similar to whites than they are to Hispanics, Native Americans, or blacks. Asian Americans are more similar to whites on both the verbal and quantitative tests of the Graduate Record Examination (GRE). Their profiles, however, differ from whites because Asian Americans have higher quantitative but lower verbal scores on the GRE than do whites. For example, the Asian American group scored highest on the GRE-Q (quantitative part), whereas whites averaged highest on the GRE-V (verbal) among the Asian Americans, blacks, Hispanics, and Native Americans.

Recent data on college student majors has tended to confirm earlier studies' findings regarding the restricted career patterns of minority youth. Thomas (1980) used data from the Office of Civil Rights to study how blacks and whites were distributed in different types of higher educational institutions and in academic major fields within higher educational institutions in the mid-1970s. The findings showed that black participation in higher education in 1977 remained largely concentrated in traditionally black 4-year Southern institutions and that in 1974 blacks and females were still overrepresented in education and the social sciences and underrepresented in the technical sciences.

According to the American Council on Education's (1977) study of bachelor degrees earned among racial minorities, members of the major groups mentioned tended to earn their degrees in selected areas. For example, from July 1973 to June 1974, almost half (48.8%) of the black and nearly one-third of the Spanish-surnamed and Native American populations obtained their bachelor degrees in one of two areas: education and the social sciences. By contrast, blacks earned only 1.8% of the total number of bachelor degrees in engineering; Spanish-surnamed, 1.4%; Native Americans, .1%; and Asian Americans, 1.7%. When these four racial minority groups were combined, the figures showed that racial minorities earned 5.0% of the undergraduate degrees in engineering; 6.6% of those in the biological sciences; and 5.3% in the physical sciences (National Center for Educational Statistics, 1977). In contrast white males earned approximately 90% of the degrees in engineering during this same period. As Smith (1980) has stated:

> Clearly, racial minorities, as a group, are underrepresented in the hard sciences and engineering. Whatever the reasons may be—racial discrimination, self-imposed cultural constraints, lack of job information, or ineffectual counseling—few minority youth either aspire to or major in science and engineering. Racial minorities are continuing to pursue courses of study in which there is a dwindling job market, the salary is low, and the chance for advancement is slim. In the social science field, the number of people seeking employment is predicted to exceed available job openings (U.S. Department of Labor, 1978). In contrast, career opportunities in scientific and technological occupations are anticipated to expand throughout the mid-1980s [p. 142].

Smith (1980) observed that: (1) a concerted national effort is needed to pull minority students, especially blacks, Spanish-surnamed, and Native Americans, out of their current restricted cycle of traditional career patterns into the more nontraditional career paths of math and science; and (2) current counseling practices need to be changed to achieve this goal.

ISSUES IN RESEARCH METHODOLOGY

Investigators have also criticized vocational psychologists for the type of studies that have been conducted. For example, Griffith (1980) and Smith (1976, 1977) have observed that many of the studies conducted on ethnic minorities have failed to take into account such variables as respondents' socioeconomic status, sex, and family background. To this extent, racial minorities have been treated as homogeneous groups. Only recently have researchers begun to investigate the inique career needs of black, Hispanic, Native American, and Asian American females. The general dearth of research on minority females stands in direct contrast to the wealth of studies conducted on white females and their career development.

In addition, the majority of studies on ethnic minorities, especially black Americans, have been conducted on those from the lower class. When findings from such studies are used to generalize to the career behavior of all black Americans, unwarranted stereotypes have resulted. Moreover, most of the studies conducted on racial minorities have been cross-sectional rather than longitudinal. There is a need for increased numbers of longitudinal studies on the career behavior of American ethnic minorities.

Generally speaking, research in vocational psychology has failed to examine the aspirations and goal-striving patterns of minority youth in relation to real opportunities in the occupational work world. The studies of economically poor racial minorities has been dominated by mainly two approaches: (1) comparative analyses of blacks (or other disadvantaged racial minorities) and majority whites; and (2) examinations of the life styles of lower-class people as an exotic or deviant subculture.

Much of the black–white comparative research has been directed by white researchers who tend to assume that the only real alternative to underclass and black life is integration into mainly white society. Hence, researchers have been concerned with such questions as: How much have racial minorities moved away from their ethnic culture and assimilated into the dominant white society? What counseling interventions could be used to change the behavior of those who have not accommodated to the values and life styles of the dominant white culture? As Glasgow (1980) has stated:

> And although strategies contend that change will occur, that openings will be made available in the mainstream when blacks show the necessary readiness, what in large measure really determines Blacks' entrance into mainstream life is whether the majority is ready to accept them and, more recently, whether real roles are available in the mainstream culture. The true impact of institutional barriers and racism is denied or ignored, and stress is placed instead on altering or "improving" individual behavior that is considered dysfunctional [pp. 20–21].

No sound evaluation of any group of minorities can be completed without relating it to what is available for all in black, Hispanic, or Native American life. This means, for example, that the behavior and aspirations of black youth should be compared with those of blacks of other social classes. Such comparative studies could reveal if the underclass striving behavior and aspirations are different from those of other black strivers or are different only from those of majority Americans. In addition, studies should determine if there are some new variables in the mobility search that did not exist for earlier strivers.

JOB PROGRAMS FOR THE POOR AND MINORITY YOUTH

Job programs in the United States have a long history. Throughout American history, job programs have been used for a number of groups, including poor majority Americans, racial minorities, and the young. Perhaps job programs reached their most widespread use during the Depression of the late 1920s and early 1930s. This section will focus on the job programs developed during the 1960s and 1970s for economically poor racial minorities in the United States. Most of the job programs during these time periods have been directed mainly toward black Americans and Hispanics, and only to a minor extent toward Native Americans. Black Americans, however, have used the job programs to a higher degree than either Hispanics or Native Americans; therefore, most of the research presented here is focused on this group. In addition, a brief historical perspective on job programs is presented.

A Brief Historical Perspective

During the 1960s, the plight of the nation's poor and racial minorities surfaced more forcifully than in the previous 2 decades. A pervasive feeling was that the nation contained "pockets of poverty" whose populations required programmatic interventions to lift them out of poverty and to help them achieve a stable income earning state. As President, John F. Kennedy had proposed an approach to ghetto revitalization. His untimely death prevented full development of his administration's proposal.

During Lyndon Johnson's tenure as president in the 1960s, the inner cities exploded in protest against continued joblessness, lack of opportunity, racism, and the anticipated demise of the civil rights movement. As Glasgow (1980) has stated: "The hoax of rehabilitation without the reality of opportunity, the years of evasive social reform, and the ultimate anger at not being able to enter the broader society, especially after having one's hopes raised, provided one of the crucial elements for rebellion [p. 174]."

In response to the unrest and turbulence in the nation's inner cities, the Johnson administration vowed to wage a "war on poverty." As a result, the Office of Economic Opportunity (OEO) was created to eliminate poverty by: (1) retraining the poor in the areas of citizen participation in the organization and affairs of the community; (2) improving access to employment opportunity through affirmative action for those minorities who had the prerequisite skills; and (3) training to upgrade the skills of racial and ethnic minorities. A major development was the Manpower Development and Training Act. Programs such as the Job Corps and WIN were also developed.

By the 1970s, there was a pronounced change in American sentiments toward the poor, and especially toward the uprisings in the inner cities of our nation. A backlash developed against blacks and other minorities, with the main view being that members of these groups were receiving too much attention from national and state governments—especially in the areas of economics and job opportunities. New administrations were voted in that promised a return to "law and order" in response to the previous inner-city unrest. Much of the direct funding for training and social rehabilitation that had gone previously to the poor and their communities were withdrawn and redistributed in lump-sum payments to the state governments under a revenue sharing plan that effectively removed control of this money from inner-city and anti-poverty groups (Glasgow, 1980). In 1973, the Comprehensive Employment and Training Act (CETA) became law.

A detailed assessment of the effects of the Great Society and the War on Poverty is beyond the scope of this chapter. Although uneven, some benefits did occur. For example, in terms of absolute numbers and in percentages, the number of Americans, black and white, who were considered to be living in poverty declined during the mid- to late-1960s. Whereas before the War on Poverty, there were approximately 38 million Americans living in poverty (9.9 million blacks and 28.3 million whites), by 1969 that figure had decreased to 24.1 million, of whom 7 million were black and 17.1 million white (U.S. Bureau of the Census, 1978b). During the mid- and late-1960s, black Americans made major social and economic advances in income, employment, and education. "It has been suggested that expanded government programs, the civil rights movements, and efforts to reduce segregation and discrimination were some of the factors which contributed to this progress [p. xx]."

In order for the American society to progress effectively, alleviating the unemployment of racial minorities has to improve significantly. Lack of critical skills is the major factor that keeps underclass people on the unemployment shuttle. One of the career development needs for black, Hispanic, and Native American adult workers is for greater skill training. Black adults need to avail themselves of every opportunity for skill training—especially in the skilled trades and technological areas.

The big issue seems to be: who will do such training and who will fund it? Prior governmental efforts have met with varying success rates. As Guzzardi (1976) has pointed out, CETA's massive educational programs are often run by teachers with little experience or firsthand knowledge about jobs. Moreover, seeing profit in poverty, many entrepreneurs have started training programs for the government that are more geared toward making money than toward training workers for specific skills.

Focusing on the severely disadvantaged adult black worker, Miller and Oetting (1977) have suggested that work programs should focus on barriers to employment. Some of the barriers these investigators listed were lack of child care facilities, transportation, job qualifications, legal and financial problems, and emotional–personal problems. According to Miller and Oetting (1977), an overall program to help the severely disadvantaged should have three major components. It should: (1) deal with the work adjustment behavior of disadvantaged workers; (2) work with local employers to change those aspects of the work environment that interact with characteristics of the disadvantaged that lead to failure; and (3) identify and attack barriers to employment.

Job Programs for Minority Youth

In response to the high unemployment of minority youth, job programs have been established. Many of these job programs have been used to collect data on the social psychological orientations of poor youth. Recently, however, the overall effectiveness of such programs has been challenged, because unemployment among poor black youth remains very high (Goodwin, 1980). An analysis of studies on job programs for low-income youth is important in providing a basis for the understanding such youth career development needs. This section examines studies on low-income youth and job programs.

Maynard (1979) examined the employment patterns of experiential and control groups of youth enrolled in the National Supported Work Demonstration program. In general, the Support Work Demonstration program provided poor persons who have experienced difficulties in finding work with employment experiences, training, and counseling. The rationale of the program was that temporary employment assistance (which might last up to a year) would help individuals to find jobs in the regular labor market. The target groups of this program consisted of out-of-school youth 17 to 20 years of age who are referred to the program from a variety of sources.

Maynard (1979) found that those individuals (90% males) who were assigned to Supported Work worked longer than did the control group. Ten months after leaving the Supported Work program, both the Supported Work youth and the control group were both working about 60 hours per month and their hourly wages were nearly the same.

Maynard (1979) was unable to offer any explanation for this change in work force participation. One possible explanation might be, however, that the attention and training provided by concerned staff might have raised the youth's confidence to work.

A study by Goldenberg (1971) has also shown that intensive support and effort of concerned staff persons does make a difference in the employment experiences of severely disadvantaged youth. Subjects in Goldenberg's study consisted of low-income youth who were referred to the Residential Youth Center. Nine months after their Residential Youth Center experience, the experimental group was much more gainfully employed than the control group.

Richardson (1975) studied the labor force participation of male and female youth (two-thirds were female) from 14 Work Incentive Program (WIN). Richardson found that young women who obtained jobs through the assistance of WIN had longer immediate post-WIN employment than did other young women studied. Labor market conditions were seen to have had an important influence on the employment of post-WIN employment of participants.

Clearly, short-term work programs that provide counseling/staff support and temporary job placements do help minority youth. Youth who participate in such programs tend to manifest greater work activity immediately following their supported work experiences. They also tend to experience a decrease in work activity over time after they leave the programs. The failure of youth to continue their work activity on a long-term basis has been cited as one of the failures of work programs for poor youth. Such a position may be shortsighted, because it does not take into account such factors as the labor market conditions (meaning the general availability of jobs), racism, or other social psychological factors related to employment of black youth.

Such a position also does not take into account sufficiently programmatic issues that might have a bearing on youth employment as a result of their experiences in work programs. For example, citing his experience with the Job Corps Program, Gottlieb (1979) has pointed out:

> In a desire to explain away high attrition rates, center disturbances, failure to achieve enrollee quotas, and to persuade Congress of the difficulties of our task, we did much to contribute to the image of enrollee as alienated, hostile, emotionally distressed, and deficient in even the most basic of cognitive and interpersonal skills. . . . The strengths and motivations of enrollees were underplayed. Rather, the prevalent theme in many centers was to stress the emotional and attitudinal dimension while sacrificing relevant job-skill training and the building of bridges between the enrollees and specific employment and job opportunities. The emphasis on the minds, heads, and internal dynamics of enrollees did little to enhance job skills or posttraining placement [pp. 101–102].

Likewise, Taggart (1976) has stressed that it was only when Job Corps began to take its legislated mission seriously that significant changes did occur. As Taggart (1976) has stated: "Second, overall Job Corps performance improved rather than deteriorated when many of the frills were slashed. Training and education were narrowed to specific requirements. The key seemed to be the ability to gain access to better jobs rather than the efforts to alter attitudes and values of enrollees [p. 121]."

In areas of youth employment, training, and job programs, an undue or disproportional emphasis has been placed on youth for the success of job programs and too little emphasis has been placed on those responsible for increasing work opportunities and on those responsible for the absorption of youth into the work force. As Gottlieb (1979) has maintained, present youth employment programs and training policies/procedures reflect either naiveté or a deliberate avoidance of data-based reality. Such policies are:

> Naive in behaving as if proper skill training and an assertive work attitude alone will lead to productive and satisfying employment; unfair in implying that the major problem is with people, young or older, who are either unwilling or unable to take on reasonable work or nondeadend employment; indifferences to the hard facts of shrinking job opportunities; increased competition in job entry; a reluctance on the part of employers to hire the young; particularly those who have not completed high school, and those who are black; and indifference to the fact that most of the jobs available to poor youth, particularly those who have not completed high school and those who are not white, do not require much in the way of skill training and do not represent an opportunity for career stability, and even less in the way of job satisfaction [p. 103].

How does one evaluate realistically the Great Society, War on Poverty, and the manpower job training programs that resulted? Have minorities really been helped by such programs? To be objective in any evaluation of job programs, one must look at both their pluses and their minuses. On the minus side, the job training programs were directed at such low-level jobs that even if the trainees had been able to obtain these jobs, they would not have attained either adequate incomes or career mobility lines. The jobs that many minorities trained for under job programs were piecemeal efforts, stopgaps that provided limited job security, benefits or mobility. Training in job programs was often limited to lower-level or dead-end jobs. Successful completion of these programs did not automatically lead to a job.

Moreover, many of the job programs for the poor and racial minorities were too simplistic. They sought quick and easy answers. They failed to realize that disadvantagement is a complex problem, created in the first place by American society, but once established it becomes self-perpetuating. Even worse yet is the realization that job programs for helping blacks and other disadvantaged racial minorities have traditionally done more to assist middle-class professions (especially in the way of jobs) than they have the recipients for whom the programs were intended.

On the positive side, job training programs for the poor and racial minorities have provided some notable successes. Enrollees in job programs have shown considerable gains in both reading and math skills. They have learned some job-related skills and social habits that are important in obtaining and maintaining a job. As Sar A. Levitan and Robert Taggart (1976) have stated in their assessment of Lyndon Johnson's War on Poverty:

> The Great Society did not eliminate poverty, but the number of poor was reduced and their deprivation significantly alleviated. The Great Society did not equalize the status of blacks and other minorities, but substantial gains were made which have not been completely eroded. Significant redistribution of income was not achieved or sought, but the disadvantaged and disenfranchised were helped. The Great Society did not have any magic formula for prosperity but its policies contributed to the longest period of sustained growth in the nation's history. It did not revamp education, or assure health care for everyone, or feed all the hungry, but as a result of its efforts, the disadvantaged were considerably better educated, fed, and cared for [pp. 274–275].

Career Development Needs of Ethnic American Minorities

The career development needs of ethnic minority Americans are both similar to and different from those of majority Americans. In general, the career development needs of ethnic minorities may be placed into three categories, those that are related to the: (1) individual and group level; (2) institutional level; and (3) societal level. Variables important at the individual and group level are those that the individual may have some control over, for example, level of educational achievement, career interests, and choices. The quality and behavior of institutions have a great deal to do with the career development of both minority and majority Americans, for example, the schools and employment institutions. Broadly based societal conditions, such as the openness of the opportunity structure and the presence of racism, also may influence the career progress of minority youth.

Most of the emphasis on the career development of ethnic minorities has tended to be at the individual level. For example, Gottlieb (1979) and Taggart (1976) have observed that in the areas of youth employment, training, and job programs, an undue or disproportional emphasis has been placed on youth for the success of job programs, and too little emphasis has been placed on those responsible for increasing work opportunities and on those responsible for the absorption of youth into the work force. As Gottlieb (1979) has maintained, present youth employment programs and training policies/procedures reflect either naiveté or a deliberate avoidance of data-based reality.

For the sake of parsimony, the career development needs that have been articulated for ethnic American minorities are listed below:

1. Need for better education and higher achievement; Asian Americans provide one exception—especially in the area of quantitative achievement.

2. Need for greater occupational awareness and more accurate occupational information on both the local and national level. Ethnic American minorities should have an updating of hazardous occupational lists.

3. Need for increased numbers and occupationally diversified role models. The presence of work role models gives hope to youngsters.

4. Need for fewer environmental and racial constraints that delimit their career development.

5. Need to change the opportunity structure of American life for ethnic minorities.

6. Need for more carefully designed research that focuses on institutional, societal, and individual variables. Thus far, too many of the studies have had small samples and focused heavily on individual/intrapsychic variables.

7. Need for increased and better-informed career counselors who are knowledgeable of cultural differences/similarities.

8. Need to take into account sex differences within ethnic groups.

9. Need to revamp current vocational theories.

10. Need to revamp/reconstruct our constructs and instruments to measure career progress.

11. Need to analyze labor market realities carefully.

12. Need to diversify career interests and choices.

13. Need for greater availability of jobs to ethnic American minorities.

14. Need to reduce the occupational segregation of ethnic minorities, particularly in job categories that have little opportunity for stability or advancement.

15. Need for higher employment rates of ethnic American minorities.

SUMMARY AND CONCLUSIONS

Research on the career behavior and cultural background of ethnic minorities has been reviewed. Several conclusions seem reasonable. Ethnic minorities are not a monolithic group; there are important differences both between and within them. Race appears to be an important variable in the career development of ethnic minorities. The interaction between race and social class is noteworthy, because it functions to delimit occupational membership and attainment. Studies regarding American ethnic minorities have produced conflicting findings. This situation may stem from a number of problems, including researchers' confounding of race, sex and social class variables, lack of a clear conceptual basis for most of the research, and small samples that delimit generalizability.

Clearly, ethnic minorities have made progress within the past two decades. That progress has not been uniform across the various ethnic groups. The degree of progress a particular ethnic group has appears to be dependent on a number of factors, including the history of the group within this country, the cultural factors that clash or mesh with the dominant American value system, the social distance majority Americans feel toward a given ethnic group, and the educational achievement and career behavior of the respective groups.

Prospects for the 1980s do not look too encouraging for those individuals who are both poor and members of ethnic minority groups. Currently, American society appears to be facing a future of shrinking job opportunities, increased credentialing requirements, and increased competition in job entry. There is also reason to believe that as the American economy becomes increasingly international rather than nationally focused as it is now, labor market competition will likewise become international in scope. The competition presently observed between the Detroit automobile workers and the automobile workers of Japan could spread or have filtering affects on other related industries.

The possibility of a permanent underclass of ethnic minority Americans from lower socioeconomic backgrounds seems to be increasing rather than decreasing. The situation of ethnic minorities from middle-class backgrounds offers chance for improvement. Members of this socioeconomic category will probably experience one of several patterns: (1) a holding pattern, which allows them to maintain themselves at their current level but offers no forward movement; (2) a downward or regressive pattern in which some occupational slippage occurs because of technological developments or personal circumstances; and (3) a forward pattern, which allows them to climb the occupational career ladder.

REFERENCES

Anadon, M. The American College Interest Inventory: Its usefulness and validity with the Native American student. Unpublished doctoral dissertation, University of North Dakota, order no. 7810309, *Dissertation Abstracts,* 122-A.

Anderson, C. H. *Toward a new sociology: A critical view.* Homewood, Ill.: Dorsey Press, 1971.

Anderson, J. G., & Johnson, W. H. Stability and change among three generations of Mexican-Americans: Factors affecting achievement. *American Education Research Journal,* 1971, *8,* 285.

Antonovsky, A. Aspirations, class, and racial-ethnic membership. *The Journal of Negro College Education,* 1967, *36,* 385–393.

Bayer, A. E. *The Black college freshman: Characteristics and recent trends.* American Counsel of Education Research Reports, Vol. 8, No. 1. ACE, 1972.

Berry, G., & Lopez, C. Testing programs and the Spanish-speaking child: Assessment guidelines for school counselors. *School Counselor,* 1977, *24,* 261–269.

Bingham, R. P., & Walsh, W. B. Concurrent validity of Holland's theory for college-degreed black women. *Journal of Vocational Behavior,* 1978, *13,* 242–250.

Bogardus, E. Measuring social distance. *Journal of Applied Sociology,* 1925, *9,* 229–308.

Borgen, F. H., & Harper, G. T. Predictive validity of measured vocational interests with black and white college men. *Measurement and Evaluation in Guidance,* 1973, *6*(1), 19-26.

Bowers, N. Young and marginal: An overview of youth employment. *Monthly Labor Review,* October 1979, 4-18.

Campbell, R. E. Special groups and career behavior: Implications for guidance. In J. Picou & R. E. Campbell (Eds.), *Career behavior of special groups: Theory, research, and practice.* Columbus, Oh.:   1975, 424-444.

Centra, J. A. Graduate degree aspirations of ethnic student groups. *American Educational Research Journal,* Winter 1980, *17*(4), 459-478.

Chandler, C. R. Value orientations among Mexican Americans in a southwestern city. *Sociology and Social Research,* 1974, *58*(3), 262-271.

Cheng, C. W., Brizendine, E., & Oakes, J. What is an equal chance for minority children? *The Journal of Negro Education,* 1979, XLVIII(3), 267-287.

Chu, P-H. Cross-cultural study of vocational interests measured by the Strong-Campbell Interest Inventory. *ACTa Psychological Taiwanica,* 1975, *17,* 69-84.

Cosby, A. Occupational expectations and the hypothesis of increasing realism of choice. *Journal of Vocational Behavior,* 1974, *5,* 53-65.

Crites, J. O. *Vocational psychology.* New York: McGraw-Hill, 1969.

Crites, J. O. Foreword. In J. Steven Picou and Robert E. Campbell (Eds.), *Career behavior of special groups: Theory, research, and practice.* Columbus, Oh.: Merrill, 1975, pp. ix-x.

Davidson, J. P. Urban black youth and career development. *Journal of Non-White Concerns in Personnel and Guidance,* 1980, *8*(3), 119-142.

Doughtie, E. B., Chang, W-N, Alston, H. L., Wakefield, J. A. Jr., & Yom, B. L. Black-white differences on the Vocational Preference Inventory. *Journal of Vocational Behavior,* 1976, *8,* 41-44.

Dreger, R. M., & Miller, K. S. *Comparative psychological studies of Negroes and whites in the United States: 1959-1965.* Psychological Bulletin Monograph Supplement, 1968, p. 70.

Farley, R. Trends in racial inequalities: Have the gains of the 1960s disappeared in the 1970s? *American Sociological Review,* April 1977, *42,* 189-208.

Freeman, R. Why is there a youth labor market problem? In Bernard Anderson & Isabel Sawhill (Eds.), *Youth employment and public policy.* Englewood Cliffs, N.J.: Prentice-Hall, 1980.

Frost, F., & Diamond, E. E. Ethnic and sex differences in occupational stereotyping by elementary school children. *Journal of Vocational Behavior,* 1979, *15,* 43-54.

Gerlach, E. *The employment of American Indians in New Mexico and Arizona.* Washington, D.C.: United States Commission on Civil Rights, 1972.

Ginzberg, E., Ginsberg, S. W., Axelrad, S., & Herma, J. L. *Occupational choices: An approach to a general theory.* New York: Columbia University Press, 1951.

Glanz, O. Locus of control and aspiration to traditionally open and traditionally closed occupations. *The Journal of Negro Education,* 1977, *46,* 278-290.

Glasgow, D. G. *The black underclass.* San Francisco, Calif.: Jossey-Bass, 1980.

Goldenberg, I. *Build me a mountain: Youth, poverty, and the creation of new settings.* Cambridge, Mass.: MIT Press, 1971.

Goodwin, L. Do the poor want to work? *A social psychological study of work orientations.* Washington, D.C.: Brookings Institution, 1972.

Goodwin, L. Do the poor want to work? A social psychological perspective. *Youth and Society,* 1980, *2,* 311-351.

Gottfredson, L. S. *Race and sex differences in occupational aspirations: Their development and consequences for occupational segregation.* The Johns Hopkins University, Center for Social Organization of Schools, Grant No. NIE-G-78-0210, National Institute of Education, Washington, D.C., 1978.

Gottlieb, L. Alienation and adjustment to limited prospects. *Youth and Society,* 1979, *2,* 92–113.

Griffith, A. R. Justification for a black career development. *Counselor Education and Supervision,* 1980, *19,* 301–310.

Guzzardi, W., Jr. How to deal with the "new unemployment." *Fortune,* October 1976, pp. 132–135; 208–215.

Haberman, M. Guiding the disadvantaged. In C. E. Beck (Ed.), *Guidelines for guidance: Readings in the philosophy of guidance.* Dubuque, Ia.: W. C. Brown, 1966.

Hager, P. C., & Elton, C. F. The vocational interests of black males. *Journal of Vocational Behavior,* 1971, *1,* 153–158.

Hansen, L. S. ACES Position Paper: Counselor preparation for career development/career education. *Counselor Education and Supervision,* 1978, *17,* 168–179.

Harrington, T. F., & O'Shea, A. J. Applicability of the Holland (1973) model of vocational development with Spanish-speaking clients. *Journal of Counseling Psychology,* 1980, *27*(3), 246–251.

Hill, R. The illusion of black progress. *Social Policy,* 1978, *9,* 14–25.

Holland, J. L. A theory of vocational choice. *Journal of Counseling Psychology,* 1959, *6,* 35–45.

Hoyt, K. *A primer for career education.* U.S. Office of Education Policy Paper. Washington, D.C.: The Office of Career Education, U.S. Office of Education, 1978.

Hoyt, L. B. *An introduction to career education.* A policy paper to the U.S. Office of Education, Washington, D.C.: The Office, 1974.

Johnson, H. W. *American Indians in transition.* Agricultural Economic Report No. 283. Washington, D.C.: United States Department of Agriculture, 1975.

Jones, B. A. Utilization of Black human resources in the United States. *The Review of Black Political Economy,* 1979, *10*(1), 79–96.

Journal of Non-White Concerns. Special Issue: Testing, April 1978, 6, 3, (Guest editors: Robert L. Williams, & Willie S. Williams), 98–156.

June, L. N., & Pringle, G. C. The concept of race in the career-development theories of Roe, Super, and Holland. *Journal of Non-White Concerns in Personnel and Guidance,* 1977, *6,* 17–24.

Kanzaki, G. A. Fifty years of stability in the social status of occupations. *The Vocational Guidance Quarterly,* 1976, *25*(2), 101–105.

Kimball, R. L., Sedlacek, W. E., & Brooks, G. C., Jr. Black and white vocational interests in Holland's Self-Directed Search. *Journal of Negro Education,* 1973, *42,* 1–4.

Kinloch, G. *The sociology of minority group relations.* Englewood Cliffs, N.J.: Prentice-Hall, 1979.

Kitano, H. L., & Matsushima, N. Counseling Asian Americans. In P. P. Pedersen, J. G. Draguns, W. J. Lonnerg, & J. E. Trimble (Eds.), *Counseling across cultures* (Rev. ed.). Honolulu: The University Press of Hawaii, 1981.

Krogman, W. M. The concept of race. In R. Linton (Ed.), *The science of man in world crisis.* New York: Columbia University Press, 1945.

Kuvlesky, W. P., & Juarez, R. Mexican American youth and the American dream. In J. S. Picou & R. E. Campbell (Eds.), *Career behavior of special groups: Theory, research, and practice.* Columbus, Oh.: Merrill, 1975.

Kuvlesky, W. P., Wright, D. E., & Juarez, R. Z. Status projections and ethnicity: A comparison of Mexican American, Negro, and Anglo youth. *Journal of Vocational Behavior,* 1971, *1,* 137–151.

Lamb, R. R. *Validity of the American College Testing Interest Inventory for minority group members.* American College Testing Research Report 72. Iowa City, Ia.: American College Testing Program, 1976.

Lefton, M. Race, expectations, and anomia. *Social Forces,* 1968, *46,* 347–352.

Levitan, S. A. Coping with teenage unemployment. In *The teenage unemployment problem: What are the options?* Washington, D.C.: U.S. Government Printing Office, 1976.

Levitan, S. A., & Taggart, R. *The promise of greatness.* Cambridge, Mass.: Harvard University Press, 1976.

Lipsman, C. K. Maslow's theory of needs in relation to vocational choice for lower socioeconomic levels. *Vocational Guidance Quarterly,* 1967, *15,* 283–288.

Littig, L. Negro personality correlates of aspiration to traditionally open and closed occupations. *The Journal of Negro Education,* 1968, *37,* 31–36.

LoCasio, R. Continuity and discontinuity in vocational development theory. *Personnel and Guidance Journal,* 1967, *46,* 32–36.

Louis Harris & Associates. Contained in National Urban League, *The State of Black America,* 1978, New York City.

Machlowitz, M. *Workaholics: Living with them, working with them.* New York: New American Mentor Books, 1980.

Mack, R. W. *Race, class, and power.* New York: American Book, 1968.

MacMichael, D. C. Work ethics: Collision in the classroom. *Manpower,* January 1974, *6*(1), 15–20.

Mangum, G. L. *Career education and the Comprehensive Employment and Training Act.* Washington, D.C.: U.S. Government Printing Office, 1978.

Maykovich, M. K. Asian Americans—quiet Americans? In Harry A. Johnson (Ed.), *Ethnic American minorities: A guide to media and materials.* New York: Bowker, 1976.

Maynard, R. *The supported work demonstration: Effects after the first 18 months after enrollment.* New York: Manpower Demonstration Research Corporation, 1979.

Merton, R. K. *Social theory and social structure* (3rd ed.). New York: Free Press, 1968.

Miller, D. C., & Oetting, G. Barriers to employment and the disadvantaged. *Personnel and Guidance Journal,* 1977, *56,* 89–93.

Murphy, G. Work and the productive personality. In H. Borow (Ed.), *Career guidance for a new age.* Boston: Houghton Mifflin, 1973.

Nafziger, D. H., Holland, J. L., Helms, S. T., & McPartland, J. M. Applying an occupational classification to the work of young men and women. *Journal of Vocational Behavior,* 1974, *5,* 381–390.

National Center for Educational Statistics. *Condition of Education,* 1977. Washington, D.C.: Author, 1977 (NCES77–400).

National Commission on Manpower Policy. Washington, D.C.: U.S. Bureau of Labor, 1976.

National Vocational Guidance Association and American Vocational Association. Career development and career guidance. *NVGA Newsletter,* 1973, *13,* No. 1, pp. 5–8.

Neff, W. S. The meaning of work to the poor. *Rehabilitation Counseling Bulletin,* 1967, *9,* 71–77.

Newman, D. K., Amidet, N. J., Carter, B. L., Day, D., Kruvant, W. J., & Russell, J. S. *Protest, politics, and prosperity: Black Americans and white institutions, 1940–1975.* New York: Pantheon Books, 1978.

Newman, M. A. A profile of Hispanics in the U.S. work force. *Monthly Labor Review,* December 1978, *101*(12), 3–14.

O'Brien, W., & Walsh, W. B. Concurrent validity of Holland's theory for non-college degreed black working men. *Journal of Vocational Behavior,* 1976, *8,* 239–246.

Oetting, E. R., & Miller, D. C. Work and the disadvantaged: The work adjustment hierarchy. *Personnel and Guidance Journal,* 1977, *56*(1), 29–35.

Osipow, S. H. *Theories of career behavior* (2nd ed.). Englewood Cliffs, N.J.: Prentice-Hall, 1973.

Osipow, S. H. The relevance of theories of career development to special groups: Problems, needed data, and implications. In J. S. Picou & R. E. Campbell (Eds.), *Career behavior of special groups: Theory, research, and practice.* Columbus, O.: Merrill, 1975.

Osipow, S. H. Vocational behavior and career development, 1975: A review. *Journal of Vocational Behavior,* 1976, *9*(2), 129–145.

Osterman, P. Racial differentials in male youth unemployment. In R. Taggert & N. Davidson (Eds.), *Conference report on youth unemployment: Its measurement and meaning.* Washington, D.C.: U.S. Department of Labor, 1978.

Picou, J. S., & Campbell, R. E. (Eds.). *Career behavior of special groups: Theory, research, and practice.* Columbus, O.: Merrill, 1975.

Prediger, D. J., Roth, J. C., & Noeth, R. J. *A nationwide study of student career development: Summary of results* (ACT Research Report No. 161). Iowa City, Ia.: American College Testing Program, 1973.

Raspberry, W. Employers ignore young urban black. *Buffalo Evening News,* June 25, 1981. (Syndicated column, Washington Post.)

Richardson, A. *Youth in the WIN program: A report on a survey of client backgrounds, program experience and subsequent labor force participation.* Bureau of Social Science Research, 1975. Washington, D.C.

Richardson, E. H. Cultural and historical perspectives in counseling American Indians. In D. W. Sue (Ed.), *Counseling the culturally different.* New York: Wiley, 1981.

Rivlin, A., & Timpane, M. *Planned variation in education: Should we give up or try harder?* Washington, D.C.: Brookings Institution, 1975.

Roe, A. *The psychology of occupations.* New York: Wiley, 1956.

Rosen, B. C. Race, ethnicity, and the achievement syndrome. *American Sociological Review,* 1959, *24,* 47–60.

Scott, T. B., & Anadon, M. A comparison of the vocational interest profiles of Native American and Caucasian college-bound students. *Measurement and Evaluation in Guidance,* 1980, *13*(1), 35–42.

Sexton, P. Negro career expectation. In H. J. Peters, & J. C. Hansen (Eds.), *Vocational guidance and career development.* New York: MacMillan, 1971.

Shlensky, B. C. Determinants of turnover in training programs for the disadvantaged.

Smith, E. J. Profile of the black individual in vocational literature. *Journal of Vocational Behavior,* 1975, *6,* 41–59.

Smith, E. J. Reference group perspectives and the vocational maturity of lower socioeconomic black youth. *Journal of Vocational Behavior,* 1976, *8,* 321–336.

Higher Education Panel Reports, No. 24. Washington, D.C.: American Council on Education, 1977. (a)

Smith, E. J. Work attitudes and job satisfactions of black workers. *Vocational Guidance Quarterly,* 1977, *25*(2), 252–263.(b)

Smith, E. J. Career development of minorities in nontraditional fields. *Journal of Non-White Concerns in Personnel and Guidance,* 1980, *8*(3), 141–156.

Spencer, B. G., Windham, G. O., & Peterson, J. H., Jr. Occupational orientations of an American group. In J. S. Picou & R. E. Campbell (Eds.), *Career behavior of special groups: Theory, research, and practice.* Columbus, O.: Merrill, 1975.

Stafford, W. Where the jobs are. *Black Enterprise,* February 1980, pp. 43–50.

Stafford, W. Youth unemployment: Needed a union of schools and community. *Urban Education,* in press, October, 1981.

Sue, D. W. Asian-Americans: Social-psychological forces affecting their life styles. In J. S. Picou and R. E. Campbell (Eds.), *Career behavior of special groups: Theory, research, and practice.* Columbus, O.: Merrill, 1975.

Sue, D. W. Cultural and historical perspectives in counseling Asian Americans. In D. W. Sue (Ed.), *Counseling the culturally different.* New York: Wiley, 1981.

Super, D. E. A theory of vocational development. *American Psychologist,* 1953, *8,* 185–190.

Super, D. E. The dimensions and measurement of vocational maturity. *Teachers College Record,* 1955, *57,* 151–163.

Super, D. E. A developmental approach to vocational guidance. *Vocational Guidance Quarterly,* 1964, *13,* 1–10.

Suzuki, R. Education and socialization of Asian-Americans: A revisionist analysis of the "Model Minority" thesis. *Amerasia Journal,* 1977, *4,* 23–52.

Taggart, R. Employment and training programs for youth. In *From school to work: Improving the transition.* Washington, D.C.: U.S. Government Printing Office, 1976.

Tauber, K. E., & Tauber, A. E. *Negroes in cities.* New York: Atheneum, 1965.

Thomas, G. E. Race and sex group equity in higher education: Institutional and major field enrollment statuses. *American Educational Research Journal,* Summer 1980, *17*(2), 171–181.

Trow, M. *Reflection on youth problems and policies in the United States.* The Carnegie Council on Policy Studies in Higher Education. San Francisco, 1980.

Tsu, J. B. The future of Asian bilingual and bicultural education. *Journal of the Chinese Language Teachers Association,* 1977, *XII*(3), 239–243.

Tyler, L. E. The encounter with poverty: Its effect on vocational psychology. *Rehabilitation Counseling Bulletin* (Fall special), 1967, 61–70.

Urban Associates. *A study of selected socioeconomic characteristics based on the 1970 census. Asian Americans, Vol. 2.* Washington, D.C.: U.S. Government Printing Office, 1974.

U.S. Bureau of the Census. Current Population Reports, Series P–20, No. 328, *Persons of Spanish origin in the United States.* Washington, D.C.: U.S. Government Printing Office, 1978.(a)

U.S. Bureau of the Census. Current Population Reports, Special Studies, Series P–23, No. 80, *The social and economic status of the black population in the United States: An historical view, 1790*-1978. Washington, D.C.: U.S. Government Printing Office, 1978.(b)

U.S. Bureau of the Census. Current Population Reports, Series P–25, No. 796, *Illustrative Projections of State Populations by Age, Race, and Sex: 1975 to 2000.* Washington, D.C.: U.S. Government Printing Office, 1979.

U.S. Commission on Civil Rights. *Social indicators of equality for minorities and women.* Washington, D.C., 1978.

U.S. Department of Health, Education, and Welfare. *Toward a social report.* Washington, D.C.: U.S. Government Printing Office, 1969.

U.S. Department of Labor. *Years for Decision, A longitudinal study of the educational and labor market experience of young women.* Washington, D.C.: 1973.

U.S. Department of Labor, Bureau of Statistics. *Employment rates by race, sex, and age,* 1977.

The underclass: Minority within a minority. *Time,* August 29, 1977, pp. 14–27.

Vondracek, S., & Kirchner, E. Vocational development in early childhood: An examination of young children's expressions of vocational aspirations. *Journal of Vocatinal Behavior,* 1974, *5,* 251–260.

Wakefield, J. A., Jr., Yom, L. B., Doughtie, E. B., Chang, W-N, & Alston, H. L. The geometric relationship between Holland's personality typology and the vocational preference inventory for blacks. *Journal of Counseling Psychology,* 1975, *22*(1), 58–60.

Ward, C. M., & Walsh, W. B. Concurrent validity of Holland's theory for non-college-degreed black women. *Journal of Vocational Behavior,* 1981, *18,* 356–361.

Warnath, C. F. Vocational theories: Direction to nowhere. *Personnel and Guidance Journal,* 1975, *53,* 422–428.

Westbrook, B. W., & Mastie, M. M. Three measures of vocational maturity: A beginning to know about. *Measurement and Evaluation in Guidance,* 1973, *6,* 8–16.

Whetstone, R. D., & Hayles, V. R. The SVIB and black college men. *Measurement and Evaluation in Guidance,* 1975, *8*(2), 105–109.

Williams, R. L. *Psychological tests and minorities.* National Institute of Mental Health.

U.S. Department of Health, Education, and Welfare. Washington, D.C.: U.S. Government Printing Office, 1975.

Williams, R. L. *Journal of Non-White Concerns in Personnel and Guidance. Special Issue: Testing* (Guest Editor with Willie Williams), 1978, *6*(3).

Wirth, L. The problem of minority groups. In R. Linton (Ed.), *The science of man in the world crisis.* New York: Columbia University Press, 1945.

Wright, D. E., Jr. Occupational orientations of Mexican American youth in selected Texas counties. Unpublished master of science thesis, Texas A & M University, 1968.

Zito, R. J., & Bardon, J. I. Negro adolescents' success and failure imagery concerning work and school. *Vocational Guidance Quarterly,* 1968, *16,* 181–184.

Zytowski, D. G. Toward a theory of career development for women. *Personnel and Guidance Journal,* 1969, *47,* 660–664.

5 Adult Vocational Behavior

Robert E. Campbell
James M. Heffernan
*The National Center for Research
in Vocational Education*

Introduction

For approximately 60 years research and practice in vocational psychology has been preoccupied with the adolescent and young adult. It was assumed that very little of interest happened after an adolescent selected and initially entered an occupation. However, the belief that a static occupational existence occurs beyond age 25 is rapidly changing. There are many key transitions and corresponding critical decisions throughout the adult life cycle. It has been noted that adults just do not stay "put" as in the past. People are discovering that there is life after 40, even after 70. Many are having at least two careers if not three or more. There are 126 million adults 25 years of age and older. Approximately one-third of them are seeking career changes. As a result, the past 10 years has seen interest in adult vocational behavior mushroom. For example, several books on adult behavior have become best sellers (Levinson, Darrow, Klein, Levinson, & McKee, 1978; Sheehy, 1976). In addition, a number of national magazines have devoted cover stories to adult development and behavior.

Although sheer demographics (i.e., the massive growing numbers of adults in our society primarily as a result of the post-World War II baby boom) have accounted for the dynamics of adult vocational behavior, a number of additional societal trends are also significantly related. These include such factors as high divorce rates, the instability of the economy, changing job opportunities, changing family patterns, the proliferation of educational opportunities, new life-styles, and the rise of women in the labor force. Each of these trends will be discussed below.

Divorce rates.   Rising divorce rates over the past decade, as high as 80% in some parts of the country, have forced women displaced as homemakers to reenter the labor force. The most frequent age range affecting this population is between 35 and 55. The incidence of displaced homemakers has become so prevalent that the Federal government has subsidized a number of centers throughout the country to assist these women in becoming prepared to reenter the labor market after years of being outside it.

The economy.   Because of the instability of the economy a number of people have been forced to change jobs and careers. A notable recent example occurred in the aerospace industry when severe cutbacks in the NASA program forced trained technicians and engineers to prepare for alternative careers.

Job opportunities.   A disinclination to stay with the same company and/or job for an indefinite period of years has given rise to horizontal and vertical occupational moves.

Family patterns.   Changes in family pattern prompted by the rise in single parent families and trends toward childless couples have caused people to question the type of career they desire as well as their involvement in work.

Educational opportunities.   Aslanian and Brickell (1980) recently completed a national study of the reasons adults pursue education. They found that approximately 50% of the American adult population age 25 and older participated in at least one educational course during the year of their survey. They also found that adults frequently entered educational programs as a result of some transition and/or triggering event in their life, such as divorce, loss of business, change of life-style. These transition events were classified into seven categories representing major life areas: changes in careers, family life, leisure, artistic life, personal health, religious life, and citizenship. The demand by adults for increased educational opportunities has become very evident throughout the country. Many of these educational settings are described in more detail later in this chapter. The settings include short programs in public institutions, private foundation, churches, community agencies, business and industry, and professional organizations.

Life-styles.   People are seriously questioning conventional life-styles. Many wonder if they would like to live the myth of the traditional life of preparing for a career, entering a career, raising a family, and living in suburbia forever and ever. Some question whether the rat race is worth it and are becoming middle-age dropouts. There appears to be intensive searches for variety in life style that has prompted major shifts in careers.

Women.   The very significant rise of the amount of women in the labor force, almost 50%, has greatly affected employment practices. There is a major move toward the renunciation of sex stereotyping, equal opportunity, and an increased incidence of women in key managerial positions.

Dual careers.   The simultaneous employment of both spouses is becoming more prevalent. Each spouse wants a satisfying career that in some instances has resulted in career compromises to accommodate both spouses working in the same geographic location. Hall (1978), in his research on dual careers, has found that a number of factors are important in achieving satisfactory dual careers. These include high energy levels, a willingness to compromise, willingness to adjust to a different style of living, and respect for each others careers. Maintaining dual careers places a heavy burden on both spouses especially when one spouse seeks a job change that would require relocation of the other spouse. In most instances spouses have to make joint relocations to obtain mutually satisfying jobs.

Midlife crisis.   Considerable attention has been given recently to the concept of midlife crisis. Midlife crisis refers to the questioning of values, attitudes, life-styles, and generally a reassessment of personal goals during the midyears 35 to 55. As a result of this reassessment, many people have undergone significant changes especially in their vocational behavior. Jobs that were once satisfying no longer seem to be as attractive. Generally, the crisis reflects a period of restlessness in personal life and career status.

Life expectancy.   The extension of life expectancy well into the seventies combined with improved health during the older years has resulted in older persons seeking second and third careers. Consequently, there is a more active organized movement toward assisting older persons in seeking employment opportunities. Many older persons retire and pursue a second career, often on a part-time basis, to supplement retirement income. The higher incidence of older persons participating in the labor force has added complexity to an already dynamic labor market.

The foregoing trends have stimulated new theoretical formulations of adult career development and the proliferation of adult counseling services. It is the purpose of this chapter to review these developments. This chapter is organized into three sections: (1) a review and synthesis of the theories of adult career development; (2) an examination of career and educational counseling services for adults; and (3) conclusions and recommendations.

THEORIES OF ADULT CAREER DEVELOPMENT

The general adult development and career development models reviewed in this section have a number of features in common (see Table 5.1). Most theorists specify that individual development proceeds through a series of stages, each of which requires the mastery of developmental tasks and/or the resolution of developmental issues unique to that stage. Movement to subsequent stages is viewed as contingent upon the satisfactory completion or resolution of previous stages. An individual's development reflects the history of successive stages.

Although the models vary as to the number of stages across the life span, each model links its stages to age ranges of varying degrees of specificity. Miller and Form (1951, 1964) and Super (1963) are most specific in the age ranges associated with each stage. Levinson, et al. (1978) and Schein (1978) are equally specific, but allow overlap in the age ranges of adjacent stages. Erikson (1950) and Havighurst (1952) specify more generalized age periods for each of their hypothesized stages.

Developmental stage tasks vary in number among models. However, most models include tasks that reflect development in social, psychological, and career areas. Erikson (1950), Havinghurst (1952), and Levinson et al. (1978) emphasize the social and psychological aspects whereas Miller and Form (1951, 1964), Super (1963), and Schein (1978) emphasize the career aspects. Most models are based on white males and do not specify different developmental tasks for different subpopulations. The tasks are the same regardless of sex, race, socioeconomic status, and occupational level.

Finally, developmental theories of this sort, with the possible exception of Miller and Form (1964), assume that stages in development are sequential and each is encountered only once. That is, individuals do not return to "lower" level stages once they have been satisfactorily negotiated.

Career Development Stages

In order to organize the review four career development stages, based upon a synthesis of the literature, were postulated. The literature seems to indicate that four major phases take place during the career development cycle: (1) preparation for an occupation and obtaining a job; (2) demonstration of competence in and adjustment to a new work environment; (3) maintenance and/or advancement of one's position in an established occupation; and (4) decline in involvement with the work place. These career development stages were named, respectively; (1) preparation; (2) establishment; (3) maintenance; and (4) retirement. This conception is consistent with that presented by Super and Hall (1978).

A significant element of the theories reviewed above is the delineation of developmental tasks associated with each stage. This model is followed in the review below. Thus, the purpose of the review is twofold: (1) to provide a full description of each stage through a comprehensive literature review; and (2) to generate a list of developmental tasks for each stage as suggested by the literature.

The resulting career development stages and tasks presented below differ from previous conceptions in several important ways. Although some stages tend to be associated with a general age span, an individual may enter or reenter any stage listed below at any point in the life span. The sequential, nonrepeatable, and age-linked aspects of career stages reported above seem to be in conflict with the fact that people are changing jobs in midlife, entering the work force during late adulthood, and coming out of retirement and starting over. Thus, in the conception presented below, an 18-year-old obtaining a first job, a 35-year-old entering the job market for the first time, a 50-year-old changing jobs, and a 65-year-old coming out of retirement could all be placed in the preparation stage so long as one is dealing with preparation for an occupation and/or obtaining a job in the work force. Furthermore, these people may cycle through the same stages several times during their lives.

Preparation stage.   The preparation stage encompasses that period of time and those activities that are relevant to preparing for an occupation and obtaining a position in the work force. Individuals pass through this stage for a variety of reasons.

The majority of people passing through this stage do so at the very beginning of the career development process. These people may not have yet held a full-time job and usually fall into the 14- to 24-year age range (Super, 1963). Through exposure to familial, subcultural, and social forces, they take part in a variety of planned and unplanned learning experiences that shape their future career preferences and choices. They also begin to make formal and informal assessments concerning their personal capabilities and the world of work in general (Krumboltz, Mitchell, & Jones, 1976).

In the later phases of this stage, individuals make tentative choices about possible occupational goals, obtain appropriate academic or vocational training, and execute a job search. This latter activity can take a variety of forms. Some people take positions that are a result of placement during academic or vocational training. Others embark upon a series of formal interviews with selected organizations and institutions offering the desired type of position. Still others may choose to become self-employed.

Although the beginning of the career development process is usually associated with young people, an increasing number of women begin this

TABLE 5.1
Adult Development Stage Theories

	ADOLESCENCE (≈ 20 and under)	EARLY ADULTHOOD (≈ 20-40)	MIDDLE ADULTHOOD (≈ 40-60)	LATE ADULTHOOD (≈ 60 and over)
Erikson	"Identity vs. Role Confusion"	"Intimacy vs. Isolation"	"Generativity vs. Stagnation"	"Ego Integrity vs. Despair"
	Determination of one's role in life	Development of intimate relationships with others	Providing guidance for younger generation	Satisfaction with past life and accomplishments
	Establishment of an identity	Fusion of identity with another	Ability to give of oneself	Fulfillment and contentment
			Teaching and leading others	Ego integrity
	vs.	vs.	vs.	vs.
	Lack of certainty regarding one's place in society	Avoidance of intimacy	Self-indulgence	Sense of meaningless and alienation
	Confusion	Inability to give fully of oneself	Preoccupation with own concerns and needs	Loneliness
	Turmoil	Isolation and alienation	Impoverishment and stagnation	Fear of death
				Despair
Havighurst	**TASKS**	**TASKS**	**TASKS**	**TASKS**
	1. Achieving mature relations with age mates	1. Selecting a mate	1. Achieving civic and social responsibility	1. Adjusting to decreasing physical strength and health
	2. Accepting one's physique	2. Learning to live with a marriage partner	2. Maintaining an economic standard of living	2. Adjusting to retirement and reduced income
	3. Achieving a social role	3. Managing a home	3. Giving guidance to adolescent children	3. Adjusting to death of one's spouse
	4. Achieving emotional independence	4. Rearing children	4. Developing leisure activities	4. Meeting social and civic obligations
	5. Selecting and preparing for an occupation	5. Beginning an occupation	5. Adjusting to physiological changes	5. Establishing an affiliation with one's age group
	6. Preparing for marriage	6. Taking on civic responsibility	6. Relating to one's spouse	
	7. Achieving socially responsive behavior	7. Finding a social group	7. Adjusting to aging parents	

Levinson

"Early Adult Transition"(18-20)

Separation from family
Desire for independence
Development of adult identity
Exploration

"Entering the Adult World"(20-27)

Exploration
Experimentation
Tentative commitments
Foundation for life structure
Vision or dream

"Age 30 Transition"(28-32)

Critical turning point
Modification of existing life
  structure
Foundation for new structure
May be somewhat stressful

"Settling Down"(30-40)

Stability
Commitments to family and work
Security and vitality
Career advancement
Termination of mentor relationship
Productivity

"Mid-Life Transition"(28-32)

Critical turning point
Disillusioning process
Reexamination of goals
  and dreams
Reevaluation of relationships
Confrontation with physical decline

"Restabilization"(46-55)

Security and stability
Achievment and productivity
Satisfaction with life vs. despair
Concerns about past mistakes

"Culmination"(55-60)

Stability

"Late Adult Transition"(60-65)

Foundation for later adult years

229

TABLE 5.1 (continued)

	Preparatory Period (0-16)	Initial Stage (16-18)	Trial Period (18-34)	Stable Period (35-retirement)	Retirement
Miller and Form	This period represents early experiences and adjustments in the home, school, and community as the young person develops physical and mental maturity.	Aside from becoming more willing and able to work, individuals begin to aquire the social and technical skills necessary for the job performance. The vocational aspirations of the individuals become more realistic. Job seeking begins and continues until the educational process is terminated.	This period begins when the worker seeks his/her first fulltime work position and continues until he/she has secured a work position in which he/she remains permanently (three years or more). During this stage, the individual tries numerous jobs by transferring, promotions, and trying another organization. When individuals find themselves, they enter into a period of stable work adjustment.	The stable period is a period of job persistence beginning when the worker finds a work position in which he/she remains more or less permanently. At this point, advancement in one's occupation to the highest level possible frequently occurs. Usually, this period extends until retirement, death, or until he/she enters another trial period.	Individuals at this period must learn to adjust to a new situation—that of being unemployed. Interests at this time tend to shift to the home. Frequently, changes take place in security, health, and friendship patterns.

Super

Exploration (15-24)	Establishment (25-44)	Maintenance (45-64)	Decline (65 on)
Self-examination, role tryouts and occupational exploration take place in school, leisure activities, and part-time work. Substages of the exploration stage are	Having found an appropriate field, effort is put forth to make a permanent place in it. There may be some trial early in this stage, with consequent shifting, but establishment may begin without trial, especially in the professions. Substages of the establishment stage are	Having made a place in the world of work, the concern is now to hold it. Little ground is broken, but there is continuation along established lines.	As physical and mental powers decline, work activity changes and due course ceases. New roles must be developed; first that of selective participant and then that of observer rather than participant. Substages of this stage are
Tentative (15-17). Needs, interests, capacities, values, and opportunities are all considered. Tentative choices are made and tried out in fantasy, discussion, courses, work, etc.	Trial and Stabilization. (25-30). The field of work presumed to be suitable may prove unsatisfactory, resulting in one or two changes before the life work is found or before it becomes clear that the life work will be a succession of unrelated jobs.		Deceleration (65-70). Sometimes at the time of official retirement, sometimes late in the maintenance stage, the pace of work slackens, duties are shifted, or the nature of the work is changed to suit declining capacities. Many individuals find part-time jobs to replace their full-time occupations.
Transition (18-21). Reality considerations are given more weight as the youth enters market or professional training and attempts to implement a self concept.	Advancement (31-44). As the career pattern becomes clear, effort is put forth to stabilize, to make a secure place in the world of work.		Retirement (71 on). As with all specified age limits, there are great variations from person to person. But, complete cessation of occupation comes for all in due course, to some easily and pleasantly, to others with difficulty and disappointment, and to some only with death.
Trial (22-24). A seemingly appropriate field having been located, a beginning job in it is found and is tried out as a life work.			

231

TABLE 5.1 (*continued*)

	Crystallization (14-18)	**Specification** (18-21)	**Consolidation** (35 plus)
	a. Awareness of the need to crystallize	a. Awareness of the need to specify	a. Awareness of the need to consolidate and advance
	b. Use of resources	b. Use of resources in specification	b. Possession of information as to how to consolidate and advance
	c. Awareness of factors to consider	c. Awareness of factors to consider	c. Planning for consolidation and advancement
	d. Awareness of contingencies which may affect goals	d. Awareness of contingencies which may affect goals	d. Executing consolidation and advancement plans
	e. Differentiation of interests and values	e. Differentiation of interests and values	
	f. Awareness of present-future relationships	f. Awareness of present-future relationships	
	g. Formulation of generalized preference	g. Specification of a vocational preference	
Super	h. Consistency of preference	h. Consistency of preference	
	i. Possession of information concerning the preferred occupation	i. Possession of information concerning the preferred occupation	
	j. Planning for the preferred occupation	j. Planning for the preferred occupation	
	k. Wisdom of the vocational preference	k. Wisdom of the vocational preference	
		i. Confidence in a specific preference	

Super
(cont'd)

Implementation
(21-24)

a. Awareness of the need to implement preference

b. Planning to implement preference

c. Executing plans to qualify for entry

d. Obtaining an entry job

Stabilization
(25-35)

a. Awareness of the need to stabilize

b. Planning for stabilization

c. Becoming qualified for a stable regular job or accepting the inevitability of instability

d. Obtaining a stable regular job or acting on resignation to instability

TABLE 5.1 (continued)

	ADOLESCENCE	EARLY ADULTHOOD	MIDDLE ADULTHOOD	LATE ADULTHOOD
	Growth, Fantasy, Exploration (0-21)	**Full Membership in Early Career** (17-30)	**Late Career in Nonleadership Role** (40 to retirement)	**Retirement** (Retirement age)
	1. Develop and discover one's own needs and interests	1. Perform effectively and learn how things are done	1. How to remain technically competent or how to learn to substitute wisdom based on experience for immediate technical skills	1. How to maintain a sense of identity and self-worth without a full-time job or organizational role
	2. Develop and discover one's own abilities and talents	2. Accept partial responsibility	2. How to develop interpersonal and group skills if needed	2. How to remain engaged up to one's level of energy and abilities in some kind of activity
	3. Find realistic role models from which to learn about occupations	3. Accept subordinate status and learn how to get along with the boss and one's peers	3. How to develop supervisory and managerial skills if needed	3. How to use one's wisdom and experience
	4. Get maximum information from testing and counseling	4. Develop initiative and realistic level of aggressiveness within the limits of the job; to show full commitment	4. How to learn to make effective decisions in a political environment	4. How to achieve a sense of fulfillment and satisfaction in one's past career
	5. Locate reliable sources	5. Find a mentor, sponsor	5. How to deal with the competitiveness and aggression of younger persons "on the way up"	
	6. Develop and discover one's own values, motives, and ambitions	6. Reassess original decision to pursue this type of work in terms of opportunities and constraints in the organization	6. How to deal with mid-life crisis and empty-nest problem at home	
	7. Make sound educational decisions	7. Prepare for long-range commitments and a period of maximum contribution or for a move to a new job or organization	7. How to prepare for senior leadership roles	
	8. Perform well enough in school to keep career options as wide open as possible	8. Deal with feelings of success or failure in the first job	**Late Career in Leadership Role** (Varies)	
	9. Find opportunities for self-tests in sports, hobbies, and school activities in order to develop a realistic self-image	**Full Membership in Mid-Career** (25+)	1. How to disengage from being primarily concerned with self to becoming more responsible for organizational welfare	
Schein	10. Find trial and part-time work opportunities to test early vocational decisions	1. Gain a measure of independence		

Schein (cont'd)

Entry Into World of Work (16-25)

1. Learn how to look for a job, how to apply, how to negotiate a job interview

2. Learn how to assess information about a job and an organization

3. Pass selection and screening tests

4. Make a realistic and valid first-job choice

Basic Training (16-25)

1. Overcome the insecurity of inexperience and develop a sense of confidence

2. Decipher the culture, "learn the ropes" as quickly as possible

3. Learn to get along with the first boss or trainer

4. Learn to get along with other trainees

5. Accept and learn from the initiation rites and other rituals associated with being a novice (doing much of the "mickey mouse" tasks, etc.)

6. Accept responsibly the official signs of entry and acceptance (uniforms, badges, identity cards, parking stickers, company manuals)

2. Develop one's own standards of performance and confidence in one's own decisions

3. Carefully assess own motives, talents, and values as basis for decision of how specialized to become

4. Carefully assess the organizational and occupational opportunities as basis for making valid decisions about next steps

5. Work through one's relationships with mentors and prepare to become a mentor to others

6. Achieve an appropriate accommodation among family, self, and work concerns

7. Deal with feelings of failure if performance is poor, tenure is denied, or challenge is lost

2. How to handle organizational secrets and resources responsibly

3. Learn to handle high-level political situations both inside and at the organization/environment boundary

4. Learn how to balance continued high commitment to career with needs of family, especially spouse

5. Learn how to handle high levels of responsibility and power without becoming paralyzed or emotionally upset

Decline and Disengagement (40 to retirement)

1. How to find new sources of satisfaction in hobbies, family, social and community activities, part-time work, etc.

2. Learn how to live more closely with spouse

3. Assess total career and prepare for retirement

process following years spent as a homemaker. Although such women may need to confront a unique set of issues surrounding the management of multiple roles, they share with younger people the demands and challenges of deciding on, and implementing, a career plan.

In addition to individuals at the beginning of their careers, many individuals in the preparation stage are negotiating major career changes. For example, self-employed persons may decide to join an organization. Individuals may choose to make a major change in their occupation or to make a change in organizational affiliation. Other individuals may choose to leave the military and to seek civilian employment. In such cases, these individuals must perform a series of self-assessments, make decisions, and locate a new position.

A final group of people in the preparation stage are those planning reentry to the work force following a period of either voluntary or forced unemployment. Women returning to the work force after fulfilling child-rearing responsibilities or following divorce or widowhood constitute an increasingly large reentry group, as do retirees and unemployed people seeking to resume part- or full-time employment.

Thus, whereas individuals in the preparation stage are most likely to be in the 14- to 24-year age range, individuals may also pass through this stage later in life. It may seem that an 18-year-old obtaining a first job, a 35-year-old reentering a job market, and a 50-year-old changing jobs would perform basically different tasks in obtaining their jobs. However, as Super (1977) notes, many career tasks are similar across the life span (i.e., although the *content* of the task may vary, the *process* remains the same).

During the preparation stage, there are two major types of tasks. The first type encompasses those activities that are part of decision making. Individuals must assess their personal attributes and the work environment, generate and evaluate alternative career options, and select one of these options. This process is unchanging and applies whether individuals are choosing occupations, college majors, training programs, or organizations.

The second major type of task encompasses those activities necessary to implement the choices that have been made. This includes obtaining appropriate occupational training (be it academic or vocational) and obtaining a position in the chosen occupation or organization.

Other tasks that seem to have less emphasis during this stage require that individuals adapt to, and perform adequately in, the organization or institution with which they are affiliated. During the preparation stage, this affiliation is usually with an educational or training institution.

Once individuals have completed these tasks, the preparation stage is considered successfully negotiated. Individuals enter the establishment stage on the first day of employment.

Goal: To prepare for an occupation and to obtain a position in the work force.

Tasks: The task of the individual is to

I. Assess personal attributes and the world of work in anticipation of work entry/reentry

    A. Possess a vocabulary with which to discuss personal attributes and the world of work

    B. Know resources for assessing personal attributes and obtaining career/occupational information

    C. Be able to make use of these resources

    D. Extract and understand information from these resources

    E. Perceive relationships among personal attributes, the world of work, and the socioeconomic environment

II. Engage in decision making for work entry/reentry

    A. Perceive a need to choose an occupation

    B. Generate appropriate occupational alternatives

    C. Evaluate alternatives on the basis of personal attributes and occupational information

    D. Make initial occupational choice

    E. Plan for implementation of occupational choice

    F. Possess ability to make alternative choices/plans if initial choices/plans are thwarted

III. Implement plans to prepare for work entry/reentry

    A. Be aware of occupational preparation requirements

    B. Identify and select appropriate sources for occupational preparation

    C. Make appropriate arrangements for obtaining occupational preparation experience

    D. Understand the relevance that preparation has for an occupation

IV. Perform adequately in and adapt to the demands of the organizational/institutional environment during preparation

    A.   Perform adequately in obtaining occupational preparation experience

    B.   Adhere to appropriate organizational/institutional regulations

    C.   Develop appropriate relationships with significant persons in the organizational/institutional environment

    D.   Operate within the environment to meet personal/professional needs

V. Obtain a position in the chosen occupation

    A.   Know where to locate employment opportunities

    B.   Extract relevant information from descriptions of employment opportunities

    C.   Select appropriate employment opportunities

        1.   Consider the match between personal attributes and requirements of employment opportunities.

        2.   Consider the organizational setting in making selections

    D.   Take appropriate action to take advantage of employment opportunities

        1.   Prepare a suitable resume of experience

        2.   Complete procedural paperwork

        3.   Display proper interview/negotiation behavior

    E.   Analyze individual employment opportunities/offers

        1.   Consider the impact of opportunity on life

    F.   Accept or reject individual employment opportunities/offers

    G.   Repeat job search tasks as necessary

Establishment stage.   The establishment stage encompasses that period of time and those activities that are relevant to demonstrating one's ability to function effectively in an occupation. This ability is demonstrated both by adequately performing one's job-related duties and by adapting to the organizational/institutional environment. This stage immediately follows the preparation stage and may be said to begin with the first day of employment.

Although most workers in the establishment stage are young, other ages and a variety of work histories may be found among individuals in this stage. The largest group is composed of newcomers to the work force. These people begin their jobs with preparatory experience from a secondary school, a vocational school, a college or university, an apprenticeship, or informal training. Many will be naive about the complexities of the work environment, and they will spend much of their time learning how to function in the world of work. They must discover how this new environment differs from those that they have known previously.

A second group of individuals in the establishment stage displays what Super, Kowalski, and Gotkin (1967) have called "floundering" behavior. Although these people are part of the work force, they never succeed in completing the tasks of the establishment stage. As Super et al. (1967) state, "floundering is defined as movement to a position which is not logical as a next step from the position being vacated, for which the subject lacks required aptitudes, interests, and preparation, or for which he is no better suited than for the position being vacated [pp. 1–9]."

The third group to be found in the establishment stage is composed of more mature workers. These are men and women who have decided to make a midlife career change or to come out of retirement and reenter the work force. The change is most likely to entail entry into a new organizational/institutional environment or into an entirely new career field. Such changes are not uncommon (Byrne, 1975; Gottfredson, 1976; Sommers & Eck, 1977).

People in this third group do not need to spend a great deal of time learning to function in the world of work. For them, the work place is not a new environment. Instead, they will direct their energies toward such tasks as learning the structure of a new organization/institution and/or demonstrating competence with skills newly acquired or recently brought up to date.

People reach the establishment stage by first passing through the preparation stage. This first step is necessary to perform the tasks of self-assessment, assessment of the world of work, decision making, and job finding. However, there is a great variability in the amount of time spent in this sort of preparation. At one extreme are persons who spend years in deciding upon, training for, and finding a job. At the other extreme are persons who enter establishment with little conscious preparation. For example, Robbins (1978) discusses the individual who takes over a business previously owned by parents or relatives not retired or deceased. For others, a job opportunity may present itself in the course of performing the requirements of a current position. With little forethought, an individual may decide to take advantage of such an opportunity.

Despite the different types of preparation and work histories of persons in the establishment stage, they must all complete the same common tasks. First, they need to become oriented and adapted to the organization/institutional environment. This includes establishing harmonious relationships with supervisors, peers, and subordinates. Second, they need to learn the requirements of the position and demonstrate competency to appropriate people. Finally, the need to examine their satisfaction with their position, consider opportunities for advancement, and develop a career plan for the future.

Whereas defining the completion of the preparation stage is relatively straightforward (i.e., as the day the individual begins employment), assessing the point at which the establishment stage has been completed is more complicated. Given the goal of this latter stage, completion can be defined as the point at which the individual has initially demonstrated his/her ability to function effectively in the occupation. However, criteria for establishing that this goal has been reached vary both across and within occupations and in both content and objectivity.

Objective indexes of goal attainment include successful completion of a probationary period, obtaining a merit raise, and being given more responsibility in the position. When such objective indexes are not available, the subjective assessment of the individual concerning his/her organizational functioning may be the salient criterion of goal attainment and, thus, successful completion of the establishment phase. Establishment may take as little as a month or as much as several years; those who complete this stage usually move to the maintenance stage, although some individuals never become fully established.

Goal: **To demonstrate initially one's ability to function effectively in an occupation.**

Tasks: **The task of the individual is to**

   I. **Become oriented to the organization/institution**

      A. **Learn the way around the physical plant**

      B. **Learn and adhere to regulations and policies**

      C. **Learn the formal and informal structure of the work environment**

         1. **Learn and utilize appropriate channels of communication**

      D. **Learn and use environmental resources appropriately**

      E. **Learn and display good work habits and attitudes**

      F. **Develop harmonious relationships with others in the work environment**

         1. **Learn and demonstrate expected social behavior**

2. Achieve acceptance of others in the work environment

3. Develop a personal support system inside work environment

G. Display flexibility in adapting to organizational/institutional changes

H. Integrate personal values with organizational/institutional values

II. Learn position responsibilities and demonstrate satisfactory performance

A. Use previously acquired skills in position performance as appropriate

B. Learn how to use job-related equipment, materials, and resources

C. Acquire new skills as tasks of position change

1. Take part in on-the-job training as appropriate

D. Learn formal and informal quality and level of productivity

E. Demonstrate adequate position performance to others in the work environment

F. Experience self-confidence in position performance

III. Explore career plans in terms of personal goals and advancement opportunities

A. Evaluate current choice of occupation

1. Determine match between personal attributes and requirements of current position

2. Assess potential of current position for satisfying personal needs

B. Evaluate advancement opportunities of current position

1. Know the requirements for advancement

2. Assess personal capacity to meet requirements for advancement

C. Develop a plan for advancement or position change

1. Survey internal and external organizational/institutional opportunities

      2. Decide upon specialization within current occupation

      3. Consider alternatives in other occupations

  D. Implement plan for advancement or position change

Maintenance stage.   The theory of work adjustment formulated by Lofquist and Dawis (1969) states that "each individual seeks to achieve and maintain correspondences with his environment. . . . Correspondence can be described in terms of the individual fulfilling the requirements of the work environment, and the work environment fulfilling the requirements of the individual [p. 45]." The achievement and maintenance of this correspondence is the general theme of the maintenance stage.

Individuals in the maintenance stage have prepared for and established themselves in an occupation. These individuals are relatively satisfied with their work and are unlikely to make radical changes unless confronted with a crisis. Thus, during the maintenance stage, individuals shift from a major focus on occupational choice, preparation, and establishment tasks to adjustment and stabilization tasks. They work toward career stability characterized by constant employment, permanence in the same occupation, maintenance and protection of acquired abilities and skills, and accrual of seniority.

The major criterion for entrance to the maintenance stage is that the individual has decided to continue in the occupation in which he or she has become established. Although age is not a major criterion, it is more of a factor than in previous stages. Theorists estimate that persons in the maintenance stage range in age from 35 to 65 years (Miller & Form, 1951; Super, 1957). These years are associated with changes in personal health, interpersonal relationships, and family structure. Changes in the work place, both objectively in terms of duties and responsibilities and subjectively in terms of personal satisfaction and fulfillment, also take place during this time.

It is within the context of these changes that the tasks of the maintenance stage are to be accomplished. There are four general types of tasks. First, a variety of assessment and decision-making tasks need to be accomplished. Assessment of personal attributes and goals continues as in previous stages. One also needs to assess one's economic status, occupational prestige, and job satisfaction. On the basis of this information, decisions are made regarding one's personal goals and strategies for achieving a specified level of performance in one's occupation. This plan for maintenance may range from a minimal level, in which a person performs at the lowest level acceptable to the organization, to an optimal level, in which a person attempts to advance within his/her occupation.

Selection of a maintenance plan is followed by activities directed at its implementation, the second type of task of this stage. The third type of task involves adjustment to the changing life and organizational events occurring during the maintenance stage. The fourth and last task is that of performing at a level consistent with organizational requirements and the individual's maintenance plan.

The maintenance stage is followed by the retirement stage. As with previous stage transition points, it is difficult to specify the exact moment at which individuals enter retirement. This is further complicated by the fact that some people plan for, others postpone consideration of, and still others never reach retirement. Furthermore, there may be a period of overlap between stages for those individuals simultaneously maintaining their occupations and planning for retirement. Individuals contemplating retirement usually begin a gradual decrease of their work activity, slowly transferring responsibility to others or acting as mentor to a potential replacement. In other instances retirement may be more abrupt (e.g., an unexpected layoff) or symbolized in a formal ceremony (e.g., a retirement banquet).

Goal: To achieve and maintain a desired level of functioning in one's established occupation.

Tasks: The task of the individual is to

I. Assess self in terms of status within one's present occupation, position, and organizational setting

    A. Reexamine initial career aspirations and assess discrepancy with present occupational status and achievements

    B. Evaluate current abilities and skills to assess discrepancy with current requirements of one's present occupation

    C. Explore opportunities in one's occupation, both within one's current organization and in other organizations

    D. Assess life goals associated with work and life values and time perspectives (e.g., age, ratio of work to nonwork empahsis, time limitations)

II. Decide on a maintenance plan

    A. Synthesize information pertaining to present status, occupational opportunities in present occupation and organizational setting, and life and work goals

B.   Generate alternative plans depending if objective is to

1.   Maintain present position at a minimum level

2.   Advance within an occupation to achieve higher level of security and comfort

3.   Make an occupational change which would require leaving the maintenance stage

C.   Assess circumstances related to alternative plans (e.g., organizational setting, economics, age, health, family status)

D.   Analyze alternatives and compare with current status

E.   Decide on maintenance plan

III.   Implement a maintenance plan

A.   Develop possible strategies to implement maintenance plan depending on objective to

1.   Maintain present position at minimal level which may require upgrading skills or developing coping behaviors

2.   Advance in occupation which may require new skills or organizational change

B.   Obtain information for implementation of different strategies to attain maintenance objective

C.   Select strategy based on efficiency and effectiveness in attaining maintenance objective

D.   Develop objectives and timetable for implementation of maintenance plan

E.   Take necessary action for maintenance plan implementation

IV.   Adjust to changing personal and organizational events arising during maintenance

A.   Assess effects of event or change

B.   Developing coping behaviors to deal with changes and events in view of maintenance objective

C.   Use coping behaviors until adjustment to the change or event occurs

D.   Reassess coping behaviors if ineffective

V. Achieve and maintain performance at a level that is consistent with organizational requirements and individual
maintenance plan

A. Determine organizational criteria for acceptable level
of performance based on current position and
maintenance objective

B. Evaluate performance in terms of organizational
criteria and maintenance objective

C. Adjust performance level to meet organizational
criteria consistent with the maintenance objective

Retirement stage.   Over the past 45 years, retirement has become an accepted custom in the United States. Consequently, retirement affects nearly
every person's career development. Unfortunately, stereotypes of retirement situations often obscure, for everyone concerned, the significance of
leaving full-time work and depending on a pension for financial support.
Whereas a great deal of attention has been paid to people entering and pro-
gressing through the working years, little attention has been given to those
people exiting the labor force.

Unlike the previous career stages, retirement is a social and economic
policy that affects individual career development. Before 1935 people were
accustomed to working as long as they were able. Retirement was uncommon until Congress passed the Social Security Act in response to economic
pressures to create jobs. This act, which was society's sanction for older
people not to work, provided governmental pensions for workers reaching
age 65, then an acceptable although arbitrary benchmark. Subsequent
private pension plans, developed after World War II, also adopted the age
of 65 as the time for retirement. Judicial decisions further ingrained pensions and retirement policies into America's work life by ruling in 1948 that
pensions were subject to collective bargaining (Woodring, 1976).

The significance of retirement, from a career development perspective, is
that it is the last major transition of one's career prior to death. Of course,
this is not true for those who choose to work full time until death or until a
severe disability overcomes them. In 1975, 86% of persons 65 or older were
retired; the number of retirement-age persons is growing (Sheppard & Rix,
1977). A retiree is typically 60 to 75 years old, healthy and independent.
Retirement is the time when self-determined leisure activities supplant the
obligations of a full-time job. Private pensions, Social Security benefits,
and investments are major sources of income. Retirement may be only part
time if part-time work is needed to supplement income. For definitional

purposes, retirement is a status people assume by leaving full-time employment with a pension income that provides for a desired lifestyle.

Not everyone wants to retire, but some have a choice in the matter; others do not. Forced, early retirements are not unusual. The ability to retire is a function of financial security that is dependent on a healthy economy. For example, it appears that an inflationary economy spurs people to continue working rather than retire. Harris et al. (1979) in a nationwide survey, found that 51% of employees who were surveyed said that they would prefer to continue with some type of employment beyond the usual retirement age of 65. In the same survey, nearly half (46%) of the retirees who responded reported that they would prefer to be working.

Note that retirement is not necessarily age-related. Although it is rare to find someone retired at age 29, it is common to find people in their late forties and fifties who are retired. Many pension programs have a "thirty and out" policy where after 30 years of service an employee may retire will full benefits. In military service the time is even less—20 years.

As for an individual's career, retirement requires planning and action under circumstances that are not always clear or predictable. In terms of career progression, the retirement and maintenance stages are overlapped when retirement planning is considered seriously during maintenance. As retirement time nears, people tend to shift interests from maintaining in what may have been a lifelong occupation to planning for retirement. If a person chooses not to retire, then he/she remains in the maintenance stage unless a career change causes the person to recycle into another stage.

Other stages could be reengaged if part-time employment is necessary to supplement pension income. For example, one may train to be a cashier in a grocery store after having worked as an automobile assembler for 30 years, thus going through preparation for, and eventually establishment in, this part-time job.

Retirement is unlike the previous stages in that this segment of the working life is a defined social policy. How people prepare for and adjust to retirement, from a career development perspective, is not widely understood. The purpose of this section is to review the retirement literature to determine appropriate career development tasks and then structure them in a way that will be useful for career counseling.

Goal: To maximize personal options in leaving full-time employment to assume a retirement role

Tasks: The task of the individual is to

I.   Decide whether or not to retire full-time or part-time

    A.   Assess values regarding work

    B.   Assess the values of leisure time

    C.   Assess personal financial situation

    D.   Assess economic climate, e.g., place of employment, national economy, economic trends

II.   Explore career options for part-time retirement

    A.   Examine new career possibilities

    B.   Identify personal skills that would transfer to new job settings

    C.   Determine barriers and facilitators to employment, e.g., health, location, and hours of employment

    D.   Determine employment possibilities

III. Assess interpersonal relationships

    A.   Judge the satisfaction and importance of interpersonal relationships on and off the job

    B.   Determine changes in relationships that full- or part-time retirement may bring, e.g., spouse, family, living alone

IV. Develop and maintain a retirement plan

    A.   Identify personal goals in retirement, e.g., level of income, use of leisure time, part-time employment

    B.   Identify required steps in negotiating the retirement process, e.g., application for private pension, filing for Social Security benefits, applying for part-time employment

    C.   Identify critical factors to monitor before and during retirement, e.g, inflation, health

    D.   Develop a contingency plan in the event of "disaster", e.g., death of spouse, forced retirement, failure of investments, depression

    E.   Periodically assess adequacy of plan

Career development adjustment problems.   Campbell, Cellini, Shaltry, Long, & Pinkos (1979) devised a diagnostic taxonomy as a means of identifying career development adjustment problems. The taxonomy is based on the assumption that problems arise when an individual experiences difficulty in coping with a career development task, when a task is only partially mastered, or when a task is not even attempted. To eliminate redundancy and achieve parsimony in constructing the taxonomy, an analysis was made of the 17 tasks and 80 subtasks of the four stages of career development to identify common tasks across the stages. Regardless of this stage content or context, four common tasks were identified as recurring across stages.

The four common tasks are listed below:

1. Decision making.   Information about the self and the environment is gathered and, based upon this information, alternatives are evaluated and selected. Hershenson (1968) and Tiedeman & O'Hara (1963) have discussed this task as it takes place during the preparation stage. It also has been identified in other stages by McCoy (1977) (establishment), Jung (1971) and Neugarten (1968) (maintenance), and Susman (1972) (retirement).

2. Implementing plans.   Activities based upon decisions are scheduled for and put into action over a period of time spanning the present and future. It has been discussed as occurring in various stages by Super (1963) and Ginzberg, Ginsburg, Axelrad, and Herma (1951) (preparation), Schein (1978) (establishment), Levinson et al. (1978) and Super (1957) (maintenance), and Atchley (1977, 1978) (retirement).

3. Organizational/institutional performance.   An acceptable level of productivity is reached. This task has been described by Havighurst (1964) (preparation), Gould (1972) (establishment), Erikson (1950) (maintenance), and Sinick (1977) (retirement).

4. Organizational/institutional adaptation.   Individuals adjust in order to take part effectively in the environment. The task has been described by Miller and Form (1964) (preparation), Schein (1978) and Van Maanen (1972) (establishment and maintenance), and Peck (1968) and Shanas (1972) (retirement).

The taxonomy was constructed to reflect the problems associated with achieving each of the four major tasks. Consequently, the taxonomy consists of four major problem categories: (1) problems in career decision making, (2) problems in implementing career plans, (3) problems in organizational/institutional performance, (4) problems in organizational/institutional adaptation.

Each major problem category is further divided into problem subcategories, that is, more specific types of problems that can be differentiated on the basis of a specific career developmental task, sharing a *common* manifestation, or having a *common* etiology. Within each problem subcategory, problem areas are further delineated with reference to distinguishing causal factor.

Several points concerning the taxonomy should be made. First, although the four major problem categories utilized appeared to minimize overlap, complete independence of problem categories was neither possible nor desirable. Thus, it may be found that problems classified within one problem category may be related to or have implications for problems within other categories.

It should be noted also that clients may have more than one type of problem at any given time and that each problem may stem from different causal factors. For example, a person's job performance may be inadequate due to skill deficits, and at the same time he or she may manifest job adjustment problems due to hostile co-workers.

The ordering of problem categories, subcategories, and causal factors within subcategories is somewhat arbitrary and does not imply that one developmental level or sequence is more important than another. Also, each of the four major problem categories describes problems that may occur at any age or stage in the career development process.

The taxonomy is intended to provide a system for the meaningful *classification* of client problems rather than a *list* of all potential problems. Thus, no attempt was made to include every problem that might arise but, rather, to provide a matrix within which the range of client problems may be classified. It is suggested, therefore, that client problems should first be classified as to problem category and then by problem subcategory. Once the latter has been designated, the range of possible causal factors provided can assist the counselor in formulating alternate diagnostic hypothesis. After determining the salient causal factor(s), appropriate treatment strategies may be formulated and implemented.

Finally, the term *organizational/institutional* is utilized throughout the taxonomy to refer to the environment in which the individual is experiencing career adjustment problems. The term *organizational* refers to the employment setting whereas the term *institutional* refers to the educational or training setting. Thus, career adjustment problems are viewed as occurring both in the actual work environment and in the environment in which the individual prepares for a career.

Table 5.2 provides an outline of the taxonomy. A synopsis of the four major problem categories follows:

1.0. Problems in career decision making.   This category includes problems that interfere with or retard satisfactory initiation and completion of the career decision-making process.

2.0. Problems in implementing career plans.   This category includes problems encountered in the process of implementing one's career plans. Individuals in this category are assumed to have a satisfactory career deci-

TABLE 5.2[a]
Diagnostic Taxonomy Outline
Problem Categories and Subcategories

1.0 Problems in Career Decision Making

   1.1 Getting Started

      A. Lack of awareness of the need for a decision

      B. Lack of knowledge of the decision-making process

      C. Awareness of the need to make a decision, but avoidance of assuming personal responsibility for decision making

   1.2 Information Gathering

      A. Inadequate, contradictory, and/or insufficient information

      B. Information overload, i.e, excessive information which confuses the decision maker

      C. Lack of knowledge as to how to gather information, i.e., where to obtain information, how to organize, and to evaluate it

      D. Unwillingness to accept the validity of the information because it does not agree with the person's self-concept

   1.3 Generating, Evaluating and Selecting Alternatives

      A. Difficulty deciding due to multiple career options, i.e., too many equally attractive career choices

      B. Failure to generate sufficient career options due to personal limitations such as health, resources, ability, and education

      C. The inability to decide due to the thwarting effects of anxiety such as fear of failure in attempting to fulfill the choice, fear of social disapproval, and/or fear of commitment to a course of action

      D. Unrealistic choice, i.e., aspiring either too low or too high, based upon criteria such as aptitudes, interests, values, resources, and personal circumstances

      E. Interfering personal constraints which impede a choice such as interpersonal influences and conflicts, situational circumstances, resources, and health

      F. The inability to evaluate alternatives due to lack of knowledge of the evaluation criteria—the criteria could include values, interests, aptitudes, skills, resources, health, age, and personal circumstances

   1.4 Formulating Plans for Implementing Decisions

      A. Lack of knowledge of the necessary steps to formulate a plan

      B. Inability to utilize a future time perspective in planning

      C. Unwillingness and/or inability to acquire the necessary information to formulate a plan

2.0 Problems in Implementing Career Plans

   2.1 Characteristics of the Individual

      A. Failure of the individual to undertake the steps necessary to implement his/her plan

TABLE 5.2 (*continued*)

B. Failure or inability to successfully complete the steps necessary for goal attainment

C. Adverse changes in the individual's physical or emotional condition

2.2 Characteristics External to the Individual

A. Unfavorable economic, social, and cultural conditions

B. Unfavorable conditions in the organization or institution central to the implementation of one's plans

C. Adverse conditions of or changes in the individual's family situation

3.0 Problems in Organization/Institutional Performance

3.1 Deficiencies in Skills, Abilities and Knowledge

A. Insufficient skills, abilities, and/or knowledge upon position entry, i.e., underqualified to perform satisfactorily

B. The deterioration of skills, abilities, and/or knowledge over time in the positions due to temporary assignment to another position, leave, and/or lack of continual practice of the skill

C. The failure to modify or update skills, abilities, and/or knowledge to stay abreast of job changes, i.e., job obsolescence due to new technology, tools, and knowledge

3.2 Personal Factors

A. Personality characteristics discrepant with the job, e.g., values, interests, and work habits

B. Debilitating physical and/or emotional disorders

C. Adverse off-the-job personal circumstances and/or stressors, e.g., family pressures, financial problems, and personal conflicts

C. The occurrence of interpersonal conflicts on-the-job which are specific to performance requirements, e.g., getting along with the boss, coworkers, customers, and clients

3.3 Conditions of the Organization/Institutional Environment

A. Ambiguous or inappropriate job requirements, e.g., lack of clarity of assignments, work overload, and conflicting assignments

B. Deficiencies in the operational structure of the organization/institution

C. Inadequate support facilities, supplies and resources, e.g., insufficient lighting, ventilation, tools, support personnel, and materials

D. Insufficient reward system, e.g., compensation, fringe benefits, status, recognition, and opportunities for advancement

4.0 Problems in Organizational/Institutional Adaption

4.1 Initial Entry

A. Lack of knowledge of organizational rules and procedures

B. Failure to accept or adhere to organizational rules and procedures

TABLE 5.2 *(continued)*

C. Inability to assimilate large quantities of new information, i.e., information overload

D. Discomfort in a new geographic location

E. Discrepancies between the individual's expectations and the realities of the institutional/organizational environment

4.2 Changes Over Time

A. Changes over the life span in one's attitudes, values, life style, career plans, or commitment to the organization which lead to incongruence between the individual and the environment

B. Changes in the organizational/institutional environment which lead to incongruence between the individual and the environment, e.g., physical and administrative structure, policies and procedures

4.3 Interpersonal Relationships

A. Interpersonal conflicts arising from differences of opinion, style, values, mannerisms, etc.

B. The occurrence of verbal or physical abuse or sexual harrassment

---

[a]Campbell, R. E., and Cellini, J. V. A Diagnostic Taxonomy of Adult Career Problems. *Journal of Vocational Behavior,* 1981, *19,* 179–180. Reproduced with permission of the *Journal of Vocational Behavior,* Academic Press.

sion and to have outlined a plan designed to implement that decision. Thus, the next critical step in their career development involves the successful implementation of the decision and the attainment of the desired career objectives.

Problems in implementation are in evidence when the individual's goals are being thwarted and/or when he/she cannot or does not orchestrate planning elements. Problems of this type typically occur due to two subcategories of factors: characteristics of the individual (e.g., lack of motivation to complete the necessary steps in implementation) and characteristics external to the individual (e.g., lack of available positions in the individual's chosen career field).

3.0. Problems in organizational/institutional performance. This category includes problems in which the individual is having difficulty achieving or maintaining an acceptable level of performance based upon either personal and/or organizational/institutional standards within an educational or work setting. The person could be satisfying work standards for the organization/institution but falling short of his/her personal standards, or the reverse (e.g., the student who is getting passing grades but aspires for much higher grades, or the mechanic who feels he/she is doing good work but is not satisfying the boss). Performance problems can be manifested in a variety of ways such as poor quality or quantity of work output, absenteeism, interpersonal conflicts, sloppy work habits, tension, dishonesty, and accidents. Performance problems can be classified under three subcategories: (1) deficits in skills, abilities, and/or knowledge; (2) personal factors (e.g., poor emotional or physical health); and (3) conditions of the organizational/institutional environment (e.g., inadequate support facilities, supplies, and/or resources).

4.0. Problems in organizational/institutional adaptation. This category includes problems in which the individual is having difficulties adjusting to and fitting into the organizational/institutional environment. Problems classified within this category involve difficulties in adjusting to organizational policies, regulations, rules, decorum, administrative structure, and to other members of the organization. The category excludes problems in performance and, rather, emphasizes the degree of adaptation of the individual to the total organizational environment. Problems in this category can be classified using three subcategories, that is, intitial entry, changes over time, and interpersonal relationships.

CAREER AND EDUCATIONAL COUNSELING SERVICES
FOR ADULTS

During the middle 1970s a number of responses to adults' career development needs emerged in this country. These responses arranged from the veritable "corn-utopia" of self-help and Starting Over guides to the profit-making career planning and job search services—including the well-known corporate "head-hunters"—to campus-based and community-based services aimed at assisting adults with both career and educational concerns. It is this latter group that is the focus of this section.

Variously called career and educational services for adults, educational brokerages, adult career advocates, and lifelong learning advisories, these programs took shape in the early 1970s as a loosely connected group of local agencies that provided information, counseling and referral services in a unique way. The first of these agencies called themselves "educational brokering services" to denote their intermediary and client-centered role. Although the more generic term "adult career and educational services" is now broadly used, the term "educational broker" was one that was useful in marking the uniqueness of the early ventures. The term is used in the discussion to follow in order to highlight the distinctiveness of these programs from school-based guidance services and from public and professional employment services.

As a generic group, educational brokers are rather a diverse lot. They offer a variety of services to a variety of clientele in a number of different settings. They are supported by a variety of sponsors and by a number of different income sources.

What makes these community-based services distinct from other types of adult counseling and information services are their purposes, organizational settings, and staffing. Educational brokering services are committed first and foremost to the needs of local communities and individuals rather than the needs of institutions or employers. They seek to serve all adults in their regions through information, referral and counseling services, and to serve special populations with such services as tutoring or rural outreach. Brokers utilize sites that are easily accessible to their clients, such as storefronts, libraries, and mobile vans. Their staffs typically are local people who, as part of the community, keep in daily job and social contact with other local people and with community needs. They usually are not "professional track" career counselors.

Characteristics of Community-Based Career and Educational Counseling Services[1]

In brief, the purposes of educational brokering services are to enable adults to develop career, personal, and educational plans, to explore alternative learning and job possibilities, to enter or reenter postsecondary education as appropriate to their plans and life situations, and to enter and reenter the world of work. Community-based counselors also seek to provide logistical and personal support for adults, remedial and tutorial assistance, and assistance with career or job development strategies. They typically do not offer instruction for credit nor help to actually place people in jobs. An unstated purpose of most of these agencies is to promote client "empowerment": to enable individuals to choose their own directions and make their own decisions in a nondependent manner and, hopefully, to learn to do so throughout their lifetimes. Effective use of information and effective inquiry and follow-through skills are the empowerment capabilities that counselors seek to enhance in their clients. Community-based agencies also seek to bring together the educational, human resources, employment, and training agencies in their communities in order to meet adults' career needs.

Services

The services of community-based educational brokering programs are essentially six: (1) information-giving; (2) assessment; (3) referral; (4)

---

[1]Portions of this section have been reported in "Community Based Information and Counseling Services," by J. M. Heffernan in *Improving Educational Information Services,* Robert I. Wise, editor, *New Directions for Education and Work* series. (San Francisco: Jossey–Bass Publishers, Inc., 1979.

counseling/advising; (5) advocacy; and (6) outreach. Although different agencies may give different emphases to these activities, and each client may require a different combination, they comprise what are considered to be the core service activities. Some examples of these activities follow: *Information giving* could involve descriptions of regional manpower conditions, training requirements for certain jobs, schedules for locally available courses, or procedures for applying for financial aid. *Referrals* may be to educational institutions, informal learning opportunities, employment services, or other community social services (i.e., training, mental health, legal). *Assessment* could involve diagnosis of basic skills, personal and vocational aptitudes or interests, or analysis of job and learning skills. *Counseling* typically revolves around career exploration, life planning and personal decision making, educational choice making, or working out problems associated with returning to school or the work force (i.e., family resistance, child care, study skills, inertia). *Advocacy* might entail gaining credits or other institutional recognition for adults' prior formal learning or their competencies attained on the job, working a special career-related major for an adult student, or, at an institutional level, securing changes in college policies for part-time students or scheduling and job-specific course offerings for adults. *Outreach* efforts would include publicity about services through local media, visits to shopping centers and neighborhoods, or actual delivery of services to adult clients via branch offices or itinerant counselors.

The National Scene: Growth of Educational and Career Services[2]

The 1980 Directory of Educational and Career Services listed 465 programs and agencies that are providing counseling, information, and support services to adults. Because most agencies have multiple sites—the median is between three and four—this means that there were nearly 700 such counseling centers in the United States in 1980. Thirty-eight states have four or more programs; New York has 54, Pennsylvania has 38, California has 35, Texas has 19, and Florida has 18.

The establishment of new programs is continuing. Although several agencies have been in operation since the 1920s and the 1940s, most of the existing ones (83%) were founded after 1972. Growth has been steady: 32 new agencies in 1977, 55 in 1978, and 44 by the end of the third quarter of 1979.

The number of persons served by such programs is large and it is increas-

---

[2]These data were first reported in the *Bulletin* of the National Center for Educational Brokering, vol. 5, no. 3, March 1980, pp. 2–3, and the *1980 Directory of Educational and Career Services,* (Syracuse, N.Y.: National Center for Educational Brokering, 1979).

ing. The total number of clients served from 1973 to 1979 was 1.9 million; the total number served in 1979 was over 763,000.

CONCLUSIONS AND RECOMMENDATIONS

This review of adult vocational behavior would be incomplete without concluding comments as to the state of our knowledge in this area. How does the future look? What needs to be done? The following are recommended:

Examination of coping techniques used by individuals in work adjustment. Individuals use a variety of techniques to cope with on-the-job adjustment and career transition problems. These individuals meet with varying degrees of success in using coping mechanisms such as seeking support from co-workers, attending courses to maintain skills, and taking medications to alleviate tension. Despite the pervasiveness of work and transition problems, there have been few systematic studies of coping techniques. Such studies might be a fruitful endeavor in identifying unique coping techniques, specifying the individual correlates of successful and unsuccessful work adjustment, and revealing maladaptive coping techniques. Once these techniques have been identified and evaluated, they can be incorporated into career counseling programs as both preventative and remedial resources available to counselors and clients.

Study of occupational differences in stress and adjustment. It is assumed that stress and adjustment problems are more pronounced in certain occupations than others (e.g., air traffic controller, physician, corporate executive). However, little research has been done to verify these assumptions. A number of questions need to be answered. For example, if differences exist among occupations in their levels of stress and adjustment, what are the reasons for these differences? Are stress and adjustment problems a function of the person or of the job? To what extent do these problems relate to organizational variables (e.g., size, organizational structure, type of operation)?

Demonstration of treatment implications of diagnostic categories. Although the diagnostic taxonomy should provide a standardized way for "labeling" career problems, this should not be its sole purpose. Experimental studies are needed to demonstrate whether or not a diagnosis as taken from the taxonomy has implications for treatment. This could be accomplished in a two-stage process. First, it would be necessary to catalogue the extant techniques for treating career development problems. Then, using the taxonomy, it will be possible to form several homogeneous groups of individuals sharing a common career problem and measure the groups' differential response to differential treatment.

Refinement of terminology and instrumentation in career development. A review of the literature in career development indicates that there is a need for increased precision in the terminology and instrumentation currently in use.

Terms and concepts exist in career development that have ambiguous or conflicting definitions (e.g., stage, vocation, career). This problem is compounded as burgeoning research produces a proliferation of new terms and concepts. Efforts need to be directed toward bringing precision to the terminology in career development.

Once this is accomplished, the development and refinement of instruments to measure concepts of career development can proceed. Theory building and counseling practice are limited by poor instrumentation of dubious validity and reliability. A lack of more precise measurement methods hinders the verification of hypotheses and the assessment of the effectiveness of our intervention strategies. A common set of terms and concepts, unambiguously defined, would also assist in ameliorating this problem.

Establishment of sound criteria for evaluating career development outcomes. To study the varied dimensions of career development effectively, there is a need for sound criteria to measure research outcomes. The experimental evaluation of career development intervention programs is especially hampered by fragile criteria. Constructs such as vocational success, job satisfaction, occupational choice, career transition, job adjustment, vocational adaptation, and career exploration are frequently mentioned as outcome criteria, but they become operationally elusive in their measurement. Although we have had reasonable success in refining some of these constructs, most of them pose problems. For example, in the study of midlife career transitions, what criteria should be used to determine if a career change has occurred? Should it be a major change of occupation or a minor shift to a related occupation? How do we determine the success of the change (transition)? Similar criterion problems can be proposed for other career development phenomena (e.g., what criteria should be used to assess the establishment of a career?). How do we know when someone has adapted vocationally? What criteria are appropriate to track career progression?

Development of techniques to improve diagnostic assessment. Although the taxonomy identified gross categories and subcategories of career development problems, it does not provide the more comprehensive diagnostic assessment that is needed for a functional diagnostic evaluation of the client's problem. Consequently, it is recommended that more effort be devoted to the development of techniques that would enhance more specific diagnostic evaluation. For example, even though the counselor may have superficially diagnosed a problem as relating to organizational adaptation, this still leaves a great deal of latitude as to the specific facets of this problem (i.e., is it a problem of work style, values, organizational commitment?). Similar questions could relate to other areas of career development.

Improved diagnostic techniques could embrace a range of information gathering approaches such as measurement, observation, and interviewing. Some promising development have been occurring in this regard, for example, adult vocational maturity (Crites, 1978; Super, 1977), vocational indecision (Holland, Gottfredson, & Nafziger, 1975; Osipow, Carney, & Barak, 1976), and organizational commitment (Mowday, Steers, & Porter, 1979). In addition to these instrumentation approaches, observation and interviewing techniques have been developed such as role playing, work evaluations, situational simulations, and structured clientself-reports.

Improved quality and support of adult brokering services.   The time for developing and testing the brokering concepts has passed. The brokering idea and practices have been adopted in a variety of settings. They have been translated into both federal and state legislation. Their utility and their impacts on adult clients have been variously demonstrated.

If the brokering "movement" is to continue to spread to new settings, new and different kinds of challenges will have to be met. The "issues of the Eighties" that will face the providers of adult vocational services will be *quality*—quality of services to clients, quality of brokerages' performance as organizations, and *support*—financial, organizational, and public policy.

Quality and support are the key concerns for the continuing expansion of brokering—type services for essentially two reasons: One, the eighties will be a time of restricted rather than expanding public expenditures for such items as education and social services. Competition for limited resources, both public and private, will increase. Secondly, individual job and career mobility will be lessened because of the combined effects of a slow growth economy and the demographic bulges in the labor supply.

ACKNOWLEDGMENTS

Preparation of this chapter was supported by a grant from the National Institute of Education and Welfare. We are grateful to the National Center for Research in Vocational Education and Robert E. Campbell, James V. Cellini, Paul E. Shaltry,

Aubrey E. Long, and Darlene Pinkos for permission to reproduce Table 1, pages 10–15, and pages 23, 30, 31, 36, 37, and 46 of "A Diagnostic Taxonomy of Adult Career Programs."

REFERENCES

Aslanian, C. B., & Brickell, H. M. *Americans in transition: Life changes as reasons for adult learning.* New York: College Entrance Examination Board, 1980.

Atchley, R. C. *The sociology of retirement.* Cambridge, Mass.: Schenkman, 1976.

Atchley, R. C. *The social forces in later life* (2nd ed.). Belmont, Calif.: Wadsworth, 1977.

Byrne, J. J. *Occupational mobility of workers* (Special Labor Force Report No. 176). Washington, D.C.: U.S. Department of Labor, Bureau of Labor Statistics, 1975.

Campbell, R. E., Cellini, J. V., Shaltry, P. E., Long, A. E., & Pinkos, D. *A diagnostic taxonomy of adult career problems.* Columbus, O.: The National Center for Research in Vocational Education, The Ohio State University, 1979.

Crites, J. O. *Theory and research handbook for the career maturity inventory.* Monterey, Calif.: CTB/McGraw-Hill, 1978.

Erikson, E. H. *Childhood and society.* New York: Norton, 1950.

Ginzberg, E., Ginsburg, S. W., Axelrad, S., & Herma, J. L. *Occupational choice: An approach to a general theory.* New York: Columbia University Press, 1951.

Gottfredson, G. D. *Career stability and redirection in adulthood* (Report No. 219). Baltimore: The Johns Hopkins University Center for Social Organization of Schools, 1976.

Gould, R. The phases of adult life: A study in developmental psychology. *American Journal of Psychiatry,* 1972, *129,* 521–531.

Hall, D. T. *Careers in organizations.* Pacific Palisades, Calif: Goodyear, 1976.

Harris & Associates, Inc. *1979 study of American attitudes toward pensions and retirement.* New York: Johnson & Higgins, 1979.

Havighurst, R. J. *Developmental tasks and education* (2nd ed.). New York: Longmans, Green, & Company, 1952.

Havighurst, R. J. Youth in Exploration and Man Emergent. In H. Borow (Ed.), *Man in a World of Work.* Boston: Houghton Mifflin, 1964.

Hershenson, D. B. Life-stage vocational development system. *Journal of Counseling Psychology,* 1968, *15,* 23–30.

Hitchcock, A. A., & Nott, W. L. *Mid-life change: An annotated bibliography.* Washington, D.C.: The National Vocational Guidance Association, 1981.

Holland, J. L., Gottfredson, G. D., & Nafziger, D. H. Testing the validity of some theoretical signs of vocational decision-making ability. *Journal of Counseling Psychology,* 1975, *22,* 411–422.

Jung, C. G. The stages of life. Translated by R. F. C. Hull. In J. Campbell (Ed.), *The portable Jung.* New York: Viking Press, 1971.

Krumboltz, J. D., Mitchell, A. M., & Jones, G. B. A social learning theory of career selection. *The Counseling Psychologist,* 1976, *6*(1), 71–81.

Levinson, D. J., Darrow, C. N., Klein, E. B., Levinson, M. H., & McKee, B. *The seasons of a man's life.* New York: Knopf, 1978.

Lofquist, L. H., & Dawis, R. V. *Adjustment to work.* New York: Appleton-Century-Crofts, 1969.

Lowenthal, M. F. Social isolation and mental illness in old age. *American Sociological Review,* 1964, *29,* 54–70.

McCoy, V. R. Adult life cycle changes. Lifelong learning: The adult years, 1977, *1*(2), 14–18.

Miller, D. C., & Form, W. H. *Industrial sociology: An introduction to the sociology of work reactions.* New York: Harper & Row, 1951.

Miller, D. C., & Form, W. H. *Industrial sociology: The sociology of work organizations.* New York: Harper & Row, 1964.

Mowday, R. T., Steers, R. M., & Porter, L. W. The measurement of organizational committment. *Journal of Vocational Behavior,* 1979, *14,* 224–248.

Neugarten, B. L. Adult personality: Toward a psychology of the life cycle. In B. L. Neugarten (Ed.), *In middle age and aging.* Chicago: University of Chicago Press, 1968.

Osipow, S. H., Carney, C. G., & Barak, A. A scale of educational-vocational undecidedness: A typological approach. *Journal of Vocational Behavior,* 1976, *9,* 233–243.

Peck, R. Psychological developments in the second half of life. In B. L. Neugarten (Ed.), *Middle age and aging.* Chicago: University of Chicago Press, 1968.

Robbins, P. I. *Successful midlife career change.* New York: AMACOM, 1978.

Schein, E. H. *Career dynamics: Matching individual and organizational needs.* Reading, Mass.: Addison–Wesley, 1978.

Shanas, E. Adjustment to retirement: Substitution or accommodation? In F. M. Carp (Ed.), *Retirement.* New York: Behavioral Publications, 1972.

Sheehy, G. *Passages: Predictable crises of adult life.* New York: Dutton, 1976.

Sheppard, H. L., & Rix, S. E. *The graying of working America: The coming crisis in retirement-age policy.* New York: Free Press, 1977.

Sinick, D. *Counseling older persons: Careers, retirement, dying.* New York: Human Sciences, 1977.

Sommers, D., & Eck, A. Occupational mobility in the American labor force. *Monthly Labor Review,* 1977, *100,* 3–19.

Super, D. E. *The psychology of careers.* New York: Harper & Row, 1957.

Super, D. E. Vocational development in adolescence and early adulthood: Tasks and behaviors. In D. E. Super, R. Starishevsky, N. Matlin, & J. P. Jordaan (Eds.), *Career development: Self concept theory* (Research monograph No. 4). New York: College Entrance Examination Board, 1963.

Super, D. E. Vocational maturity in mid-career. *Vocational Guidance Quarterly,* 1977, *25,* 294–302.

Super, D. E., Kowalski, R. S., & Gotkin, E. H. *Floundering and trial after high school* (Cooperative Research Report No. 1393). New York: Columbia University Press, 1967.

Super, D. E., & Hall, D. T. Career development: Exploration and planning. *Annual Review of Psychology,* 1978, *29,* 333–372.

Sussman, M. B. An analytic model for the sociological study of retirement. In F. M. Carp (Ed.), *Retirement.* New York: Behavioral Publications, 1972.

Tiedeman, D. V., & O'Hara, R. P. *Career development: Choice and adjustment.* New York: College Entrance Examination Board, 1963.

Van Maanen, J. *Breaking-In: A Consideration of Organizational Socialization* (Technical Report No. 10). Irvine, Calif.: University of California, Graduate School of Administration, August 1972.

Woodring, P. Why 65? The case against mandatory retirement. *Saturday Review,* August 7, 1976, pp. 18–20.

III
RESEARCH ISSUES IN VOCATIONAL PSYCHOLOGY

Two chapters make up the final part of the *Foundations* volume of the *Handbook of Vocational Psychology*. The first chapter is by Bert Westbrook on Career Maturity: The Concept, the Instruments and the Research. The second chapter by John O. Crites focuses on the Research Methods in Vocational Psychology.

Westbrook, in his chapter on Career Maturity, reviews the concept, the instruments, and the research related to career maturity. Westbrook notes that he specifically reviews career maturity models and instruments that deal with variables such as occupational information, occupational exploration, career awareness, career planning, career decision making, self-knowledge, career exploration activities, and career indecision. To Westbrook, the words *Vocational Maturity* or *Career Maturity* are associated primarily with Donald E. Super and his associates, particularly John O. Crites and the Career Pattern Study. Thus, a first section reviews and discusses John Crites' Model of Career Maturity. A third section reviews a variety of other models that have developed over the years: The Gribbons and Lohnes' Readiness for Vocational Planning Variables, the Vocational Maturity Project Variables, the National Assessments Career and Occupational Development Objectives, Healy and Klein's Career Education Objectives, the American College Testing Programs Career Development Variables, Fadale's Career Awareness Variables, the Career Indecision Construct, and the College Board's Career Skills. After the Models of Career Maturity have been discussed, Westbrook examines the reliability and validity of various career maturity measures.

John Crites' chapter on Research Methods in Vocational Psychology makes the point that the central focus of research in the field of vocational psychology has been upon theoretical issues and hypothesis testing. In the main, this emphasis has not necessarily been cumulative and frequently has lacked the time consuming studies needed to identify an operationally defined variables of interest. To support this conclusion and to provide an overview of research methods in vocational psychology, his chapter is divided into three sections. As noted by Crites, the first section classifies the research strategies that have been used in the field into categories that are appropriate for different kinds of research purposes: survey, technique, theoretical, and applied. Crites comments on each of these, with illustrative examples of studies which provide models for exemplary research procedures and practices. The second section reviews contemporary approaches to experimentation designed to establish causal connections between independent and dependent variables, with particular emphasis upon what legitimate conclusions may be drawn when randomization cannot be accomplished in field settings. The third and last section is more speculative in nature. It proposes a model of research methods for a vocational psychology based upon an integration of philosophy of science, research design, and statistical analysis.

6 Career Maturity: The Concept, the Instruments, and the Research

Bert W. Westbrook
North Carolina State University

Introduction

The purpose of this chapter is to review the concept, the instruments, and the research related to career maturity. The writer recognizes that the terms vocational maturity and career maturity do not have universal meaning. For the purposes of this chapter, career maturity models and measuring instruments are included in our discussion if they deal with variables such as occupational information, occupational exploration, career awareness, career planning, career decision making, self-knowledge, career exploration activities, and career indecision. Several variables and instruments are specifically excluded in our discussion: interests, values, abilities, and aptitudes.

THE CONCEPT OF CAREER MATURITY

The words vocational maturity or career maturity are associated primarily with Donald E. Super and his associates, particularly John O. Crites, from the Career Pattern Study. The first part of this section reviews the work of Super and his associates. The second part discusses Crites' model of career maturity. This is followed by a review of the work of other researchers.

The Work of Super and His Associates

Although the term *career maturity* was first coined by Crites when he published the Career Maturity Inventory (Crites, 1973a), the concept was introduced 18 years earlier by Super (1955), who called it vocational maturity and defined it conceptually as "the place reached on the continuum of vocational development from exploration to decline [p. 153]." In his article, Super (1955) specified the "dimensions of vocational maturity [p. 154]" that should be applicable during adolescence:

1. *Orientation to vocational choice* includes concern with choice, use of resources, and general occupational information.

2. *Information and planning about preferred occupation* includes the specificity of information one has about his/her preferred occupation, the specificity of planning that the individual has done for his/her preferred occupation, and whether the individual has a vocational preference.

3. *Consistency of vocational preference* was defined as the extent to which one's vocational preferences are consistent over a period of time, within occupational fields, within occupational levels, and within occupational families.

4. *Crystallization of traits* includes seven indices such as interest maturity, vocational independence, realism of attitudes toward work, and degree of patterning of measured interests and work values.

5. *Wisdom of vocational preferences* consists primarily of the relationship between preferences and abilities, activities, and interests.

Super's (1955) idea was that a vocational maturity quotient (VMQ) could be developed to indicate: "whether or not the vocational development of an individual is appropriate for his age and how far below or beyond his chronological age his vocational development is [p. 153]."

In 1957 Super, Crites, Hummel, Moser, Overstreet, and Warnath published the first monograph on the Career Pattern Study, "a longitudinal research project in vocational development [p. vii]." The monograph describes the planning for the study and the initial phases of the project that used 142 eighth-grade boys and 134 ninth-grade boys when the study began in the fall of 1951. Data collection methods included: (1) tests, questionnaires, and ratings; (2) interviews with the boys; and (3) interviews with the parents of the boys. The monograph includes the "interview outlines" for the four semistructured interviews that consist of lead questions and primer questions designed to elicit information about the individual's vocational maturity. For example, one lead question is: "What would you like to be by the time you're thirty? [p. 122]." A primer for that question is: "How do you expect to achieve that ambition? [p. 122]." The interviewer is told to "be sure to get [p. 122]" certain things such as work values and attitudes, alternatives, and planfulness. The titles of the four interviews are free time, school, family, and plans.

Perhaps the most significant achievement of the 1957 monograph is its elaboration of the concept of vocational maturity. The brief discussion in this chapter does not do justice to Super's elucidation of the construct of vocational maturity.

In the second monograph of the Career Pattern Study, Super and Overstreet (1960) report the results of the first year of research, based primarily on data from a group of 105 boys who were in the ninth grade when the study began. In the 1960 monograph Super and Overstreet (1960) defined vocational maturity as comprising six dimensions and 20 indices. Some of the indices contain components and some of the components contain elements, making a total of 77 vocational maturity variables.

As Super and Overstreet (1960) have indicated, the domain of vocational maturity variables was "logically refined [p. 32]" and "strictly hypothetical [p. 34]." When the 77 variables were assessed and subjected to various analyses, Super and Overstreet (1960) concluded that only one major dimension had been established for ninth-grade boys. This dimension "is primarily orientation to the need to make educational and vocational choices including acceptance of responsibility for choosing and planning, and a planning and information-getting approach to the orientation and choice process: it is, essentially, planfulness [p. 150]." In addition to the general vocational maturity trait, Super and Overstreet (1960) reported five factors that could be interpreted: (1) planning orientation; (2) independence of work experience; (3) long view ahead; (4) short view ahead' and (5) intermediate view ahead. Super and Overstreet (1960) conclude that "Vocational maturity in the ninth grade appears to consist of one general factor, Planning Orientation, and three group factors which contribute differently to the four indices [p. 75]."

About 10 years later Super and his colleagues developed the Career Development Inventory (Super, Bohn, Forrest, Jordaan, Lindeman, & Thompson, 1971) and made it available in mimeographed form to other researchers. The Career Development Inventory's preliminary manual (Super & Forrest, 1972) indicated that Super and his associates had narrowed vocational maturity down to three major variables:

1. *Planning orientation* includes concern with choice, specificity of planning, and self-estimated amount of occupational information. It represents the degree of the student's awareness of and inclination toward planning and choice.

2. *Resources for exploration* refers to the quality of the actually used and potentially useful resources for career exploration.

3. *Information and decision making* refers to the student's possession of actual occupational information and his knowledge of how to integrate personal and occupational information into educational and vocational decisions.

In a 1979 article Super and Thompson report that research with Form III of the Career Development Inventory suggests that vocational maturity is comprised of "six psychologically meaningful dimensions [p. 13]":

1. *Extent of planning* refers to planfulness.
2. *Use and evaluation of resources in exploration.*
3. *Career decision making* refers to the students' knowledge and application of career decision-making principles.
4. *Career development information.*
5. *World of work information.*
6. *Information about the preferred occupation.*

In the spring of 1981 Consulting Psychologists Press, Inc. announced the publication of the most recent version of the Career Development Inventory (CDI) (Super, Thompson, Lindeman, Jordaan, & Myers, 1979). The CDI is supplemented by a User's Manual (Thompson, Lindeman, Super, Jordaan, & Myers, 1981) that is "designed to facilitate research and field use [p. iii]."

The CDI yields eight scores: career planning, career exploration, decision-making, world-of-work information, knowledge of preferred occupational group, career development attitudes, career development knowledge and skills, and career orientation total, comprised as follows:

Career planning (20-item score)
Career exploration (20-item score)
Decision-making (20-item score)
World-of-work information (20-item score)
Knowledge of preferred occupation (40-item score)
Career development attitudes (40-item score)
Career development knowledge and skills (40-item score)
Career orientation total (80-item score)

This score is obtained by combining the scores on all CDI scales except the knowledge of the preferred occupational group. The career orientation total score, according to Thompson, Lindeman, Super, Jordaan, and Myers (1981) "approaches a measure of career or vocational maturity [p. 3]."

Super's model of career maturity, with the development and changes over the years, should be recognized for its significance as a first step and as a model that continues to impact on career development theory even as it evolves.

Crites' Model of Career Maturity

In 1961 Crites wrote a paper on the measurement of vocational maturity (Crites, 1961). In this article Crites analyzed and critiqued the various definitions of vocational maturity and consolidated them into "two independent measurable constructs [p. 255]", degree and rate of vocational development:

1. Degree of vocational development "refers to the maturity of an individual's vocational behavior as indicated by the similarity between his behavior and that of the oldest individuals in his vocational life stage [p. 259]." For example, if a student in tenth grade takes an inventory designed for students in the exploratory life stage and scores at the 25th percentile when compared to the oldest students (twelfth graders), then this would be his "degree" of vocational maturity.

2. Rate of vocational development "refers to the maturity of an individual's vocational behavior in comparison with that of his own age group [p. 259]." In other words, how does the student compare with other students his/her own age?

Although this article provided a very helpful synthesis of the various definitions of vocational maturity, it was not clear how Crites' two proposed definitions were "independent" of one another nor did the definitions indicate what variables should be included in the model.

In 1965 Crites reorganized and revised the Career Pattern Study dimensions of vocational maturity into a model of vocational maturity (Crites, 1965). The 1965 model included 18 vocational maturity variables organized under four dimensions: *consistency of vocational choices, realism of vocational choices, vocational choice competencies,* and *vocational choice attitudes.* Sample items were included for the vocational choice attitudes variables in the 1965 (Crites) article. Sample items for vocational choice competencies were presented in a later article (Crites, 1972).

In 1973 Crites published the Career Maturity Inventory and made the following changes in his model of vocational development: He substituted the term *career* for the term *vocational,* he dropped the family variable from the consistency dimension, the wisdom of vocational choices dimension was changed to realism of career choices, and a personality variable was substituted for the activities variable.

The handbook for the Career Maturity Inventory (Crites, 1973a) presents definitions and sample items for the career choice attitudes variables along with a thorough description of the rationale for the career choice competency variables. The handbook does not discuss the variables subsumed under the consistency of career choices and realism of career choices dimensions.

When Crites published the revised edition of the Career Maturity Inventory (Crites, 1978) he made the following changes in the "model of career maturity [p. 4]." The social class variable was dropped from the realism of career choices dimension. Under the career choice attitudes dimension, decisiveness and compromise variables were substituted for the preference and conception variables. Hence, the most recent Crites model of career maturity in adolescence is shown in Fig. 6.1. The 1978 model introduces a distinction among the dimensions in the model of career maturity between career choice *content* and career choice *process* (Crites, 1978a). Career choice *content* includes the consistency of career choices and realism of career choices dimensions in the model. Career choice *process* includes the dimensions of career choice competencies and career choice attitudes in the model of career maturity. According to Crites (1978a): "process and content are largely distinct, must as the assembly line and the product are [p. 5]."

The availability of objective measures of the career choice process variables of the Crites' model has made it possible to investigate the internal validity of the model (Westbrook, 1976a, 1976b, 1976c, 1976d; Westbrook, Cutts, Madison, & Arcia, 1980; Crites, 1978a).

The Career Maturity Inventory (CMI) (Crites, 1965, 1973, 1978), which has probably been the most widely used standardized measure of career maturity, consists of the *attitude scale* and the competence test and is comprised as follows:

Attitude Scale, Screening Form (50-Item Score)

The screening form of the attitude scale (Crites, 1965, 1973, 1978) contains 50 true–false items. Although this scale was designed to measure five attitudinal clusters, it yields only a total score.

Attitude Scale, Counseling Form

The counseling form of the attitude scale (Crites, 1978) contains 75 true–false items and yields scores on five attitude variables. It does not yield a total score and only 47 of the 75 items are scored.

Decisiveness (10-item score).   The extent to which an individual is definite about making a career choice.

Involvement (10-item score).   The extent to which the individual is actively participating in the process of making a choice.

Independence (10-item score).   The extent to which the individual relies upon others in the choice of an occupation.

Orientation (10-item score).   The extent to which the individual is task- or pleasure-oriented in his or her attitudes toward work and the values he or she places upon work.

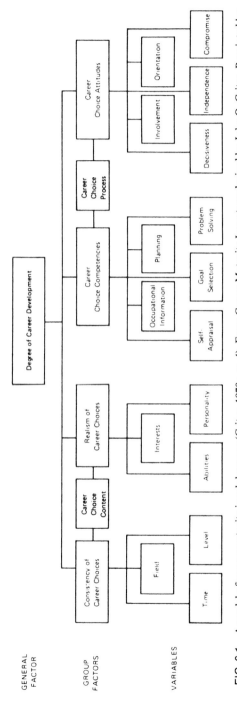

FIG. 6.1 A model of career maturity in adolescence (Crites, 1978a, p. 4). From Career Maturity Inventory devised by John O. Crites. Reprinted by permission of the publisher, CTB/McGraw-Hill, Del Monte Research Park, Monterey, Calif. 93940. Copyright © 1973, 1978 by McGraw-Hill, Inc. All rights reserved. Printed in the United States of America.

Compromise (7-item score). ' The extent to which the individual is willing to compromise between needs and reality.

Competence Test

The competence test is comprised of 100 multiple-choice items that yield five 20-item subtest scores. Scores are *not* combined to give a Competence Test total score.

Self-appraisal (20-item score). Given a description of the characteristics of an individual and a list of conclusions the student is instructed to identify the conclusion that represents the most accurate appraisal of the individual.

Occupational information (20-item score). Given a brief description of a job performed by an individual and a list of occupational titles, the respondent is instructed to identify the correct occupational title for the given job description.

Goal selection (20-item score). Given a description of the characteristics and background of an individual, the student should be able to identify, from a list of jobs, the job that would be most appropriate for the individual.

Planning (20-item score). Given an occupational title and a list of steps that a person could complete to prepare for and enter the given occupation, the student must identify the correct sequence of steps required to enter the given occupation.

Problem solving (20-item score). Given a description of a problem that a person is having in school or in choosing an occupation, the student is instructed to identify, from a list of solutions, the best solution to the given problem.

Clearly, the developing Crites model and the extensive research spawned by his Career Maturity Inventory have both helped to further our understanding of the concept of career maturity and helped to sharpen our questions about it.

Gribbons and Lohnes' Readiness for Vocational Planning Variables

The Career Development Study was a small-sample longitudinal study initiated by Warren Gribbons in 1957 (Gribbons & Lohnes, 1968). This study resembles the Career Pattern Study in some respects, but the 110 subjects in the Career Development Study are equally split between males and females.

The major purpose of the Career Development Study according to Gribbons and Lohnes (1968) was "to test and contribute to the growing body of knowledge on career development [p. 1]." One focus of the study was to assess "readiness for vocational planning." The model for the Career Development Study includes the eight variables "which are considered to represent eight dimensions of a domain of Readiness for Vocational Planning traits [p. 15]."

The Readiness for Vocational Planning (RVP) questionnaire (Gribbons & Lohnes, 1968, pp. 119–121) consists of 47 open-ended questions that were designed "to gather data for the study of pupil progress in career planning [p. 12]" and "to accomplish a successful multidimensional scaling of early vocational maturity [p. 5]." The 47 questions were asked orally in private interviews with the pupils. Responses are written out verbatim by the interviewers and most interviews were tape-recorded. The responses to all questions were assigned scores by using the scoring manual that had been developed during a pilot study (Gribbons & Lohnes, 1968, pp. 137–154). The responses to most questions "fell into clear-cut categories resulting in three, four, or five point scales [p. 15]." The scores were then grouped into the following set of eight variables.

Factors in Curriculum Choice (11-Item Score)

These questions deal with the subject's awareness of relevant factors, including one's abilities, interests, and values and their relation to curriculum choice, curricula available, courses within curricula, and the relation of curriculum choice to occupational choice.

Factors in Occupational Choice (9-Item Score)

These questions assess the student's awareness of relevant factors, including abilities, interests, values; educational requirements for choice; relation of specific high school courses to choice; accuracy of description of occupation.

Verbalized Strengths and Weaknesses (5-Item Score)

These questions are designed to reveal student's ability to verbalize appropriately the relation of personal strengths and weakenesses to educational and vocational choices.

Accuracy of Self-Appraisal (3-Item Score)

These questions with the subject's estimates of his general scholastic ability, verbal ability, and quantitative ability with his actual attainments on scholastic aptitude tests, English grades, and mathematics grades.

Evidence for Self-Rating (3-Item Score)

These questions attempt to determine the quality of the evidence cited by the subject in defense of his appraisal of his own abilities.

Interests (4-Item Score)

These questions are designed to measure the subject's awareness of interests and their relation to occupational choices.

Values (4-Item Score)

Measures awareness of values and their relation to occupational choices.

Independence of Choice (3-Item Score)

Attempts to reveal the subject's willingness to take personal responsibility for his choices.

The scores for the eight variables were subjected to principal components analyses based upon longitudinal data from 110 male and female subjects tested in the eighth and tenth grades. Gribbons and Lohnes (1968) conclude that the eight scales "exhibited enough mutual independence to guarantee the multidimensionality of the measurement space [p. 35]."

The Gribbons and Lohnes work, with its own unique variables and measurement techniques, introduced the variety of career maturity models and instruments that would follow, as the next several sections document.

The Vocational Maturity Project Variables

As a part of the research program of the Center for Occupational Education, Westbrook initiated the Vocational Maturity Project to construct and validate measures of vocational maturity. The Cognitive Vocational Maturity Test (CVMT) (Westbrook, 1970) was designed to measure variables that may be classified in the career choice competency group of the Crites (1965) model of career maturity. Although the psychometric characteristics of the CVMT are presented in several sources (Clemmons, 1973; Westbrook, 1971; Westbrook, 1974; Westbrook, 1977; Westbrook & Mastie, 1973; Westbrook & Mastie, 1974; Westbrook & Parry-Hill, 1973a; Westbrook & Parry-Hill, 1973b; Westbrook & Parry-Hill, 1975), its basic components are:

Fields of Work (20-Item Score)

These items are designed to reveal whether the student has knowledge of the occupations that are available in different fields of work.

Job Selection (15-Item Score)

These items are designed to measure the subject's ability to choose the most realistic occupation for a hypothetical student who is described in terms of his/her abilities, interests, values, etc.

Work Conditions (20-Item Score)

Designed to measure knowledge of work schedules, income level, physical condition, job location, etc.

Education Required (20-Item Score)

These items assess knowledge of educational requirements of jobs.

Attributes Required (20-Item Score)

This subtest is designed to reveal the student's knowledge of the abilities, interests, and values generally required for various occupations.

Duties (25-Item Score)

These items assess the student's knowledge of the principal duties performed in various occupations.

Total Score (120-Item Score)

This score is the sum of all six subtest scores and can be considered to be a geneal measure of occupational information, a component of cognitive vocational maturity.

Results of research on the above variables using the Cognitive Vocational Maturity Test have been reported in several sources (Westbrook, 1976a; Westbrook, 1976b; Westbrook, 1976d; Westbrook & Mastie, 1973; Westbrook & Mastie, 1974; Westbrook & Parry-Hill, 1973a; Westbrook & Parry-Hill, 1973b; Westbrook & Parry-Hill, 1975). As of this writing Westbrook is adding several other vocational maturity variables to his "model." They include variables such as career indecision, career salience, career decision-making principles, involvement, self-knowledge, independence and planfulness.

National Assessment's Career and Occupational Development Objectives

Although the terms vocational maturity or career maturity are not found in National Assessment's literature, their *career and occupational development* objectives include many variables that can be classified clearly as career maturity variables. The National Assessment of Educational Progress published an extensive list of objectives for the area of career and occupational development (1971). The following outline is only a brief summary of the 43-page listing of career and occupational development objectives:

1. Prepare for making career decisions.
   (a) Know own characteristics relevant to career decisions.
   (b) Know the characteristics and requirements of different careers and occupations.
   (c) Relate own personal characteristics to occupational requirements.
   (d) Plan for career development or change.
2. Improve career and occupational capabilities.
3. Possess skills that are generally useful in the world of work.
   (a) Have generally useful numerical skills.
   (b) Have generally useful communication skills.
   (c) Have generally useful manual-perceptual skills.
   (d) Have generally useful information-processing and decision-making skills.
   (e) Have generally useful interpersonal skills.
   (f) Have employment seeking skills.
4. Practice effective work habits.
   (a) Assume responsibility for own behavior.
   (b) Plan work.
   (c) Use initiative and ingenuity to fulfill responsibilities.
   (d) Adapt to varied conditions.
   (e) Maintain good health and grooming.
5. Have positive attitudes toward work.
   (a) Recognize the bases of various attitudes toward work.
   (b) Hold competence and excellence in high regard.
   (c) Seek personal fulfillment through own achievement.
   (d) Value work in terms of societal goals.

Objectives 1a, 1b, and 1c are roughly equivalent to Frank Parson's model of vocational counseling: self-analysis (1a), occupational information (1b), and matching oneself to the best-fitting job (1c). These three areas are also nearly identical to Crites' self-appraisal, occupational information, and goal selection variables. The revised set of objectives, including age-specific objectives, are contained in a 92-page objectives document (National Assessment of Educational Progress, 1977a) that retains these same critical first three objectives while embodying a number of other changes.

The National Assessment of Education Progress developed exercises to assess the achievement of students aged 9, 13, and 17 and young adults aged 26–35 in career and occupational development during 1973–1974 (National Assessment of Educational Progress, 1977b). These types of item formats were used in the National Assessment exercises: (1) multiple-choice items designed to be administered to groups of students; (2) open-ended items to be administered to groups of students; and (3) items administered in an interview situation to one student at a time. Individually administered questions are generally open-ended. Because only a sample of students were administered only a sample of the exercises, scores are not available for individual students. Also, total scores and subtest scores are not available, only percentage scores for each individual exercise.

Healy and Klein's Career Education Objectives

Healy and Klein (1973) drew up a detailed outline of career education objectives that served as the basis for their New Mexico Career Education Test Series (NMCETS). These objectives are "thought to be significantly involved in career success and frequently incorporated into career-education programs [p. 1]." The New Mexico Career Education Test Series was designed to measure those objectives and is comprised as follows:

NM Attitude Toward Work Test (25-Item Score)

Designed to determine whether the student appreciates the personal and social significance of work, the items are written around five clusters of attitudes.

NM Career-Planning Test (20-Item Score)

This test is designed to determine whether the student is able to make appropriate decisions about preparing for an occupation. Half of the items deal with sources of information. The other half are similar to Crites' problem-solving items.

NM Career-Oriented Activities Checklist (25-Item Score)

This is a self-report ineventory that is designed to reveal whether the student has taken important steps in order to help make an occupational decision.

NM Knowledge of Occupations Test (25-Item Score)

This test is designed to reveal whether the student understands the characteristics and requirements of different occupations.

NM Job Application Procedures Test (20-Item Score)

This test is designed to reveal whether the student knows how to apply for a job.

NM Career Development Test (25-Item Score)

This test is designed to determine whether the student knows and appreciates what is required to hold a job and to advance in an occupation.

American College Testing Program's Career Development Variables

In 1974 the Assessment of Career Development (ACD) was published (The American College Testing Program, 1974) to provide measures of occupational characteristics, occupational preparation requirements, career planning knowledge, career planning involvement, and exploratory occupational experiences.

These five areas are considered by the American College Testing Program (1974) to be "core aspects of career development that can be economically and objectively measured through use of standardized group assessment procedures [p. 1]." Although these variables do not claim to represent "the psychological dimensions of vocational maturity [p. 1]", they certainly do cover many behaviors that are included in various models of career maturity such as knowledge of duties required in different occupations, knowledge of the educational requirements of jobs, and involvement in exploratory activities.

The Assessment of Career Development provided measures of the variables that follow. Because redevelopment is now underway, the original form is probably not available. Some elements of some of these components are retained in more recent instruments from ACT such as VIESA:

Occupational characteristics (54-item score)
Occupational preparation requirements (18-item score)
Career planning knowledge (40-item score)
Career planning involvement (32-item score)
Exploratory occupational experiences (90-item score)

Fadale's Career Awareness Variables

The Career Awareness Inventory (Fadale, 1974a) was designed to assess the career awareness element of the Comprehensive Career Education School-Based Model (Fadale, 1974b) for elementary students. The Career Awareness Inventory consists of the seven areas, although only a total score is generated.

The Career Indecision Construct

Still another construct related to career maturity was introduced with the Career Decision Scale (CDS) (Osipow, Carney, Winer, Yanico, & Koschier,

1976), designed according to Osipow (1979) "to identify barriers preventing individuals from making career decisions [p. 1]." The first published version of the Career Decision Scale (Osipow et al., 1976) appears in an article describing the psychometric characteristics of the scale (Osipow, Carney, & Barak, 1976). The third revision of the Career Decision Scale (Osipow, Carney, Winer, Yanico, & Koschier, 1976) appears in a manual for the Career Decision Scale (Osipow, 1980). The Career Decision Scale contains 19 statements that students make about their educational and occupational plans. Students are asked to indicate how closely each item describes them in their thinking about a career or a college major.

College Board's Career Skills

When they published the *Career Skills Assessment Program* (CSAP) (1978a, 1978b), The College Entrance Examination Board revealed a very extensive list of objectives. Although they are called career skills rather than vocational or career maturity variables, they cover many of the same behaviors that are included in career maturity models such as self-evaluation and occupational information. The specifications of career skills are extensive. The list of 259 objectives (sample tasks) covers 17 pages in the handbook (College Entrance Examination Board, 1978b). The career skills are divided into six content areas: self-evaluation and development skills, career awareness skills, career decision-making skills, employment-seeking skills, work effectiveness skills, and personal economics skills. Each of the six areas is described later. Each content area is divided into skills, each skill is divided into objectives, and each objective is divided into tasks measured by multiple-choice items:

> *Self-evaluation and development skills (60-item score)*
> *Career awareness skills (60-item score)*
> *Career decision-making skills (60-item score)*
> *Employment-seeking skills (70-item score)*
> *Work effectiveness skills (60-item score)*
> *Personal economics skills (60-item score)*

Other Concepts/Models of Career Maturity

The present discussion of career maturity does not claim to cover all of the many related concepts and models of career maturity and career education. For the most part, the discussion in this chapter is limited to career maturity models for which standardized measures are available. In addition to those discussed in this chapter there are several local, state, and national models of career education that are not dealt with in this chapter. The reader who is interested in career education models should consult sources such as Taylor, Montague, & Michaels (1972), Miller (1972), and Bonnett (1978).

Similarly, readers interested in fuller reviews of the cited measures themselves are encouraged to consult Hansen, 1974; Katz, 1978; Sorenson, 1974; Westbrook and Mastie, 1973; Westbrook and Mastie, 1974; Westbrook, 1976e; Westbrook and Rogers, 1980; Westbrook, in press; and Zytowski, 1978. In addition to the reviews appearing in *Measurement and Evaluation in Guidance,* the *Journal of Counseling Psychology,* and Buros' *Mental Measurements Yearbooks,* a forthcoming book from the National Vocational Guidance Association, entitled *Counselors' Guide to Career Guidance Measures,* will contain an extensive collection of test reviews.

Despite the limitations of this discussion, a clear picture emerges of a concept and models still in development and of instruments still in refinement. The remainder of this chapter summarizes the ongoing research into the psychometric properties of these instruments.

RELIABILITY AND STABILITY OF CAREER MATURITY MEASURES

Reliability of Career Maturity Measures

Interview techniques.   Data for several of Super's indices of vocational maturity were obtained from content analysis of typescripts of recorded interviews. Super and Overstreet (1960) report reliability estimates based upon agreement between two judges for 10 of the 20 indices. The estimates range from .78 to .84 with an N of 10 to 30 subjects taking each measure. Because some of the indices are based on objective measures or standardized measures or because of inconvenience (Super & Overstreet, 1960), reliability estimates were not reported for half (10 out of 20) of the indices. Super and Overstreet (1960) concluded that "the indices of vocational maturity were reliable enough for use in the study of group trends at the ninth-grade level [p. 49]."

The reliability estimates for the Gribbons and Lohnes Readiness for Vocational Planning instrument (Gribbons & Lohnes, 1968) based on 111 eighth-graders and using interjudge agreement ranged from .70 to .90. All interviews in the Gribbon and Lohnes (1968) sample were scored twice, once by the senior investigator and a second time by another independent judge. It should be emphasized that reliability estimates based upon interjudge agreement provide an estimate of scorer reliability for items, not reliability estimates for the variables assessed by the instrument. The scoring of about half of the items in Super's indices and all of the items in Gribbons and Lohnes' instrument requires a subjective judgment on the part of the tester as to whether the examinee passed or failed the item. For example, in the Gribbons and Lohnes' Readiness for Vocational Planning instrument

(1968), the tester has to decide whether to give a score of 4, 3, 2, 1, or 0 to most items, depending on the "quality and accuracy of information [p. 137]."

Group measures of career maturity.   Unlike interview techniques, most group measures of career maturity have completely objective scoring, so there is usually no question of scoring reliability. The reliability coefficients for several group measures of career maturity are shown in Table 6.1. Because equivalent forms of the instruments are not available, internal consistency reliabilities are estimated by split-half or Kuder–Richardson formulas. Where a range of values is given for a test, it indicates the range of reliabilities in different grades and/or for various subscores. The median reliabilities reported in Table 6.1 range from .61 to .91, but the median of the medians is approximately .75, 15 points lower than the reported average reliability ($r = .90$) of group mental ability tests and standardized achievement tests. An examination of the data in Table 6.1 shows that the median reliability coefficients of the Career Maturity Inventory, Career Development Inventory and Assessment of Career Decision Making scales reported in 14 studies are, with only one exception, in the .60s and .70s. That one exception is the median reliability of the CMI competence test subtests ($r = .83$) reported by Crites (1973, 1978). The reported median reliabilities of scales on the Assessment of Career Development, the Career Decision Scale, the Cognitive Vocational Maturity Test, and the Career Skills Assessment Program are in the .80s and .90s.

Most test experts are critical of using tests with reliability of less than .90 as a basis for individual decisions. It seems apparent that career maturity scales with reliabilities in the .60s and .70s will probably be hard pressed to demonstrate their validity. From a statistical point of view, it is more than a cliché to say that a test cannot be valid unless it is reliable. If it is true that "science flies on the wings of its measurement instruments," then the scientific basis of career maturity, like the instruments themselves, may be in jeopardy. Several writers have expressed a great deal of concern about the less-than-acceptable reliability of career maturity measures (Hanna & Neely, 1978; Moore & McLean, 1977; Prediger, 1979; Westbrook, Cutts, Madison, & Arcia, 1980; Zytowski, 1978). Westbrook, Cutts, Madison, and Arcia (1980) have discussed some of the implications of using unreliable career maturity profile scores for individual interpretation. If the separate scales are unreliable, then the difference scores will be even more unreliable. For example, in the Westbrook et al. (1980) study the reliabilities of the Career Maturity Inventory Competence Tests of goal selection and problem solving were found to be .73 and .64, respectively. The reliability of the difference score is only .30. The low reliability of profile scores has particular implications for the counselor (Westbrook et al., 1980):

TABLE 6.1

Internal Consistency Reliability Coefficients for Group Measures of Career Maturity

Investigator	Test Title	r [a]	
		Range	Median
College Entrance Examination Board (1978)	Career Skills Assessment Program	.85–.93	.91
Westbrook and Parry-Hill (1973)	Cognitive Vocational Maturity Test	.67–.91	.84
Prediger (1979)	Career Decision Scale		.84
Crites (1973, 1978)	CMI Competence Test, 5 Subtests	.58–.90	.83
American College Testing Program (1974)	Assessment of Career Development	.61–.93	.80
Prediger (1979)	Career Development Inventory	.78–.90	.79
Westbrook, Cutts, Madison, and Arcia (1980)	CMI Attitude Scale, Form A-1		.78
Westbrook, Cutts, Madison, and Arcia (1980)	CMI Competence Test, 5 Subtests	.65–.80	.76
Mowsesian and Holley (1977)	CMI Attitude Scale, Form A-1	.70–.81	.75
Crites (1978a)	CMI Attitude Scale, Form A-2	.73–.75	.74
Crites (1973, 1978)	CMI Attitude Scale, Form A-1	.65–.84	.72
Hanna and Neely (1978a)	CMI Attitude Scale, Form A-1	.70–.71	.71
Neely (1981)	CMI Competence Test, 5 Subtests	.51–.80	.70
Prediger (1979)	Assessment of Career Decision Making	.32–.73	.69
Crites (1978a)	CMI Attitude Scale, Counseling Form	.50–.72	.67
Moore and McLean (1977)	CMI Attitude Scale, Form A-1	.58–.64	.61
Median			.75

The low reliability that tends to characterize difference scores on the Competence Test is something to which the counselor must always be sensitive. It becomes a problem whenever the counselor wishes to use test patterns on the Career Maturity Profile for diagnosis. Thus, the judgment that the clients' Goal Selection lags behind his/her Problem Solving is a judgment that has to be made a good deal more tentatively than a judgment about his/her Goal Selection score or his/her Problem Solving score taken separately. Any difference needs to be interpreted in light of the standard error of measurement of that difference. Many differences will be found to be quite small relative to their standard error of measurement, and consequently undependable (Zytowski, 1978). The interpretation of the Career Maturity Profile is where the caution especially applies [p. 273].

The results of reliability studies suggest that investigators should concentrate on increasing the reliability of career maturity measures before becoming engaged in extensive validity studies.

Stability of Career Maturity Measures

The reliability coefficient indicates how accurately a test score measures whatever trait it measures at a given point in time. The stability coefficient, however, indicates how consistent or stable the test scores are from one occasion to another. Stability is an important consideration when a test is designed to measure a trait, because we think of a trait as being a relatively stable and enduring characteristic of persons that should not change frequently. When we obtain a person's score on a career maturity measure today, we would like to have some assurance that the person's score is likely to be very similar if tested again tomorrow, or next week, or even after several months. The stability coefficient for career maturity measures tells us the degree to which the person's score is likely to remain the same over a period of time. The stability coefficients reported in the literature are simply the correlations between scores on the same career maturity scale obtained at two points in time.

How stable are scores on career maturity measures? A review of the literature revealed some but not much evidence on this point. Table 6.2 shows some test–retest stability coefficients that are reported in the literature. It is very difficult to draw firm conclusions about the stability of scores on career maturity measures because the few reported studies differ greatly in terms of number of subjects, level of subjects, test–retest interval, and perhaps a variety of other factors. However, a few observations can be made. The reported median coefficients range from .55 to .90, but the median of the medians ($r = .71$) is considerably less than the median coefficient ($r = .93$) for high school students on the Otis–Lennon Mental Ability Test, a well-established measure of mental ability, over a time interval of 12

TABLE 6.2
Stability Coefficients of Career Maturity Measures

Investigator	Measure	Grade	N	Test-retest Interval	r Range	r Median
Osipow, Carney, and Barak (1976)	Career Decision Scale	13+	56	2 weeks		.90
Osipow, Carney, and Barak (1976)	Career Decision Scale	13+	59	2 weeks		.82
Forrest and Thompson (1974)	Career Development Inventory Scales, Form I	10	82	2–4 weeks	.71–.85	.82
Mowsesian and Holley (1977)	CMI Attitude Scale, Form A-1	8	155	3 months		.78
American College Testing Program (1974)	Assessment of Career Development	11	340	9 weeks	.44–.87	.76
American College Testing Program (1974)	Assessment of Career Development	9	445	9 weeks	.56–.86	.71
Crites (1973a)	CMI Attitude Scale, Form A-1	6–12	1648	12 months		.71
Forrest and Thompson (1974)	Career Development Inventory Scales, Form I	10	1000	6 months	.63–.71	.67
Westbrook, Cutts, Madison, and Arcia (1980)	CMI Attitude Scale, Form A-1	9	193	5 months		.67
Mowsesian and Holley (1977)	CMI Competence Test Subtests	8	155	3 months	.58–.66	.64
Moore and McLean (1977)	CMI Attitude Scale, Form A-1	14–15	202	4 months		.60
Westbrook, Cutts, Madison, and Arcia (1980)	CMI Competence Test Subtests	9	193	5 months	.47–.65	.55

months. Also, none of the coefficients are greater than the .70s if the time between testing is greater than 1 month. The coefficients reported in the literature are relatively low considering the short time interval. The relatively low coefficients may be due to the instability of the trait itself or the methods used to measure the trait. Whatever the explanation, it seems obvious that we do not have evidence that career maturity measures provide scores that are dependable and enduring throughout the course of career development. Perhaps the most important issue posed by these results is whether career maturity scales can be used as measures of individual or group change (Zytowski, 1978). It seems apparent that the stability of career maturity measures needs to be investigated more thoroughly than it has been.

VALIDITY OF CAREER MATURITY MEASURES

This section examines, in turn, the evidence pertaining to the content, concurrent, and construct validity of career maturity measures.

Content Validity of Career Maturity Measures

There are several general statements that can be made about the content of career maturity measures. Each statement is listed, followed by a discussion of the evidence related to the statement:

1. There is very little consensus as to the number of career maturity variables that can be reliably measured, the best organization of them, or their most appropriate names. Nearly all the investigators give somewhat different names to their scales. The number of scales range from one for the 1965 Vocational Development Inventory Attitude Scale and the Career Decision Scale to ten for the Assessment of Career Development. With only two exceptions (career planning and career decision making), none of the investigators use identical scale names. The word *career* appears in several scale names but the item content is not identical.

2. Career maturity measures differ substantially in their coverage of cognitive, affective, and psychomotor behaviors. Using the criteria suggested by Baker and Schutz (1972), Westbrook (1970) drew up a list of 54 instructional objectives by analyzing the content of several career maturity measures. Analyzing the content of six career maturity measures, he found that the measures differ: (1) in their coverage of cognitive, psychomotor, and affective behaviors; (2) in terms of the range of behaviors in the three domains; and (3) in their coverage of specific behaviors.

Even within the same instrument there is an extremely wide range of behaviors. This is illustrated by the Assessment of Career Development (The American College Testing Program, 1972), which covers the affective, cognitive, and psychomotor domains. Westbrook (in press) prepared a detailed content analysis of the Assessment of Career Development and identified 71 independent behaviors covering the three domains.

3. Some instructional objectives are assessed by nearly all career maturity measures. Although different authors of career maturity measures do not agree on all behaviors that constitute career maturity, several authors do agree on a few areas. The five instructional objectives that are assessed most often by career maturity measures can be briefly described as follows: (1) the ability to make appropriate vocational choices; (2) the ability to identify valid sources of occupational information; (3) knowledge of educational requirements of jobs; (4) knowledge of job duties; and (5) the ability to identify the most appropriate solution to a problem that a student is having in school or in choosing a career. These are objectives 38, 6, 16, 22, and 46 in Westbrook's (1970) catalog of instructional objectives in career development.

4. Career maturity instruments vary considerably in their coverage of a particular career development objective. Some tests include only one item to assess a particular objective, whereas other instruments provide separate subtests of 20 or more items to assess the same objective. The Assessment of Career Development includes only five items to measure an objective whereas the Career Maturity Inventory provides a separate subtest of 20 items to assess the same objective.

5. Career maturity instruments vary in their emphasis on occupational information. In a content analysis of career maturity measures, Westbrook (1974) estimated that the Cognitive Vocational Maturity Test is heavily loaded with occupational information items (87%), whereas the Assessment of Career Development focuses less (23%) on occupational information.

6. The jingle and jangle fallacies represent a problem in the measurement of career maturity. The jangle fallacy refers to the fact that two tests with different names do not necessarily measure different things (Hills, 1976). The jingle fallacy refers to the fact that two tests with the same name do not necessarily measure the same thing (Hills, 1976). The jingle fallacy is illustrated by the different types of "planning" items on four different instruments. Crites' planning items present the career goal of a hypothetical individual and a set of unordered steps necessary to attain it. The learner is required to indicate the correct order of these steps.

Super's planning orientation items ask the learner to report how much thinking and planning he/she has done in different areas. The career planning knowledge part of the Assessment of Career Development includes items that deal with trends in the labor force. Finally, the career planning subtest of the New Mexico Career Education Tests includes occupational information items.

Although all four scales claim to provide measures of "planning," the items on each scale clearly differ. Whether these scales are measuring the same or different behaviors is certainly a debatable question. However, they appear to assess different instructional objectives. We might ask ourselves whether these items represent the most appropriate concept of planning and, if not, what an acceptable substitute would be.

7. On many career maturity measures, there are discrepancies between the name of the scale and the behavior actually assessed by the items that comprise the scale. A typical example of this problem is illustrated by the items on the CMI self-appraisal test. The entire test consists of 20 multiple-choice questions that assess the subject's ability to recognize accurate conclusions about hypothetical people whose characteristics have been described; but can we assume that the items measure one's ability to appraise oneself?

In the opinion of Martin Katz (1978), the items "cannot serve as work samples of CDM (career decision making) because they do not engage each person in CDM in his or her own identity [p. 223]." Katz recommends that we measure career decision making by assessing whether students know what information they need, whether they can get the information they want, and whether they can use the information (Katz, 1978).

8. Career maturity instruments vary considerably in terms of how clearly they define the domain being assessed. At one extreme is the Cognitive Vocational Maturity Test that describes the domain by naming and giving a brief description of each of the six career maturity variables in the cognitive domain. At the other extreme is the Career Skills Assessment Program that defines the domain by presenting a total of 259 different instructional objectives, each of which is assessed by one or more items.

In summary, the analysis of career maturity measures reveals that there is very little consensus regarding what should be covered on career maturity measures.

Concurrent Validity of Career Maturity Measures

How well do scores on different career maturity measures agree with one another? Do different career maturity instruments measure one and the same career maturity? There are only a few studies of correlations between different career maturity measures that can shed light on concurrent validity questions such as these.

The correlations among various career maturity measures reported in five studies (Forrest & Thompson, 1974; Prediger, 1979; Westbrook, 1976a; Westbrook, 1976d; Westbrook, Cutts, Madison, & Arcia, 1980) were found to vary widely. Because of space limitations, the summary table has been omitted. The unpublished table shows a total of 21 *different* median correlations that range from −.18 to .62. The median of the medians is .18, which is considerably lower than the typical range of correlations (+.67 to .77) between different mental ability tests (Jensen, 1980).

Is it possible that .18 is a misleading index of the relationship between different career maturity measures because some of the scales are affective and others are cognitive? To provide a partial answer to this question, all of the scales in the Prediger (1979) study were classified as a measure of typical performance or maximum performance, using Cronbach's (1970) definitions.

The data suggest that scores on different measures of career maturity in the affective domain (measures of typical performance) do not agree with one another, because the median correlation attained in a very extensive investigation (Prediger, 1979) is only .25.

The correlations among cognitive career maturity scales (i.e., measures of maximum performance) developed by different investigators range from .45 to .65, but most of them are in the .50s with a median of .56.

Table 6.3 presents a summary of the correlations among different career maturity measures compared to the correlations among different mental maturity measures. The lowest correlation was obtained whenever career maturity measures were compared to other career maturity measures without taking into account the type of career maturity scale. The data suggest that, in general, scores on different career maturity measures do not agree with one another.

Because studies in the literature indicate that there is only moderate agreement between scores on different cognitive measures of career maturity, one might conclude that different cognitive career maturity scales are not measuring the same thing. However, one study (Westbrook, 1976d) demonstrates that *reliable* scores on different cognitive measures of career maturity strongly agree ($r = .88$) with one another. In the Westbrook (1976d) study a correlation of .88 was obtained between the total score on the Cognitive Vocational Maturity Test and a total score on the CMI competence test. These findings, along with the marginal reliability estimates reported for most career maturity subtests, suggest that the concurrent validity of career maturity scales could be improved, perhaps substantially, if the reliability of career maturity scales were increased.

In summary, the results of studies suggest that scores on different career maturity measures do not agree with one another when all scales on each instrument are compared with all scales on other instruments (median r = .18) or when different affective career maturity scales are compared with one another (median r = .25). Although there is moderate agreement between scores on different career maturity scales in the cognitive domain (median r = .56), the agreement is less than the agreement between different mental ability tests (typical range = .67 to .77). The much higher correlation between highly reliable scores on different cognitive career maturity total scores (r = .88) (Westbrook, 1976d) suggests that different cognitive career maturity scales may measure the same thing whenever reliable scores are obtained.

One obvious implication of these results is that test constructors should increase the length of their scales as necessary to yield reliability in the high .80s at least. Until the longer scales are developed and standardized, users of existing career maturity scales should not expect to find very much agreement among them unless the scales are combined to produce more reliable scores.

Construct Validity of Career Maturity Measures

The construct validity of career maturity measures will be examined by reviewing studies of: (1) intercorrelations of career maturity competencies; (2) correlation between career maturity attitudes and career maturity

TABLE 6.3
Summary of Comparisons of Correlations Among Different Mental Maturity Measures and Among Different Career Maturity Measures

Comparison	r
Correlation Between the CMI Competence Test Total Score and CVMT Total Score (Westbrook, 1976d)	.88
Correlations Among Mental Maturity Measures Reported in the Literature (Jensen, 1980)	.67–.77
Correlations Among Different Career Maturity Scales in the Cognitive Domain (Measures of Maximum Performance (Prediger, 1979)	.56
Correlations Among Different Career Maturity Scales in the Affective Domain (Measures of Typical Performance (Prediger, 1979)	.25
Correlations Among Different Career Maturity Scales Irrespective of Domain	.18

competencies; (3) factorial analyses of career maturity measures; (4) correlation between career maturity measures and other variables; and (5) the effects of different treatments on career maturity.

Intercorrelation of Career Choice Competencies

The term *career choice competencies* was introduced by Crites (1973a) to refer to one of the four major dimensions in the model of career maturity. In the Crites (1973a) model, career choice competencies include self-appraisal, occupational information, goal selection, planning, and problem solving. Career choice competencies can be viewed as measures of maximum performance (Cronbach, 1970) or measures in the cognitive domain (Bloom, 1956). Most cognitive career maturity scales can be considered career choice competencies because they are measures of maximum performance and they (like Crites' competence test scales) deal with various aspects of occupational information.

According to Crites, career choice competencies are significantly related to each other, the hypothesized *r* values ranging "between the .40s and .60s (1973a, p. 36; 1978a, p. 35)." The correlations reported in previous studies range from .41 to .88 with a median of .58, which is the approximate theoretical expectation (American College Testing Program, 1974; Crites, 1973a; Forrest & Thompson, 1974; Gasper & Omvig, 1976; Westbrook, 1976a, 1976c, 1976d; Westbrook, Cutts, Madison, & Arcia, 1980). The highest correlation was obtained with the two scales that are probably most reliable, the CMI competence test total score and the CVMT total score.

This finding suggests that it might be appropriate to think of the intercorrelations of more reliable measures of career choice competencies as being in the .60s, .70s, and .80s rather than the .40s, .50s, and .60s. Of course, this is only a hypothesis that should be investigated in future research, but these results are consistent across studies.

Relationship Between Career Maturity Attitudes and Career Maturity Competencies

According to Crites (1965, 1974a), competencies and attitudes are somewhat positively related to each other, probably "in the mid-.30s [1972, p. 4]." However, the correlations reported in some investigations (Westbrook, 1976c, 1976d) range from .56 to .64 and suggest that career maturity competencies and career maturity attitudes are more highly related to each other than hypothesized. More recently, Westbrook et al. (1980) have reported higher correlations (*r* = .47, .59) than the predicted mid-.30s. When the correlations were corrected for attenuation, they increased to .57 and .70.

A review of the literature revealed 38 reported correlations between career maturity attitude measures and career maturity competency measures

(Forrest & Thompson, 1974; Gasper & Omvig, 1976; Hanna & Neely, 1978; Hansen & Ansell, 1973; Super & Thompson, 1979; Westbrook, 1976a, 1976b, 1976c, 1976d; Westbrook, Cutts, Madison, & Arcia, 1980). The coefficients range from a low of .17 to a high of .64, with a median of .40, which is only somewhat higher than Crites' estimate of the mid-.30s. Perhaps the most significant finding is the wide range of coefficients. There is a tendency for Crites' measures of attitudes and competencies to be more highly related to each other than Super's measures of attitudes and competencies are related to each other.

There is a possibility that Super's coefficients tend to be lower because some of his Career Development Inventory scales have lower reliabilities. For example, Thompson and Lindeman (1981) reported the reliability estimates range from .55 to .89, but the median is only .77, which is lower than what is desired for an individual interpretation. If the reliabilities of Super's attitudinal measures and cognitive measures were .90 rather than .77, then the correlation between the attitudinal measures and the cognitive measures might be higher.

In summary, the research data suggest that career maturity attitudes are more highly related to career maturity competencies than the .30s as suggested by Crites (1972). Highly reliable measures in the affective domain are probably correlated in the .50s and .60s with highly reliable cognitive measures.

Factorial Validity of Career Maturity Measures

Both Super and Crites have contended that career maturity is multidimensional (Crites, 1965, 1973, 1978; Super, 1955; Super & Overstreet, 1960). What is the evidence regarding this issue? There have been only a few investigations of the factorial validity of career maturity measures. This part of the chapter will review the published research that speaks to the multidimensionality of career maturity.

The Super and Overstreet study.   One of the earliest studies was reported by Super and Overstreet (1960). They factored 27 indices of vocational maturity derived from psychometric and interview data on 140 ninth-grade boys in the Career Pattern Study.

Five factors were extracted and rotated to simple structure by the quartimax procedure. Although five factors were extracted, they accounted for only 38% of the total variance. There is a good possibility that the large percentage of remaining variance was due to errors of measurement.

The five reported factors are described as follows:

1. Planning orientation—acceptance of responsibility for choice and planning, specificity of information, and extent of planning activity.

2. Independence of work experience—defined by the index of the same name.
3. Long view ahead—awareness of need for ultimate choices, specificity of information and planning.
4. Short view ahead—specificity of high school plans.
5. Intermediate view ahead—awareness of factors in choice.

Super and Overstreet (1960) conlcude that "Vocational maturity in the ninth grade thus appears to consist of one general factor, Planning Orientation, and three group factors which contribute differently to the four indices [p. 75]."

The Gribbons and Lohnes' study.   The findings of Gribbons and Lohnes (1968) are difficult to interpret. Their eight Readiness for Vocational Planning scales were subjected to principal components analyses based upon longitudinal data from 110 male and female subjects tested in the eighth and tenth grades. All scales except accuracy of self-appraisal had high loadings on the first component, but some of them were loaded on the second component. Gribbons and Lohnes (1968) concluded that "the eight RVP scales exhibited enough mutual independence to guarantee the multidimensionality of the measurement space [p. 35]."

The 1976 Westbrook study.   More recently, there have been some studies that have used objective measures of career maturity to investigate career maturity dimensions (Prediger, 1979; Super & Thompson, 1979; Westbrook, 1976a; Westbrook, Cutts, Madison, & Arcia, 1980; Wilton, 1979).
    Westbrook (1976a) factored 10 objective measures of career maturity that were administered to 90 ninth-grade pupils. Three of the measures were classified in the affective domain (attitudes) based upon their content: Crites' Career Maturity Inventory attitude scale, Super's Career Development Inventory planning orientation, and Super's Career Development Inventory resources for exploration. The other seven measures were classified in the cognitive domain (competencies): Super's Career Development Inventory information and decision-making, and the six part scores on Westbrook's Cognitive Vocational Maturity Test (fields of work, job selection, work conditions, education required, attributes required, and duties). The 10 variables were intercorrelated and factor analyzed. Two factors were extracted and rotated to simple structure by the Direct Oblimin procedure (Harman, 1967).
    One factor was defined by eight scales: the seven scales that require the learner to provide accurate occupational information and the Career Maturity Inventory attitude scale. The second factor was defined by the two

scales that ask the subject to provide self-reports of the things they have done or things that they would do about their career development.

The Wilton study.   Wilton (1979) factor analyzed eight measures that were administered to 89 sixth-graders and 94 eighth-graders. The measures included five of the Career Maturity Inventory scales (attitude scale, self-appraisal, occupational information, planning, and problem solving), the Children's Social Desirability Questionnaire (Crandall, Crandall, & Katkovsky, 1965), the Children's Nowicki–Strickland Locus of Control Scale (Nowicki & Strickland, 1973) and the Different Situations Inventory (Gardner & Warren, 1977). Two factors were extracted.

The five career maturity scores loaded by Wilton (1979) on one factor, "an indication that they represented one overall dimension of factor of career maturity [p. 7]."

The Super and Thompson study.   Super and Thompson (1979) factored the six scales that comprise the Career Development Inventory, Form III (Super, Thompson, Lindeman, Jordaan, & Myers, 1979): (1) extent of planning; (2) use and evaluation of resources in exploration; (3) career decision making; (4) career development information; (5) world-of-work information; and (6) information about the preferred occupation. Separate factor analyses were carried out for ninth-graders ($N = 195$) and eleventh-graders ($N = 147$).

Two factors were extracted in both grades. Super and Thompson (1979) conclude that the results "clearly yield a two-factor structure, with the attitudinal Scales (1 and 2) in one cluster and the cognitive Scales (3 to 6) in the other [p. 13]." These results agree with those of Westbrook (1976a) who found that the Career Development Inventory affective scales loaded on one factor and the cognitive scales loaded on a different factor.

The Prediger study.   Prediger (1979) factor analyzed 19 scales from several major instruments assessing various aspects of career development and decision making: Harren's Assessment of Career Decision Making (ACDM) (seven scales), Crites' Career Maturity Inventory (CMI) attitude scale and goal selection test; the career decision making skills test of College Boards' Career Skills Assessment Program (CSAP), Osipow et al.'s Career Decision Scale (CDS); the quantitative thinking scale and the reading total scale of the Iowa Tests of Educational Development, Form Y-6 (ITED); three shortened scales of Super's Career Development Inventory (CDI) (extent of planning, career decision making, world-of-work information); and three scales from American College Testing Program's Assessment of Career Development (ACD) (career planning knowledge, career planning involvement, certainty of choice).

Four factors were derived via the principal-factor procedure. The first factor is defined primarily by the following scales, which are listed in descending order according to size of factor loading:

1. CSAP career decision making skills
2. ITED reading total
3. CDI world-of-work information
4. ACD career planning knowledge
5. CDI career decision making
6. ITED quantitative thinking
7. CMI goal selection
8. CMI attitude scale

What do the above measures have in common? They all require the subject to be able to read; the reading load is heaviest on the measures at the top of the list: CSAP career decision making skills and ITED reading total. Of course, all 19 measures included in the study require reading. However, the above eight scales involve a higher level of reading comprehension than the other 11 scales. In addition, having knowledge and general mental ability appears to contribute to performance on the above eight scales.

Another common characteristic of all the scales is that they are all measures of maximum performance (Cronbach, 1969) because they require the learner to try to attain the highest score possible. All eight scales are measures in the cognitive domain (Bloom, 1958) rather than the affective or psychomotor domain.

An additional thing that can be said about the eight scales is that none of them is a self-report measure whereas all the other 11 scales are self-report scales. Thus, although the name of the first factor is debatable, it might be referred to as "the cognitive domain."

The second, third, and fourth factors are comprised of variables that can be described as self-report affective measures. All the variables that load on the second factor are decision-making style measures.

The third factor is defined primarily by measures that ask the subject to provide a self-report of how much thinking, exploring, and planning he/she has engaged in (i.e., involvement).

The fourth factor appears to be a career indecision factor because it is defined primarily by Osipow's Career Decision Scale.

In summary, there seems to be some evidence for a cognitive factor, an indecision factor, an involvement factor, and a decision-making style factor.

The 1980 Westbrook studies.   In an investigation of the Crites' model of career maturity using 312 ninth-graders, Westbrook (1980) factored the six scales on the Career Maturity Inventory: attitude scale, self-appraisal, occupational information, goal selection, planning, and problem solving. Only one factor was extracted because there was only one factor with an eigenvalue greater than 1.00. In a separate analysis with the same sample (Westbrook, 1980), the same six career maturity scales, an ability measure and two achievement measures were factored. All nine measures loaded heavily on one factor.

Westbrook (1980) also carried out a factor analysis of career maturity measures with 200 technical college students. When Crites' six Career Maturity Inventory scales were factor analyzed, only one factor yielded an eigenvalue greater than one. When the six career maturity scales and three other scales were factored, only one factor was obtained having an eigenvalue greater than one.

In sum, the Westbrook (1980) factor analyses provided no evidence to support the multidimensional theory of the Crites' model.

Summary of factorial studies.   The results of the factor analytic studies suggest that career maturity measures of maximum performance (the cognitive domain) tend to load on the same factor. The studies do not provide evidence that there are different cognitive career maturity factors. Also, there is no evidence that cognitive career maturity scales are measuring anything different from cognitive measures of ability and achievement.

There are some data to support the idea of "domain" factors, at the very least a cognitive domain factor and a noncognitive domain factor (Prediger, 1979; Super & Thompson, 1979; Westbrook, 1976a).

Finally, there is some evidence (Prediger, 1979) that there may be different noncognitive career maturity factors in the affective domain. These noncognitive factors are based on self-reports and may be referred to as an indecision factor, an involvement factor, and a decision-making style factor, etc. Of course, generalizations cannot be made until these studies are replicated.

Correlations of Career Maturity Measures
With Other Variables

This section will present the results of studies of the relationship between career maturity and mental ability, scholastic achievement, sex, and race.

Correlations with mental ability measures.   To shed light on the construct validity of career maturity measures, the American Psychological Association (1974) states that authors of career maturity measures should report "correlations between the test and other relevant tests for which interpretations are relatively clear [p. 47]." Such information enables us to determine the extent to which constructs other than career maturity account for variance in scores on the test.

Authors of career maturity measures should present data relevant to those counter-hypotheses most likely to account for variance in test scores. Test authors should report correlations of career maturity measures with well-established standardized measures of mental ability and educational achievement because ability and achievement are recognized for their importance in educational performance and often account for much of total test variance.

To be of practical value, career maturity measures must not closely duplicate the measurement of mental ability and educational achievement.

The term *career maturity* refers to a psychological construct that presumably differs from mental ability. Theoretically, a person could be high on career maturity and low on mental maturity, or vice versa. If the construct of career maturity is meaningful, then we should be able to demonstrate empirically the relative independence of career maturity and mental maturity.

A review of the literature revealed 46 reported correlations between measures of career maturity and measures of mental ability. Because of space limitations, the lengthy table reporting the investigator, grade level, number of subjects, and names of the instruments could not be included. The unpublished table shows that the correlations range from .08 to .86 with a median of .54.

However, the median of .54 does not tell the full story. The correlations between the cognitive measures of career maturity and mental ability measures among secondary school (grades 6–12) students are higher, ranging from .43 to .86, with a median of .61.

Furthermore, the data show that the longer, more reliable scores (such as the CMI competence test total score and the CVMT total scores correlate in the .70s and .80s with mental ability measures.

In addition, when the correlations are corrected for attenuation, their size increases substantially in some cases. The data suggest that highly reliable cognitive measures of career maturity duplicate, to some extent, the measurement of mental ability.

Career maturity measures in the affective domain (measures of typical performance) correlate much lower with mental ability measures, ranging from .08 to .49 with a median of .32.

Correlations with scholastic achievement. If career maturity is something different from educational achievement, then scores on career maturity measures should not be correlated highly with scores on standardized achievement measures. Theoretically, it should be possible for a student to be a low or average achiever in his/her school work, but have high scores on career maturity measures. If career maturity and educational achievement are truly different constructs, then it should be possible for a student with low career maturity scores to have high scores on standardized achievement tests.

The correlations reported in previous studies of the relationship between career maturity and educational achievement range from $-.10$ to $.77$ with a median of $.57$. The data show some fairly consistent trends:

1. Career maturity measures of typical performance (the affective domain measures) are practically uncorrelated with standardized achievement tests, the r's ranging from $-.10$ to $.08$.

2. Career maturity measures of maximum performance (the cognitive domain measures) are correlated substantially with standardized achievement tests, ranging from $.37$ to $.77$ with a median of $.64$.

3. In several samples, career maturity measures in the cognitive domain are correlated in the $.70$s with standardized achievement measures of reading and language.

4. The correlations corrected for attenuation are higher and indicate that we can think of the correlation of cognitive career maturity measures with reading and language measures in some cases as the low $.80$s.

Correlations with Holland's congruency variable.   Several studies have reported a significant relationship between congruent person–environment interactions and career maturity (Walsh & Barrow, 1971; Walsh & Hanle, 1975; Walsh & Osipow, 1976). Congruency occurs when a person is in a like environment. An example of a high level of congruency would be an artistic person in an artistic environment. An artistic person in a conventional environment represents incongruency.

Relationship between career maturity and sex.   Several investigators have found that secondary school females are more career mature, on the average, than males (Omvig & Thomas, 1977; Smith & Herr, 1972; Westbrook, 1980).

The ninth-grade females in Westbrook et al.'s (1980) study attained significantly higher scores than males on all the Career Maturity Inventory competence test subtests as well as the total score. Females also scored higher than males on the Career Maturity Inventory attitude scale, but the difference was not significant.

The technical college female students in Westbrook et al.'s (1980) study attained higher scores than male students on all career maturity measures. The differences were significant on all tests except goal selection.

Similar results have been reported by Thompson et al. (1981). Career orientation total scores on the Career Development Inventory are higher for females at all grade levels.

In summary, the evidence reported in the literature suggests that females are more career mature than males.

Relation between career maturity and race.   A review of the literature revealed a few studies that investigated the relationship between career maturity and ethnic background. Lawrence and Brown (1976) found significant race differences on all career maturity measures employed in their study. Crites (1978b) reported that black students attained lower scores than the standardization sample of white ninth-graders.

These results were confirmed by Westbrook et al. (1980) who found that white students attained significantly higher scores than black students in grade 9 and in college. The white students in grade 9 scored significantly higher on all tests. Similar results were found among technical college students. The research evidence shows consistently that whites score significantly higher than blacks on career maturity measures.

Effects of Different Treatments on Career Maturity Scores

Career maturity measures have been used in numerous studies and evaluation projects as criterion measures to assess the effectiveness of some sort of treatment, program, or activity. Some reports of these studies can be found in government technical documents, theses and dissertations, and journal reports. A review of these studies revealed that the studies are so different from each other that it is difficult to draw conclusions. Perhaps the most extensive review was carried out by Bonnet (1978) who found that only a small fraction of career education programs reported statistically significant results using career maturity measures.

The Bonnet (1978) analysis shows that when the CMI attitude scale was used as a criterion measure only two out of 34 studies yielded significant results. Similarly low success rates were obtained with the CMI competence test subtests. The success rates were as follows: goal selection, only three out of 25 successes; problem solving, two out of 18; self-appraisal, two out of 19; occupational information, two out of 20; and planning, two out of 25.

Whether or not the low success rate is due to the inadequacy of the measures or of the programs remains to be determined.

SUMMARY, CONCLUSIONS, SUGGESTIONS FOR RESEARCH

A review of career maturity instruments and research suggests that a number of generalizations can be made, some of which have been discussed elsewhere (Westbrook, in press):

1. There is very little consensus as to the number of career maturity variables that can be reliably measured, the best organization of them, or their most appropriate names.

2. Career maturity tests differ substantially in their coverage of cognitive, psychomotor, and affective behavior.

3. Some instructional objectives in the cognitive domain are assessed by nearly all career maturity tests.

4. Career maturity tests vary enormously in their coverage of a particular objective. Some tests include only one item to measure a particular objective, whereas other tests provide separate subtests of 20 or more items to assess the same objective.

5. Career maturity measures vary in their emphasis on occupational information. Some tests appear to be overloaded with occupational information items, whereas other tests are comprised of items in a variety of areas.

6. Although several scales from different tests have similar names, the items do not look as if they are measuring the same behavior.

7. We have a tendency to overgeneralize regarding the domain sampled by career development tests. A multiple-choice question may measure the ability to recognize accurate conclusions about hypothetical people whose characteristics have been described, but can it be assumed that such a test also measures the ability to accurately appraise one's own career-relevant capabilities?

8. There is no evidence that variables called career maturity have more in common with each other than they have in common with non career-maturity variables.

9. Many career maturity tests yield several scores that are not distinguishable from each other statistically. What is the rationale and the justification for dividing career development knowledge into so many differently named parts? Research results indicate that part scores are so highly intercorrelated that, for the most part, they are probably measuring the same thing.

10. There is very little sound evidence that career maturity is a multidimensional construct. A review of the literature revealed only one study (Super & Thompson, 1979) that yielded more than one factor, but the second factor (a noncognitive factor) consists of two self-report scales that have not yet proven themselves as reliable and valid measures of significant career maturity constructs.

11. We need a stronger research base before we use these instruments for differential diagnosis in career counseling. To illustrate this point, one Career Maturity Inventory is recommended by Crites (1973b) as "an assessment device which might be useful to the practicing counselor [p. 34]." The instrument could be used for differential diagnosis if evidence could be marshalled to support Super's (1974) contention that it "yields scores for six major aspects of vocational maturity [p. 164]."

12. There is evidence that there is a relationship between career maturity and sex. Females score higher than males and, for the most part, the differences are statistically significant. Although the scores are significantly different, it is yet to be determined whether these results should be attributed to real differences between males and females or to the test.

13. There is some evidence that there is a relationship between career maturity and ethnic background. A review of the literature revealed that whites score significantly higher than blacks on all the measures. Whether these results are due to real differences in the career maturity of blacks and whites or to the test has not yet been determined.

14. The reliability of many career maturity measures has not been firmly established. Until the reliability of most career maturity measures has been improved, we cannot place a great deal of confidence in the results.

15. Career maturity attitude variables have less in common with reading ability than do career maturity competency variables. Scales that are least highly correlated with reading seem to have different characteristics: They do not attempt to measure what the learner knows; they tend to be self-report measures in which the learner reports how he/she feels, what the learner thinks he/she can do, or what the learner says he/she is actually doing to facilitate his/her career maturity.

Some very promising measures of career maturity appear to be those that are: (1) highly reliable; and (2) uncorrelated with reading. The following scales have reliabilities of at least .84 and correlate less than .10 with the ITED Reading Test: Career Development Inventory Planning, Career Decision Scale, and Assessment of Career Development Involvement.

16. Career maturity measures have been used widely as a criterion measure for career education programs, but Bonnet's (Note 1) analysis revealed that only a small fraction of the programs reported statistically significant results.

Studies Needed

Westbrook et. al. (1980) have suggested a number of research studies that might shed light on the construct of career maturity:

1. Administer separate measures of all 16 variables in the Crites (1978a) model and intercorrelate and factor analyze the scores to determine whether the model is multidimensional.

2. Use the multitrait–multimethod matrix design (Campbell & Fiske, 1959) to investigate the construct validity of vareer maturity measures.

3. Administer career maturity measures/indicators to students at dif-

ferent ability levels to determine which items and indicators are highly correlated with each other but uncorrelated with mental ability.

4. Construct and tryout new measures of career maturity that are less demanding in reading, verbal, and language skils; that have fewer occupational information items than existing measures; and that include variables such as career indecision, career salience, and realism or career choice.

5. Investigate procedures for increasing the reliability of existing career maturity measures such as increasing the length of the attitude scale or combining the scores on the subtests of the competence test.

6. Administer career maturity measures to students and ask the students' teachers or counselors to provide independent ratings of each pupil's career maturity level.

7. Conduct studies of the relationship between career maturity and career adjustment.

8. Carry out studies to determine the relationship between career maturity and appropriateness of vocational choices (Westbrook, 1976b), particularly simulated occupational choice (Katz, Norris, & Pears, 1978).

9. Perhaps an updated content analysis (Westbrook, 1974) or a comparative test review (Westbrook & Mastie, 1973) would be helpful if it included more recent measures of career maturity.

10. A recent nationwide assessment (Westbrook, 1978a) indicates the need for studies of adult career maturity.

Westbrook et. al. (1980) have suggested that the concept of career maturity is an endangered species:

A major goal of future investigations should be to collect more evidence of the construct validity of career maturity measures. If over the course of numerous investigations career maturity measures produce theoretically parsimonious findings that fit the construct name *career maturity* applied to them, then investigators will be encouraged to continue using them in research, and to use the name *career maturity* to refer to the instruments. On the other hand, if the evidence is dismal in this regard, it will discourage scientists from investing in additional research with the instruments, and we will continue to wonder if the instruments really fit the trait name that has been employed to describe them [p. 278].

REFERENCES

The American College Testing Program. *Assessment for career development, form B.* Iowa City, Ia.: Author, 1972.

The American College Testing Program. *Handbook for the assessment of career development.* Boston: Houghton Mufflin, 1974.

American Psychological Association. *Standards for educational and psychological tests.* Washington, D.C.: American Psychological Association, 1974.

Bloom, B. S., Engelhart, M. D., Furst, E. J., Hill, W. H., & Krathwohl, D. R. *Taxonomy of educational objectives, handbook I: Cognitive domain.* New York: D. McKay, 1956.

Bonnett, D. G. *A synthesis of results and programmatic recommendations emerging from career education evaluation in 1975-76.* Washington, D.C.: U.S. Government Printing Office, 1978.

Campbell, D. T., & Fiske, D. W. Convergent and discriminant validation by the multitrait-multimethod matrix. *Psychological Bulletin, 1959, 56,* 81-105.

Clemmons, J. S. *Attributes associated with career awareness among North Carolina sixth graders. Unpublished manuscript, Division of Research, State Department of Public Instruction, Raleigh, N.C., 1973.*

College Entrance Examination Board. Career skills assessment program. New York: Author, 1978. (a)

College Entrance Examination Board. *Implementing the career skills assessment program: A handbook for effective use.* New York: Author, 1978. (b)

Crites, J. O. A model for the measurement of vocational maturity. *Journal of Counseling Psychology,* 1961, *8,* 255-259.

Crites, J. O. Measurement of vocational maturity in adolescence: I. Attitude Test of the Vocational Development Inventory. *Psychological Monographs,* 1965, *79* (2, Whole No. 595).

Crites, J. O. Career maturity. *Measurement in Education,* 1972, *4*(2), 1-8.

Crites, J. O. *Theory and research handbook for the Career Maturity Inventory.* Monterey, Calif.: CTB/McGraw-Hill, 1973. (a)

Crites, J. O. *Administration and use manual for the Career Maturity Inventory.* Monterey, Calif.: CTB/McGraw-Hill, 1973. (b)

Crites, J. O. Career development processes: A model of career maturity. In E. L. Herr (Ed.), *Vocational guidance and human development.* Boston: Houghton Mifflin, 1974. (a)

Crites, J. O. *Theory and research handbook for the Career Maturity Inventory* (2nd ed.). Monterey, Calif.: CTB/McGraw-Hill, 1978. (a)

Crites, J. O. *Administration and use manual for the Career Maturity Inventory* (2nd ed.). Monterey, Calif.: CTB/McGraw-Hill, 1978. (b)

Cronbach, L. J. *Essentials of psychological testing* (3rd ed.). New York: Harper & Row, 1970.

Fadale, L. M. *Career Awareness Inventory, student book.* Bensenville, Ill.: Scholastic Testing Service, 1974. (a)

Fadale, L. M. *Teacher's manual for the Career Awareness Inventory.* Bensenville, Ill.: Scholastic Testing Service, 1974. (b)

Forrest, D. J., & Thompson, A. S. The Career Development Inventory. In D. E. Super (Ed.), *Measuring vocational maturity for counseling and evaluation.* Washington, D.C.: National Vocational Guidance Association, 1974.

Gasper, T. H., & Omvig, C. P. The relationship between career maturity and occupational plans of high school juniors. *Journal of Vocational Behavior,* 1976, *9,* 367-375.

Gribbons, W. D., & Lohnes, P. R. *Emerging careers.* New York: Teachers College Bureau of Publications, 1968.

Hanna, G. S., & Neely, M. A. Reliability of the CMI attitude scale. *Measurement and Evaluation in Guidance,* 1978, *11,* 114-116.

Hansen, J. C. Review of Career Maturity Inventory by J. Crites. *Journal of Counseling Psychology,* 1974, *21,* 168-172.

Hansen, J. C., & Ansell, E. M. Assessment of vocational maturity. *Journal of Vocational Behavior,* 1973, *3,* 89-94.

Healy, C. C., & Klein, S. P. *Manual for the New Mexico Career Education Test Series.* Hollywood, Calif.: Monitor, 1973.

Hills, J. R. *Measurement and evaluation in the classroom.* Columbus, O.: Merrill, 1976.

Katz, M. R. Review of the Career Maturity Inventory by J. O. Crites. In O. K. Buros (Ed.), *The eighth mental measurements yearbook.* N.J.: Gryphon Press, 1978.

Katz, M., Norris, L., & Pears, L. Simulated occupational choice: A diagnostic measure of competencies in career decision-making. *Measurement and Evaluation in Guidance,* 1978, *10,* 222-232.

Lawrence, W., & Brown, D. An investigation of intelligence, self-concept, socioeconomic status, race, and sex as predictors of career maturity. *Journal of Vocational Behavior,* 1976, *9,* 43-52.

Miller, A. J. *The emerging school-based comprehensive career education model.* Presented at National Conference on Career Education for Deans of Colleges of Education, Columbus, Ohio, 1972.

Moore, T. L., & McLean, J. E. A validation study of the Career Maturity Inventory attitude scale. *Measurement and Evaluation in Guidance,* 1977, *10,* 113-116.

Mowsesian, R., & Holley, S. I. *Reliability and validity of the CMI by sex, ethnicity and time.* Paper presented at the annual meeting of the American Educational Research Association, New York, April 1977.

National Assessment of Educational Progress. *Objectives for career and occupational development.* Denver: Education Commission of the States, 1971.

National Assessment of Educational Progress. *Career and occupational development kit.* Denver: National Assessment of Educational Progress, 1977. (a)

National Assessment of Educational Progress. *Objectives for career and occupational development* (Second Assessment). Denver: Education Commission of the States, 1977. (b)

Omvig, C. P., & Thomas, E. G. Relationship between career education, sex, and career maturity of sixth and eighth grade pupils. *Journal of Vocational Behavior,* 1977, *11,* 322-331.

Osipow, S. H. *Manual for the Career Decision Scale.* Columbus, O.: Marathon Consulting & Press, 1980.

Osipow, S. H., Carney, C. G., & Barak, A. A scale of educational–vocational undecidedness: A typological approach. *Journal of Vocational Behavior,* 1976, *9,* 233-243.

Osipow, S. H., Carney, C. G., Winer, J., Yanico, B., & Koschier, M. *The Career Decision Scale* (3rd Rev.), Columbus, O.: Marathon Consulting & Press, 1976.

Prediger, D. *Career decision-making measures in the context of Harren's model.* Paper presented at the meeting of the American Personnel and Guidance Association, Las Vegas, April 1979.

Smith, E. D., & Herr, E. L. Sex differences in the maturation of vocational attitudes among adolescents. *Vocational Guidance Quarterly,* 1972, *20,* 177-182.

Sorenson, G. Review of the Career Maturity Inventory. *Measurement and Evaluation in Guidance,* 1974, *7,* 54-57.

Super, D. E. The dimensions and measurement of vocational maturity. *Teachers College Record,* 1955, *57,* 151-163.

Super, D. E. Retrospect, circumspect, and prospect. In D. E. Super (Ed.), *Measuring vocational maturity for counseling and evaluation.* Washington, D.C.: National Vocational Guidance Association, 1974.

Super, D. E., Bohn, M. J., Jr., Forrest, D. J., Jordaan, J. P., Lindeman, R. H., & Thompson, A. S. *Career Development Inventory.* Unpublished test, Columbia University, 1971.

Super, D. E., Crites, J. O., Hummel, R. C., Moser, H. P., Overstreet, P. L., & Warnath, C. F. *Vocational development: A framework for research.* New York: Bureau of Publications, Teachers College, Columbia University, 1957.

Super, D. E., & Forrest, D. J. *Preliminary manual: Career Development Inventory.* New York: Columbia University, Teachers' College, 1972, mimeo.

Super, D. E., & Overstreet, P. L. *The vocational maturity of ninth-grade boys.* New York: Teachers College Bureau of Publications, 1960.

Super, D. E., & Thompson, A. S. A six-scale, two factor measure of adolescent career or vocational maturity. *Vocational Guidance Quarterly,* 1979, *28*(1), 6–15.

Super, D. E., Thompson, A. S., Lindeman, R.H., Jordaan, J. P., & Myers, R. A. *Career Development Inventory.* Palo Alto, Calif.: Consulting Psychologists Press, 1979.

Taylor, J. E., Montogue, E. K., & Michaels, E. R. *An occupational clustering system and curriculum implications for the comprehensive career education model.* Alexandria, Va.: Human Resources Research Organization, 1972.

Thompson, A. S., Lindeman, R. H., Super, D. E., Jordaan, J. P., & Myers, R. A. *Users' manual for the Career Development Inventory.* Palo Alto, Calif.: Consulting Psychologists Press, 1981.

Walsh, W. B., & Barrow, C. A. Consistent and inconsistent career preferences and personality. *Journal of Vocational Behavior,* 1971, *1,* 271–278.

Walsh, W. B., & Hanle, N. A. Consistent occupational preferences, vocational maturity, and academic achievement. *Journal of Vocational Behavior,* 1975, *7,* 89–97.

Walsh, W. B., & Osipow, S. H. Career preferences self-concept and vocational maturity. *Research in Higher Education,* 1976, *1,* 287–295.

Westbrook, B. W. (Ed.). *The Cognitive Vocational Maturity Test.* Unpublished test, Department of Psychology, North Carolina State University, Raleigh, N.C., 1970.

Westbrook, B. W. *Toward the validation of the construct of vocational maturity* (Center Technical Paper No. 6). Raleigh, N.C.: North Carolina State University, Center for Occupational Education, 1971.

Westbrook, B. W. Content analysis of six career development tests. *Measurement and Evaluation in Guidance,* 1974, *7*(3), 172–180. (a)

Westbrook, B. W. *Item numbers of test items on career development tests that can be used to assess specific instructional objectives in the cognitive domain.* Mimeographed. Raleigh, N.C.: North Carolina State University, Department of Psychology, 1974. (b)

Westbrook, B. W. Interrelationship of career choice competencies and career choice attitudes of ninth-grade pupils: Testing hypotheses derived from Crites' model of career maturity. *Journal of Vocational Behavior,* 1976, *8,* 1–12. (a)

Westbrook, B. W. The relationship between vocational maturity and appropriateness of vocational choices of ninth-grade pupils. *Measurement and Evaluation in Guidance,* 1976, *9,* 75–80. (b)

Westbrook, B. W. The relationship between career choice attitudes and career choice competencies of ninth-grade pupils. *Journal of Vocational Behavior,* 1976, *9,* 119–125. (c)

Westbrook, B. W. Criterion-related and construct validity of the Career Maturity Inventory competence test with ninth-grade pupils. *Journal of Vocational Behavior,* 1976, *9,* 377–383. (d)

Westbrook, B. W. Review of the New Mexico career education test series. *Measurement and Evaluation in Guidance,* 1976, *8,* 263–266. (e)

Westbrook, B. W. Content analysis of career development tests. In H. J. Peters & J. C. Hansen (Eds.), *Vocational guidance and career development.* New York: Macmillan, 1977.

Westbrook, B. W. *Career development needs of adults.* Washington, D.C.: The National Vocational Guidance Association and The Association for Measurement and Evaluation in Guidance, 1978. (a)

Westbrook, B. W. Construct validation of career maturity measures. In J. D. Krumboltz & D. A. Hamel (Eds.), *Assessing career development.* Palo Alto, Calif.: Mayfield Publishing, 1982.

Westbrook, B. W., Cutts, C. C., Madison, S. S., & Arcia, M. the validity of the Crites model of career maturity. *Journal of Vocational Behavior,* 1980, *16,* 249–281.

Westbrook, B. W., & Mastie, M. M. Three measures of vocational maturity: A beginning to know about. *Measurement and Evaluation in Guidance,* 1973, *6,* 8–16.

Westbrook, B. W., & Mastie, M. M. The Cognitive Vocational Maturity Test. In D. E. Super (Ed.), *Measuring vocational maturity for counseling and evaluation.* Washington, D.C.: National Vocational Guidance Association, 1974.

Westbrook, B. W., & Parry-Hill, J. W. *The construction and validation of a measure of vocational maturity* (Center Technical Paper No. 16). Raleigh, N.C.: North Carolina State University, Center for Occupational Education, 1973. (a)

Westbrook, B. W., & Parry-Hill, J. W. The measurement of cognitive vocational maturity. *Journal of Vocational Behavior,* 1973, *3,* 239–252. (b)

Westbrook, B. W., & Parry-Hill, J. W. The construction and validation of a measure of vocational maturity. *JSAS Catalog of Selected Documents in Psychology,* 1975, *5,* 256. (Ms. No. 968)

Westbrook, B. W., & Rogers, B. Review of the Career Skills Assessment Program by the College Board. *Measurement and Evaluation in Guidance,* 1980, *13,* 107–115.

Wilton, T. L. *Sex differences in career development: Social desirability as a cultural role mediator in analyzing locus of control and career maturity of middle school students.* Paper presented at the meeting of the Eastern Educational Research Association, Kaiwah Island, South Carolina, February 22, 1979.

Zytowski, D. G. Review of the Career Maturity Inventory by J. O. Crites. In O. K. Buros (Ed.), *The Eighth Mental Measurements Yearbook.* N.J.: Gryphon Press, 1978, 1565–1567.

7 Research Methods in Vocational Psychology*

John O. Crites
Kent State University

Introduction

The field of vocational psychology has a long and distinguished history on career choice and work adjustment phenomena as well as career counseling and vocational guidance interventions. Crites (1969) has delineated four *eras* in the development of vocational psychology as a field of scientific inquiry:

> The first might be called the *observational,* which embraced the period from Parsons and his precursors to World War I, when knowledge of vocational behavior phenomena was largely qualitative; the second would be the *empirical,* which spanned the years between the two world wars, when variables were quantified and empirical laws were established: ... the third might be termed the *theoretical,* which characterizes the present concern of the field with formulating and testing hypotheses [and] in the not too distant future we may envision still another era, best described as *experimental,* in which our research will be conducted in the laboratory as well as in the field [p. 9].

Although written over a decade ago, the prediction of experimental/laboratory research in vocational psychology, with a few notable exceptions, has not come true. Clearly, the central focus of research in the field

---

*With the exception of a section on "Survey Research," this chapter presents an overview of primarily quantitative research methods. It should be recognized that a wide range of qualitative methods are also available that might be applicable to research in vocational psychology. For an overview, see Cook and Reichardt (1979) and Patton (1980).

has been upon theoretical issues and hypothesis testing. This emphasis has not necessarily been cumulative, building upon observational and empirical research, but rather *de novo* attempts at new lines of inquiry, often without the tedious and time-consuming studies needed to identify and operationally define variables of interest.

To explicate this conclusion and to provide an overview of this chapter, surveying the past as well as the present and projecting into the future, this chapter has been divided into three sections: the first classifies the research strategies that have been used in the field into categories that are appropriate for different kinds of research purposes—survey, technique, theoretical, and applied. Critical comment is offered on each of these, with illustrative examples of studies that provide models for exemplary research procedures and practices. The second section discusses contemporary approaches to experimentation designed to establish *causal* connections between independent and dependent variables with particular emphasis upon what legitimate conclusions can be drawn when randomization cannot be accomplished in field settings. Within-group as compared with between-group analyses are also discussed as instances of general data systems, and a taxonomy for selecting appropriate statistical analyses is presented. The third, and last section, is more speculative and hortatory—it proposes a model of research methods for vocational psychology based upon an integration of philosophy of science, research design, and statistical analysis.

RESEARCH METHODS IN VOCATIONAL PSYCHOLOGY: STRATEGIES AND TYPE

A convenient taxonomy for classifying research methods that have been used in vocational psychology comes from Edwards and Cronbach's (1952) and Edwards' (1954) delineation of four types of research depending upon what the purpose of a study is. Definitions of each follow:

1. *Survey research:* to discover relevant variables for more systematic study and to establish the parameters of known variables.
2. *Technique research:* to develop methods, whether test or nontest, for making observations which are quantifiable.
3. *Theoretical research*[1]: to test hypotheses that have been deduced from theories or that have been formulated to account for empirical laws.
4. *Applied research:* to determine what course of action should be taken.

---

[1]Originally, this category was called "Critical Research" by Edwards and Cronbach (1952) and Edwards (1954), but the term *theoretical research* seems to describe it more accurately.

Although these categories are treated as discrete, Edwards (1954) notes that there may be considerable overlapping among them:

> Survey research [for example] may have practical or applied aspects, once it is completed. Examination of the results of survey research may provide a basis for administrative decisions, although this was not contemplated when the research was planned. Technique research may also have applied aspects, and applied research may also have theoretical as well as practical implications [p. 260].

For the purposes of choosing appropriate research methods for investigating a problem, however, the initial question is: Which type of research is being conducted?

Survey Research

The research methods most appropriate for this type of research are those that allow maximal "bandwidth" in the identification of variables of interest for further study. Not to deny the efficacy of intuition and serendipity, it is usually necessary to use more systematic methods to identify and define phenomena that have high heuristic value. There is no one approach that is most productive for this purpose, but there are several widely used ones that have initiated significant programs of research. Foremost among these is the open-ended or semistructured interview. Although it is typically designed to survey certain preconceived topical areas (e.g., vocational decisionmaking), it is unstructured and flexible enough to elicit free responses that can be followed up by the interviewer with additional questions for explication and elaboration. Illustrative of this technique in survey research is the interview schedule devised for collecting data on the vocational development of ninth-grade boys in the Career Pattern Study (Super, Crites, Hummel, Moser, Overstreet, & Warnath, 1957). This interview was one of four from which several of the variables in Super's (1955) concept of vocational maturity were extrapolated, the most important in subsequent research being the "planning" factor in career choice (Super & Overstreet, 1960). That is, through the relatively unstructured and subjective interview method, some variables were identified that have become central to models of career maturity (Crites, 1973, 1978; Super, 1974).

Not only does survey research serve as a modus operandi for identifying salient variables for further study, but it often generates hypotheses about possible relationships among variables that can be more systematically investigated in theoretical research. Probably the outstanding example of this function of survey research is Roe's[2] studies of eminent scientists. In these,

---

[2]See Crites (1969) for references to Roe's research.

she gathered survey data with a variety of methods, including projective techniques and standardized tests, but her principal technique was an in-depth interview of a subject's personal and professional life. From these, she extrapolated what she considered to be a critical variable not only in the career choices of eminent scientists but also in the vocational decisions of others. Roe (1957) hypothesized from her survey interview findings that early childhood experiences in the family directly affect later career choices. More specifically, from her data on eminent scientists augmented by her general theoretical predilections, she conceptually linked the parental attitudes of acceptance, avoidance, and concentration to differential fields of career choice (e.g., avoidance leads to choice of physical science). Empirically, these hypothesized relationships have been only minimally confirmed,[3] but their heuristic value was unquestionably great. They stimulated both theoretical speculations and empirical studies and, although the latter failed to support the former, new hypotheses (e.g., parental attitudes in relation to problems in career choice) and new instruments (viz., the Family Relations Inventory) have emanated from Roe's survey research on eminent scientists.

In addition to the identification of variables and the formulation of hypotheses, survey research sometimes suggests further lines of inquiry that were not originally anticipated or intended. For example, it was mentioned above that an unexpected outcome of Roe's research on parental attitudes was the implication that these variables might be related to problems in vocational choice, whereas they have not been demonstrated to be cor-relates of field of vocational choice. Crites (1969) has hypothesized the following relationships among parental attitudes and choice problems, which have received preliminary support from research by Goen (1963):

1. *Parental acceptance* is related to realism in career choice.
2. *Parental concentration* is related to indecision in career choice.
3. *Parental avoidance* is related to unrealism in career choice.

Also generated from Roe's research on eminent scientists and her theory of vocational choice has been the Family Relations Inventory (FRI) (Brunkan & Crites, 1964) and the studies that have been conducted with it, most of which have been on vocational phenomena (Brunkan, 1965, 1966) but some of which have been on variables of more general interest (Medvene, 1969). Thus, survey research is not necessarily limited to its original focus upon variables and hypotheses in a particular area of investigation. It may have broader implications for research in related or even remote areas of inquiry.

---

[3]More precisely, they have been largely disconfirmed (see discussion in next section on infer-ring causal relationships).

Comment. It should be noted that, although most of this discussion of survey research has focused upon the interview for identifying variables and generating hypotheses, it is by no means the only method available for this purpose. Case studies, for example, are often a rich source of survey data as are verbatim protocols from career counseling interviews. Both have been used to provide item content for inventories and tests in technique research (Crites, 1973, 1978). Another technique is to administer standardized or tailor-made measures to establish base rates for phenomena that have been observed with less objective techniques. Not infrequently, the central tendencies and distribution characteristics of such data suggest further research (Crites, 1969):

> Likewise, correlational and factorial analyses are sometimes classified as survey reseach, if they are made to open up new lines of inquiry. Following Tucker (1955), Bechtoldt (1961) has pointed out, for example, that factor analysis may be *exploratory* or *confirmatory*. The distinction rests upon what is known about an area of investigation: "The exploratory factor analysis, being the first, is used to generate hypotheses while a confirmatory factor analysis is designed subsequently to test these hypotheses" (Bechtoldt, 1961, p. 407) [p. 587]." Implicit in this distinction is a more widely applicable caveat, which should be made about survey research in vocational psychology. Its interpretation should be circumscribed by its purpose—the identification of variables and generation of hypotheses. It should not be interpreted as if it is confirmatory (theoretical) research, which is too often the practice in the field.

Technique Research

Once variables are identified and hypotheses formulated from survey research, technique research should be conducted to give the variables operational definitions. Much controversy has surrounded the concept of operationalizing variables (Cook & Campbell, 1979), but whatever philosophical position is assumed to engage in empirical research it is necessary first to measure the phenomena of interest. Three approaches have generally been used for this purpose: (1) tests and questionnaires; (2) scales; and (3) experimental procedures. Paper-and-pencil instruments have varied from highly sophisticated aptitude tests and interest inventories—the products of many years' research—to homemade measures devised specifically for a given study without much psychometric development. The difficulty with the latter is tha their psychometric characteristics are usually unknown and, as a consequence, they may be confounded with the other variables in a study. For example, if a measure of undetermined reliability is used in an experiment to assess the dependent variable, and if the results are negative (i.e., no significant difference between the experimental and control groups), it may be due to the unreliability of the measure rather than no treatment effect. In this case, the results are equivocal, and the experiment is indeterminate—no definitive conclusions can be drawn. Yet it is seldom recognized that the psychometric properties of an instrument, such as reliability, actually constitute control variables, every bit as much as possible subject and environmental "confounds" (Underwood, 1957), and therefore should be established *before* a study is undertaken.[4]

How technique research should be pursued, however, has raised many theoretical and methodological issues in general and in the field of vocational psychology in particular. One issue revolves around the difference in the orientations of those trained in intellectual measurement (aptitude and achievement tests) and those versed in nonintellectual assessment (interest and personality inventories). For example, standards of high internal consistency expected of aptitude or achievement tests do not necessarily apply to measures of such nonintellective vocational behaviors as career choice attitudes because they are factorially complex variables (Crites, 1978; Cattell & Tsujioka, 1964). If they are purified factorially, as some have proposed (Westbrook, Cutts, Madison, & Arcia, 1980), then, although their reliability (homogeneity) would be greater, their validity for composite nontest behavioral criteria would be less. Thus, for many vocational behaviors, particularly nonintellective ones, the usual psychometric canons of high reliability[5] and high validity may not apply. Another issue, tangentially related to this one but more fundamental, concerns the rational versus empirical methods of constructing tests. Crites (1961, 1973, 1978) has argued that neither is sufficient although elements of both are necessary to construct valid measures. Rationally derived tests and inventories, especially those developed to assess nonintellective behaviors, typically have low empirical validity, and empirically constructed measures often lack content or construct validity. To resolve this dilemma, Crites (1965, 1978) has proposed a combined rational–empirical approach that includes in a test or inventory only those items that are both theoretically meaningful and empirically valid. Experience indicates that measures constructed by this method enter into a more explicable and extensive nomological network than those based upon either method used separately.[6]

---

[4]See Cook and Campbell's (1979, chap. 7) discussion of autocorrelations and error variance as threats to causal inferences from passive-observational studies.

[5]More precisely, the term *reliability,* as referred to by Westbrook et al. (1980), is actually *internal consistency. Ceteris paribus,* a scale or inventory should have sufficient test–retest *stability* to define reliable individual differences in a behavioral phenomenon but not be so stable that there is no possiblity of measuring systematic maturational variance (Karren, Crites, & Bobko, 1979).

[6]See fuller discussion of this point in following section on construct validity. Suffice it to state here that the combined rational–empirical method of test construction circumvents some of the logical fallacies in construct validity.

Illustrative of a set of measures constructed by the rational-empirical method is the Career Maturity Inventory (CMI), which was developed to operationally define the career choice attitudes and career choice competencies delineated in contemporary concepts of career maturity (Crites, 1974a; Super, 1974). Cognate inventories developed rationally *and* empirically, but not using the combined method, are the Career Development Inventory (CDI) (Forrest and Thompson, 1974) and the Assessment of Career Development (ACD) (American College Test Program, 1974). The former emanated from the Career Pattern Study, focusing principally upon the planning and informational variables, in career development, and the latter was based upon Westbrook and Mastie's (1973) Cognitive Vocational Maturity Test (CVMT), although it also included items to survey high school students' opinions about the availability and need for different guidance services. Also promising as a measure of what Crites (1978) has called *career choice process* is the Career Decision Scale constructed by Osipow, Carney, Winer, Yanico, and Koschier (1976). This scale assesses the extent to which an individual is decisive and identifies the factors which produce indecisiveness. In contrast, measures of career choice content (Crites, 1978) quantify the outcomes of the decisional process—which occupation the individual intends to enter after schooling or training. Foremost among these instruments in vocational psychology are the Self-Directed Search (SDS) Holland, 1979) and the Strong-Campbell Interest Inventory (SCII) (Campbell & Hansen, 1981). Even though these are well-established and heavily researched inventories, however, they should be used with cognizance of their limitations (Buros, 1978).

Comment.   Despite the long tradition of psychometric commitment and productivity in vocational psychology (Super & Crites, 1962), current research in the field is not technique oriented. It is disproportionately focused upon theory testing and practical applications, yet without adequate instrumentation little or nothing can be concluded from these studies because of the confounded psychometric properties of the measures. In both theoretical and applied research the main purpose is to attribute some effect to a putative cause (Cook & Campbell, 1979), but this cannot be done particularly if technique research is not sufficient to rule out instrument threats to the validity of the experiment. Especially with respect to the so-called construct validity of an experiment it is essential to control extraneous sources of variance in total score on the dependent variable. As mentioned above, to the extent that the reliability and/or validity of a dependent measure are unknown, the interpretation of the experimental results is compromised. There is no gainsaying, therefore, the necessity of conducting the often painstaking and time-consuming technique research on an instrument's psychometric characteristics prior to running an experiment on a causal connection between X and Y.

Theoretical Research

What is generally referred to as theoretical research has dominated the field of vocational psychology since the early 1950s when a spate of theories appeared, stimulated by the work of Ginzberg, Ginsberg, Axelrad, and Herma (1951), to explain a variety of vocational choice phenomena. In retrospect these theories have fared more or less well for several reasons not the least of which has been a lack of sophistication among vocational psychologists in integrating and implementing the canons and concepts of philosophy of science, experimental design, and statistical analysis in their research. In no other type of research (with the possible exception of applied) is it more important to effect this integration and implementation than in theoretical research if causal conclusions are to be drawn. This is the intent even though the methodology is typically inappropriate. Only if theoretical research is experimental is there the possibility of drawing causal inferences and, then, only probabilistically to the extent that "threats" to the validity of the experiment have been eliminated (Cook & Campbell, 1979). It is widely recognized, from introductory statistics courses to paper presentations at professional meetings, that "causes cannot be inferred from correlations"; yet most of the theoretical research in vocational psychology is correlational.[7] Almost without exception, the major theories of career choice and adjustment (Bordin, Holland, Roe, Super, and Tiedeman) have been "tested" with data from what Cook and Campbell (1979, chap. 7) refer to as passive observational studies.

Studies of this type should be clearly distinguished from forecasting studies, which constitute the bulk of research in predicting high school or college academic achievement and training or on-the-job performance. According to Cook and Campbell (1979): "For purely forecasting purposes, it does not matter whether a predictor works because it is a symptom or a cause [p. 296]." In contrast, it is of central interest in passive observational studies that, for example, socioeconomic status or parental attitudes or needs causally influence career choice or vocational adjustment (Osipow, 1973). By in large, the research methods used by vocational psychologists to establish these causal connections have been zero-order or multiple correlation, even though the so-called independent variables have not been actively manipulated.[8] Sometimes analysis of variance designs have been employed thereby creating the illusion of an experiment but without random assign-

---

[7]More accurately, this research has usually been "non-manipulative." As Cook and Campbell (1979) correctly note: "Correlations in the technical statistical sense could be used to analyze data from experiments as well as from nonintrusive observational studies [p. 295]."

[8]Unfortunately, the terminology here is misleading and confusing, because predictors in regression analyses are often referred to as the "independent" variables even though they have not been actively manipulated.

ment to groups and direct intervention in some but not others. The effect has been seductive—to draw causal conclusions when these are not justified logically or methodologically. Nowhere has this tendency been more apparent in recent years in vocational psychology than in the application of path analysis to choice and adjustment phenomena. Cook and Campbell (1979) are skeptical, however, that path models offer a panacea for passive observational studies: "The estimates of specific causal paths may occasionally be plausible and valid, but the pressure to come up with a model permitting their estimation results in omissions which render most of these conclusions suspect [p. 308]." In general, path analysis is subject to the same third-variable causation flaws that beset other correlational techniques, particularly when, as has frequently been the practice in career research (Card, 1978), the data are cross sectional and hence not even temporal priority is established.

These shortcomings of passive-observational studies in conducting theoretical research on vocational phenomena would be prohibitive were it not that all theoretical research need not necessarily be what Marx (1963) has termed *functional,* as has largely been true in the field. It may be in the model-fitting mode of theory construction, which seeks explanation through establishing an isomorphism between the conceptual-language and data-language levels of scientific discourse (Brodbeck, 1957). In this approach, demonstrating causal relationships among variables is neither the primary objective nor a *sine qua non* of answering why questions. Model fitting nevertheless serves many explanatory functions (Chapanis, 1961; Lachman, 1960). Among these are the following, enumerated by Crites (1969, p. 625) for evaluating theory construction in vocational psychology: (1) subsumptive value; (2) parsimony; (3) internal consistency; (4) heuristic value; and (5) predictive value. To illustrate, consider Crites' (1974b; 1978) model of career maturity. Derived initially from Vernon's (1950) work on the structure of abilities, but found also to fit many vocational phenomena (Crites, 1969), it subsumes Super's (1955) concept of vocational maturity but extends it to include additional dimensions and to specify the relationships among them as expected from a hypothesized hierarchical structure of career choice content and process variables. In other words, it has predictive as well as subsumptive value, and it is internally consistent by analogy to an explicit factor analytic model. Whether it is parsimonious remains to be tested because it has not been compared as yet to the only other model of career maturity that has been proposed (Super, 1974), but it does have heuristic value as numerous studies of its variables (Crites, 1974a, 1978) and recent studies of its structure attest (Westbrook et al., 1980).

Comment. The prospect for theoretical research in vocational psychology from which causal inferences might be drawn would be bleak were it not for a paradigm that Cook and Campbell (1979) do not consider.

This is the strong inference model, originally suggested by Platt (1964) and exemplified by the Taylor–Spence studies of anxiety and learning (Spielberger, 1966). It is a two-stage design, in which differential predictions are made for the outcomes of Study 1 and Study 2. In the Taylor–Spence series of investigations, for example, the hypothesis in Study 1 was that high-anxious S's would condition faster on a simple learning task (eye-blink) than low-anxious S's. In Study 2, the hypothesis was that low-anxious S's would learn a complex task (paired-associates) better than high-anxious S's. In other words, although both studies compared high- and low-anxious S's, the exact opposite results were predicted, depending upon whether the learning task was simple or complex. The causal inference drawn was that the findings confirmed Taylor–Spence theory that posits an interactive (nonlinear) relationship between anxiety and learning, and the inference was strong because the differential prediction presumptively precludes all competing third-variable explanations that are linear or monotonic. Such a strong inference paradigm is extremely powerful logically without instituting the usual experimental or statistical controls. Moreover, it is peculiarly suited to passive observational studies, because what amounts to the independent variable in this design can be a subject characteristic (e.g., anxiety); yet it provides for active manipulation by the experimenter in the choice of the dependent variable, exactly the reverse of classic experimental procedure. If there is any limitation to this design, it is the necessity of an explicit theory from which differential predictions can be deduced. This should, however, be a *sine qua non* for any theoretical research.

Applied Research

As a research strategy, applied research has been much maligned but probably as much misused. It has most likely been maligned because it has been misused. Applied research arises from the need to solve practical problems—which test interpretation method is most effective, which interview techniques are most facilitative, which kinds of occupational information are most useful, etc.? It is sometimes treated, however, as if it is theoretical research and then neither serves the purpose for which it was intended. Certainly theoretical research can guide applied research, and applied research often has implications for theoretical research, but the strategies for each, despite generic communalities, are discernably different. Only occasionally can true experiments be conducted on applied problems in the field, and when they are they often interfere with service exigencies or acquire an aura of artificiality that attenuates their applicability and significance. Often the only resort is what Cook and Campbell (1979) call 'quasi-experiments'' (see next section on experimental research). Because they usually do not involve random assignments to experimental and control conditions, they cannot be classified as true experiments. Often too, they do not even incorporate active manipulation of the independent variable. These are what Underwood (1957) calls *ex post facto* studies and as such are open to many of the threats to the validities of experiments enumerated by Cook and Campbell (1979) [and discussed below]. Spokane and Oliver (in Chapter 4, vol. 2) also note the methodological "flaws" that have beset applied research on the outcomes of vocational interventions (e.g., career counseling).

It is possible to design applied research, however, to minimize some of these problems and, through a series of successive approximations, produce results that contribute to a greater understanding of the vocational phenomena of interest. The applied research that is proposed here is based upon a different premise than classical experimental design. Rather than attempting to eliminate as many extraneous variables as possible by instituting pretreatment controls, a task that is often extremely difficult in field settings, certain contingencies are built into the experimental design, in order to allow for their statistical evaluation as variables that might be confounded with the effects of the intervention(s). Figure 7.1 outlines a "testable experimental design for research on vocational interventions", which illustrates how some possible confounds can be assessed and possibly eliminated from consideration as threats to experimental validity. One of these factors is time, because in a field setting subjects may start interventions at different times. Provision for this variable is made in the applied design in the replicated time blocks shown in Fig. 7.1. If there are no significant differences between them on the pretests, there is at least presumptive evidence that they are from the same population on time, and they can be combined to gain N. Within blocks, some of the experimental and control groups are pretested and others are not in order to assess the possible interaction of pretesting and treatment (X). If there are no effects due to time and pretesting, then at the beginning of every Nth week, where N equals the member of weeks of intervention, two additional experimental-control group comparisons are gained. In Fig. 7.1, these are for groups $2G_{t2}$ and $10G_{t1}$, and groups $4G_{t1}$ and $12G_{nt}$ in the third week and will occur for comparable groups as each cycle is completed. In short, the design is adapted to ongoing service activities; yet by incorporating checks on confounds approximations can be made to an ideal or true experiment (Ackoff, 1953; Campbell & Stanley, 1966).

The research design shown in Fig. 7.1, or closely related versions of it, can be translated into a data collection flow in a service agency, as outlined in Fig. 7.2. This plan for collecting data (both test and nontest) on Personal-Adjustment (PA) and Vocational-Educational (VE) clients is a variation on the Solomon Four-Group design (Campbell & Stanley, 1966), the pretest being administered to one-third rather than one-half of the subjects at a time.

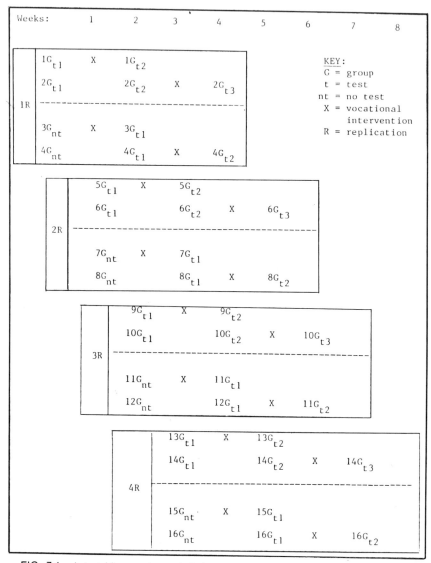

FIG. 7.1 A testable experimental design for research on vocational interventions. (From "Research on Vocational Guidance: Status and Prospect. Part II: Proposals for a New Criterion Measure and Improved Research Design" by J. O. Crites, in *Man in a World at Work,* H. Borow (Ed.), 1964, p. 335. Copyright 1964 by Houghton Mifflin. Reprinted by Permission.)

The time blocks shown on the left side of the figure are defined by the client's contacts with the agency. In the first block, for example, the client applies for counseling and is either accepted or referred to another, more appropriate service. Those who are accepted take the intake battery, which may be comprised of various and sundry forms and inventories to gather data on personal background (PDB) and general adjustment status (e.g., Lanyon's *Psychological Screening Inventory*). Designation as a PA or VE client is based upon presenting problem and subsequently verified by the intake interviewer, who asks the client whether she/he wants to participate in the service's ongoing research project. Those who opt not to participate become one control group; the remainder are tested with the research battery at staggered intervals during periods of subsequent contacts. All clients eventually take the posttest, and they are all followed up after their counseling but again at staggered intervals to assess the possible interaction between treatment and testing (see discussion in next section on external validity of experiments). From data collected in this flow, any number of analyses can be made depending upon the researcher's substantive hypotheses. Methodologically, checks and balances are built into the data collection to estimate, if not control, many of the threats (e.g., reactivity of pretesting) to the validity of experiments in field settings (Cook & Campbell, 1979).

Comments. The research design presented in Fig. 7.1 and the data collection flow chart shown in Fig. 7.2 conform closely to many of the check points for design and analysis and criteria enumerated by Spokane and Oliver in Chapter 4, Vol. 2. Among these, the following stand out: First, real clients are used as subjects in the experimental and control groups, and they are equated on motivation for counseling. Second, they can be randomly assigned to treatment and control conditions, but all clients eventually receive treatment, even though it may be delayed.[9] Third, client problems are diagnosed and they are classified according to the diagnosis, which involves their judgments as well as the intake interviewer's assessment. Fourth, appropriate data are collected to make analysis of Attribute by Treatment Interactions (ATI's). These analyses can either be built in as factors in the experiment or be handled as covariates. Fifth, the possible reactive effects of pretesting can be determined with the modified Solomon Four-Group design. Moreover, many of the other points on Spokane and Oliver's checklist can be covered and incorporated into the proposed research design, such as "studying drop outs," "considering differences among counselors," and "multiple measurements taken at post-treatment and follow-up." Probably the main consideration, however, is that the research design and data collection flow chart can be implemented in an agency setting without disrupting service processes. Thus, there is no excuse for not conducting research on career interventions in the field because it might interfere with assisting clients.

---

[9]One possible disadvantage or shortcoming of the proposed research design is that there are no untreated (uncounseled) S's upon follow-up unless possible comparisons can be made with dropouts before their counseling starts.

Data Collection

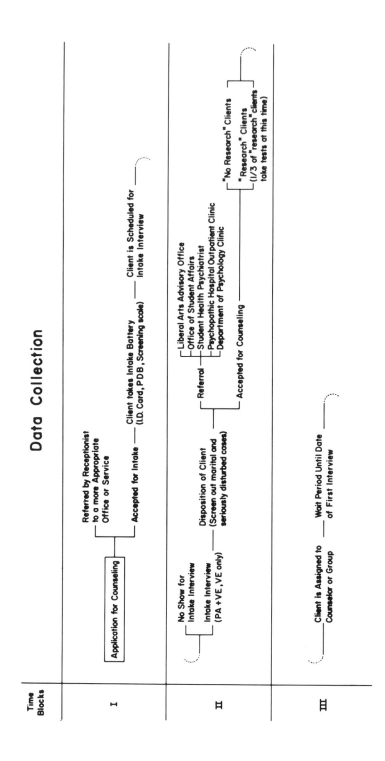

318

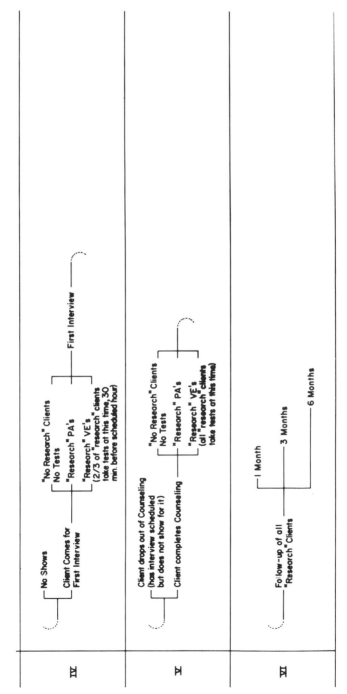

FIG. 7.2 Data collection flow chart for research on vocational and personal adjustment counseling.

319

RESEARCH METHODS IN VOCATIONAL PSYCHOLOGY:
DESIGN AND ANALYSIS

In the foregoing discussions of theoretical and applied research it was emphasized that if causal inferences are to be drawn about an hypothesized relationship between an independent and dependent variable, then as many threats to the validity of the experiments as possible must be eliminated. Even in true experiments, where subjects have been assigned at random to the experimental and control (or comparison) conditions, not all threats are precluded, and particularly in quasi-experimentation in field settings, which is usually the case in vocational psychology, threats to causal inferences are typically present. It is possible to identify these threats, however, and sometimes adjust for their effects in the interpretation of the results from an investigation. Different types of statistical analyses, both between- and within-group techniques, can be used for this purpose and for data reduction from passive observational studies. How design relates to analysis in conducting relatively valid experiments, and how between- and within-group analyses related to each other are the questions addressed in this section, which discusses first the validity of experiments and then reviews certain widely used correlational techniques. It closes with a presentation of a general data analytic system and a taxonomy for between- and within-group types of statistical analysis as a basis for integrating different kinds of techniques.

Experimental Research

Following Campbell and Stanley (1966), but elaborating upon and revising their criteria for the validity of experiments, Cook and Campbell (1979, pp. 37–39) enumerate and define four kinds of validity applicable to experiments designed to investigate causal relationships among variables: (1) statistical conclusion validity; (2) internal validity; (3) construct validity; and (4) external validity. The first of these, statistical conclusion validity, essentially concerns whether any relationship exists between the independent and dependent variables. More specifically, Cook and Campbell (1979) address three questions: "(1) Is the study sensitive enough to permit reasonable statements about covariation? (2) If it is sensitive enough, is there any reasonable evidence from which to infer that the presumed cause and effect covary? and (3) If there is such evidence, how strongly do the two variables covary? [p. 39]." These are largely questions of the power of the statistical tests used, which is a function of: (1) the alpha (∞) level selected; (2) sample size (N); and (3) the variances of the variables involved. The essential problem is to fix these parameters so that power is optimal. Assuming that the variances of X and Y are sufficiently large (and typical of the population) to control for restricted range in the bivariate distribution, then the optimal power for the statistical significance of the correlation coefficient, as probably the most widely used index of covariation, can be described as shown in Fig. 7.3. When the values of r at the .05 and .01 points are plotted against varying df ($N - 2$), it becomes apparent that, in a "mini-max" sense, the optimal power for the correlation coefficient is at approximately df = 125. It is at this point that statistical significance and magnitude estimate appear to be balanced. Smaller samples usually produce such wide confidence intervals that the modal tendency for r across accumulated studies is close to .00 (Ghiselli & Brown, 1955), and larger samples yield statistically significant r's that are so small in magnitude that they have neglible predictive and questionable theoretical value (Cottle, 1950). To achieve at least a modicum of statistical conclusion validity as far as detecting a putative causal relationship of sufficient magnitude to interpret meaningfully, the rule of thumb in correlational analysis is to use samples with approximately 125 df.

Cook and Campbell (1979, pp. 42–44) enumerate seven possible threats

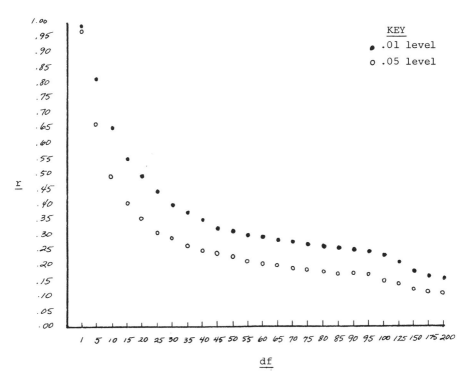

FIG. 7.3   Values of r at the .05 and .01 levels for degrees of freedom 1–200.

to statistical conclusion validity: (1) low statistical power; (2) violated statistical assumptions; (3) multiple comparisons and error rate; (4) reliability of measures; (5) reliability of treatment implementation; (6) random irrelevancies in the experimental setting; and (7) random heterogeneity of respondents. Statistical power, too much as well as too little, has already been discussed. Of the remaining threats, the following appear to be the most serious in vocational research. First, there is a widespread practice in the field to conduct multiple comparisons among groups on several different variables when an overall statistical test was not made or planned comparisons (with directional hypotheses) were not pursued, thus increasing Type I errors and producing more significant results than justified (Norrell & Grater, 1960). A similar effect occurs when the assumption of homogeneous variances is violated in t- or F-tests for occupational and other group differences. Second, related to the error rate and statistical assumptions problems are the random heterogeneity of respondents and random irrelevancies in the experimental setting threats. Both can be illustrated by experimental/control (E/C) studies of career counseling. If they involve college students as clients (or S's) as many do (Crites, 1981), it can be expected that results will differ depending upon when data are collected. During midterm and final examination periods when anxiety is higher, to the extent that it is related to the dependent variables (e.g., career maturity; Crites, 1969), the findings will be different than at other times during the term (Crites, 1964). The other phenomenon that can occur in such studies is a nonsignificant difference between the means of the E and C groups but a significant difference between their variances, with that for the E group being larger. This so-called *fan effect* results from the random heterogeneity of S's in the E group who differentially respond to the treatment. Not that this is not an important finding per se, but the heterogeneity violates a statistical assumption and equivocates the original intention of the experiment—to draw causal inferences about the effects of the independent variable upon the dependent variable.

Even more critical than these threats are two that plague research in vocational psychology: reliability of measures and reliability of treatment implementation. There are two facets to the problem of measurement realibility: First, the measure must have sufficient test-retest[10] reliability to operationally define stable (nonrandom) behavioral phenomena. Too often, homemade instruments with unknown reliability are used to measure vocational behaviors and, when negative findings are obtained from an in-

---

[10]Internal consistency coefficients, which are sometimes cited for this purpose, are not estimates of the stability of a behavioral phenomenon, because they are based upon scores from only one testing, and hence are inappropriate as a *sine qua non* for defining vocational behaviors.

vestigation, it is indeterminate whether they are a function of measurement error or failure to reject the null hypothesis. Moreover, no amount of post hoc equivocation about the inadequacy of the measures can substitute for their thorough and painstaking a priori construction and development. Second, to the extent that measures are unreliable, the reliability of any difference scores derived from subtracting one from the other, depending upon their intercorrelation, is adversely affected. Particularly in pretest–posttest designs this consideration is a central one. The threat of reliability of treatment implementation poses a somewhat different problem. Here the reliability is that of the experimenter or whoever is administering the treatment. If the treatment is not constant across experimental conditions, systematic variance may be spuriously increased. In a replicated analysis of a study of traditional and client-centered counseling by Barahal, Brammer, and Shostrum (1949), for example, Forgy and Black (1954) found an interaction between counselor and type of counseling. In other words, counselors were not reliable (standard or uniform) across counseling approaches. Conversely, counselors (or experimenters) may artifactually increase error variance by differentially responding to S's within groups, thus possibly masking or counteracting significant differences between groups. Statistical conclusion validity, therefore, can be affected by a variety of extraneous factors. To conclude statistically that there is a real (nonchance, nonartifactual) relationship between an independent and dependent variable, much less a causal one, necessitates eliminating as many of these threats as possible—and even then the inference is only probabilistic.

The second kind of experimental validity delineated by Cook and Campbell (1979) is internal validity. It is defined as follows: "Once it has been established that two variables covary, the problem is to decide whether there is any causal relationship between the two and, if there is, to decide whether the direction of causality is from the measured or manipulated A to the measured B, or vice versa [p. 59]." That a researcher can infer with a relative degree of confidence that a causal connection exists between an independent and dependent variable, and what the direction of the relationship is, depends essentially upon the extent to which third-variable explanations can be eliminated. Third variables can either contrive relationships that do not exist (false positives) or they can countervail relationships that do exist (false negatives). Illustrative of a false positive relationship in vocational research is one reported by Campbell (1965) on the long-term effects of career counseling. From a quasi-experiment, with no randomly constituted control group, he concluded that career counseling had a salubrious effect upon career choice when this effect might have equally well been attributable to any number of other third variables, such as maturation. Conversely, false negative conclusions are exemplified by the accumulated research on the relationship between job satisfaction and job success, which generally indicates that they are unrelated (Crites, 1969). When this relationship is projected over time as a third variable, there is evidence that job satisfaction and job success may be related during certain stages in career development but not others (Crites, 1979). In other words, not considering the possible effects of career developmental stages upon the relationship between job satisfaction and job success has previously led to the conclusion that they are unrelated.

These examples of alternative third-variable explanations of putative causal relationships between variables of interest in vocational psychology illustrate only a few of the threats to the internal validity of experiments as explicated by Cook and Campbell (1979, pp. 51–55). They enumerate thirteen threats in all: (1) history; (2) maturation; (3) testing; (4) instrumentation; (5) statistical regression; (6) selection; (7) mortality; (8) interactions with selection; (9) ambiguity about the direction of causal inference; (10) diffusion or imitation of treatments; (11) compensatory equalization of treatments; (12) compensatory rivalry by respondents receiving less desirable treatments; and (13) resentful demoralization of respondents receiving less desirable treatments. Not all of these are directly relevant to vocational research, but several stand out as recurring threats to quasi-experimentation in the field about which vocational psychologists might be more cognizant and self-conscious. History and maturation plague the one-sample longitudinal studies of career development that have been so celebrated since the early 1950s, because they fail to control for the effects of concurrent or intervening events (history) or to assess maturation unconfounded with error variance from repeated measures. Closely related to these problems are those of reactive testing, which may either change the phenomenon being studied or additively combine with the independent variable, and instrument decay that may occur over the course of the experiment or time and become confounded with the process or variable being investigated. All of these extraneous factors are threats to the internal validity, for example, of experiments on the effectiveness of career counseling in service agencies when the so-called *own-control* group design is used with paper-and-pencil repeated measures (Crites, 1964).

Often compounded with these time-related and testing threats are those of statistical regression, selection, and mortality. When subjects are classified into groups on the basis of their pretest scores (or correlates of them) and the measures are relatively unreliable, statistical regression to the mean on posttest may occur. Because of ceiling and floor effects on the measuring scale, high scorers obtain lower scores on posttest and low scorers receive higher scores. To conclude, therefore, that this differential change was attributable to the treatment would be erroneous. In a true experimental design this problem can be precluded by matching subjects on the pretest and then randomly assigning them to the E and C groups. There might still be statistical regression but its contribution would be controlled for by the C group. Similarly, selection of subjects from intact groups almost invariably introduces extraneous factors into a quasi-experiment that are confounded with the treatment effects. This problem is accentuated in what Underwood (1957) has called *ex post facto* studies, in which a treatment is not even actively manipulated yet causal inferences are drawn. In vocational psychology, the most obvious examples are studies of occupational differences in which it is usually assumed that the traits of workers in given occupations caused them to choose those occupations. Finally, mortality or the differential dropping out of subjects from the experimental and comparison groups may influence or bias the results of a study. Not infrequently in both studies of career counseling and career development fewer subjects are available on posttest than pretest.

The concept of construct validity, as originally formulated in test psychology (Cronbach & Meehl, 1955) and as applied by Cook and Campbell (1979) to experimentation refers to the degree of correspondence between a construct and its operational definition. In other words, a construct is presumably more or less valid to the extent that it is isomorphic with the operational procedures used to define or measure it. Given this meaning of construct validity, it can apply to the independent variable (X) as well as the dependent variable (Y), although it has traditionally referred to the latter. For example, a particular approach to career counseling may be theoretically defined by differentiable concepts of diagnosis, process, and outcomes (Crites, 1981). Its use as an intervention to increase the career choice realism of clients has more or less construct validity depending upon how closely its implementation corresponds to the conceptual model. Similarly, measures of dependent variables such as career maturity have greater or less construct validity depending upon how closely the conceptual and operational definitions conform. Cook and Campbell (1979) point out that there are two possible sources of error or variance that can adversely affect construct validity: (1) "construct underrepresentation"; and (2) "surplus construct irrelevancies [p. 64]." The former arises when operations are not as inclusive as the construct, as in a measure of career maturity (dependent variable) that assesses only the cognitive aspects of decision making and omits the attitudinal (Westbrook & Mastie's Cognitive Vocational Maturity Test, 1973). The latter arise when operations include extraneous factors, as in career counseling (independent variable) by a counselor who prefers a different approach (Forgy & Black, 1954).

These sources of error or variance can be cross-classified with the independent and dependent variables as shown in Fig. 7.4. The cell entries are confounds identified by Cook and Campbell (1979, p. 64, *et passim*) that equivocate interpretations of the effects of the independent variable upon

	Independent Variable	Dependent Variable
Construct Underrepresentation	Mono-operation bias Confounding- constructs and levels of constructs	Mono-operation bias Restricted generaliza- bility across constructs
Surplus Construct Irrelevancies	Mono-operation bias Mono-method bias Hypothesis - guessing Evaluation Apprehension Experimenter Expectancies 'Interaction' of different treatments	Mono-operation bias Mono-method bias Hypothesis - guessing Evaluation Apprehension Interaction of testing and treatment

FIG. 7.4   Classification of threats to the construct validity of independent and dependent variables.

the dependent variable. They are like third variables that introduce competing explanations of the experimental findings. Mono-operation and mono-method biases reduce the construct validity of both the X and Y variables, for example, by introducing either derepresentation or irrelevancies or both. Cook and Campbell (1979) subscribe to what they call "multiple formal definitionalism" and "multiple operationalism", which stated more simply mean define and measure constructs, whether independent or dependent, in as many ways as possible—preferably before an experiment is undertaken. Also, precautions should be taken to eliminate possible hypothesis guessing (or ingratiation effects) by subjects and biases by experimenters (Rosenthal, 1966). Evaluation apprehension on the part of subjects (i.e., being evaluated unfavorable by the experimenter) may compromise the construct validity of the dependent variable, as the interaction of treatments (i.e., several administered serially) may for the independent variable. Probably more salient threats to construct validity in vocational psychology, however, are confounding constructs and levels of constructs and interaction of testing and treatment. The former is a common flaw in studies where an extreme group analysis is used, and there is a nonlinear relationship between X and Y that might have been detected had the excluded middle group been used. The latter was discussed as a potential threat to internal validity but it may also affect construct validity, particularly if repeated posttests are made. They can then become confounded with the treatment construct, and it is indeterminate which (either singly or combined) has an effect upon the behavioral construct.

Since its introduction by Cronbach and Meehl (1955), the concept of construct validity, whether used in test psychology or experimental research, has raised more logical and philosophical issues than it has resolved (Bechtoldt, 1959; Campbell, 1960; Guion, 1977; Loevinger, 1957). At one extreme are those who abjure the concept entirely (Bechtoldt, 1959) and who argue that not only is construct validity simply a special case of theory testing, and therefore unnecessary, but that it leaves the definition of variables open-ended, as determined by relationships (rather than operations) in the "nomological network" (Brodbeck, 1959). Given this premise, construct validity is subject to the logical fallacy of infinite regress—or, stated psychometrically, "what is the *criterion* for the criterion?". The proposed alternative to construct validity, however, stated in ultraoperational terms, suffers from the theoretical barrenness of a "dustbowl empiricism" designed to eliminate any surplus meaning associated with the definition of variables. If the MMPI item "I think Washington is greater than Lincoln" differentiates schizophrenics from normals, as it does, then it is considered a "useful" item and is keyed to the schizophrenia scale, regardless of whether it can be related conceptually (linguistically) to some construct of schizophrenia. Cook and Campbell (1979) take a position between these extremes but obviously closer to those who advocate construct validity. Were they to combine constructs and operations methodologically, as Crites (1965, 1973, 1978) has proposed in the rational–empirical method of test construction, a construct would be defined conceptually (linguistically) from relevant theory and/or observation and measured operationally only by those test items or experimental procedures that empirically fit the construct. Thus, in developing the Career Maturity Inventory, for example, all items were rationally derived from career development concepts (Crites, 1964) but only those that differentiated empirically among grades 5 through 12 were retained to measure the developmental variable career maturity (Crites, 1965, 1973, 1978).

There are several logical and methodological advantages to the rational–empirical method as an alternative to both ultraoperationalism and construct validity. First, by rationally deriving test items and experimental procedures, substantive and theoretical meaning is given to constructs. No longer is the construct of intelligence, for example, reduced to the circular (and nonsensical) definition that it is "what an intelligence test measures." Nor is theory construction practically precluded from the outset. Second, by empirically building the criterion into a construct not only is it given operational definition, but its theoretical meaning is preserved. In the Career Maturity Inventory, for example, all items make sense conceptually, and they are all empirically valid by the criterion of being time related, a sine qua non for the measurement of any developmental phenomenon. Third, by rationally and empirically defining a construct, two logical fallacies in the nomological network are eliminated. One of these mentioned previously, infinite regress, is no longer a problem because relevant criteria for constructs are built in by the rational–empirical method. The nomological network is used to explore and establish the relational parameters of a construct but not to define it. A related problem is also resolved. The logic of construct validity has always left the investigator in the untenable position according to Bechtoldt (1959) of: "affirming an antecedent by its consequences [p. 620]." That is, a prediction from a construct is confirmed, it is inferred (backwards) that the measure of the construct is valid, yet any number of alternative hypotheses or third variables might equally well account for the results. To be faithful to Cook and Campbell's (1979) critical realism, which incorporates Popper's (1959, 1972) principles of falsification, only evidence that disconfirms the consequences of a construct would be relevant to its validity. At best, this procedure is unsatisfying philosophically and constrictive psychometrically.

The rational–empirical method was originally conceived for test construction (i.e., measurement of dependent variables), but there is no reason that it is not also applicable to experimental interventions (i.e., formulation of independent variables). More effort than is typically expended on treatment interventions needs to be given to their rational conceptualization and explication. Nowhere is this truer than in the literary definition of career counseling processes. Too often studies of the effects of career counseling are reported with no more description of what was done than "clients received traditional vocational-educational counseling." Even when it can reasonably be assumed that this is trait-and-factor career counseling (Crites, 1981), the definition is inadequate for analysis and replication. At least a manipulation check by independent observers and/or clients should be made, if not the more desirable collection and classification of process data on counselor behaviors. Much as rationally derived items for a test are validated empirically against a relevant criterion, counselor behaviors can be identified that either correspond or do not to the model and methods of a particular approach to career counseling. Similarly, programmatic interventions (e.g., career kits, computer-assisted decision-making systems, workshops) designed to facilitate career development can be checked to determine their rational–empirical congruence as they are implemented.

Also, nothing in this approach contradicts Cook and Campbell's (1979, p. 63) advocacy of multiple formal definitionalism and operationalism. The rational–empirical method incorporates these principles but, unlike construct validity, it does so before theoretical or applied research are undertaken, not afterward. Thus, controls upon confounds of definitions and relationships are effectively instituted.

The last type of experimental validity delineated by Cook and Campbell (1979) is external validity. Essentially, it concerns the extent to which the results of an experiment can be generalized. Cook and Campbell (1979) make the very useful distinction, graphically represented in Fig. 7.5, between generalizing to and across three population parameters: (1) person; (2) settings; and (3) times. Statistical theory assumes random sampling from and generalizing to general target populations, but in practice this is seldom, if ever, possible to accomplish. Consequently, Cook and Campbell stress generalizing across populations: "The rationale for this is that formal random sampling for representativeness is rare in field research, so that strict generalizing to targets of external validity is rare. Instead, practice is more one of generalizing across haphazard instances where similar-appearing treatments are implemented [p. 73]." Methods for summarizing findings from what Cook and Campbell (1979, p. 71) call achieved samples in field research have been largely intuitive and narrative until recently. Schmidt and Hunter (1977) have attempted to synthesize validity coefficients for personnel selection tests, and Spokane and Oliver (see Vol. II, Chapter 4) have used metaanalysis, as developed by Smith and Glass (1977) and Smith, Glass, and Miller (1980) to integrate the research on the outcomes of career counseling. More generally, Glass, McGaw, and Miller (1981) explicate how meta-analysis procedures can be applied to almost any problem of summarizing results from several and sundry studies, taking into consideration similarities and differences along the dimensions of persons, settings, and times.

Threats to external validity are defined as interactions of population parameters (persons, settings, and times) with treatment effects. Stated as a question, it can be asked: "To or across which categories or classes of persons, settings, and times can presumed cause-effect relationships be generalized? Drawing inferences about the causal effects of career counseling interventions upon the decision-making process across clients with different problems (e.g., vocational–educational vs. personal adjustment) illustrates the problem of generalizing across subgroups of persons. Research on the outcomes of employee development programs, for example, in different organizations poses the problem of generalizing across settings. Do the findings obtained in a research and development installation (Hanson, 1981) apply to a commercial enterprise (e.g., an insurance company)? Passive-observational studies pose a similar problem: What is the transport-

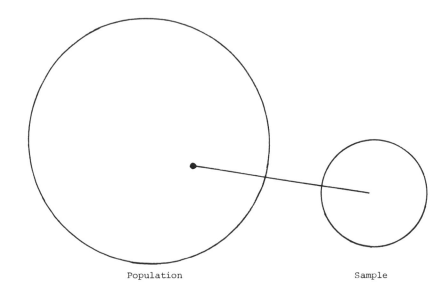

Population   Sample

(a) Generalizing *to* population parameters

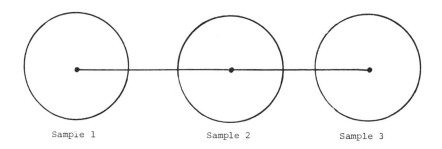

Sample 1   Sample 2   Sample 3

(b) Generalizing *across* sample parameters

FIG. 7.5   Two types of generalization in external validity.

ability, for example, of job analyses and test validities from one organization to another? Causal inference is not involved in this question but generalization is. Finally, generalizations across periods of time can either increase or decrease the external validity of an experiment. Although Cook and Campbell (1979, p. 74) do not give an extended discussion of the problems involved in generalizing from one point in time to another (see section on developmental designs), they do isolate one of the principal issues—the possible confounding (interactive) effects of historical events or prevailing Zeitgeist. Experimental studies of career counseling in higher education, for example, must contend with the confounding effects of examinations, typically administered at the middle and end of a term. At these times anxiety is almost always higher on the average and may interact with the treatment to spuriously influence outcomes.

To counteract these threats to external validity Cook and Campbell (1979, pp. 74–77, *et passim*) recommend three sampling models: (1) random sampling for representativeness; (2) deliberate sampling for heterogeneity; and (3) impressionistic model instances. The first model is the most familiar in which, if practical exigencies permit, a probability sample within known limits of error is drawn from a population so that it can be considered representative. This procedure is depicted in Fig. 7.5a. This stage of the randomization enhances the external validity of the experiment, in this instance generalization to a population, and the subsequent stage of randomization, assignment of subjects to the experimental (E) and control (C) groups, increases the internal validity of the experiment. The second model, graphically represented in Fig. 7.5b, is conceived by Cook and Campbell (1979): "to define target classes of persons, settings, and times and to ensure that a wide range of instances from within each class is represented in the design [p. 75]." This sampling design is preferably planned before experiments are conducted, for example, in several different industrial organizations, but if studies have already been run it is possible to summarize their results across population parameters by using the meta-analysis procedures discussed previously. In the third and last Cook and Campbell (1979) model, impressionistic instances of model tendencies:" the concern is to explicate the kinds of persons, settings, or times to which one most wants to generalize and then to select at least one instance of each class that is impressionistically similar to the class mode [p. 77]." Information about the class mode, of course, is essential for this procedure as is selecting schools for career maturity interventions that appear similar to benchmark or exemplary schools in a system or possibly from a national composite.

Comment. This discussion of experimental research methods in vocational psychology has ranged far and wide across a considerable array of issues relevant to drawing conclusions about causal relationships from studies conducted in field settings. If there is any conclusion that can be drawn from quasi-experiments, it is that conclusions concerning causality, in particular, are extremely difficult to draw legitimately. This does not mean, however, that such experimentation should be abandoned, but it does underscore the necessity for vocational researchers to be as conscious as possible of the threats to the validity of experiments. To facilitate awareness of the constraints and limitations imposed by conducting field studies Ackoff (1953) recommends that, in the planning stage, an investigator conceptualize the "ideal" experiment and then approximate it as closely as conditions permit. Discrepancies between the ideal and real experiment can consequently be more easily detected and taken into consideration when drawing conclusions. Another check on what can legitimately be concluded is replication (and possibly extension) of the experiment (Campbell, 1957). Although seldom done (Smith, 1970), replication may rule out some third variable explanations, because the probability of their recurring effects across occasions is unlikely unless there is some systematic confound involved. If so, then replication may identify it as a factor to either manipulate or control in future experimentation.

Passive–Observational Studies

This rubric is taken from Cook and Campbell (1979) to sharpen the differences between experimental research, which should involve random assignment and active manipulation of the independent variable(s), and largely field studies that incorporate neither but rather collect data on existing groups and variables. Illustrative of this type of study in vocational psychology is the analysis of occupational differences in traits and factors and the correlation of tests with any number of vocational behaviors (e.g., realism of career choice, job satisfaction, vocational motivation). As mentioned previously in this chapter, the predilection in passive observational studies is to infer some causal connection among variables, even though neither logic nor methodology justifies such reasoning. The designs and analyses available for passive observational studies are nevertheless highly useful to identify and extrapolate systematic (functional) relationships among vocational behaviors of both theoretical and applied interest. This section examines, therefore, some of these research methods and suggests how they might be applicable to problems in vocational psychology. The discussion begins with a presentation of hierarchical factor analysis as a summative and heuristic model, continues with a survey of complex correlational techniques, including the multitrait–multimethod matrix, crosslagged panel correlation, and path analysis, and it closes with a presentation of some developmental data designs.

Hierarchical factor analysis.   Factor analysis has long occupied a central place in differential and test psychology and to a lesser extent in vocational psychology. That it has not found greater application as a research method in the latter is probably because factor analysis in this country has been dominated by the work of Thurstone (1947) and his followers (Guilford, 1959), who have steadfastly advocated multiple factor solutions based upon rotations to orthogonality and simple structure. In contrast, the British school of factor analysts, under the leadership of Spearman, (1904), Burt (1954), and Vernon (1950), have emphasized the importance of oblique factors and hierarchical structures. Until recently, with the possible exception of the development of cluster analysis techniques by Tryon and Bailey (1970) and others (Fruchter, 1954), there has been little or no rapproachement between the American and British factor analytic traditions. Beginning with seminal papers by Schmid and Leiman (1957) and particularly Wherry (1959) in the late 1950s, however, there has been an emerging synthesis between the two points of view, best represented by the research of Wherry (in press) in explicating and refining factor methods that yield hierarchical structures but that use orthogonal rather than oblique solutions, thus making interpretation of lower-order factors less equivocal. Whereas the hierarchy developed by Schmid and Leiman (1957) might be graphically represented as shown in Fig. 7.6a, the structure obtained from Wherry's approach is depicted by Fig. 7.6b. Because the factors at each level of the latter are orthogonal, their substantive interpretation and interrelationship is considerably clarified.

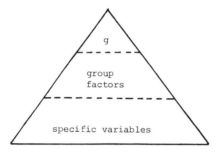

(a) Oblique hierarchical factor structure

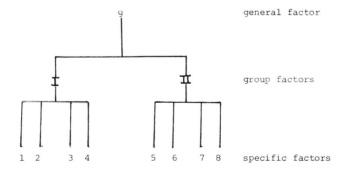

(b) Orthogonal hierarchical factor structure

FIG. 7.6   Oblique and orthogonal hierarchical factor analytic structures.

The salience of hierarchical factor analysis for vocational psychology was highlighted in Crites' (1969) review of theory and research in the field that indicated that most vocational behavioral phenomena fit a hierarchical model better than a multiple factor model. Vocational motivation, vocational success, vocational satisfaction: All are hierarchical in the structure of their dimensions. More recently it has become increasingly clear that career maturity also can be conceptualized hierarchically (Crites, 1974b), although initially only its dimensions were identified, without specifying the nature of their interrelationships (Super, 1955). As it has been most recently proposed (Crites, 1978), the hierarchical model of career maturity is as shown in Fig. 7.7. The interrelationships of the factors in the model are depicted as they would be toward the end of adolescence (i.e., at their most highly differentiated state in career development). It is hypothesized in the model that correlations within group and subgeneral factors are greater on the average than those between factors. For example, it is expected that the inter-r's among the career choice attitude clusters (involvement, independence, etc.) are in the .40–.60 range (modal $r = .50$), whereas the central tendency for correlations between this group factor and career choice competencies is in the .30s. These are the predicted intercorrelations late in career development during adolescence. Extrapolating from Garrett's (1946) differentiation hypothesis concerning the growth of intelligence, however, it is expected that the model of career maturity is much less differentiated early in career development (e.g., at the beginning of high school). At this point in time, the general (g) factor would be much more dominant, and there would be few, if any, subgeneral or group factors.[11]

Unfortunately, tests of the model of career maturity have not used appropriate factor analytic methodology. Studies by both Prediger (1979) and Westbrook et al. (1980) have used principal components analysis of the career choice attitude and competence variables in the model rather than hierarchical solutions, and they have erroneously concluded from their results, which yielded one principal factor (as the procedure is designed to do), that the model is not multidimensional as hypothesized. Compounding this flaw in methodological decision making, Westbrook et al. (1980) conducted their analyses on one group (not sample) of disadvantaged rural ninth-graders and another group of "technical, vocational, and general education students at a public technical college located in central North Carolina, [p. 259]", hardly what might be considered representative or even heterogeneous samples. But even so, for the ninth-graders, if the ap-

---

[11]One implication of this hypothesis, which has not been previously drawn or tested, is that the hierarchical structure for undecided or unrealistic individuals, even though chronologically in late adolescence, would be more like that of early adolescents, because the undecided and unrealistic are less career mature.

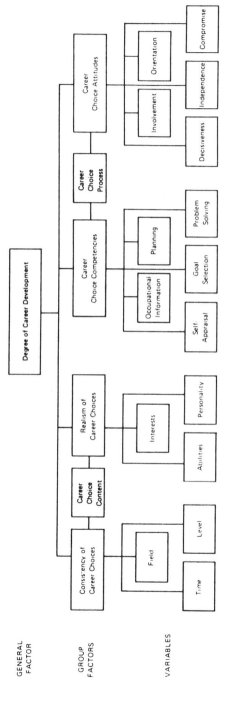

FIG. 7.7 A model of career maturity in adolescence. (From *The Career Maturity Inventory* by J. O. Crites, 1978, p. 4. Copyright 1978 by McGraw-Hill, Inc. Reprinted by permission.)

propriate hierarchical factor analysis had been performed, the expected results would have been a predominant, undifferentiated general factor, because at that stage of career development, as noted above, the model is not highly differentiated. Throughout their research, although they selectively cite other references in support of it, Westbrook and his associates have repeatedly ignored, or possibly have been ignorant of, the differentiation hypothesis, which Crites (1971, 1973, 1974b) has clearly stated in several papers.

Complex correlational designs.   One design that utilizes complex sets of correlations among variables that has obvious applicability to research in vocational psychology, particularly measurement problems, is the multitrait–multimethod matrix formulated by Campbell and Fiske (1959). It is based upon the concepts of convergent and divergent validity. The former is demonstrated when two or more methods of measuring the same trait (behavior) are substantially intercorrelated. In Fig. 7.8, which is reproduced from Campbell and Fiske (1959, p. 82), the italicized r's in the diagonals are congruent validity coefficients. The latter (divergent validity) is established by three criteria (Campbell and Fiske, 1959):

1. The validities in the diagonals are higher than "the correlations obtained between that variable and any other variable having neither trait nor method in common [p. 82-83]." (e.g., A, A_2 (.57) > A_1 B_2 (.22), A_1 C_2 (.11), and A_2 C_1 (.09))
2. The validities in the diagonals are higher than the correlations obtained between the variable and any other variable having method in common (e.g., A_1 A_2 (.57 > A_2 B_1 (.51) and A_1 C_1 (.38).
3. The same pattern of interrelationships should obtain among variables regardless of method.

Presumably when these rules hold, measures have both convergent and divergent validity, although (as Campbell and Fiske note) this is rare in test psychology, possibly because, as Humphreys (1960) observes, the matrix is limited by how many different methods to measure traits can be devised. Humphreys (1960) concludes that: "The number of methods required in any particular situation will depend on how low the intercorrelations are when trait is held constant and methods vary, as opposed to how high the intercorrelations are when method is held constant and traits vary [p. 87]." Another consideration is that there may be only one useful method for measuring a trait (e.g., inventorying vocational interests [Super & Crites, 1962]) or that different methods for measuring the same trait, which are not highly correlated (e.g., Strong–Campbell Interest Inventory vs. Kuder Occupational Interest Survey), may each be useful in a given behavioral domain.

	Traits	A_1	B_1	C_1	A_2	B_2	C_2	A_3	B_3	C_3
		Method 1			Method 2			Method 3		
Method 1	A_1	(.89)								
	B_1	.51	(.89)							
	C_1	.38	.37	(.76)						
Method 2	A_2	.57	.22	.09	(.93)					
	B_2	.22	.57	.10	.68	(.94)				
	C_2	.11	.11	.46	.59	.58	(.84)			
Method 3	A_3	.56	.22	.11	.67	.42	.33	(.94)		
	B_3	.23	.58	.12	.43	.66	.34	.67	(.92)	
	C_3	.11	.11	.45	.34	.32	.58	.58	.60	(.85)

FIG. 7.8 Multitrait-multimethod matrix (Campbell & Fiske, 1959, p. 82). (From "Convergent and Discriminant Validation by the Multitrait-multimethod Matrix" by D. T. Campbell and D. W. Fiske, *Psychological Bulletin,* 1959, *56,* 81-105. Copyright 1959 by the American Psychological Association. Reprinted by permission.)

Another complex correlational design that has been used in other fields but not extensively in vocational psychology is cross-lagged panel correlation. The basic setup is illustrated in Fig. 7.9 with fictitious data on parental attitudes and career choice attitudes. Suppose the attitudes (acceptance, avoidance, and concentration; Roe, 1957) of the parents of a group of fifth-graders are assessed by judges (e.g, teachers), and the children also take the CMI attitude scale. Assume further that the latter are followed up when they are twelfth-graders, with a measure of perceived parental attitudes (e.g, the Family Relations Inventory; Brunkan & Crites, 1964) and the CMI attitude scale (retest). The correlations between the variables on the two occasions might be as shown in Fig. 7.9. Of central interest in the cross-lagged correlational panel are the r's on the diagonals. If parental attitudes toward fifth-graders are causally related to their career choice attitude maturity as twelfth-graders, then this correlation (.35) should be higher than that between career choice attitude maturity in the fifth grade and perceived parental attitudes in the twelfth grade (.01). This is what the ficticious data in Fig. 7.10 show. Because of the temporal priority of parental attitudes on occasion 1 over career choice attitudes on occasion 2 and because of the difference between the lagged correlations, the presumption is that parental attitudes causally affect the subsequent maturation of career choice attitudes.

This conclusion would appear to be legitimate (i.e., logically valid) were it not for a competing interpretation. There is another path in the panel that may also explain the data. It is possible that parental attitudes in fifth grade

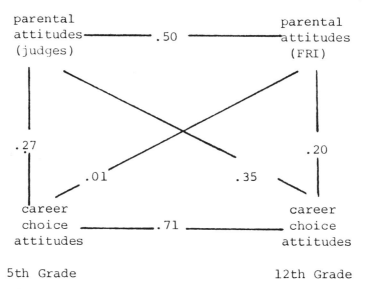

FIG. 7.9   Example of cross-lagged panel correlation for parental attitudes and career choice attitudes.

causally affect career choice attitude maturity in fifth grade which, in turn, is related to career choice attitude maturity in twelfth grade. The technique of path analysis provides a method for tracing these effects for complex sets of both endogenous and exogenous variables and to estimate, using standardized partial correlation coefficients, the contributions of each as exemplified by the path models for occupational aspiration and attainment utilized by Sewell, Haller, and Portes (1969).

Although Blalock (1971), Heise (1975), and others have argued that causal inferences can be drawn from such path models, Cook and Campbell (1979) are more skeptical, pointing out that third variable interpretations are still not ruled out. There is one use of path analysis proposed by Heise (1969), however, which is not subject to this criticism: estimating that part of the total score variance in a test or inventory that is attributable to systematic changes in behavior as contrasted with error. Given at least three waves of testing (i.e., repeated measurements) on the same S's, it is possible to calculate a path coefficient that express systematic change variance, an advantage that is particularly useful for measures of development and variables that are expected to mature over time. This procedure was applied to longitudinal data on the CMI attitude scale, for example, and the test–retest stability coefficient for the inventory increased from .71 to .82 when maturational variance was taken into consideration (Karren, et al., 1979).

Developmental data designs. Although the field of vocational psychology has been dominated by the developmental point of view for the past 30 years (Crites, 1969; Ginzberg et al., 1951; Super, 1957), sophistication in developmental data designs has lagged far behind conceptualization. The most widely used design has been the cross-sectional (O'Hara & Tiedeman, 1959), with a few simple (one-sample) longitudinal studies (Gribbons & Lohnes, 1966; Super et al., 1957). Crites' (1974b) career maturity project has combined the cross-sectional with the longitudinal, but is only an approximation to the possible combinations of developmental design parameters enumerated by Schaie (1965) and others (Baltes, Reese, & Nesselroade, 1977). This project combines the cross-sectional and longitudinal designs, but the data collection was not time lagged. As a consequence, the design does not allow for a control on time of measurement, although the reactivity of repeated measurement can be checked by comparing core and noncore samples at different points in time (Crites, 1971). Also, it is possible to construct a composite longitudinal gradient from observations at only two points in time (Crites, 1978; Meade, 1974), which, given certain assumptions, greatly collapses the time dimension in conducting developmental research. Perhaps this and other "shortcuts" to the study of long-term career developmental change will serve to close the gap

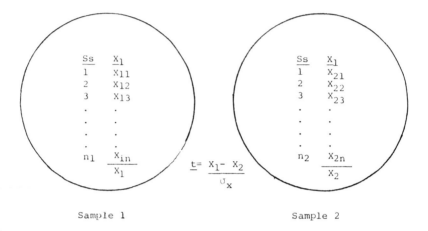

(a) Prototypic *between - groups* data analysis

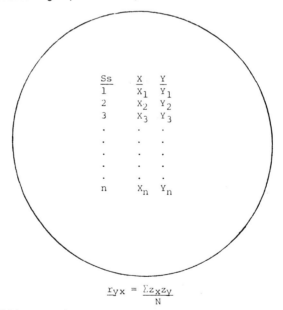

(b) Prototypic *within* group data analysis

FIG. 7.10   Between- and within-group data analysis prototypes.

between theory construction and research methodology in vocational psychology.

Comment. Passive–observational research is the mode in the field of vocational psychology. Like quasi-experimental research, it poses almost insurmountable logical and methodological problems in making causal inferences; yet it nevertheless yields highly useful data on systematic relationships among variables of interest. Perhaps the establishment of a network of statistically significant and replicable relationships among the variables in a field, as it is in astronomy, for example, may become as psychologically satisfying to the investigator as the demonstration of causal functions. If there is a problem with passive–observational research in vocational psychology, it is probably less one of its general usefulness than it is one of doing it properly. How many studies are reported, using factor analysis or complex correlational designs or developmental paradigms, which have methodological flaws? Perhaps part of the problem is the indiscriminate use of computer programs (the SPSS packages) without a basic understanding of the research methodology involved. Anyone can run a computer program but only a very few can say why. The study and understanding of research methods applicable to problems in vocational psychology is a *sine qua non* for elevating the quality of results and knowledge in the field.

General Data Analytic Systems

The two disciplines of research in vocational psychology in particular and in psychology generally, the experimental (active manipulation) and correlational (passive–observational) (Cronbach, 1957), have traditionally been associated with what have been presumed to be two fundamentally different types of data analysis. One of these is between-groups analysis, and the other is within-group analysis. The former includes t tests, Critical Ratio (CR), F tests, and any parametric and nonparametric statistical technique that involves contrasts between (or among) groups. At whatever level of complexity, the basic paradigm demands the classification of S's into two or more different categories, usually that are independent and mutually exclusive but which in mixed designs (Lindquist, 1953) includes repeated measurements on the same S's. The basic logic of the statistical tests is to compare the magnitude of differences between measures of central tendency (or comparable indices, e.g., expected vs. observed frequencies in chi square) with the magnitude of differences due to chance sampling fluctuations. The prototypic setup for this type of data analysis is shown in Fig. 7.10a. In contrast, within-group analysis, in the simplest case, is as depicted in Fig. 7.10b, where it can be seen that there are two observations (X and Y) on at least two S's, whereas in Fig. 7.10a there is, in the limiting case, only one observation on S's in at least two groups. For the within-group analysis, the usual statistical test is for degree of relationship between X and Y, as compared with no relationship, indexed by coefficients such as r, rho (ρ), and C.

That the between- and within-group data analysis techniques have been considered independent or mutually exclusive is less a matter of paradigmatic considerations than it is convention. It has simply been assumed, at least in vocational psychology, that either one statistical analysis or the other must be used, although the confusion between using analysis of variance (ANOVA), for example, as if active manipulation had been involved, has been noted. No instances of the analysis of the same data with between- and within-group statistics has been found in the literature of vocational psychology, although examples are common in general psychology (Spence, 1960). Consider the data setups in Figs. 7.10a and 7.10b, however, as examples of how the same data can be analyzed by both between- and within-group statistics. In Fig. 7.10a, either a t test or CR can be calculated, depending upon N, and a statement can be made about whether the difference between the means is significant or not. However, a within-group analysis can also be made, following the matrix in Fig. 7.10b where either a biserial or point–biserial correlation can be calculated, depending upon whether the groups can be considered as continuous or discrete. Thus, the means for the group (t test) might be significantly different at the .01 level and the biserial correlation might be .25 ($p \leq .05$). The same grouped data can be analyzed meaningfully by both between- and within-group statistical techniques.

This interface between these two types of statistical analysis has been articulated and explicated by Cohen (1968), Cohen and Cohen (1975), and Kerlinger and Pedhazur (1973). It is not a complementary one, however, because it can be shown that between-group analysis is a special case of within-group analysis. Or, more accurately, that multiple regression/correlation analysis (MRC) subsumes ANOVA, ANCOVA, etc. Cohen and Cohen (1975) state that: "Multiple regression/correlation is a highly general and therefore very flexible data-analytic system that may be used whenever a quantitative variable (the dependent variable) is to be studied as a function of, or in relationship to, any factors of interest (expressed as independent variables) [p. 3]." Probably the point of central contention in making this translation is that those versed in between-groups analysis question the limitations imposed by the linearity assumption underlying correlational analysis (i.e., method of least squares). Cohen and Cohen (1975) respond:

Most readers will know that MRC is often (and properly) referred to as *linear* MRC and may well be under the impression that correlation and regression are restricted to the study of straight-line relationships. This mistaken impression is abetted by the common usage of "linear" to mean "rectilinear", and "nonlinear" to mean "curvilinear". We are thus confounded by what is virtually a pun. What is literally meant by "linear" is any relationship of the form (1. 1. 1) $Y = a + bu + cv + dw + ext \ldots$, where the lowercase letters are constants (either positive or negative) and the capital letters are variables [p. 11].

In other words, this equation accommodates any manner of variable (including membership in E/C groups) and consequently expresses a general data-analytic system that not only incorporates between-group contrasts (as dummy variables) but also provides an index of relationship magnitude (correlation coefficient) and proportion of variance accounted for (beta weights).

RESEARCH METHODS IN VOCATIONAL PSYCHOLOGY: A SYNTHESIS

In other fields of psychology, there has been a self-conscious concern about research methods as modus operandi for the investigation of indigenous problems, but not in vocational psychology. Either "method has set the tune", as Tiedeman (1965) has put it, or substantive hypotheses have predominated. There has seldom been an articulated synthesis of subject matter and methodology in the field. Such a synthesis necessitates an integration among: (1) the canons of philosophy of science; (2) the principles of research design; and (3) the techniques of statistical analysis. In this last, summary section on research methods in vocational psychology, an attempt (provisional try) is made to conceptualize a model for the field based upon philosophical, methodological, and statistical tenets that are relevant to the study of vocational behavior and development.

Philosophy of Science

If there is any philosophy of science in the field of vocational psychology it is an expedient one born of the necessity to deal with the problems of everyday life. Probably the earliest instance of any philosophical orientation in what has become known as vocational psychology was the Minnesota point of view. Even though it contrasted sharply with the idiographic position of Allport (1937) and others, including Super (1954) to a certain extent, it held sway for many years and still does at Minnesota, even though Ginzberg (1950) accused the field of having no theory of vocational choice in his address at APGA in 1950. Super (1953) retaliated, as did Kitson (1951), not only with a critique of Ginzberg, but for Super with *A Theory of Vocational*

Development, which has been a landmark over the years. Yet Darley and Hagenah (1955), as well as others (Crites, 1969), have questioned whether Super's theory is a theory, at least as evaluated by the canons of philosophy of science. Many of what have passed as theories in the field since 1950 have not been theories by the usual standards of philosophical discourse. If the field is going to progress beyond intuitive insight, which is essential of course to logical inference in the first instance but not sufficient, then some grasp of the hypothetical sylloqism and its four figures of valid deduction must be attained (McCall, 1952). The essence of this type of reasoning is probabilistic, but even more important is the recognition than an antecedent cannot necessarily be confirmed by its consequent (Bechtoldt, 1959). In other words, we cannot reason backward from the data-language level to the theory-language level.[12]

We can, however, move inductively from data to theory or deductively from theory to data, and we can combine these two types of reasoning, alternatively, in what Marx (1963) has termed *functional* theory construction. The starting point in this process may be on either the data-language level or the theory-language level. In either case, the movement is logical and should be governed by the rules of logic. These include the definition of terms, the statement of propositions, and the extrapolation of relationships among them (Cohen & Nagel, 1934). Assumptions underlying these elements of logical reasoning vary widely among philosophers of science, an excellent review of which is provided by Cook and Campbell (1979). They choose to adopt an orientation called *critical-realism,* which addresses principally the issues of causality—how to validly conclude that X causes Y. Cook and Campbell (1979) define critical-realism as follows: "The perspective is realist because it assumes that causal relationships exist outside of the human mind, and it is critical-realist because it assumes that these valid causal relationships cannot be perceived with total accuracy by our imperfect sensory and intellective capacities [p. 29]." Implicit in this position is a recognition of the lack of correspondence between the theory- and data-language levels.

Combining the empirical tradition of the Minnesota point of view with the hypothetical syllogism of probabilistic logic underlying theory construction, with extrapolations and emendations of Cook and Campbell's critical-realism, a philosophical orientation for research in vocational psychology can be formulated and articulated. It encompasses both the functional and model-building modes of theory construction and has several basic tenets:

---

[12]For example, in empirically testing the consequent in the following syllogism can the antecedent be inferred even though the consequent is confirmed? "If the house is red (antecedent), then the house is colored "(consequent)." That the house is found to be "colored" does not necessarily mean that it is "red"!

1. Establish reliable empirical laws.   Although research may begin with deductively derived hypotheses, the preferred starting point is with what is known—and not through one-shot studies but replicated results. This sequence also pertains to building a model, although, if there is prior experience with an existing model in another area of investigation, it may usefully be tested deductively in vocational psychology (Crites, 1978; Vernon, 1950).

2. Reason syllogistically between the data- and theory-language levels. The conditional "if, then" proposition is the means for both drawing inferences from data and then deriving hypotheses for testing. Combinatory rules can be used to relate propositions to each other and thereby check the parsimony and internal consistency of a theory (Crites, 1969). The line of reasoning should always be made explicit. It is highly unlikely that even the most intuitive hypothesis (or research question) arises *de novo*—it comes from somewhere and should be articulated logically.

3. Test hypothesis by a process of elimination.   The scientific attitude is one of disproving hypotheses, not proving them. This disposition is consistent with Popper's (1959) "principle of falsification" and the elimination of third variable explanations among the variables of interest. Cook and Campbell (1979) conclude: "From Popper's work, we recognize the necessity to proceed less by seeking to confirm theoretical predictions about causal connections than by seeking to falsify them [p. 31]." This rational–empirical philosophy of science for vocational psychology is obviously incomplete, but perhaps it provides a starting point for reflection on such issues in a field that has not systematically addressed them in the past.

Research Design

The principal implication of a rational–empirical philosophical orientation in vocational psychology for decisions concerning research design is a heightened awareness of how competing interpretations of data can be identified and appraised. In classical experimental design, the obvious option is to eliminate as many extraneous factors as possible by random assignment of subjects to experimental and control groups, although as Cook and Campbell (1979) point out not all third variables are controlled by even this procedure. The external validity of true experiments also poses the additional problems of generalizing to and across populations as previously discussed. In quasi-experimentation, characteristic of research in field settings, Cook and Campbell (1979) provide an extensive enumeration of threats to drawing causal inferences, each of which should be considered as a matter of course in conducting and reporting studies on vocational psychological phenomena. Finally, in passive–observational research, probably the most common type in vocational psychology, there are at least three methodological strategies for eliminating alternative interpretations of findings. One is to replicate and extend studies across as many parameters as possible, thereby not only increasing the probability of the stability of the hypothesized relationships but also assessing the effects of other variables upon these relationships (Campbell, 1957). A second strategy is to plan for the statistical control or contribution of third variables. Illustrative of these approaches in vocational psychology are the many studies on the relationship between job satisfaction and success and the research on "moderator variables" in the prediction of job success (Ghiselli, 1960a, 1960b).

Still another strategy in passive–observational research, mentioned earlier but deserving more extended discussion, is the strong inference paradigm. Platt (1964) summarizes the steps in the logic underlying it as follows:

1. Devising alternative hypotheses;
2. Devising a crucial experiment (or several of them), with alternative possible outcomes, each of which will, as nearly as possible, exclude one or more of the hypotheses;
3. Carrying out the experiment so as to get a clean result;
4. Recycling the procedure, making subhypotheses or sequential hypotheses to refine the possibilities that remain; and so on [p. 34].

This approach incorporates not only the process of elimination explicated above, but it also provides a foundation for stong inference by controlling third variables. In the example cited previously on the Iowa studies of anxiety and learning, competing interpretations of the findings were virtually eliminated because differential predictions were made in the paradigm, which hypothesized directly opposite results for simple and complex learning for exactly the same extremes in anxiety. To conceive of third variables from which identical results might be obtained thus becomes extremely difficult. With ingenuity and imagination, there is no reason why this strategy cannot be adopted as a central one in vocational psychological research where between-groups comparisons (e.g., occupational difference studies) have predominated.

Statistical Analysis

Underwood (1957) has stated a principle of statistical analysis that may not be statistically pure but is highly pragmatic: "Analyze your data every way you can." Although statisticians may wince at this exhortation, researchers find it repeatedly revealing, not only in planning analyses but also in post

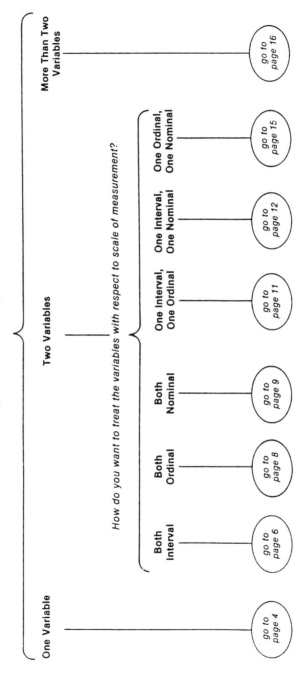

FIG. 7.11 The Decision Tree: Questions and Answers Leading to Appropriate Statistics or Statistical Techniques. (From *A Guide for Selecting Statistical Techniques for Analyzing Social Science Data* by F. M. Andrews, L. Klem, T. N. Davidson, P. M. O'Malley, & W. L. Rodgers, 1981, p. 3. Copyright 1981 by The University of Michigan. Reprinted by permission.)

ONE VARIABLE

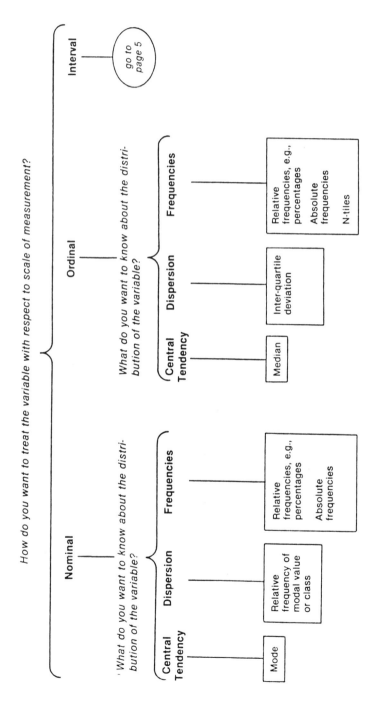

FIG. 7.12   One-variable statistical techniques. (From *A Guide for Selecting Statistical Techniques for Analyzing Social Science Data* by F. M. Andrews, L. Klem, T. N. Davidson, P. M. O'Malley, & W. L. Rodgers, 1981, p. 4. Copyright 1981 by the University of Michigan. Reprinted by permission.)

hoc analyses (replicated, hopefully, upon independent samples). Conceptualizing a problem in terms of both between- and within-group analyses expands the possibilities for discovering possible causal relationships among variables, as well as winnowing out the effects of extraneous or nuisance factors. As an aid in this process, a taxonomy of statistical techniques compiled by the Institute for Social Research (Andrews, Klem, Davidson, O'Malley, & Rodgers, 1981) is extremely helpful. It is based upon the decision tree depicted in Fig. 7.11 and illustrated for one variable in Fig. 7.12. It includes most of the statistical techniques available to researchers and indicates some of their interrelationships. It is noteworthy that these statistical analyses, in general, are independent of research designs. With certain exceptions, both mean difference and correlational analyses can be used with a between-group design. Multiple regression/correlation (MRC) analysis can be used to integrate between- and within-group designs. MRC is also highly useful for controlling and estimating the contribution of third variables. Thus, as a general data-analytic system, it is proposed that MRC is a modus operandi for synthesizing philosophy of science and research design into a systematic approach to the investigation of problems in vocational psychology.

REFERENCES

Ackoff, R. L. *The design of social research.* Chicago: University of Chicago Press, 1953.

Allport, G. W. *Personality: A psychological interpretation.* New York: Holt, 1937.

American College Testing Program. *Handbook for the assessment of career development.* Boston: Houghton Mifflin, 1974.

Andrews, F. M., Klem, L., Davidson, T. N., O'Malley, P. M., & Rodgers, W. L. A guide for selecting statistical techniques for analyzing social science data. (2nd ed.) Ann Arbor: Institute for Social Research, University of Michigan, 1981.

Baltes, P. B., Reese, H. W., & Nesselroade, J. R. *Lifespan developmental psychology: Introduction to research methods.* Monterey, Ca.: Brooks/Cole, 1977.

Barahal, G. D., Brammer, L. M., & Shostram, E. L. A client-centered approach to vocational counseling. *Journal of Consulting Psychology,* 1949, *14,* 256–260.

Bechtoldt, H. P. An empirical study of the factor analysis stability hypothesis. *Psychometrika,* 1961, *26,* 405–432.

Bechtoldt, H. P. Construct validity: A critique. *American Psychologist,* 1959, *14,* 619–620.

Blalock, H. M., Jr. (Ed.). *Causal models in the social sciences.* Chicago: Adline-Atherton, 1971.

Brodbeck, M. The philosophy of science and educational research. *Review of Educational Research,* 1957, *27,* 427–440.

Brodbeck, M. Logic and scientific method in research on teaching. In N. L. Gage (Ed.), *Handbook of research on teaching.* Chicago: Rand McNally, 1963, pp. 44–93.

Burnkan, R. J. Perceived parental attitudes and parental identification in relation to field of vocational choice. *Journal of Counseling Psychology,* 1965, *12,* 39–47.

Burnkan, R. J. Perceived parental attitudes and parental identification in relation to problems in vocational choice. *Journal of Counseling Psychology,* 1966, *13,* 394–402.

Brunkan, R. J., & Crites, J. O. A family relations inventory to measure perceived parental attitudes. *Journal of Counseling Psychology,* 1964, *11,* 3–12.

Buros, O. H. (Ed.). *Eighth mental measurements yearbook.* New Brunswick, N.J.: Gryphon Press, 1978.

Burt, C. The differentiation of intellectual ability. *British Journal of Educational Psychology,* 1954, *24,* 76-90.

Campbell, D. P. *The results of counseling: Twenty-five years later.* Philadelphia: Saunders, 1965.

Campbell, D. P., & Hansen, J. C. *Manual for the SVIB-SCII.* (3rd ed.). Stanford, Ca.: Stanford University Press, 1981.

Campbell, D. T. Factors relevant to the validity of experiments in social settings. *Psychological Bulletin,* 1957, *54,* 297-312.

Campbell, D. T. Recommendations for APA test standards regarding construct, trait or discriminant validity. *American Psychologist,* 1960, *15,* 546-553.

Campbell, D. T., & Fiske, D. W. Convergent and discriminant validation by the multitrait-multimethod matrix. *Psychological Bulletin,* 1959, *56,* 81-105.

Campbell, E. T., & Stanley, J. C. *Experimental and quasi-experimental designs for research.* Chicago: Rand McNally, 1966.

Card, J. J. Career commitment processes in the young adult years: An illustration from the ROTC/Army career path. *Journal of Vocational Behavior,* 1978, *12,* 53-75.

Cattell, R. B., & Tsujioka, B. The importance of factor-trueness and validity, versus homogeneity and orthogonality in test scales. *Educational and Psychological Measurement,* 1964, *24,* 3-30.

Chapanis, A. Men, machines and models. *American Psychologist,* 1961, *16,* 113-131.

Cohen, J. Multiple regression as a general data-analytic system. *Psychological Bulletin,* 1968, *70,* 426-443.

Cohen, J., & Cohen, P. *Applied multiple regression/correlation analysis for the behavioral sciences.* Hillsdale, N.J.: Lawrence Erlbaum Associates, 1975.

Cohen, M. R., & Nagel, E. *An introduction to logic and scientific method.* New York: Harcourt, Brace & World, 1934.

Cook, T. D., & Campbell, D. T. *Quasi-experimentation: Design & analysis issues for field settings.* Chicago: Rand McNally, 1979.

Cook, T. D., & Reichardt, C. S. (Eds.). *Qualitative and quantitative methods in evaluation research.* Beverly Hills, Ca.: Sage, 1979.

Cottle, W. C. A factorial study of the Multiphasic, Strong, Kuder, and Bell inventories using a population of adult males. *Psychometrika,* 1950, *15,* 25-47.

Crites, J. O. A model for the measurement of vocational maturity. *Journal of Counseling Psychology,* 1961, *8,* 255-259.

Crites, J. O. Research on vocational guidance: Status and prospect. Part II: Proposals for a new criterion measure and improved research design. In H. Borow (Ed.), *Man in a world at work.* Boston: Houghton Mifflin, 1964, 324-340.

Crites, J. O. Measurement of vocational maturity in adolescence: I. Attitude Test of the Vocational Development Inventory. *Psychological Monographs,* 1965, *79,* (2, Whole No. 595).

Crites, J. O. *Vocational psychology: The study of vocational behavior and development.* New York: McGraw-Hill, 1969.

Crites, J. O. *The maturity of vocational attitudes in adolescence.* American Personnel and Guidance Association Inquiry Series, Monograph, No. 2, Washington, D.C.: APGA, 1971.

Crites, J. O. *The Career Maturity Inventory.* Monterey, Ca.: CTB/McGraw-Hill, 1973.

Crites, J. O. The Career Maturity Inventory. In D. E. Super (Ed.), *Measuring vocational maturity in counseling and evaluation.* Washington, D.C.: National Vocational Guidance Association, 1974. (a)

Crites, J. O. Career development Processes: A model of vocational maturity. In E. L. Herr (Ed.), *Vocational guidance and human development.* Boston: Houghton Mifflin, 1974, 296-320. (b).

Crites, J. O. A developmental theory of the relationship between vocational success and vocational satisfaction. Paper presented at the annual convention of the American Psychological Association, New York, August, 1979.

Crites, J. O. *The Career Maturity Inventory.* (Rev. ed.) Monterey, Ca.: CTB/McGraw-Hill, 1978.

Crites, J. O. *Career counseling: Models, methods, & materials.* New York: McGraw-Hill, 1981.

Cronbach, L. J. The two disciplines of scientific psychology. *American Psychologist,* 1957, *12,* 671-684.

Cronbach, L. J., & Meehl, P. E. Construct validity in psychological tests. *Psychological Bulletin,* 1955, *52,* 281-302.

Darley, J. G., & Hagenah, T. *Vocational interest measurement.* Minneapolis: University of Minnesota Press, 1955.

Edwards, A. L. Experiments: Their planning and execution. In G. Lindzey (Ed.), *Handbook of social psychology.* (Vol. I.) Cambridge, Mass.: Addison-Wesley, 1954, pp. 259-288.

Edwards, A. L., & Cronbach, L. J. Experimental design for research in psychotherapy. *Journal of Clinical Psychology,* 1952, *8,* 51-59.

Frogy, E. W., & Black, J. D. A follow-up after three years of clients counseled by two methods. *Journal of Counseling Psychology,* 1954, *1,* 1-8.

Forrest, D. J., & Thompson, A. S. The Career Development Inventory. In D. E. Super (Ed.), *Measuring vocational maturity for counseling and evaluation.* Washington, D.C.: American Personnel and Guidance Association, 1974, pp. 53-66.

Fruchter, B. *Introduction to factor analysis.* New York: Van Nostrand-Reinhold, 1954.

Garrett, H. E. A developmental theory of intelligence. *American Psychologist,* 1946, *1,* 372-378.

Ghiselli, E. E. Differentiation of tests in terms of the accuracy with which they predict for a given individual. *Educational and Psychological Measurement,* 1960, *20,* 675-684. (a).

Ghiselli, E. E. The prediction of predictability. *Educational and Psychological Measurement,* 1960, *20,* 3-8. (b).

Ghiselli, E. E., & Brown, C. W. *Personnel and industrial psychology.* New York: McGraw-Hill, 1955.

Ginzberg, E. Toward a theory of occupational choice. *Occupations,* 1950, *30,* 491-494.

Ginzberg, E., Ginsburg, S. W., Axelrad, S., & Herma, J. L. *Occupational choice.* New York: Columbia University Press, 1951.

Glass, G. B., McGaw, B., & Miller, T. I. *Meta-analysis in social research.* Beverley Hills, Ca.: Sage Publications, 1981.

Goen, J. C. *Personality correlates of vocational problem categories.* Unpublished doctoral dissertation, University of Iowa, 1963.

Gribbons, W. D., & Lohnes, P. R. *Career development.* Weston, Mass.: Regis College, 1966.

Guilford, J. P. *Personality.* New York: McGraw-Hill, 1959.

Guion, R. M. Content validity—the source of my discontent. *Applied Psychological Measurement,* 1977, *1,* 1-10.

Hanson, M. C. Career counseling in organizational groups. In D. H. Montross & C. J. Shinkman (Eds.), *Career development in the 1980's: Theory and practice.* Springfield, Ill.: Charles C. Thomas, 1981, 379-392.

Heise, D. R. Separating reliability and stability in test-retest correlation. *American Sociological Review,* 1969, *34,* 93-101.

Heise, D. R. *Causal analysis.* New York: Wiley, 1975.

Holland, J. L. *The Self-Directed Search:* Professional manual. (1979 ed.) Palo Alto, Ca.: Consulting Psychologists Press, 1979.

Humpreys, L. G. Note on the multitrait-multimethod matrix. *Psychological Bulletin,* 1960, *57,* 86-88.

Karren, R. J., Crites, J. O., & Bobko, P. Path analysis of the Career Maturity Inventory to estimate maturational variance. (Unpublished manuscript, University of Maryland, 1979.)

Kerlinger, F. N., & Pedhazur, E. J. *Multiple regression in behavioral research.* New York: Holt, Reinhart & Winston, 1973.

Kitson, H. D. Review of Ginzberg, E., Ginsburg, S. W., Axelrad, S., & Herma, J. L. Occupational choice: An approach to a general theory. *Personnel and Guidance Journal,* 1951, *29,* 611–613.

Lachman, R. The model in theory construction. *Psychological Review,* 1960, *67,* 113–129.

Lindquist, E. F. *Design and analysis of experiments in psychology and education.* Boston: Houghton Mifflin, 1953.

Loevinger, J. Objective tests as instruments of psychological theory. *Psychological Reports Monograph Supplement No. 9,* 1957, *3,* 635–694.

Marax, M. H. (Ed.). *Theories in contemporary psychology.* New York: Macmillan, 1963.

Meade, C. J. *A comparison of the cross-sectional and longitudinal data on the Career Maturity Inventory Attitude Scale.* Unpublished manuscript, 1974.

Medvene, A. Occupational choice of graduate students in psychology as a function of early parent-child interactions. *Journal of Counseling Psychology,* 1969, *16,* 385–389.

McCall, R. J. *Basic logic* (2nd ed.). New York: Barnes & Noble, 1952.

Norrell, G., & Grater, H. Interest awareness as an aspect of self-awareness. *Journal of Counseling Psychology,* 1960, *7,* 289–292.

O'Hara, R. P., & Tiedeman, D. V. Vocational self-concept in adolescence. *Journal of Counseling Psychology,* 1959, *6,* 292–301.

Osipow, S. H. *Theories of career development.* (2nd ed.). New York: Appleton–Century–Crofts, 1973.

Osipow, S. H., Carney, C. G., Winer, J., Yanico, B., & Koschier, M. *The Career Decision Scale.* Columbus, Ohio: Marathon Consulting and Press, 1976, 3rd rev.

Patton, M. Q. *Qualitative evaluation methods.* Beverly Hills, Ca.: Sage, 1980.

Platt, J. R. Strong inference. *Science,* 1964, *146,* 347–353.

Popper, K. R. *The logic of scientific discovery.* New York: Basic Books, 1959.

Popper, K. R. *Objective Knowledge: An evolutionary approach.* Oxford, England: Clarendon Press, 1972.

Prediger, D. *Career decision-making measures in the context of Harren's model.* Paper presented at the meeting of the American Personnel and Guidance Association, Las Vegas, April 1979.

Roe, A. Early determinants of vocational choice. *Journal of Counseling Psychology,* 1957, *4,* 212–217.

Rosenthal, R. *Experimenter bias in behavioral research.* New York: Appleton–Century–Croft, 1966.

Schaie, K. W. A general model for the study of developmental problems. *Psychological Bulletin,* 1965, *64,* 92–107.

Schmid, J., & Leiman, J. M. The development of hierarchical factor solutions. *Psychometrika,* 1957, *22,* 53–61.

Schmidt, F. L., & Hunter, J. E. Development of a general solution to the problem of validity generalization. *Journal of Applied Psychology,* 1977, *62,* 529–540.

Sewell, W. H., Haller, A. O., & Portes, A. The educational and early occupational attainment process. *American Sociological Review,* 1969, *34,* 82–92.

Smith, M. L., & Glass, G. V. Meta-analysis of psychotherapy outcome studies. *American Psychologist,* 1977, *32,* 752–760.

Smith, M. L., Glass, G. V., & Miller, T. I. *The benefits of psychotherapy.* Baltimore: Johns Hopkins University Press, 1980.

Smith, N. C., Jr. Replication studies: A neglected aspect of psychological research. *American Psychologist,* 1970, *25,* 970–975.

Spearman, C. General intelligence objectively determined and measured. *American Journal of Psychology,* 1904, *15,* 201-293.

Spence, K. W. *Behavior theory and learning: Selected papers.* Englewood Cliff, N.J.: Prentice-Hall, 1960.

Spielberger, C. D. (Ed.). *Anxiety and behavior.* New York: Academic Press, 1966.

Super, D. E. A theory of vocational development. *American Psychologist,* 1953, *8,* 185-190.

Super, D. E. Career patterns as a basis for vocational counseling. *Journal of Counseling Psychology,* 1954, *1,* 12-20.

Super, D. E. The dimensions and measurement of vocational maturity. *Teachers College Record,* 1955, *57,* 151-163.

Super, D. E. *The psychology of careers.* New York: Harper & Row, 1957.

Super, D. E. (Ed.). *Measuring vocational maturity for counseling and evaluation.* Washington, D.C.: American Personnel and Guidance Association, 1974.

Super, D. E., & Crites, J. O. *Appraising vocational fitness.* (Rev. ed.). New York: Harper & Row, 1962.

Super, D. E., Crites, J. O., Hummel, R. C., Moser, H. P., Overstreet, P. L., & Warnath, C. F. *Vocational development: A framework for research.* New York: Teachers College Bureau of Publications, 1957.

Super, D. E., & Overstreet, P. L. *The vocational maturity of ninth grade boys.* New York: Teachers College Bureau of Publications, 1960.

Tiedeman, D. V. Career pattern studies: New directions. In E. Landy & A. M. Kroll (Eds.), *Guidance in American education III: Needs and influencing forces.* Cambridge, Mass.: Harvard University Press, 1965, 116-128.

Thurstone, L. L. *Multiple-factor analysis.* Chicago: University of Chicago Press, 1947.

Tryon, R. C., & Bailey, D. E. *Cluster analysis.* New York: McGraw-Hill, 1970.

Tucker, L. R. The objective definition of simple structure in linear factor analysis. *Psychometrika,* 1955, *20,* 209-225.

Underwood, B. J. *Psychological research.* New York: Appleton-Century-Crofts, 1957.

Vernon, P. E. *The structure of abilities.* London: Methuen, 1950.

Westbrook, B. W., Cutts, C. C., Madison, S. S., & Arcia, M. A. The validity of the Crites model of career maturity. *Journal of Vocational Behavior,* 1980, *16,* 249-281.

Westbrook, B. W., & Mastie, M. M. Three measures of vocational maturity: A beginning to know about. *Measurement and Evaluation in Guidance,* 1973, *6,* 6-16.

Wherry, R. J., Sr. Hierarchical factor solutions without rotation. *Psychometrika,* 1959, *24,* 45-51.

Wherry, R. J., Sr. *Contributions to correlational analysis.* Columbus, Ohio: The Ohio State University Press, (in press).

Author Index

C

Subject Index